THE NEW AVENGERS

NEW AVENGERS BY BRIAN MICHAEL BENDIS VOL. 1. Contains material originally published in magazine form as NEW AVENGERS #1-6. First printing 2011. Hardcover ISBN# 978-0-7851-4872-2. Softcover ISBN# 978-0-7851-4873-9. Published by MARVEL WORLDWIDE, INC., a subsidiary of MARVEL ENTERTAINMENT, LLC. OFFICE OF PUBLICATION: 135 West 50th Street, New York, NY 10020. Copyright © 2010 and 2011 Marvel Characters, Inc. All rights reserved. Hardcover: $24.99 per copy in the U.S. and $27.99 in Canada (GST #R127032852). Softcover: $19.99 per copy in the U.S. and $22.50 in Canada (GST #R127032852). Canadian Agreement #40668537. All characters featured in this issue and the distinctive names and likenesses thereof, and all related indicia are trademarks of Marvel Characters, Inc. No similarity between any of the names, characters, persons, and/or institutions in this magazine with those of any living or dead person or institution is intended, and any such similarity which may exist is purely coincidental. Printed in the U.S.A. ALAN FINE, EVP - Office of the President, Marvel Worldwide, Inc. and EVP & CMO Marvel Characters B.V.; DAN BUCKLEY, Chief Executive Officer and Publisher - Print, Animation & Digital Media; JIM SOKOLOWSKI, Chief Operating Officer; DAVID GABRIEL, SVP of Publishing Sales & Circulation; DAVID BOGART, SVP of Business Affairs & Talent Management; MICHAEL PASCIULLO, VP Merchandising & Communications; JIM O'KEEFE, VP of Operations & Logistics; DAN CARR, Executive Director of Publishing Technology; JUSTIN F. GABRIE, Director of Publishing & Editorial Operations; SUSAN CRESPI, Editorial Operations Manager; ALEX MORALES, Publishing Operations Manager; STAN LEE, Chairman Emeritus. For information regarding advertising in Marvel Comics or on Marvel.com, please contact Ron Stern, VP of Business Development, at rstern@marvel.com. For Marvel subscription inquiries, please call 800-217-9158. Manufactured between 11/22/10 and 12/29/10 (hardcover), and 11/22/10 and 6/29/10 (softcover), by R.R. DONNELLEY, INC., SALEM, VA, USA.

10 9 8 7 6 5 4 3 2 1

THE NEW AVENGERS

WRITER **BRIAN MICHAEL BENDIS**

PENCILER **STUART IMMONEN**

INKER **WADE VON GRAWBADGER**

COLORIST **LAURA MARTIN** WITH **MATT MILLA** & **RAIN BEREDO**

LETTERER **CHRIS ELIOPOULOS**

ASSOCIATE EDITOR **LAUREN SANKOVITCH**

EDITOR **TOM BREVOORT**

Collection Editor: JENNIFER GRÜNWALD
Editorial Assistants: JAMES EMMETT & JOE HOCHSTEIN
Assistant Editors: ALEX STARBUCK & NELSON RIBEIRO
Editor, Special Projects: MARK D. BEAZLEY
Senior Editor, Special Projects: JEFF YOUNGQUIST
Senior Vice President of Sales: DAVID GABRIEL
Book Design: JEFF POWELL

Editor in Chief: JOE QUESADA
Publisher: DAN BUCKLEY
Executive Producer: ALAN FINE

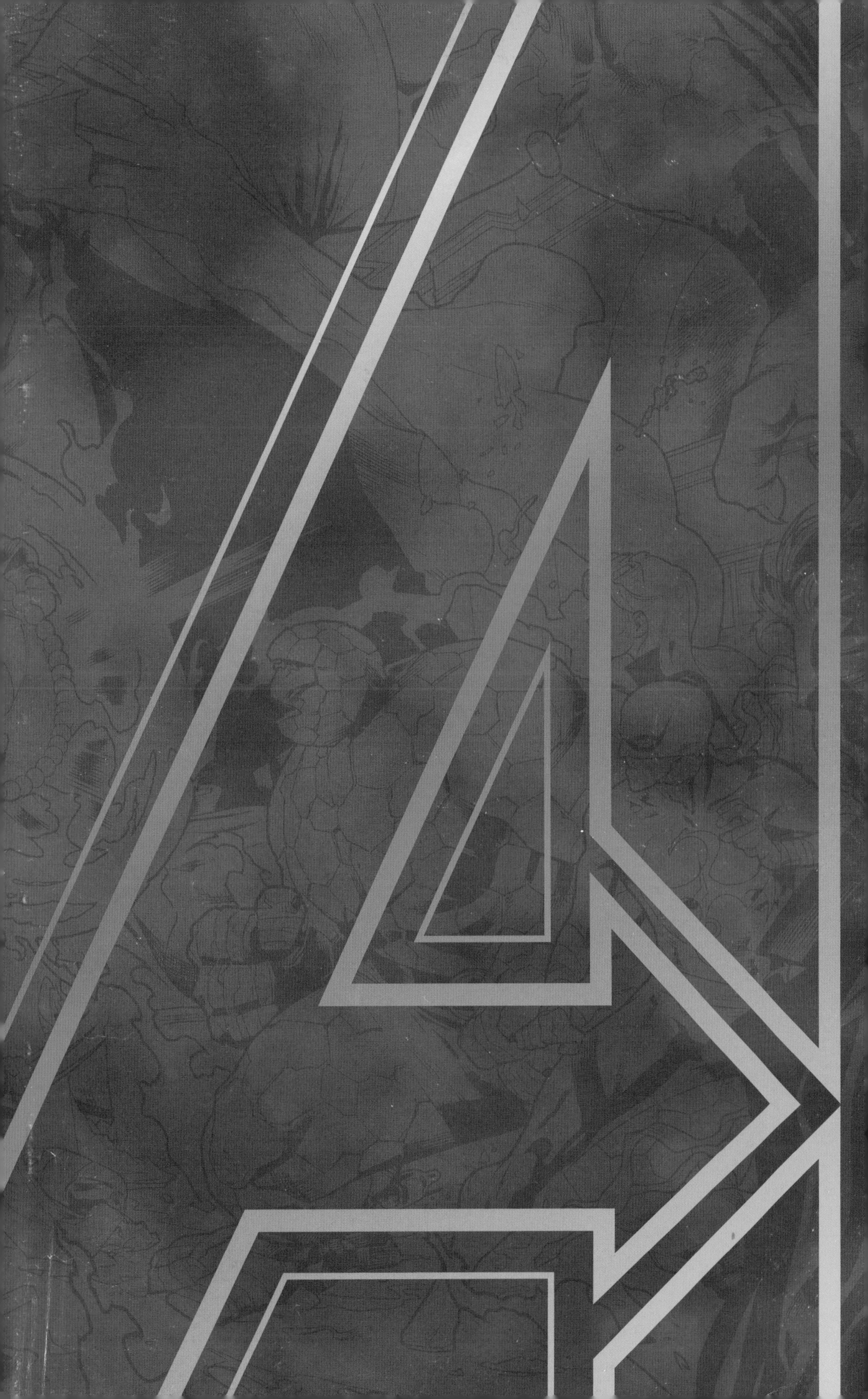

1

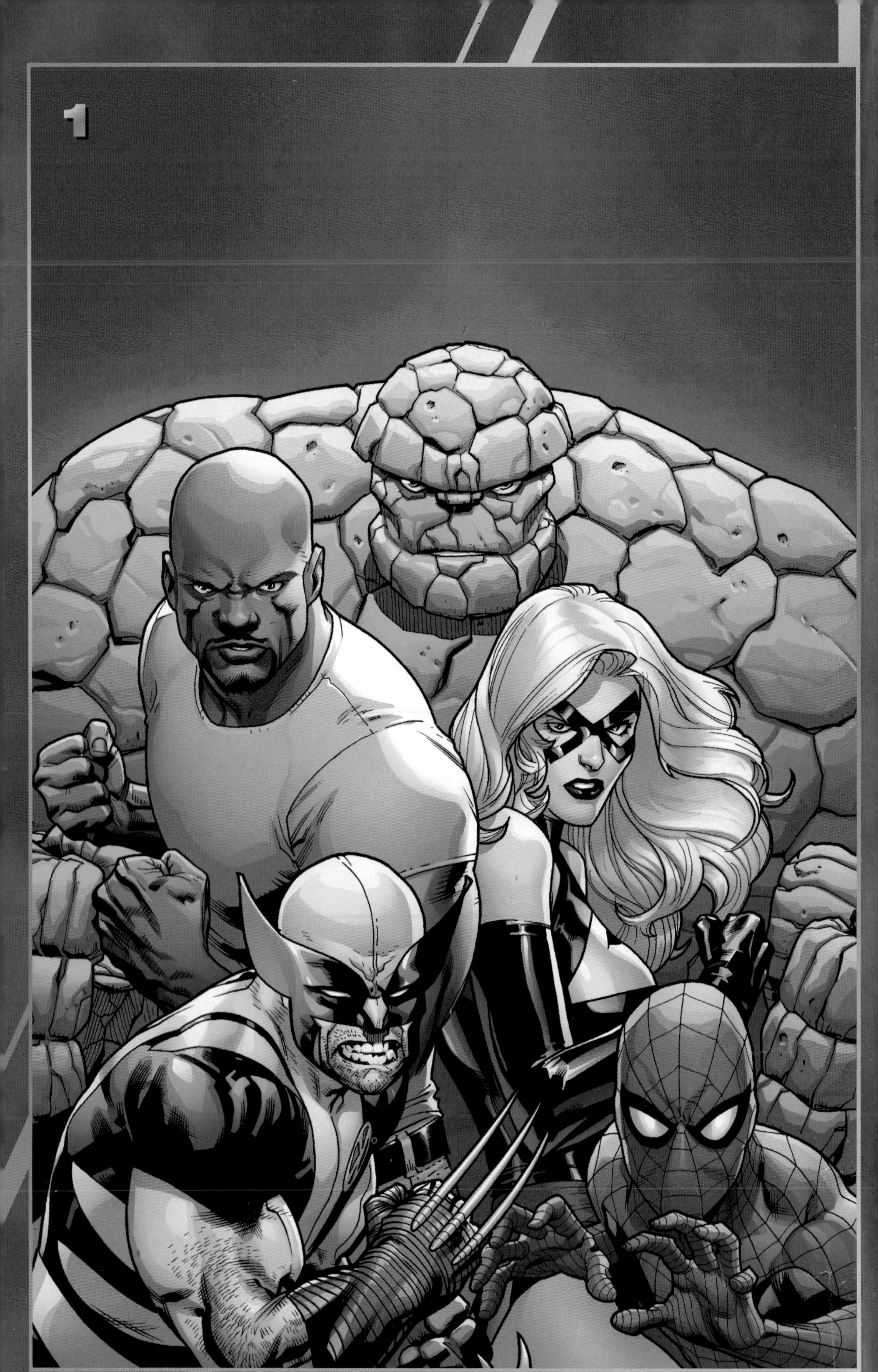

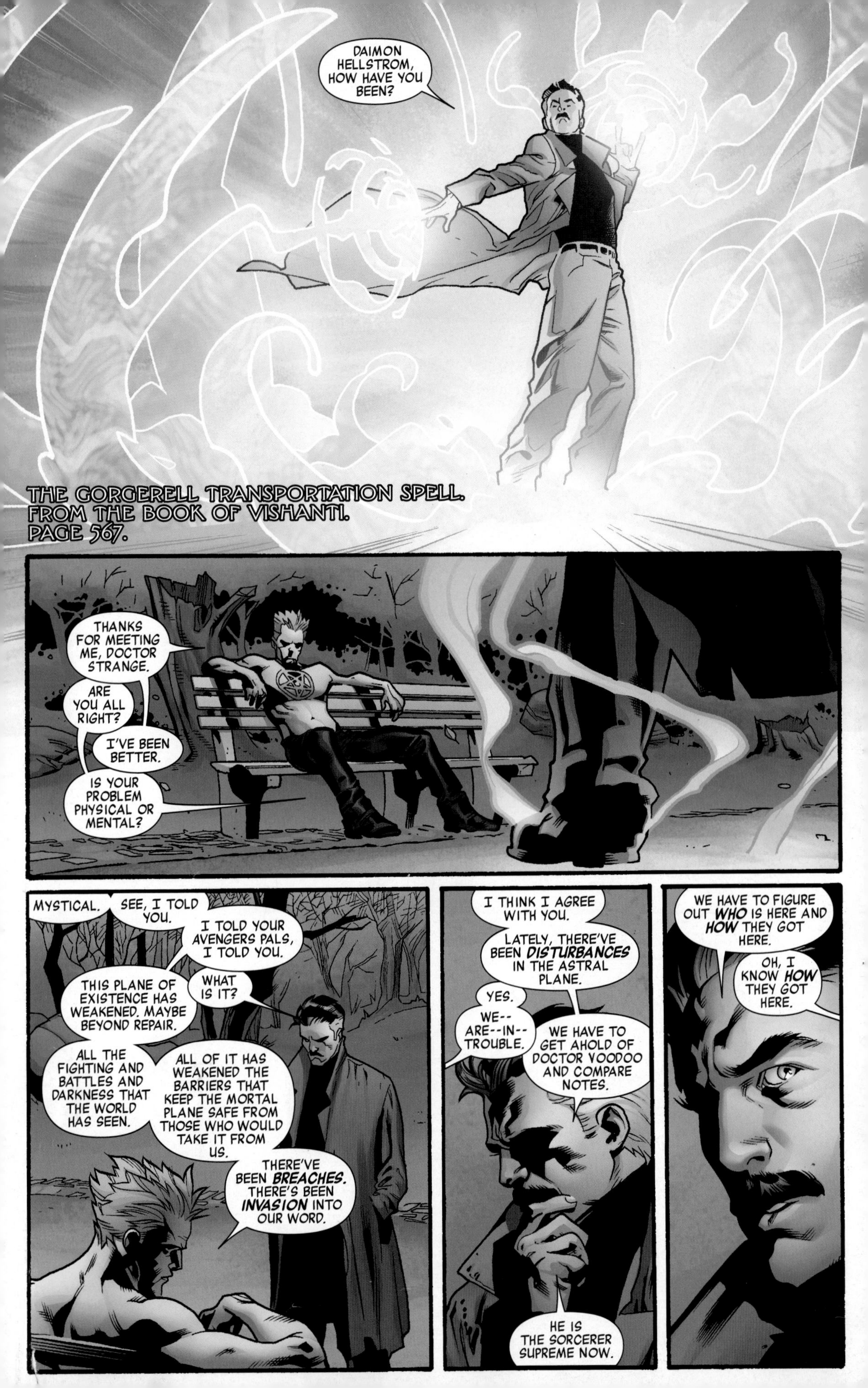
DAIMON HELLSTROM, HOW HAVE YOU BEEN?
THE GORGERELL TRANSPORTATION SPELL. FROM THE BOOK OF VISHANTI. PAGE 567.
THANKS FOR MEETING ME, DOCTOR STRANGE.
ARE YOU ALL RIGHT?
I'VE BEEN BETTER.
IS YOUR PROBLEM PHYSICAL OR MENTAL?
MYSTICAL.
SEE, I TOLD YOU.
I TOLD YOUR AVENGERS PALS, I TOLD YOU.
WHAT IS IT?
THIS PLANE OF EXISTENCE HAS WEAKENED. MAYBE BEYOND REPAIR.
ALL THE FIGHTING AND BATTLES AND DARKNESS THAT THE WORLD HAS SEEN.
ALL OF IT HAS WEAKENED THE BARRIERS THAT KEEP THE MORTAL PLANE SAFE FROM THOSE WHO WOULD TAKE IT FROM US.
THERE'VE BEEN BREACHES. THERE'S BEEN INVASION INTO OUR WORD.
I THINK I AGREE WITH YOU.
LATELY, THERE'VE BEEN DISTURBANCES IN THE ASTRAL PLANE.
YES.
WE-- ARE--IN-- TROUBLE.
WE HAVE TO GET AHOLD OF DOCTOR VOODOO AND COMPARE NOTES.
HE IS THE SORCERER SUPREME NOW.
WE HAVE TO FIGURE OUT WHO IS HERE AND HOW THEY GOT HERE.
OH, I KNOW HOW THEY GOT HERE.

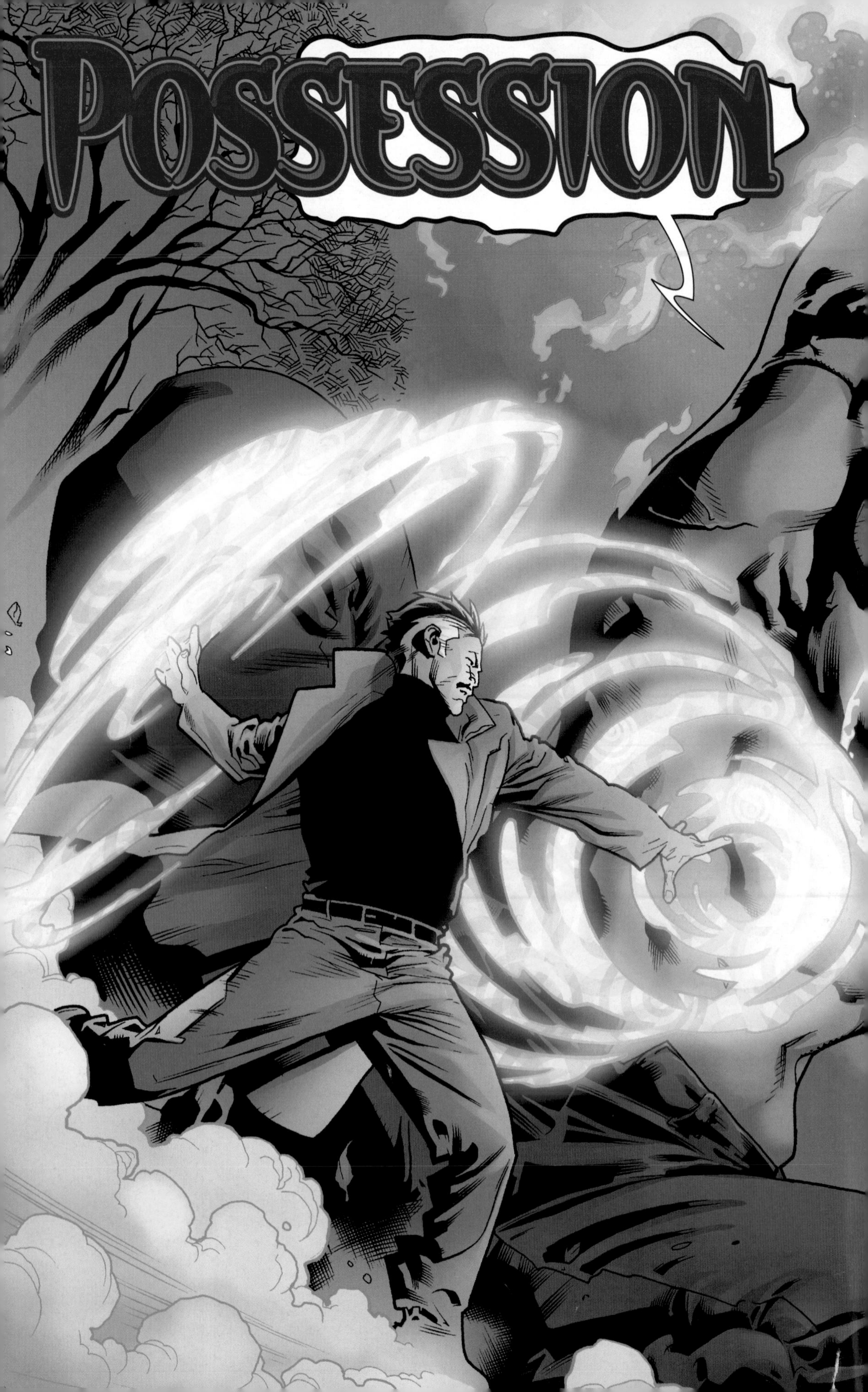
POSSESSION

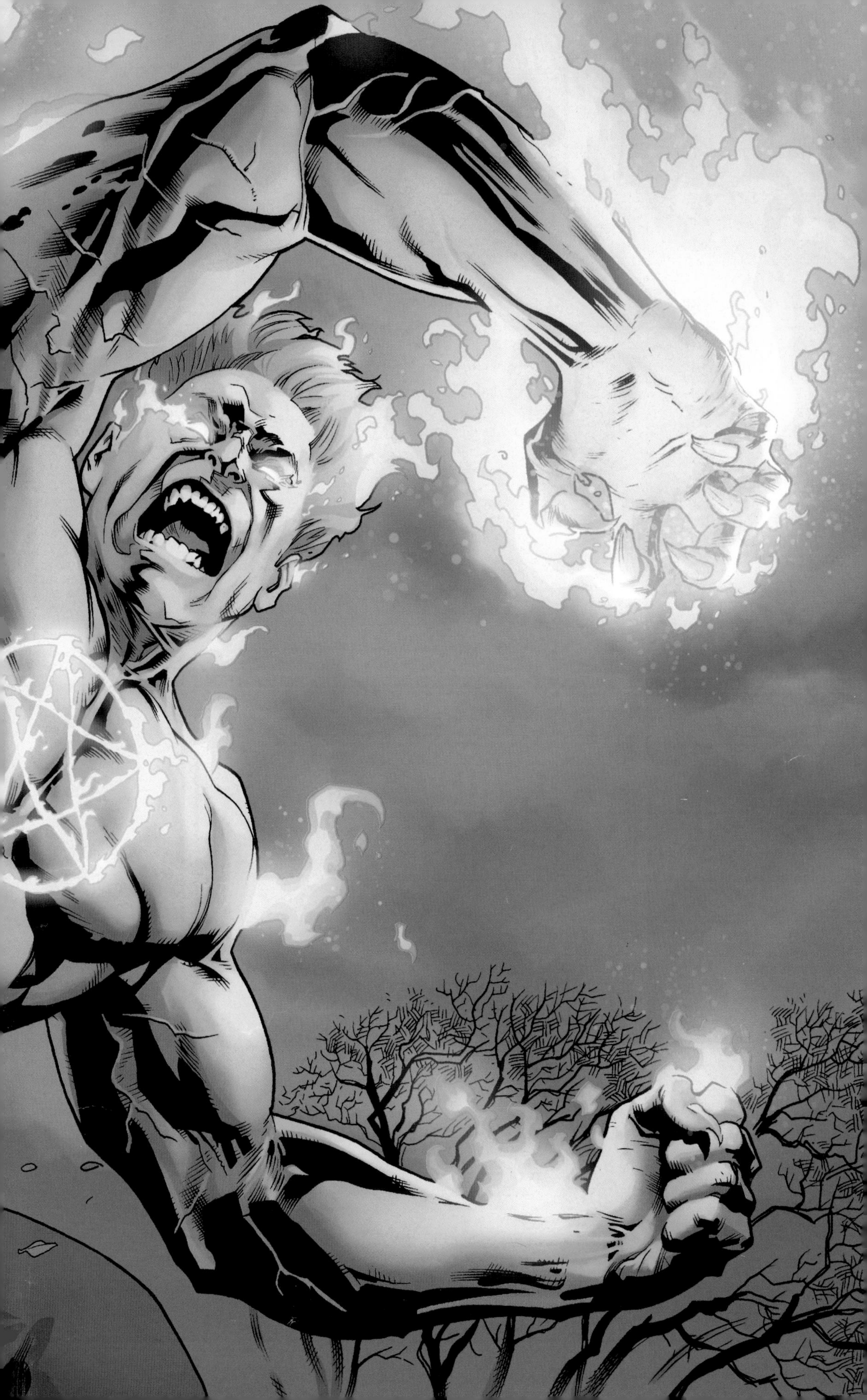

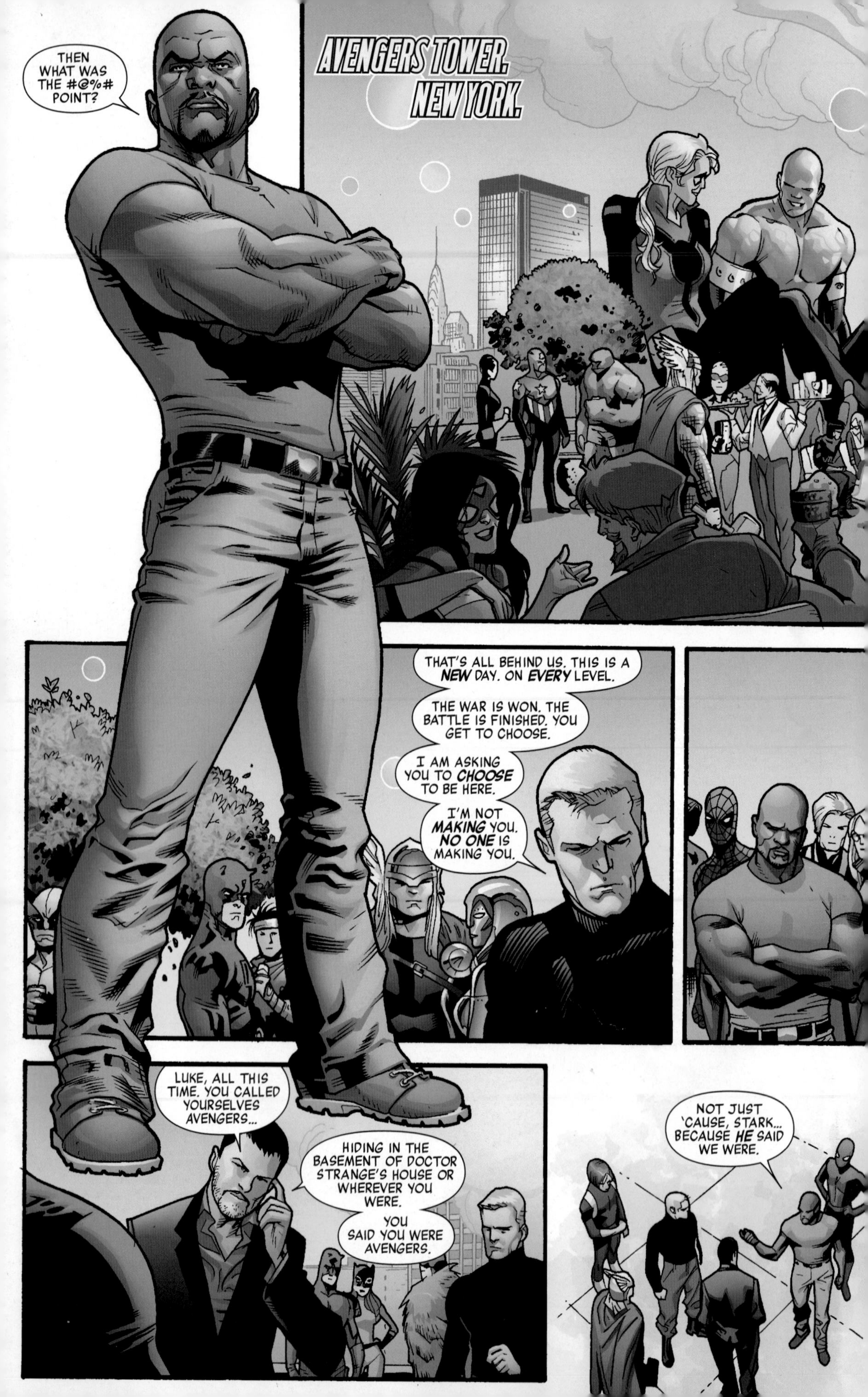
THEN WHAT WAS THE #@%# POINT?
AVENGERS TOWER. NEW YORK.
THAT'S ALL BEHIND US. THIS IS A NEW DAY. ON EVERY LEVEL.
THE WAR IS WON. THE BATTLE IS FINISHED. YOU GET TO CHOOSE.
I AM ASKING YOU TO CHOOSE TO BE HERE.
I'M NOT MAKING YOU. NO ONE IS MAKING YOU.
LUKE, ALL THIS TIME. YOU CALLED YOURSELVES AVENGERS...
HIDING IN THE BASEMENT OF DOCTOR STRANGE'S HOUSE OR WHEREVER YOU WERE.
YOU SAID YOU WERE AVENGERS.
NOT JUST 'CAUSE, STARK... BECAUSE HE SAID WE WERE.

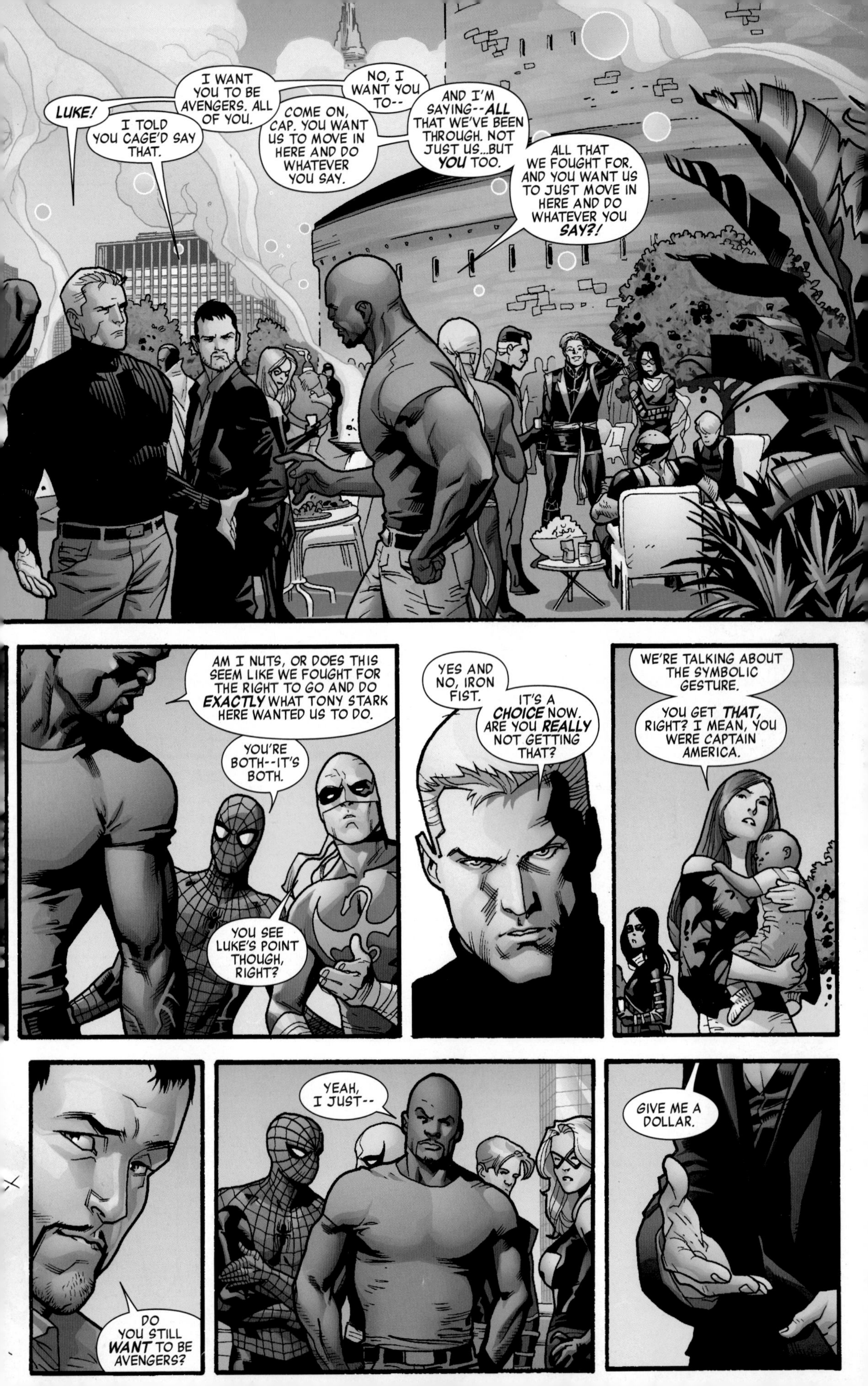
LUKE!
I TOLD YOU CAGE'D SAY THAT.
I WANT YOU TO BE AVENGERS. ALL OF YOU.
COME ON, CAP. YOU WANT US TO MOVE IN HERE AND DO WHATEVER YOU SAY.
NO, I WANT YOU TO--
AND I'M SAYING--ALL THAT WE'VE BEEN THROUGH. NOT JUST US...BUT YOU TOO.
ALL THAT WE FOUGHT FOR. AND YOU WANT US TO JUST MOVE IN HERE AND DO WHATEVER YOU SAY?!
AM I NUTS, OR DOES THIS SEEM LIKE WE FOUGHT FOR THE RIGHT TO GO AND DO EXACTLY WHAT TONY STARK HERE WANTED US TO DO.
YOU'RE BOTH--IT'S BOTH.
YOU SEE LUKE'S POINT THOUGH, RIGHT?
YES AND NO, IRON FIST.
IT'S A CHOICE NOW. ARE YOU REALLY NOT GETTING THAT?
WE'RE TALKING ABOUT THE SYMBOLIC GESTURE.
YOU GET THAT, RIGHT? I MEAN, YOU WERE CAPTAIN AMERICA.
DO YOU STILL WANT TO BE AVENGERS?
YEAH, I JUST--
GIVE ME A DOLLAR.

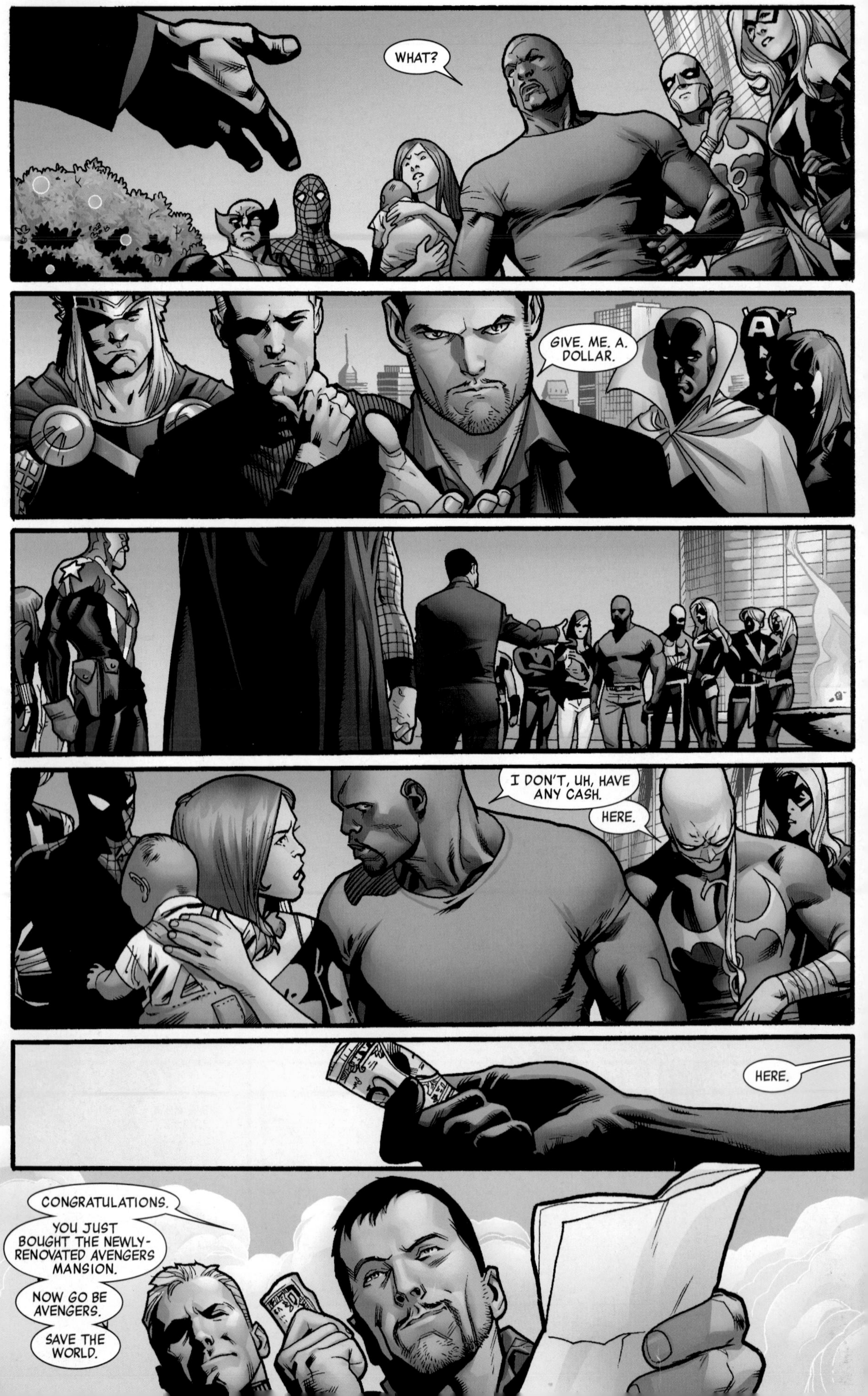
WHAT?
GIVE. ME. A. DOLLAR.
I DON'T, UH, HAVE ANY CASH.
HERE.
HERE.
CONGRATULATIONS.
YOU JUST BOUGHT THE NEWLY-RENOVATED AVENGERS MANSION.
NOW GO BE AVENGERS.
SAVE THE WORLD.

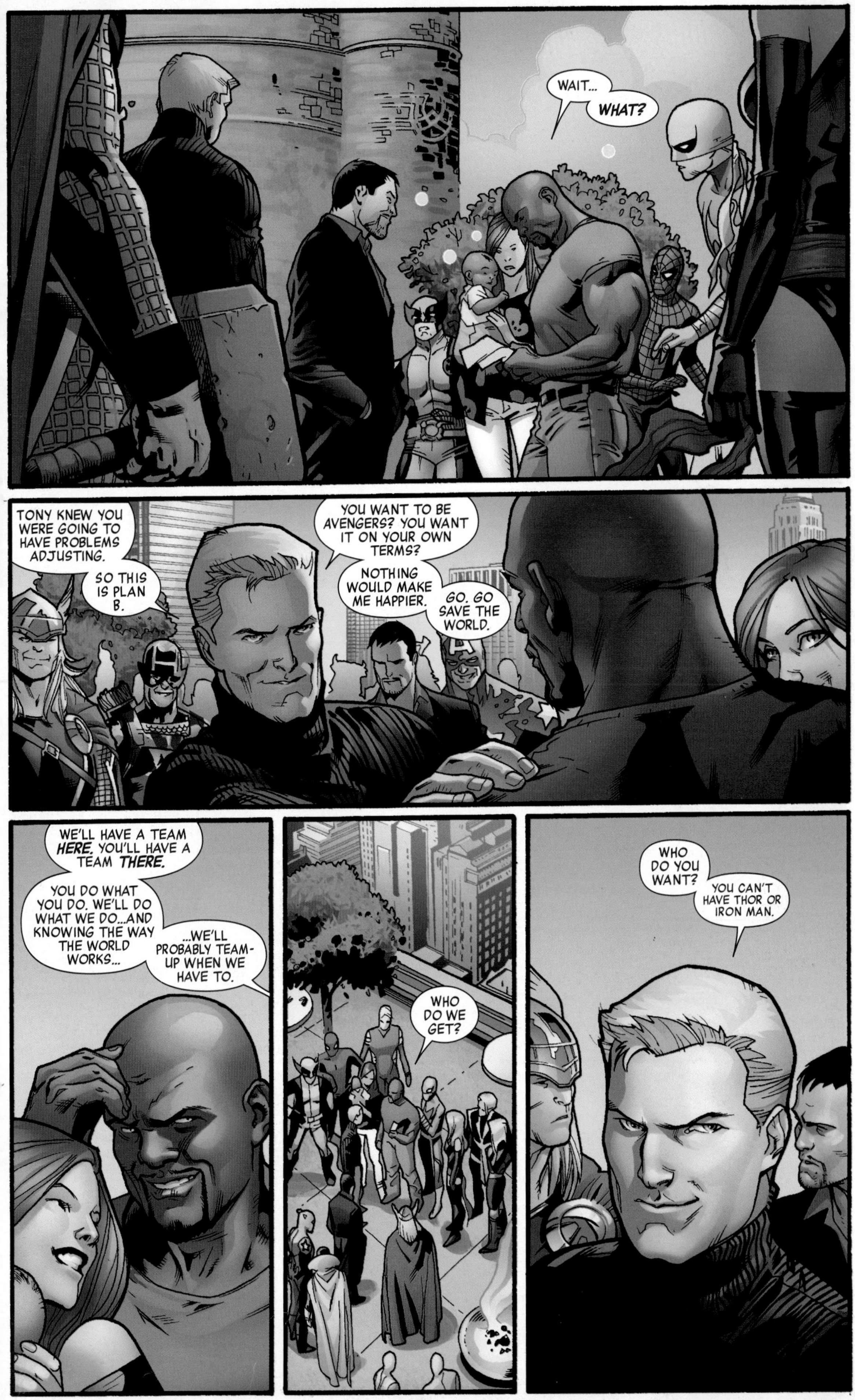
WAIT... WHAT?
TONY KNEW YOU WERE GOING TO HAVE PROBLEMS ADJUSTING.
SO THIS IS PLAN B.
YOU WANT TO BE AVENGERS? YOU WANT IT ON YOUR OWN TERMS?
NOTHING WOULD MAKE ME HAPPIER.
GO. GO SAVE THE WORLD.
WE'LL HAVE A TEAM HERE. YOU'LL HAVE A TEAM THERE.
YOU DO WHAT YOU DO. WE'LL DO WHAT WE DO...AND KNOWING THE WAY THE WORLD WORKS...
...WE'LL PROBABLY TEAM-UP WHEN WE HAVE TO.
WHO DO WE GET?
WHO DO YOU WANT?
YOU CAN'T HAVE THOR OR IRON MAN.

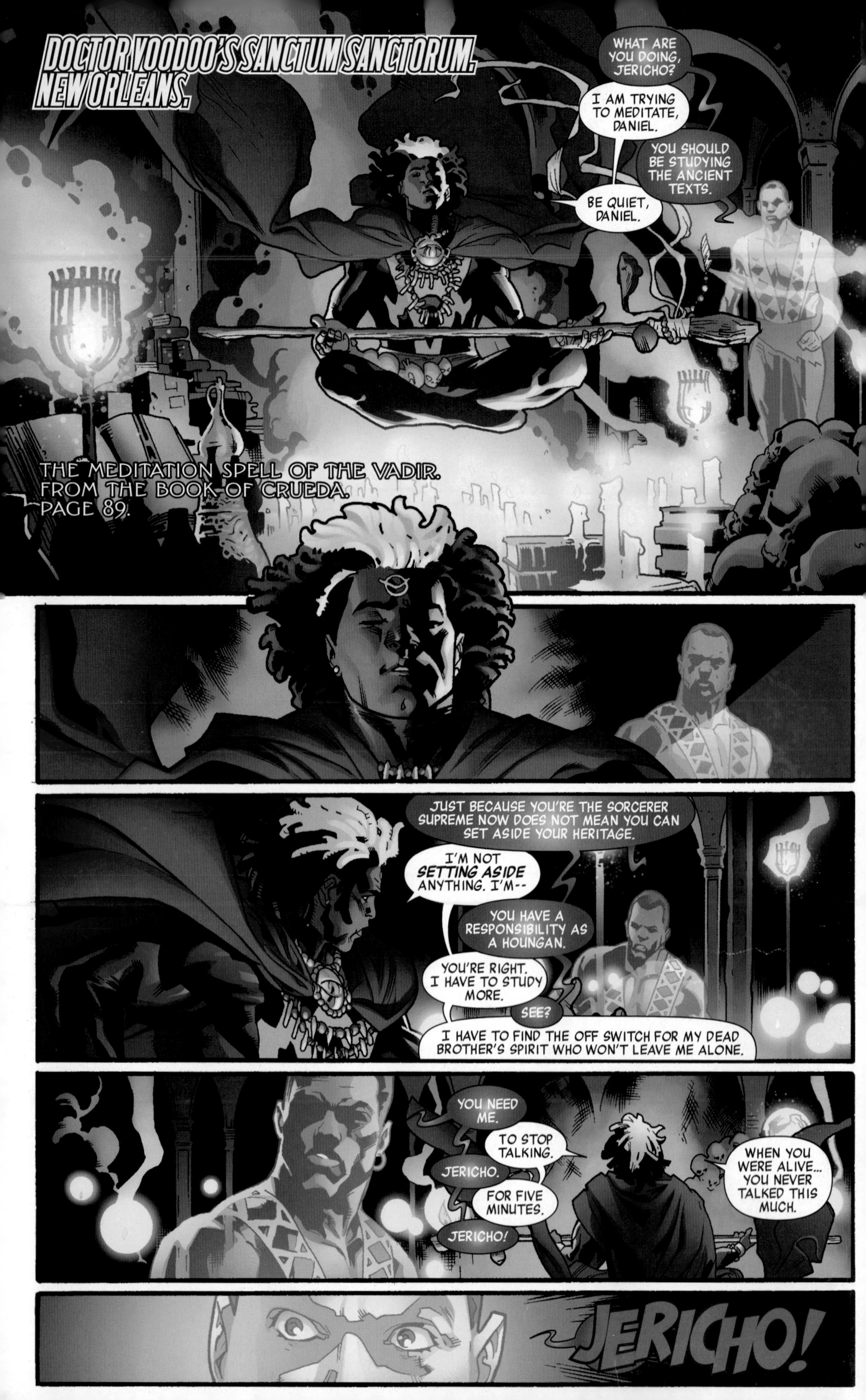
DOCTOR VOODOO'S SANCTUM SANCTORUM. NEW ORLEANS.
WHAT ARE YOU DOING, JERICHO?
I AM TRYING TO MEDITATE, DANIEL.
YOU SHOULD BE STUDYING THE ANCIENT TEXTS.
BE QUIET, DANIEL.
THE MEDITATION SPELL OF THE VADIR. FROM THE BOOK OF CRUEDA. PAGE 89.
JUST BECAUSE YOU'RE THE SORCERER SUPREME NOW DOES NOT MEAN YOU CAN SET ASIDE YOUR HERITAGE.
I'M NOT SETTING ASIDE ANYTHING. I'M--
YOU HAVE A RESPONSIBILITY AS A HOUNGAN.
YOU'RE RIGHT. I HAVE TO STUDY MORE.
SEE?
I HAVE TO FIND THE OFF SWITCH FOR MY DEAD BROTHER'S SPIRIT WHO WON'T LEAVE ME ALONE.
YOU NEED ME.
TO STOP TALKING.
JERICHO.
FOR FIVE MINUTES.
JERICHO!
WHEN YOU WERE ALIVE... YOU NEVER TALKED THIS MUCH.
JERICHO!

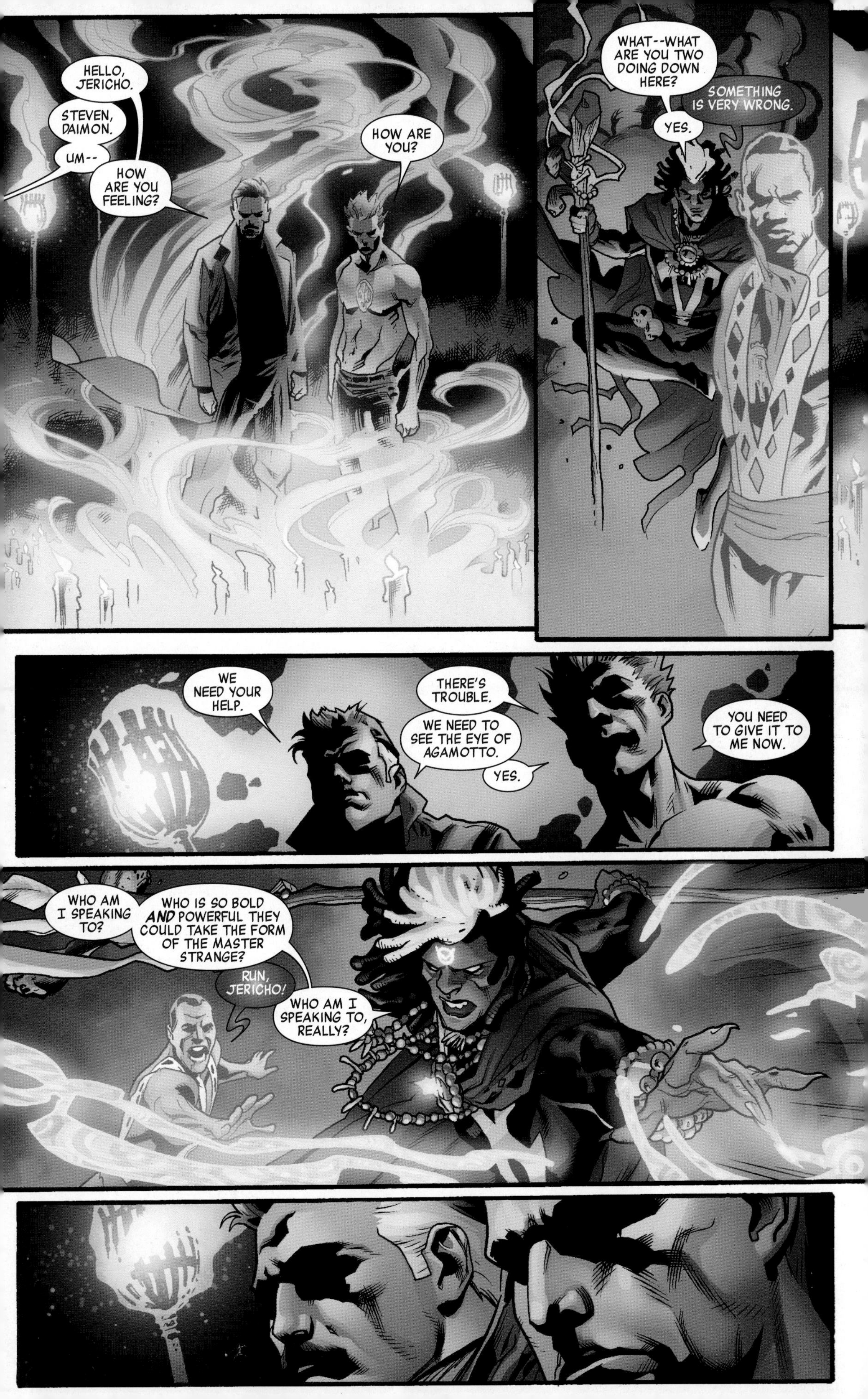
HELLO, JERICHO.
STEVEN, DAIMON.
UM--
HOW ARE YOU FEELING?
HOW ARE YOU?
WHAT--WHAT ARE YOU TWO DOING DOWN HERE?
YES.
SOMETHING IS VERY WRONG.
WE NEED YOUR HELP.
THERE'S TROUBLE.
WE NEED TO SEE THE EYE OF AGAMOTTO.
YES.
YOU NEED TO GIVE IT TO ME NOW.
WHO AM I SPEAKING TO?
WHO IS SO BOLD AND POWERFUL THEY COULD TAKE THE FORM OF THE MASTER STRANGE?
RUN, JERICHO!
WHO AM I SPEAKING TO, REALLY?

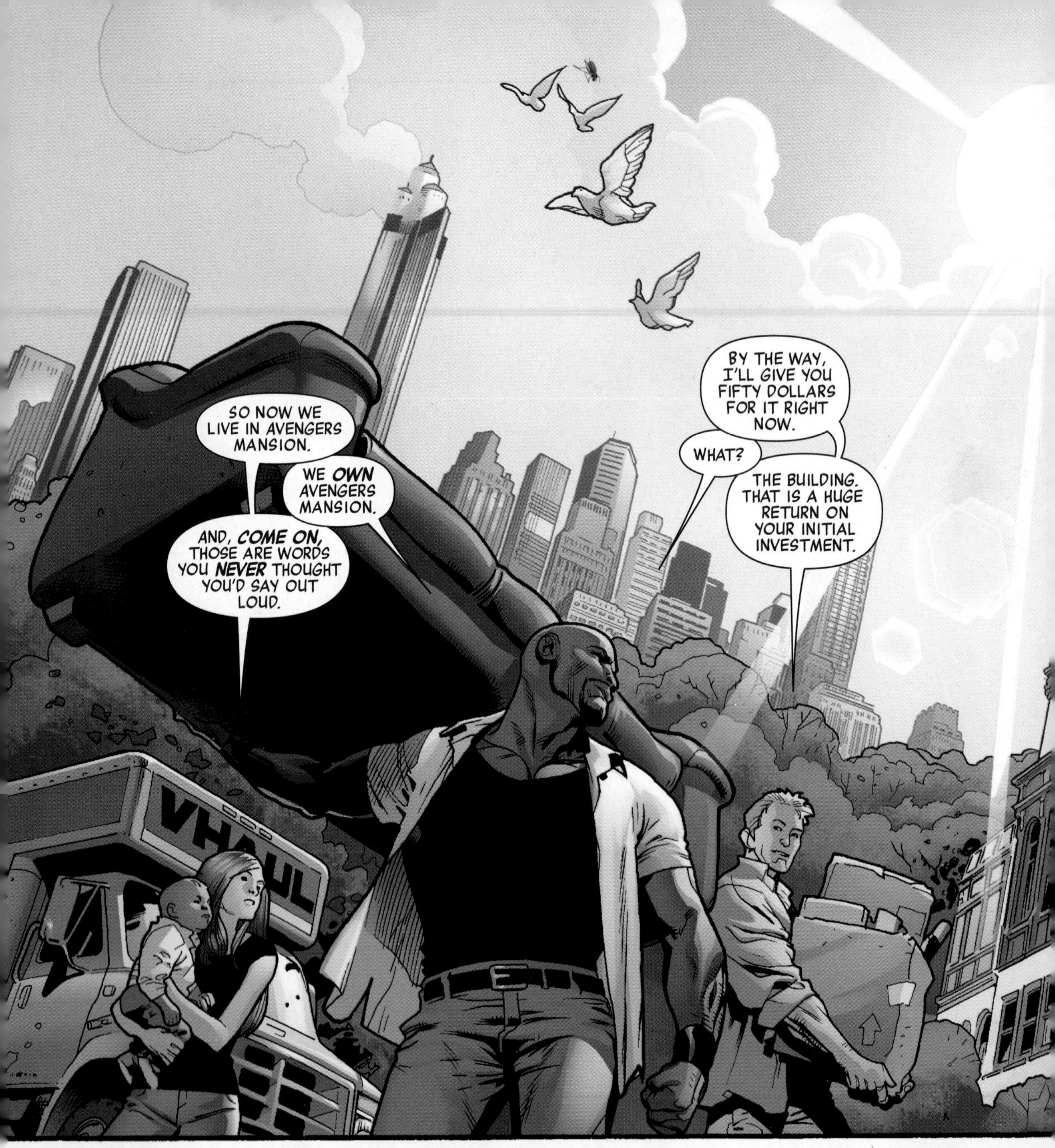
SO NOW WE LIVE IN AVENGERS MANSION.
WE OWN AVENGERS MANSION.
AND, COME ON, THOSE ARE WORDS YOU NEVER THOUGHT YOU'D SAY OUT LOUD.
BY THE WAY, I'LL GIVE YOU FIFTY DOLLARS FOR IT RIGHT NOW.
WHAT?
THE BUILDING. THAT IS A HUGE RETURN ON YOUR INITIAL INVESTMENT.
VHAUL

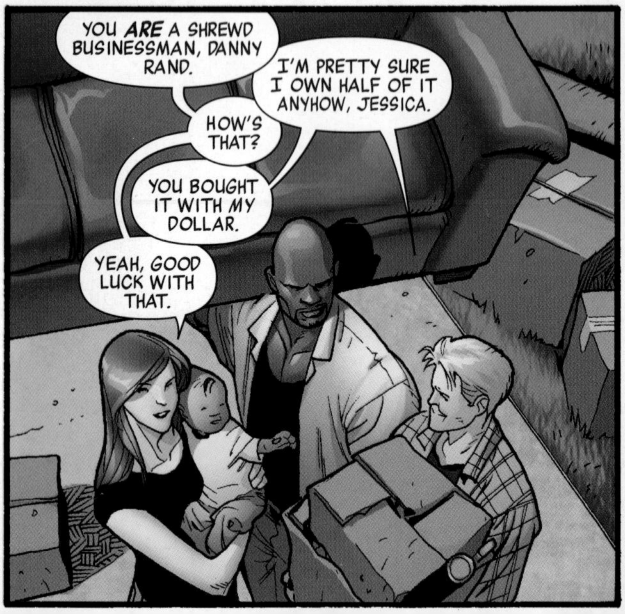
YOU ARE A SHREWD BUSINESSMAN, DANNY RAND.
I'M PRETTY SURE I OWN HALF OF IT ANYHOW, JESSICA.
HOW'S THAT?
YOU BOUGHT IT WITH MY DOLLAR.
YEAH, GOOD LUCK WITH THAT.

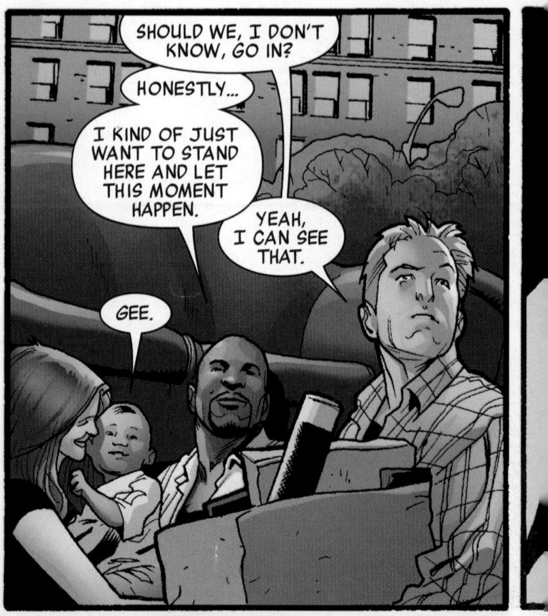
SHOULD WE, I DON'T KNOW, GO IN?
HONESTLY...
I KIND OF JUST WANT TO STAND HERE AND LET THIS MOMENT HAPPEN.
YEAH, I CAN SEE THAT.
GEE.

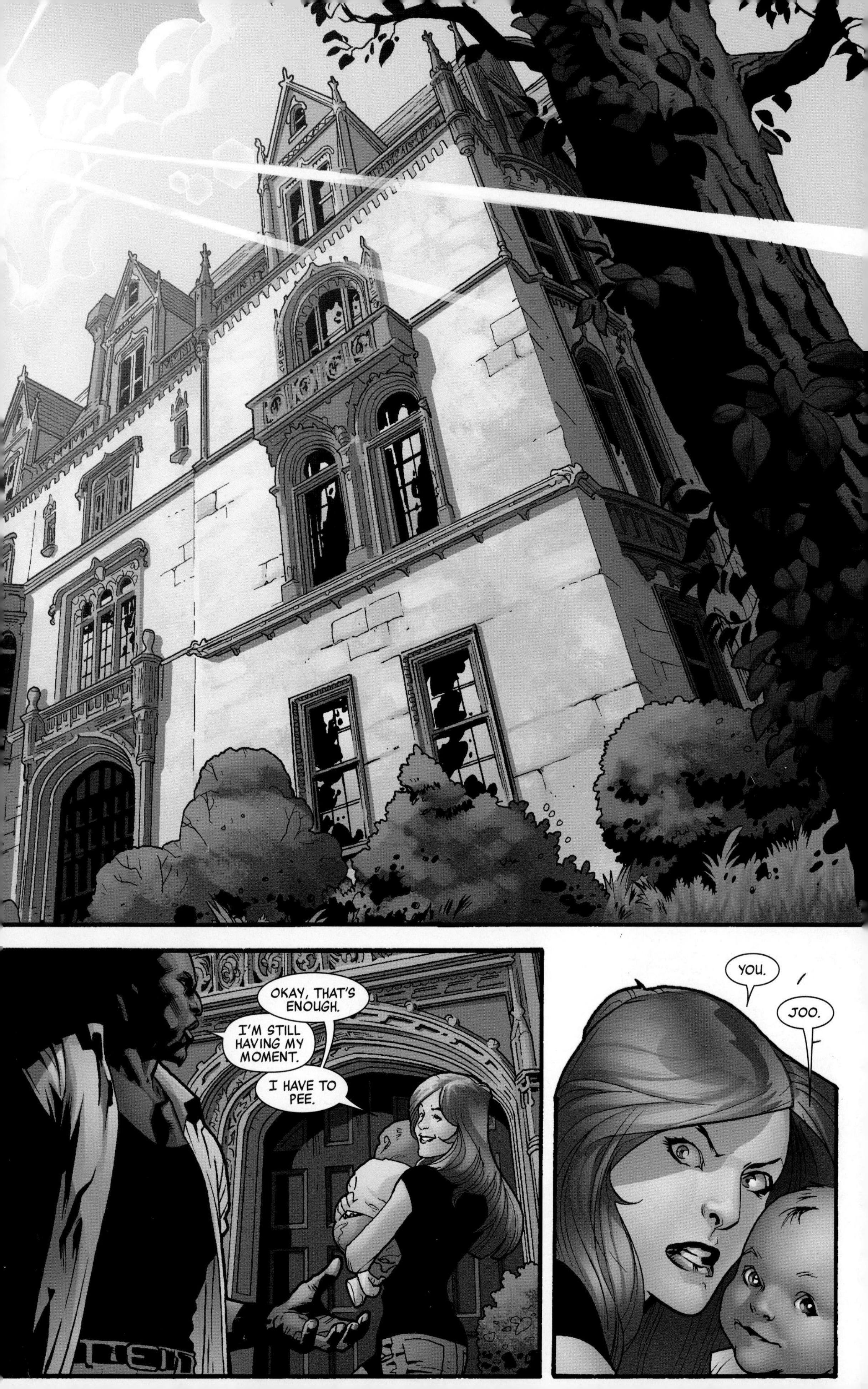
OKAY, THAT'S ENOUGH.
I'M STILL HAVING MY MOMENT.
I HAVE TO PEE.
YOU.
JOO.

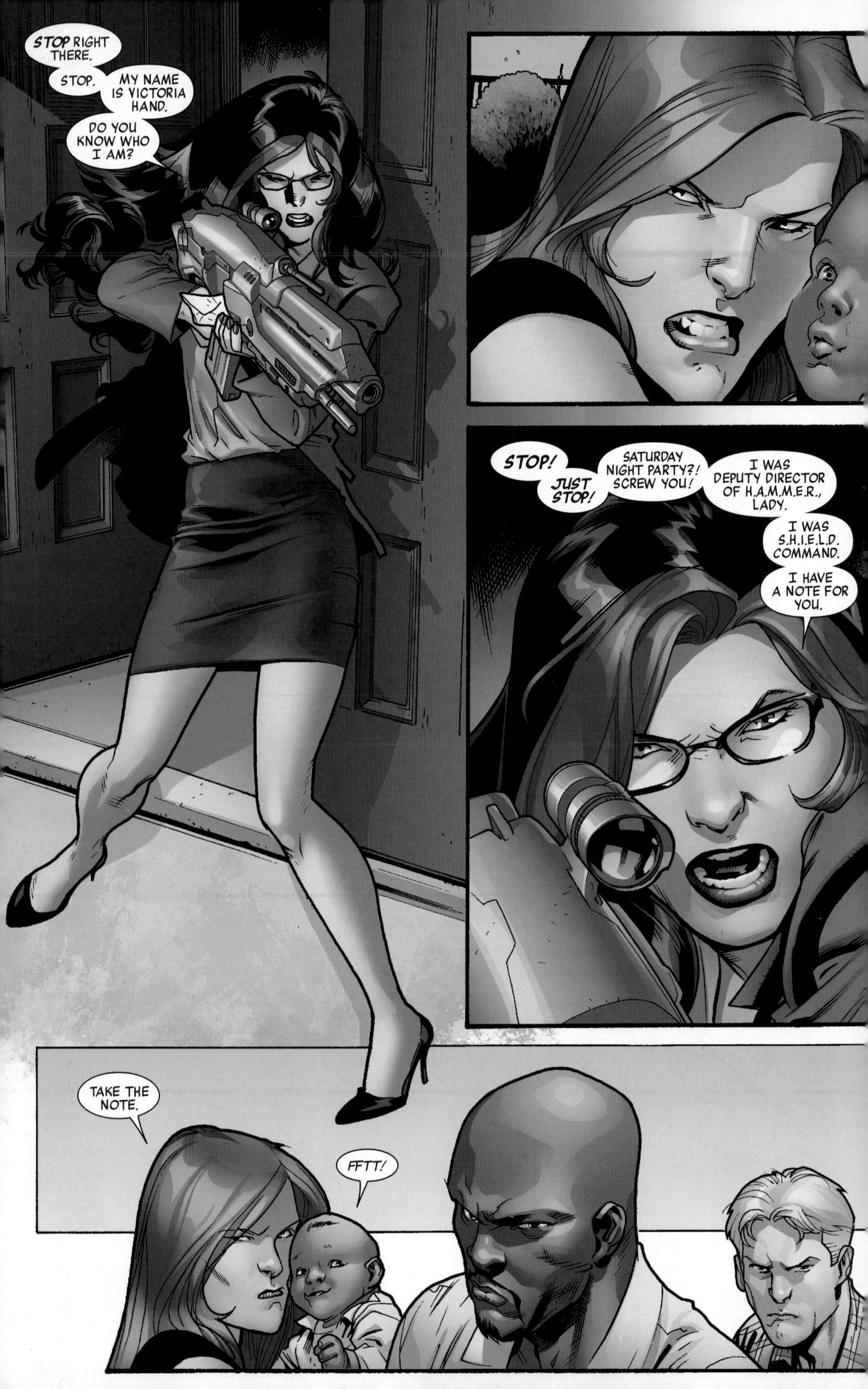
STOP RIGHT THERE.
STOP.
MY NAME IS VICTORIA HAND.
DO YOU KNOW WHO I AM?
STOP!
JUST STOP!
SATURDAY NIGHT PARTY?! SCREW YOU!
I WAS DEPUTY DIRECTOR OF H.A.M.M.E.R., LADY.
I WAS S.H.I.E.L.D. COMMAND.
I HAVE A NOTE FOR YOU.
TAKE THE NOTE.
FFTT!

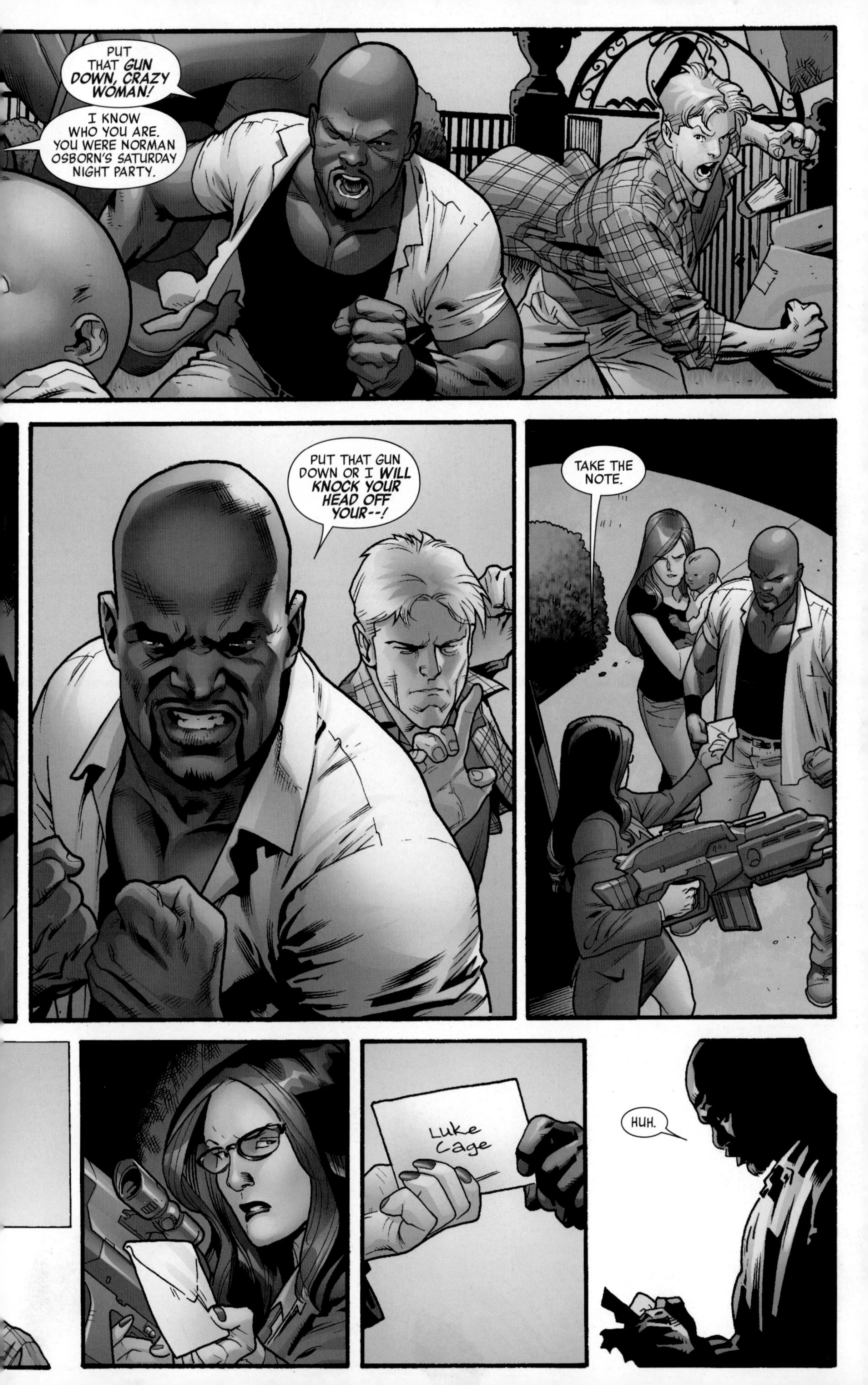
PUT THAT GUN DOWN, CRAZY WOMAN!
I KNOW WHO YOU ARE. YOU WERE NORMAN OSBORN'S SATURDAY NIGHT PARTY.
PUT THAT GUN DOWN OR I WILL KNOCK YOUR HEAD OFF YOUR--!
TAKE THE NOTE.
Luke Cage
HUH.

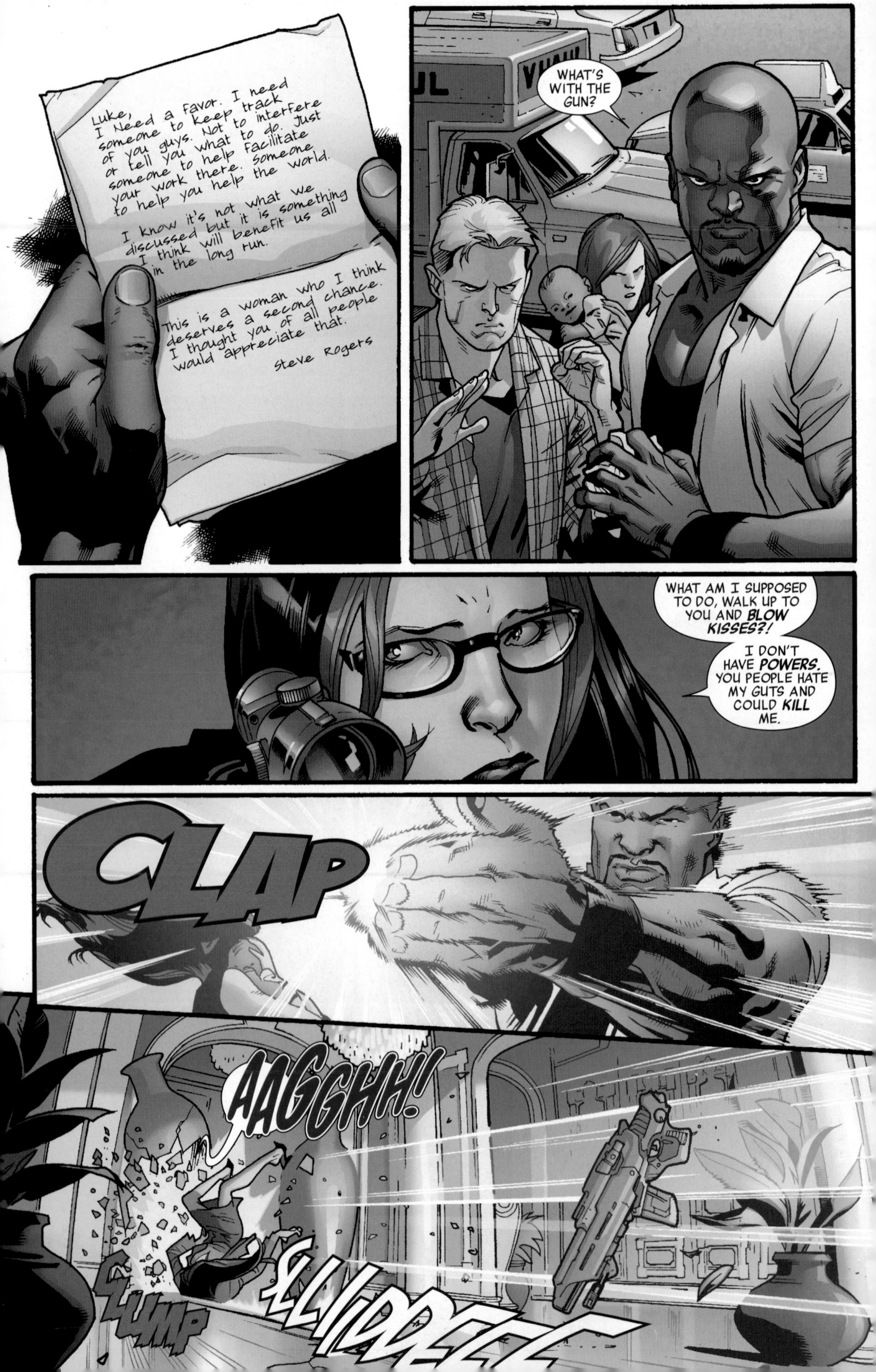
Luke,
I Need a Favor. I need someone to keep track of you guys. Not to interfere or tell you what to do. Just someone to help facilitate your work there. Someone to help you help the world.
I know it's not what we discussed but it is something I think will benefit us all in the long run.
This is a woman who I think deserves a second chance. I thought you of all people would appreciate that.
Steve Rogers
WHAT'S WITH THE GUN?
WHAT AM I SUPPOSED TO DO, WALK UP TO YOU AND BLOW KISSES?!
I DON'T HAVE POWERS. YOU PEOPLE HATE MY GUTS AND COULD KILL ME.
CLAP
AAGGHH!
CLUMP

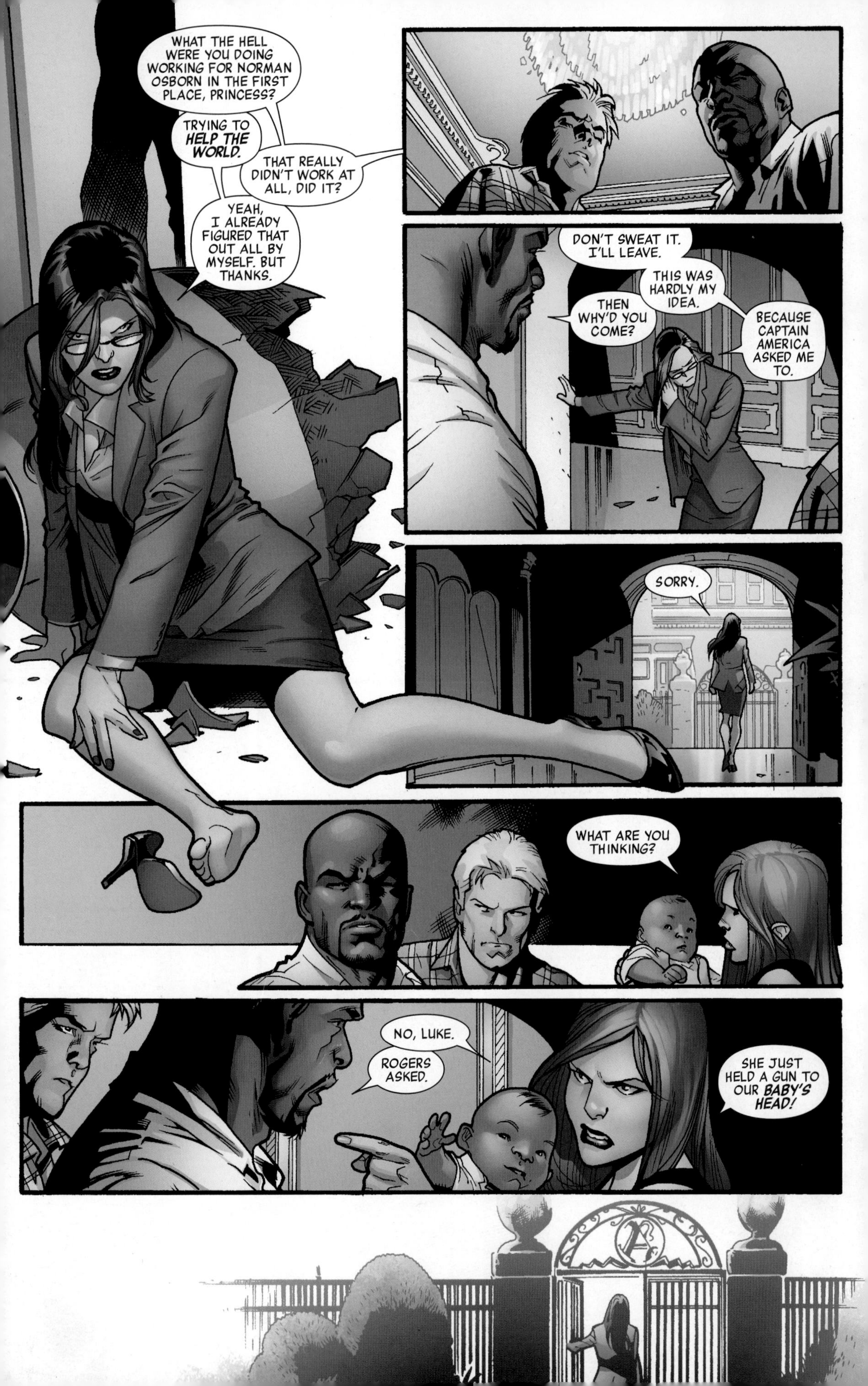
WHAT THE HELL WERE YOU DOING WORKING FOR NORMAN OSBORN IN THE FIRST PLACE, PRINCESS?
TRYING TO HELP THE WORLD.
THAT REALLY DIDN'T WORK AT ALL, DID IT?
YEAH, I ALREADY FIGURED THAT OUT ALL BY MYSELF. BUT THANKS.
DON'T SWEAT IT. I'LL LEAVE.
THIS WAS HARDLY MY IDEA.
THEN WHY'D YOU COME?
BECAUSE CAPTAIN AMERICA ASKED ME TO.
SORRY.
WHAT ARE YOU THINKING?
NO, LUKE.
ROGERS ASKED.
SHE JUST HELD A GUN TO OUR BABY'S HEAD!

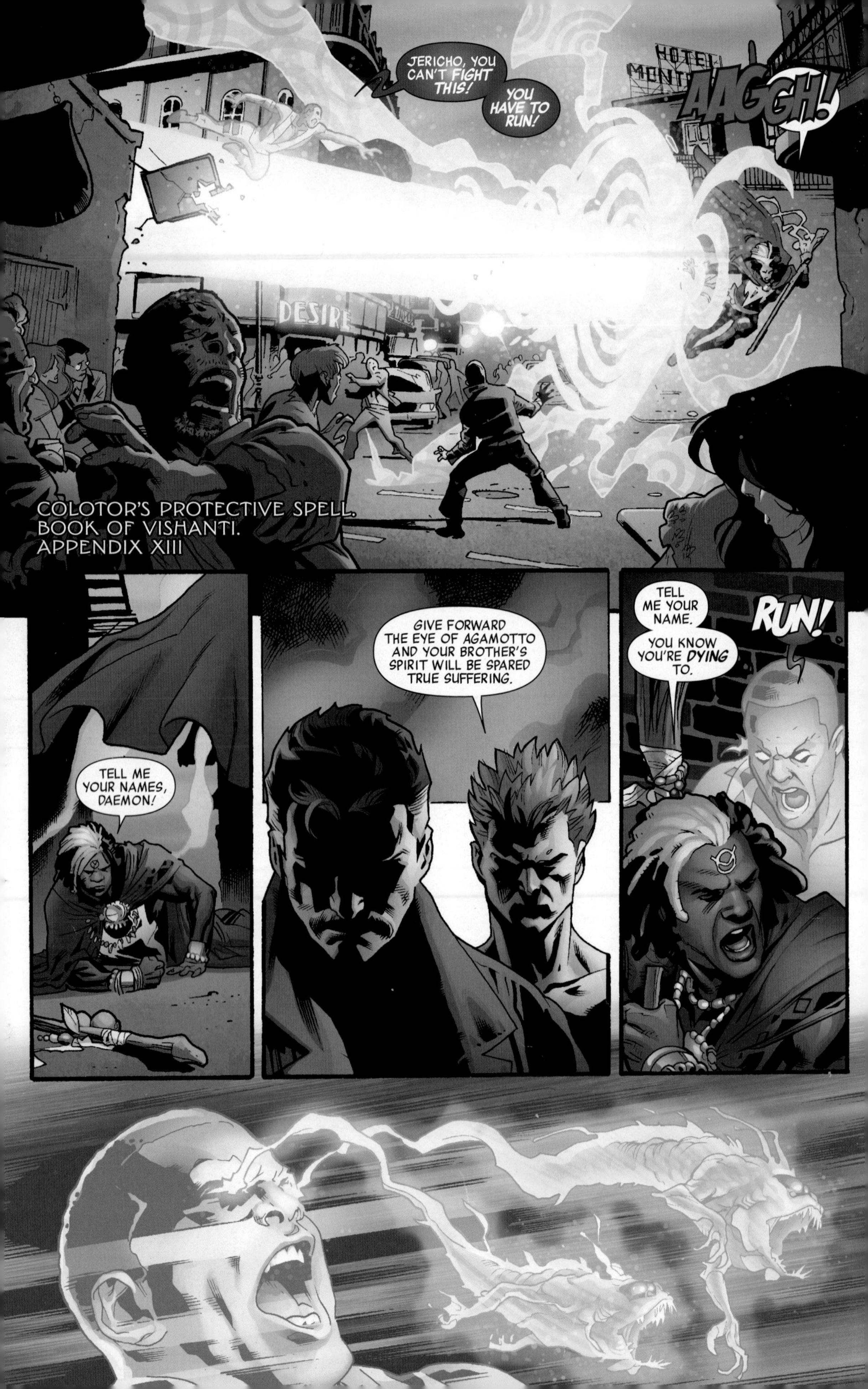
JERICHO, YOU CAN'T FIGHT THIS!
YOU HAVE TO RUN!
HOTEL MONTE
AAGGH!
DESIRE
COLOTOR'S PROTECTIVE SPELL. BOOK OF VISHANTI. APPENDIX XIII
TELL ME YOUR NAMES, DAEMON!
GIVE FORWARD THE EYE OF AGAMOTTO AND YOUR BROTHER'S SPIRIT WILL BE SPARED TRUE SUFFERING.
TELL ME YOUR NAME.
YOU KNOW YOU'RE DYING TO.
RUN!

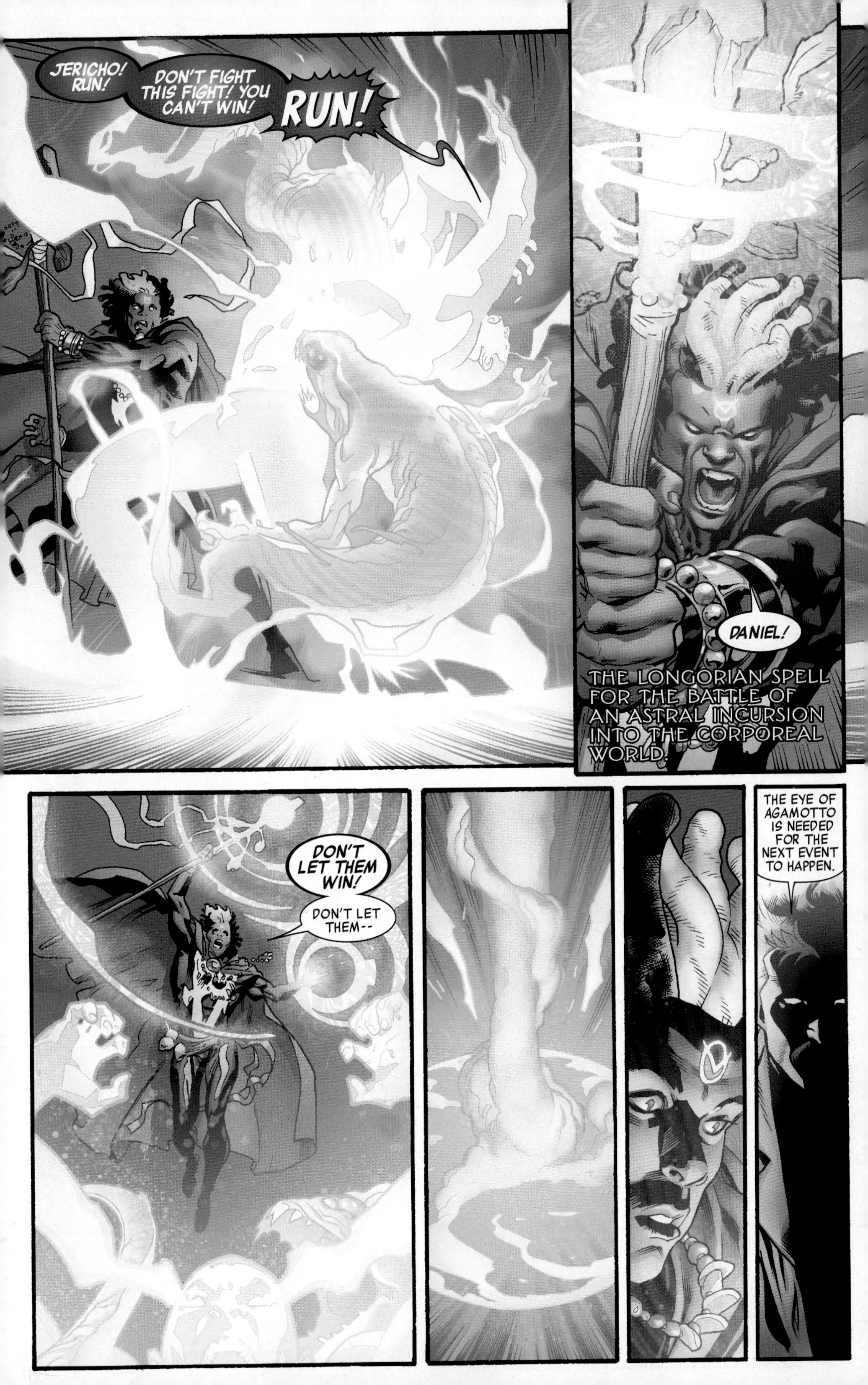
JERICHO! RUN!
DON'T FIGHT THIS FIGHT! YOU CAN'T WIN!
RUN!
DANIEL!
THE LONGORIAN SPELL FOR THE BATTLE OF AN ASTRAL INCURSION INTO THE CORPOREAL WORLD.
DON'T LET THEM WIN!
DON'T LET THEM--
THE EYE OF AGAMOTTO IS NEEDED FOR THE NEXT EVENT TO HAPPEN.

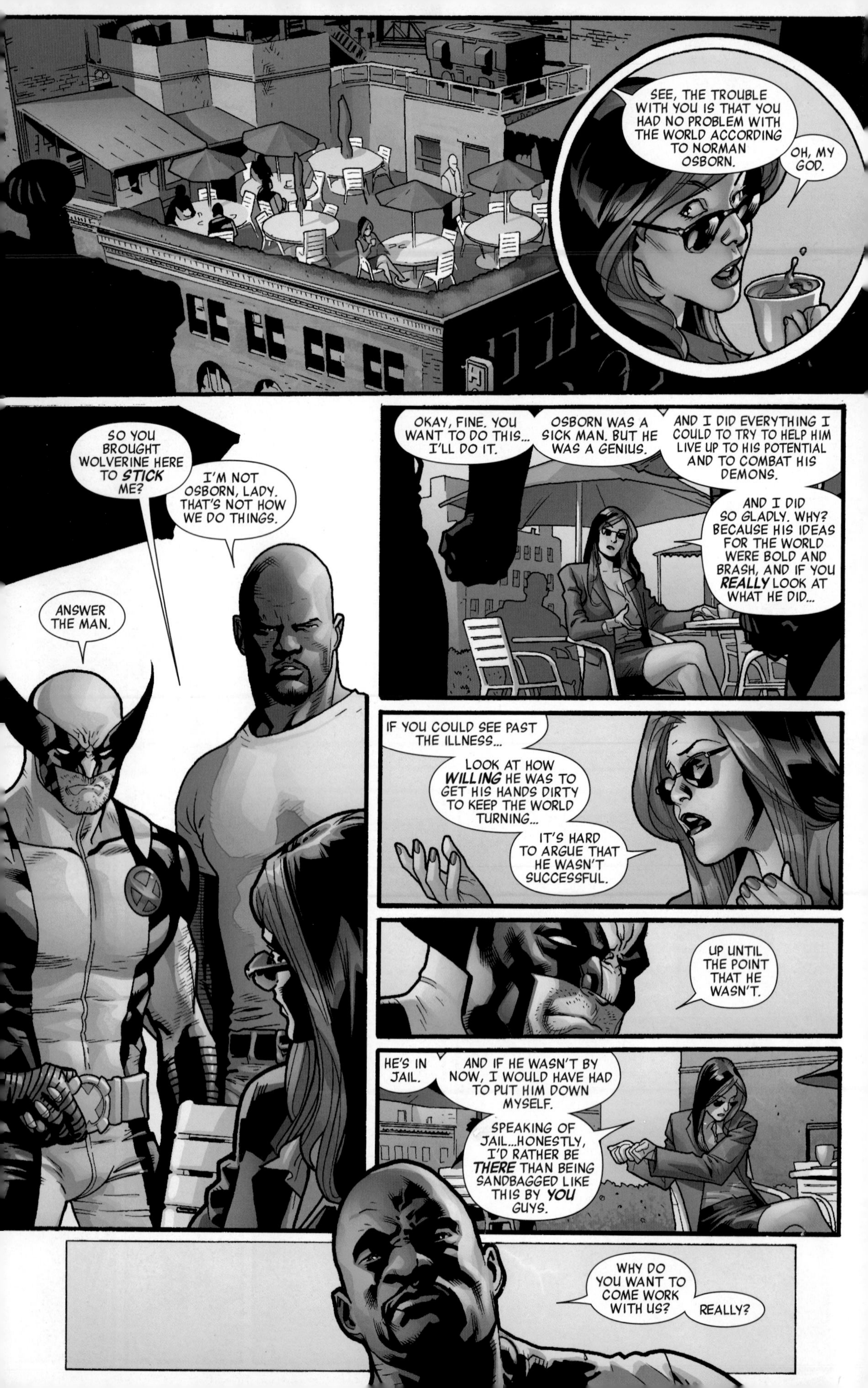
SEE, THE TROUBLE WITH YOU IS THAT YOU HAD NO PROBLEM WITH THE WORLD ACCORDING TO NORMAN OSBORN.
OH, MY GOD.
SO YOU BROUGHT WOLVERINE HERE TO STICK ME?
I'M NOT OSBORN, LADY. THAT'S NOT HOW WE DO THINGS.
ANSWER THE MAN.
OKAY, FINE. YOU WANT TO DO THIS... I'LL DO IT.
OSBORN WAS A SICK MAN. BUT HE WAS A GENIUS.
AND I DID EVERYTHING I COULD TO TRY TO HELP HIM LIVE UP TO HIS POTENTIAL AND TO COMBAT HIS DEMONS.
AND I DID SO GLADLY. WHY? BECAUSE HIS IDEAS FOR THE WORLD WERE BOLD AND BRASH, AND IF YOU REALLY LOOK AT WHAT HE DID...
IF YOU COULD SEE PAST THE ILLNESS...
LOOK AT HOW WILLING HE WAS TO GET HIS HANDS DIRTY TO KEEP THE WORLD TURNING...
IT'S HARD TO ARGUE THAT HE WASN'T SUCCESSFUL.
UP UNTIL THE POINT THAT HE WASN'T.
HE'S IN JAIL.
AND IF HE WASN'T BY NOW, I WOULD HAVE HAD TO PUT HIM DOWN MYSELF.
SPEAKING OF JAIL...HONESTLY, I'D RATHER BE THERE THAN BEING SANDBAGGED LIKE THIS BY YOU GUYS.
WHY DO YOU WANT TO COME WORK WITH US?
REALLY?

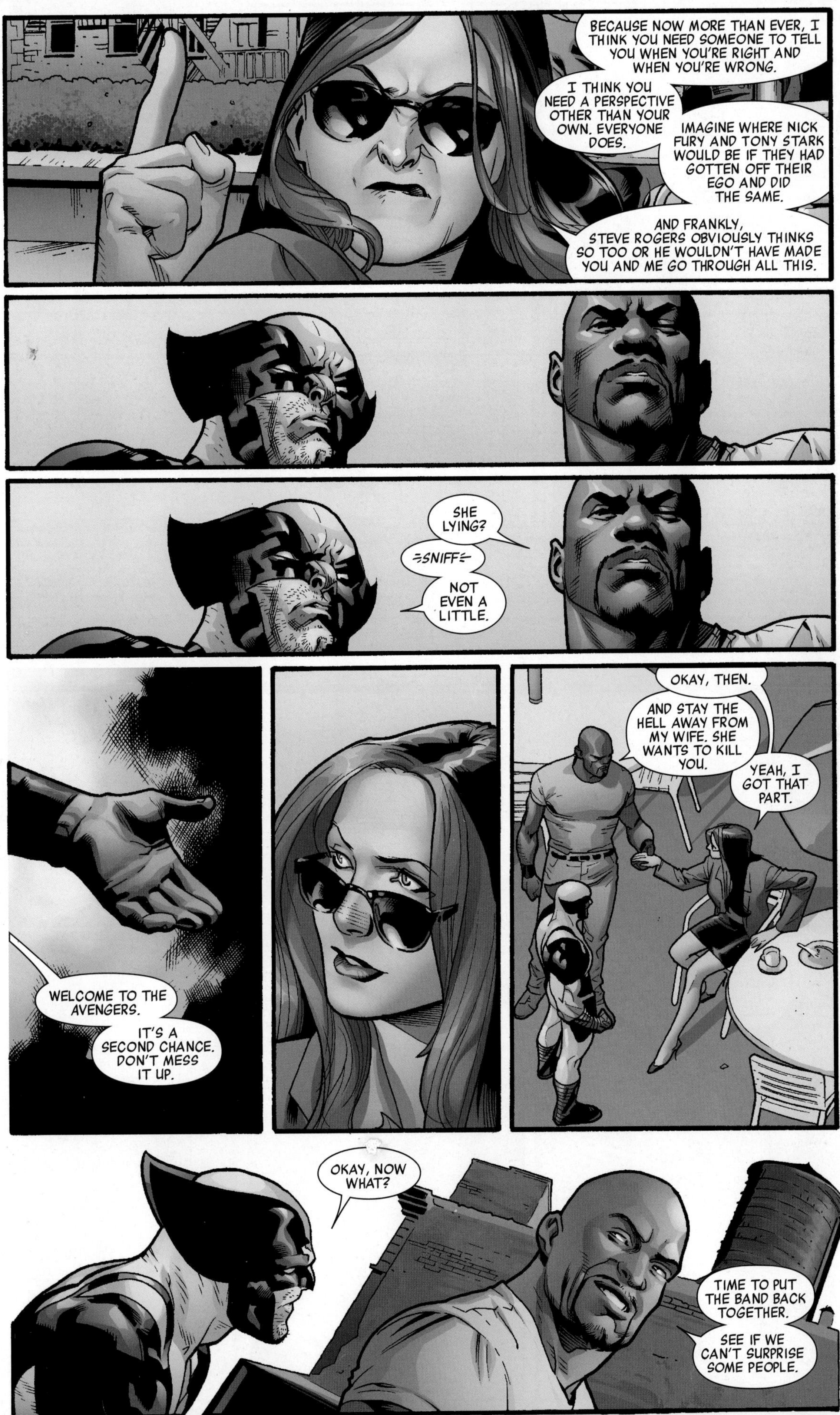

BECAUSE NOW MORE THAN EVER, I THINK YOU NEED SOMEONE TO TELL YOU WHEN YOU'RE RIGHT AND WHEN YOU'RE WRONG.
I THINK YOU NEED A PERSPECTIVE OTHER THAN YOUR OWN. EVERYONE DOES.
IMAGINE WHERE NICK FURY AND TONY STARK WOULD BE IF THEY HAD GOTTEN OFF THEIR EGO AND DID THE SAME.
AND FRANKLY, STEVE ROGERS OBVIOUSLY THINKS SO TOO OR HE WOULDN'T HAVE MADE YOU AND ME GO THROUGH ALL THIS.
SHE LYING?
SNIFF
NOT EVEN A LITTLE.
WELCOME TO THE AVENGERS.
IT'S A SECOND CHANCE. DON'T MESS IT UP.
OKAY, THEN.
AND STAY THE HELL AWAY FROM MY WIFE. SHE WANTS TO KILL YOU.
YEAH, I GOT THAT PART.
OKAY, NOW WHAT?
TIME TO PUT THE BAND BACK TOGETHER.
SEE IF WE CAN'T SURPRISE SOME PEOPLE.

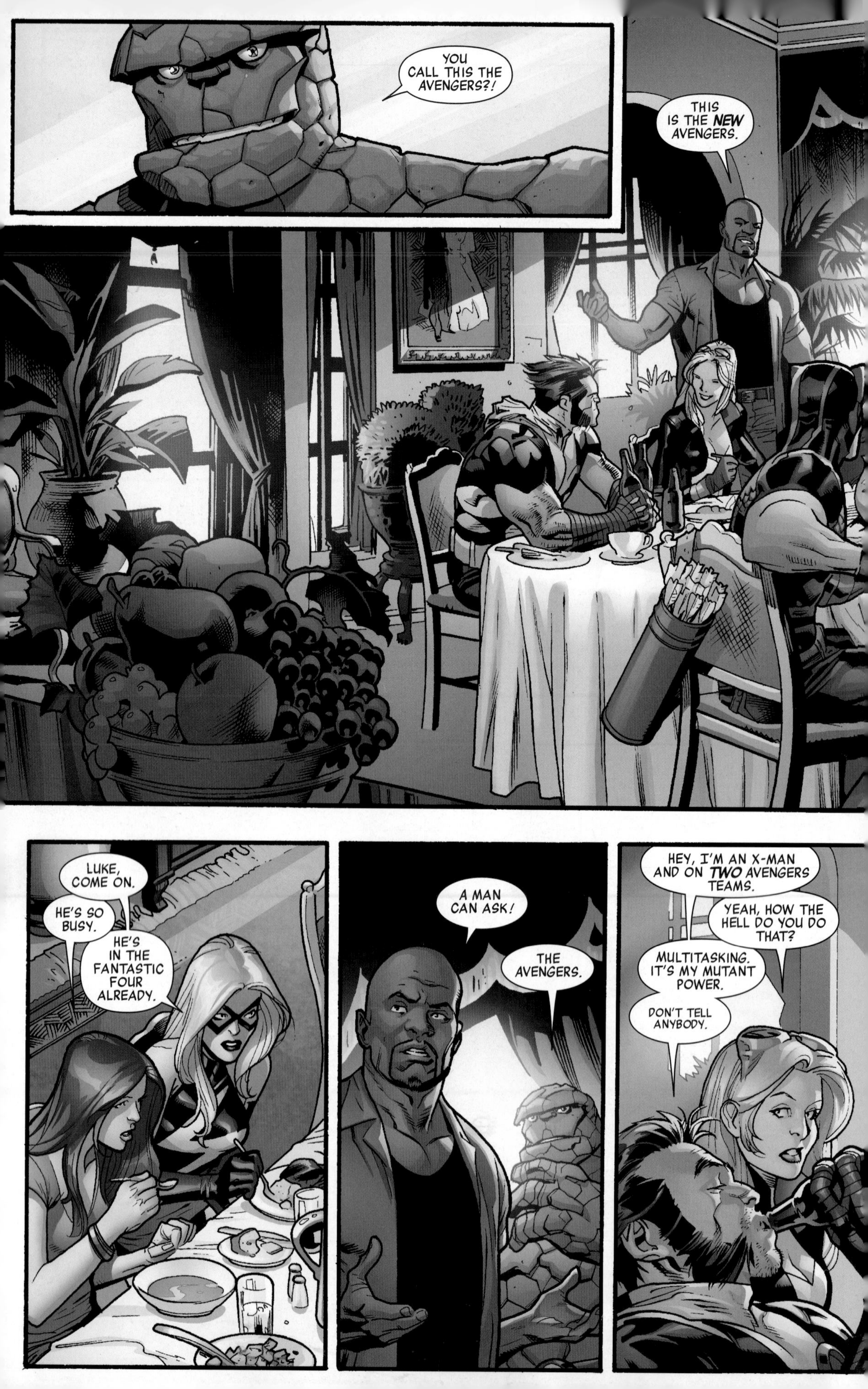
YOU CALL THIS THE AVENGERS?!
THIS IS THE NEW AVENGERS.
LUKE, COME ON.
HE'S SO BUSY.
HE'S IN THE FANTASTIC FOUR ALREADY.
A MAN CAN ASK!
THE AVENGERS.
HEY, I'M AN X-MAN AND ON TWO AVENGERS TEAMS.
YEAH, HOW THE HELL DO YOU DO THAT?
MULTITASKING. IT'S MY MUTANT POWER.
DON'T TELL ANYBODY.

BENJAMIN J. GRIMM!

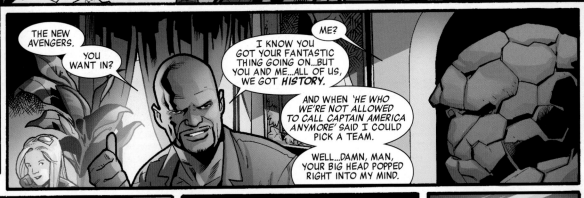

THE NEW AVENGERS.

YOU WANT IN?

ME? I KNOW YOU GOT YOUR FANTASTIC THING GOING ON...BUT YOU AND ME...ALL OF US, WE GOT *HISTORY*.

AND WHEN 'HE WHO WE'RE NOT ALLOWED TO CALL CAPTAIN AMERICA ANYMORE' SAID I COULD PICK A TEAM.

WELL...DAMN, MAN, YOUR BIG HEAD POPPED RIGHT INTO MY MIND.

I DO LOVE MY FAMILY... SUSIE, REED, THAT OTHER GUY...

BUT THEY ARE DRIVING ME ABSOLUTELY INSANE LATELY.

I'M NOT SAYING YOU *QUIT* THEM. I'M JUST SAYING, WHEN YOU'RE NOT THERE...COME HERE.

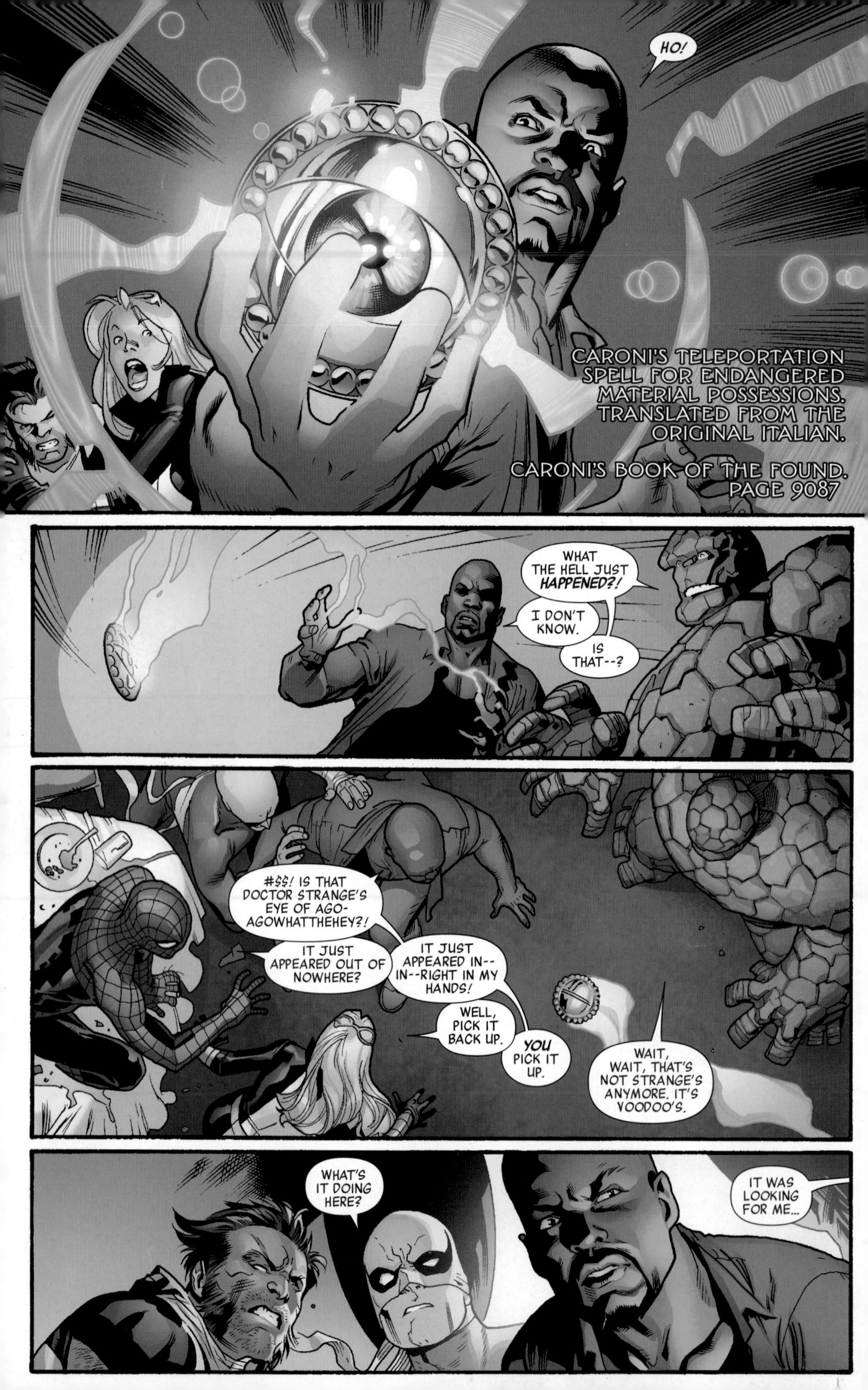

HO!
CARONI'S TELEPORTATION SPELL FOR ENDANGERED MATERIAL POSSESSIONS. TRANSLATED FROM THE ORIGINAL ITALIAN.
CARONI'S BOOK OF THE FOUND. PAGE 9087
WHAT THE HELL JUST HAPPENED?!
I DON'T KNOW.
IS THAT--?
#$$! IS THAT DOCTOR STRANGE'S EYE OF AGO-AGOWHATTHEHEY?!
IT JUST APPEARED OUT OF NOWHERE?
IT JUST APPEARED IN-- IN--RIGHT IN MY HANDS!
WELL, PICK IT BACK UP.
YOU PICK IT UP.
WAIT, WAIT, THAT'S NOT STRANGE'S ANYMORE. IT'S VOODOO'S.
WHAT'S IT DOING HERE?
IT WAS LOOKING FOR ME...

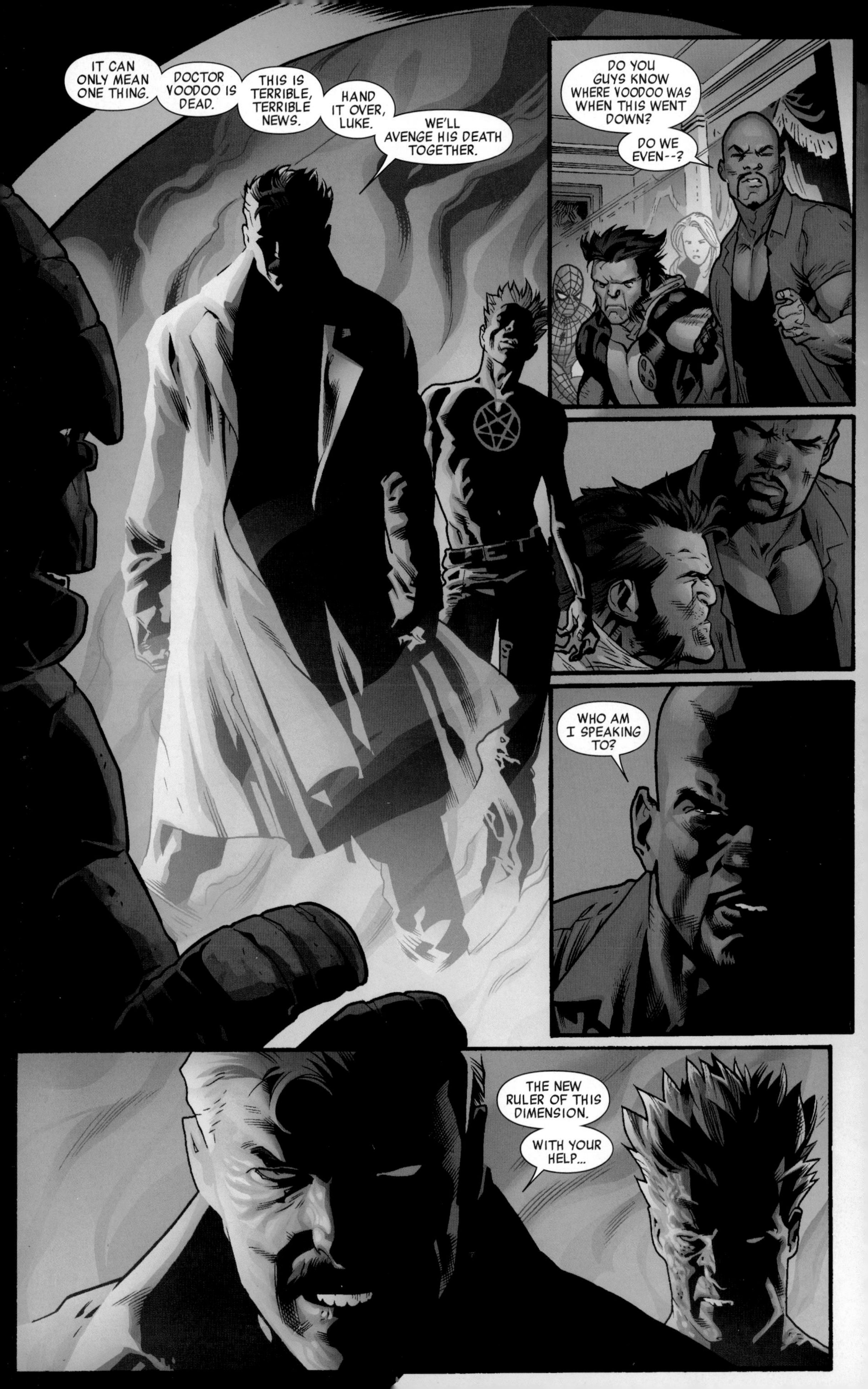
IT CAN ONLY MEAN ONE THING.
DOCTOR VOODOO IS DEAD.
THIS IS TERRIBLE, TERRIBLE NEWS.
HAND IT OVER, LUKE.
WE'LL AVENGE HIS DEATH TOGETHER.
DO YOU GUYS KNOW WHERE VOODOO WAS WHEN THIS WENT DOWN?
DO WE EVEN--?
WHO AM I SPEAKING TO?
THE NEW RULER OF THIS DIMENSION.
WITH YOUR HELP...

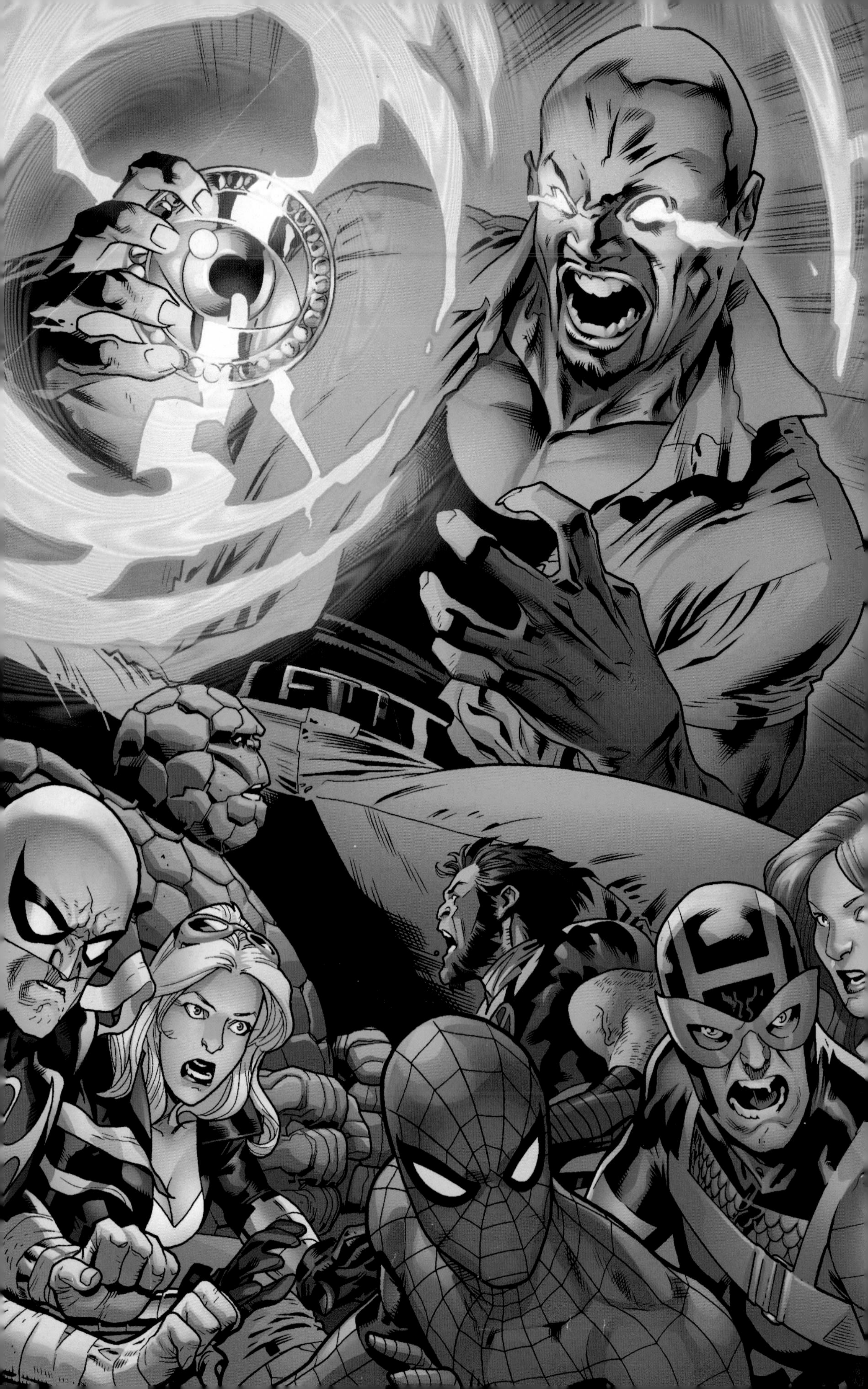

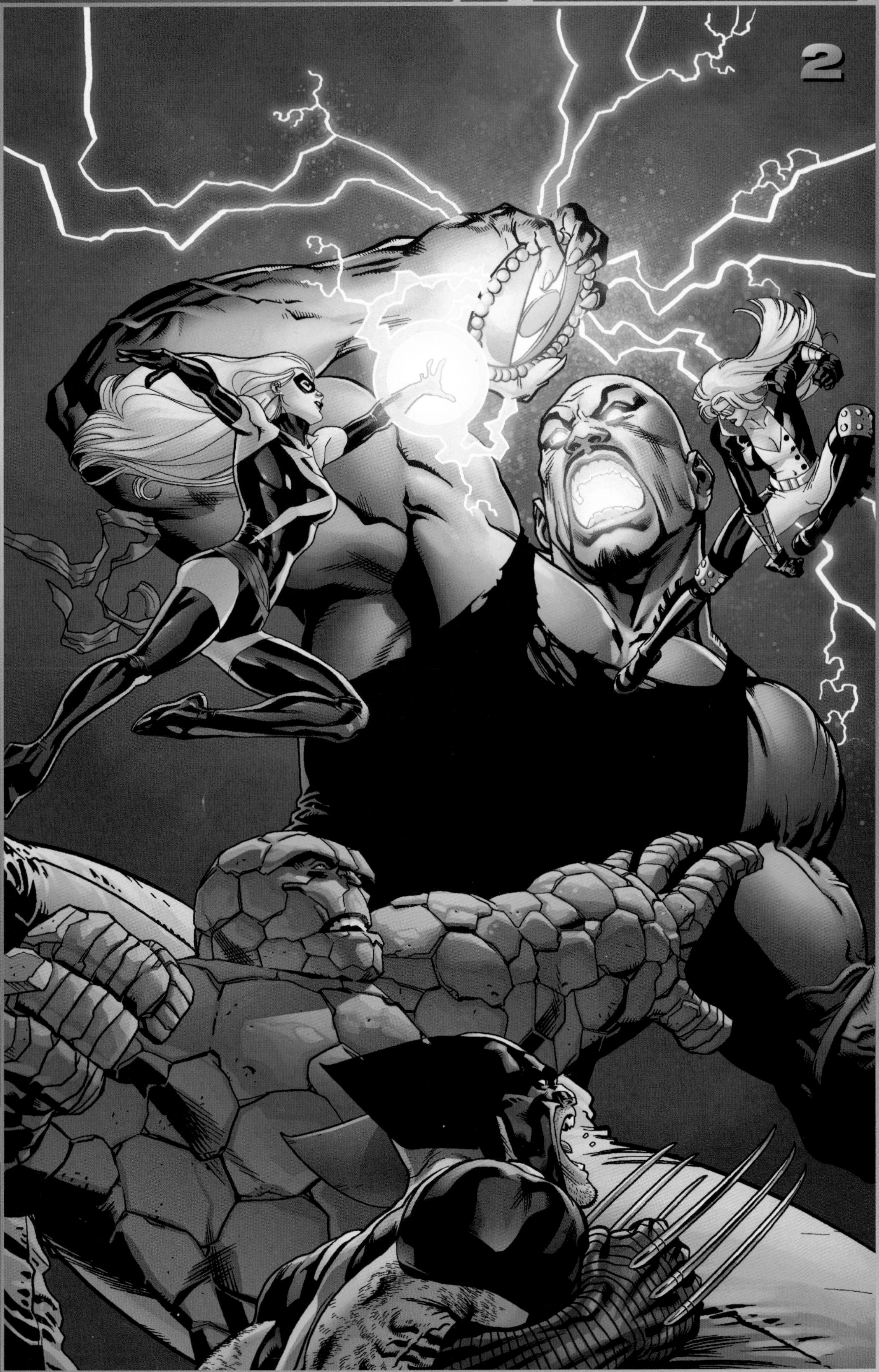
2

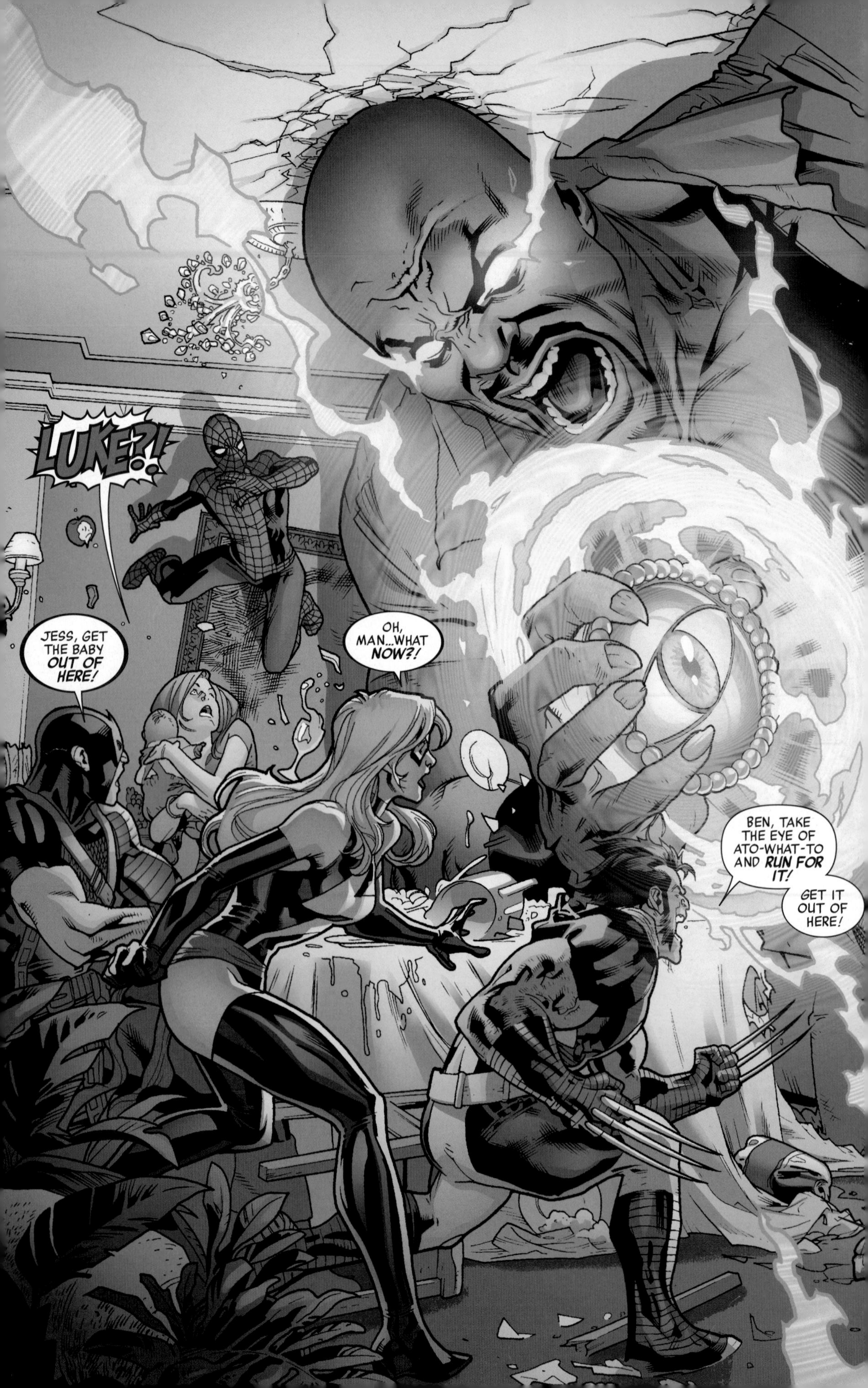
LUKE?!
JESS, GET THE BABY OUT OF HERE!
OH, MAN...WHAT NOW?!
BEN, TAKE THE EYE OF ATO-WHAT-TO AND RUN FOR IT!
GET IT OUT OF HERE!

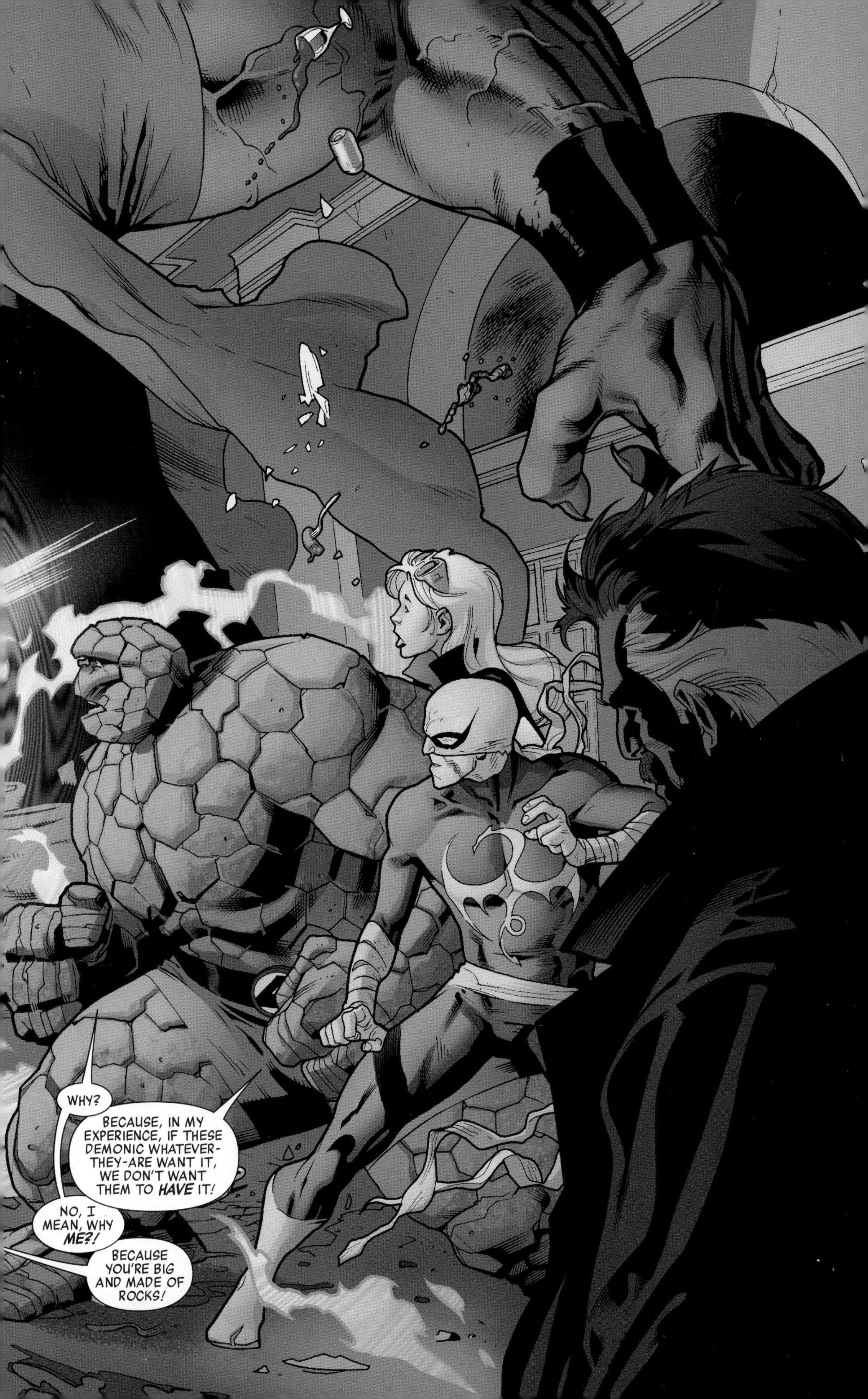
WHY?
BECAUSE, IN MY EXPERIENCE, IF THESE DEMONIC WHATEVER-THEY-ARE WANT IT, WE DON'T WANT THEM TO HAVE IT!
NO, I MEAN, WHY ME?!
BECAUSE YOU'RE BIG AND MADE OF ROCKS!

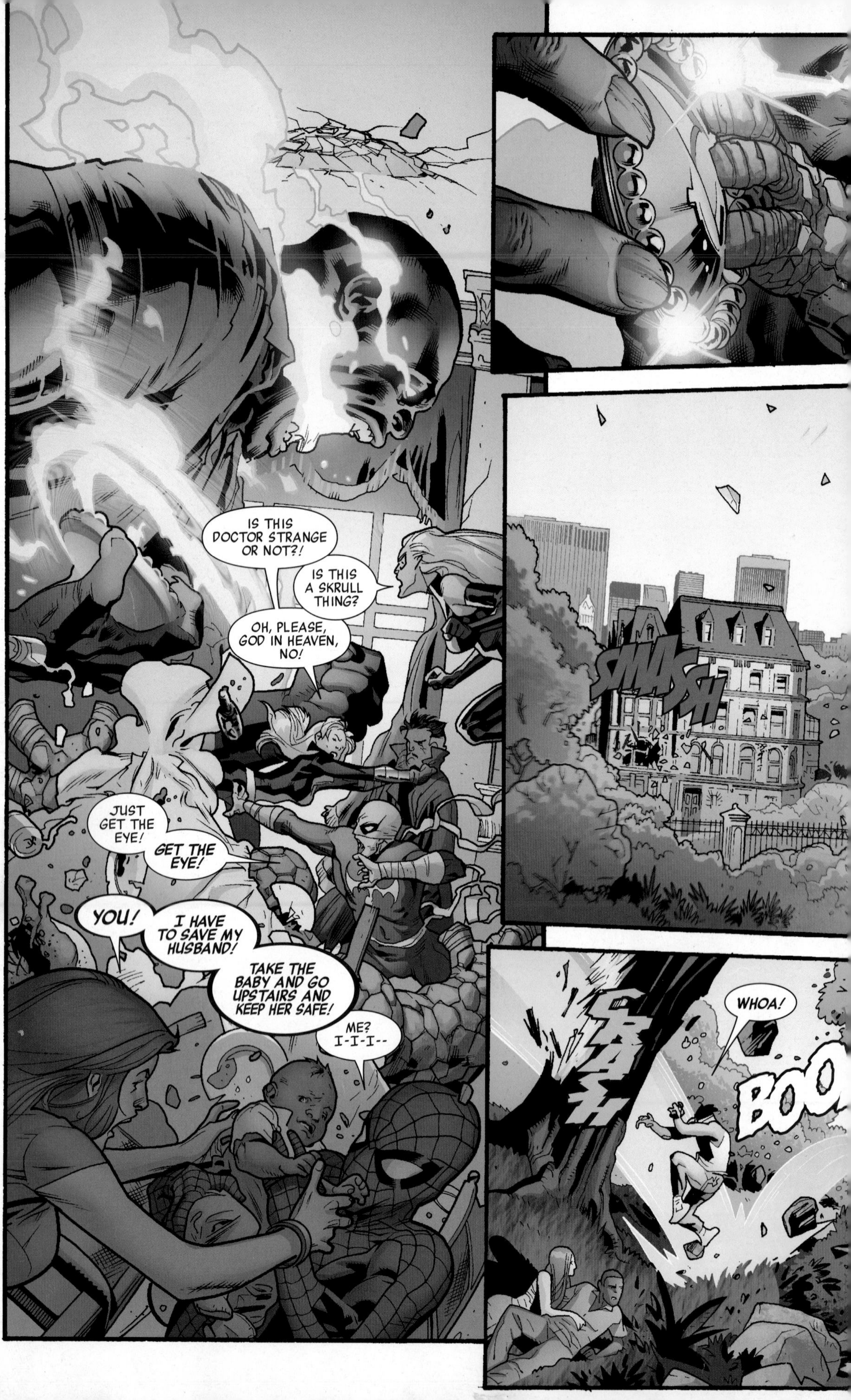

IS THIS DOCTOR STRANGE OR NOT?!
IS THIS A SKRULL THING?
OH, PLEASE, GOD IN HEAVEN, NO!
JUST GET THE EYE!
GET THE EYE!
YOU!
I HAVE TO SAVE MY HUSBAND!
TAKE THE BABY AND GO UPSTAIRS AND KEEP HER SAFE!
ME? I-I-I--
SMASSH
CRASH
WHOA!
BOO

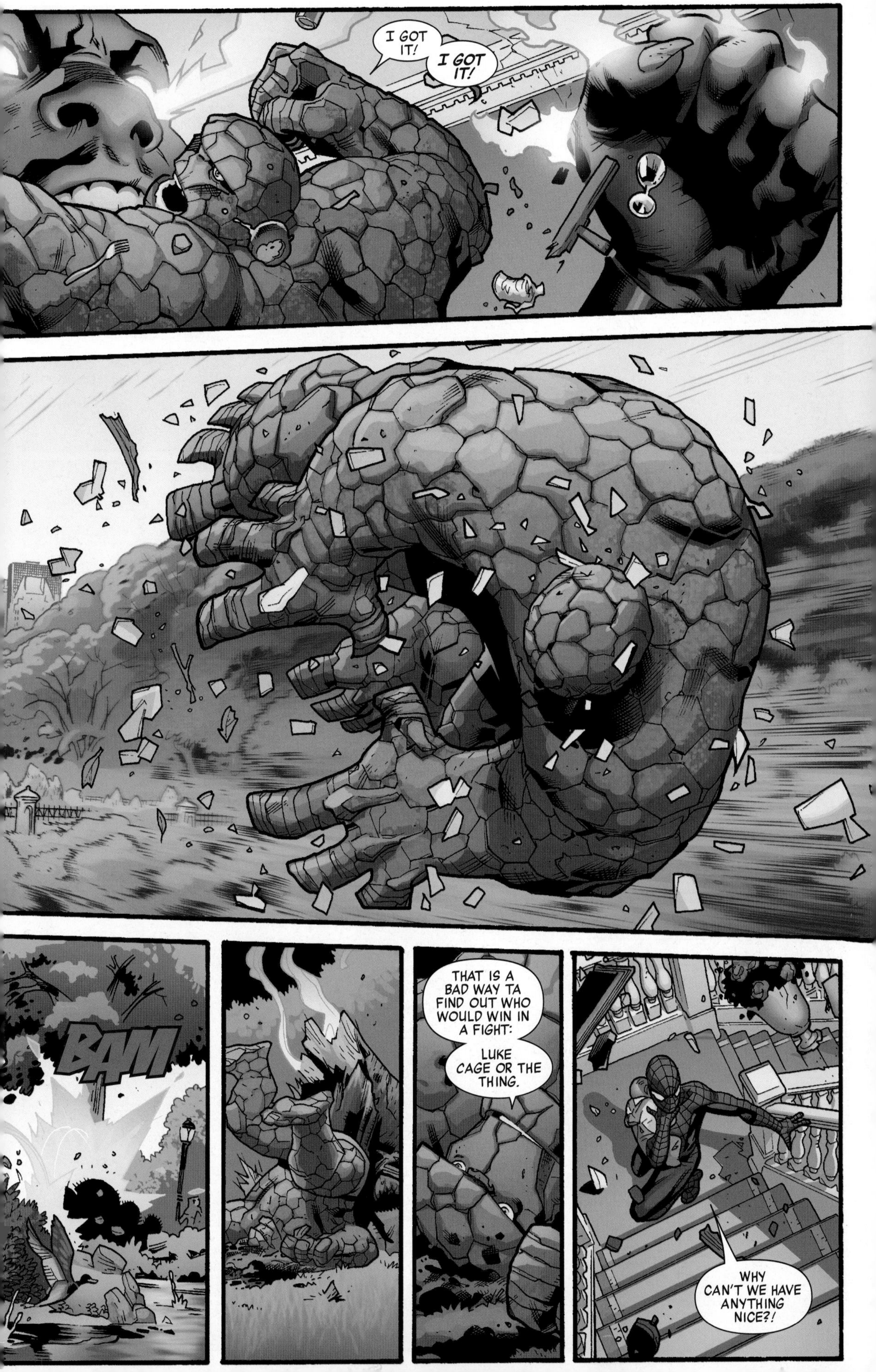
I GOT IT!
I GOT IT!
BAM
THAT IS A BAD WAY TA FIND OUT WHO WOULD WIN IN A FIGHT:
LUKE CAGE OR THE THING.
WHY CAN'T WE HAVE ANYTHING NICE?!

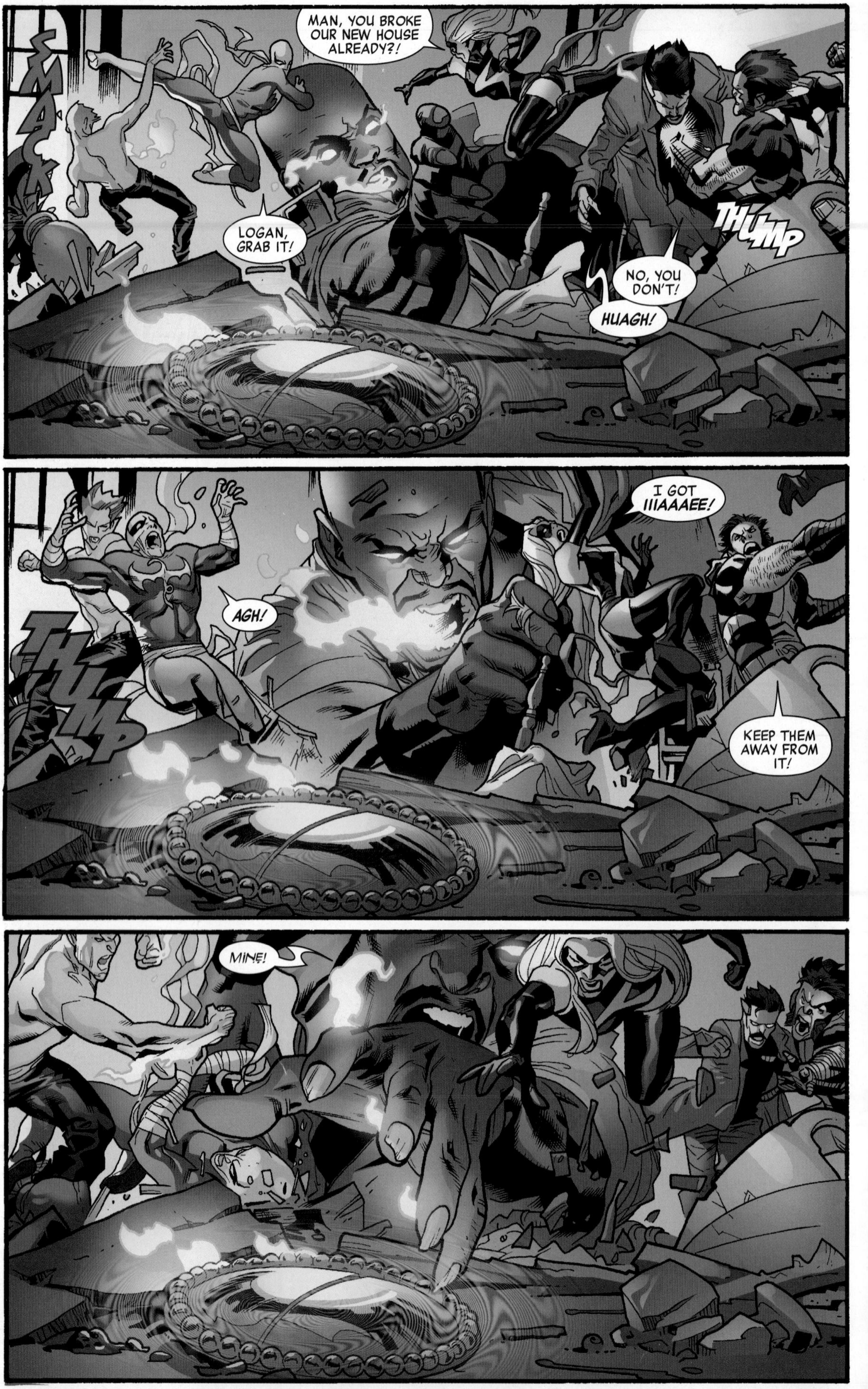
SMACK
MAN, YOU BROKE OUR NEW HOUSE ALREADY?!
LOGAN, GRAB IT!
THUMP
NO, YOU DON'T!
HUAGH!
THUMP
AGH!
I GOT IIIAAAEE!
KEEP THEM AWAY FROM IT!
MINE!

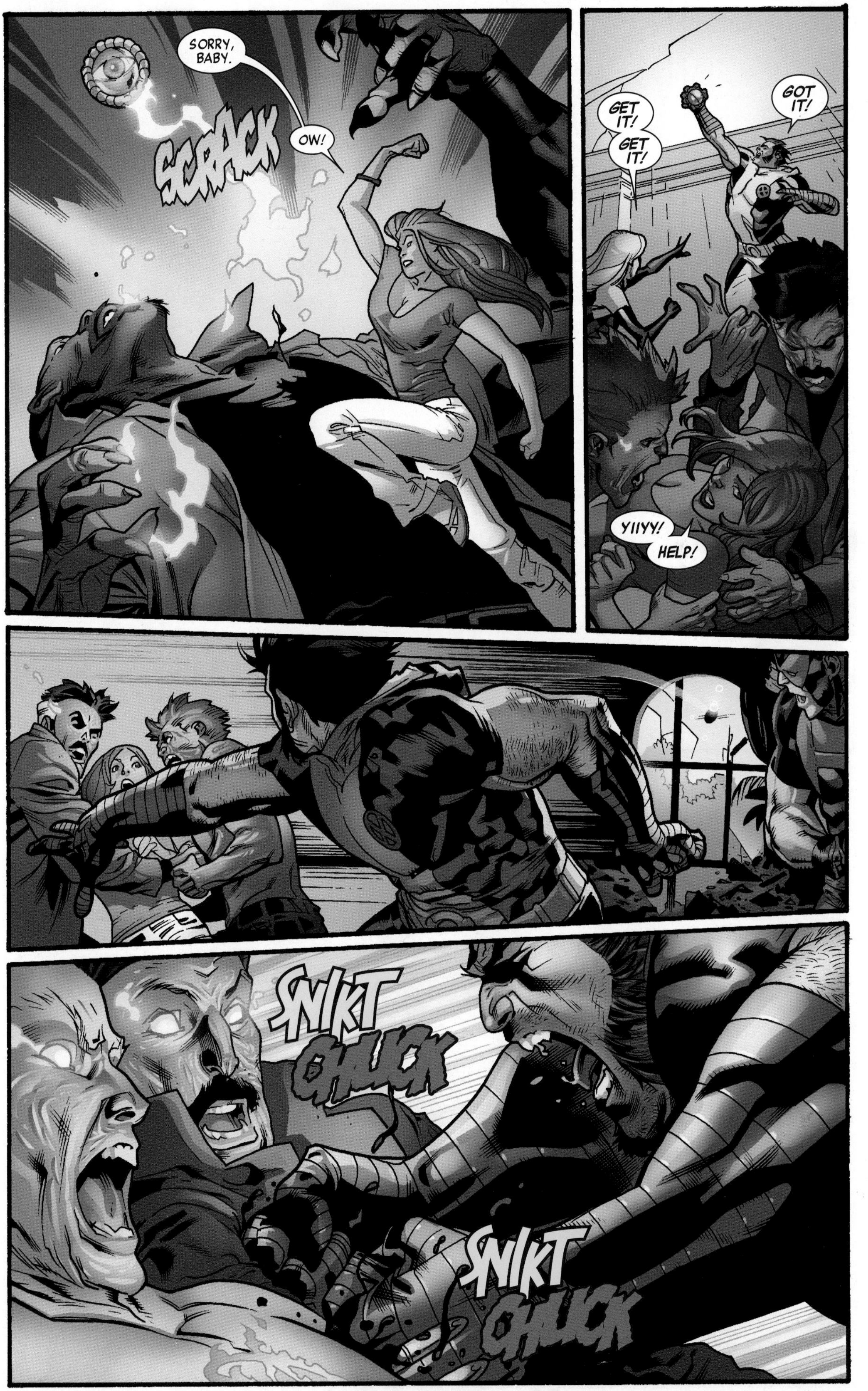
SORRY, BABY.
SCRACK
OW!
GET IT!
GET IT!
GOT IT!
YIIYY!
HELP!
SNIKT
CHUCK
SNIKT
CHUCK

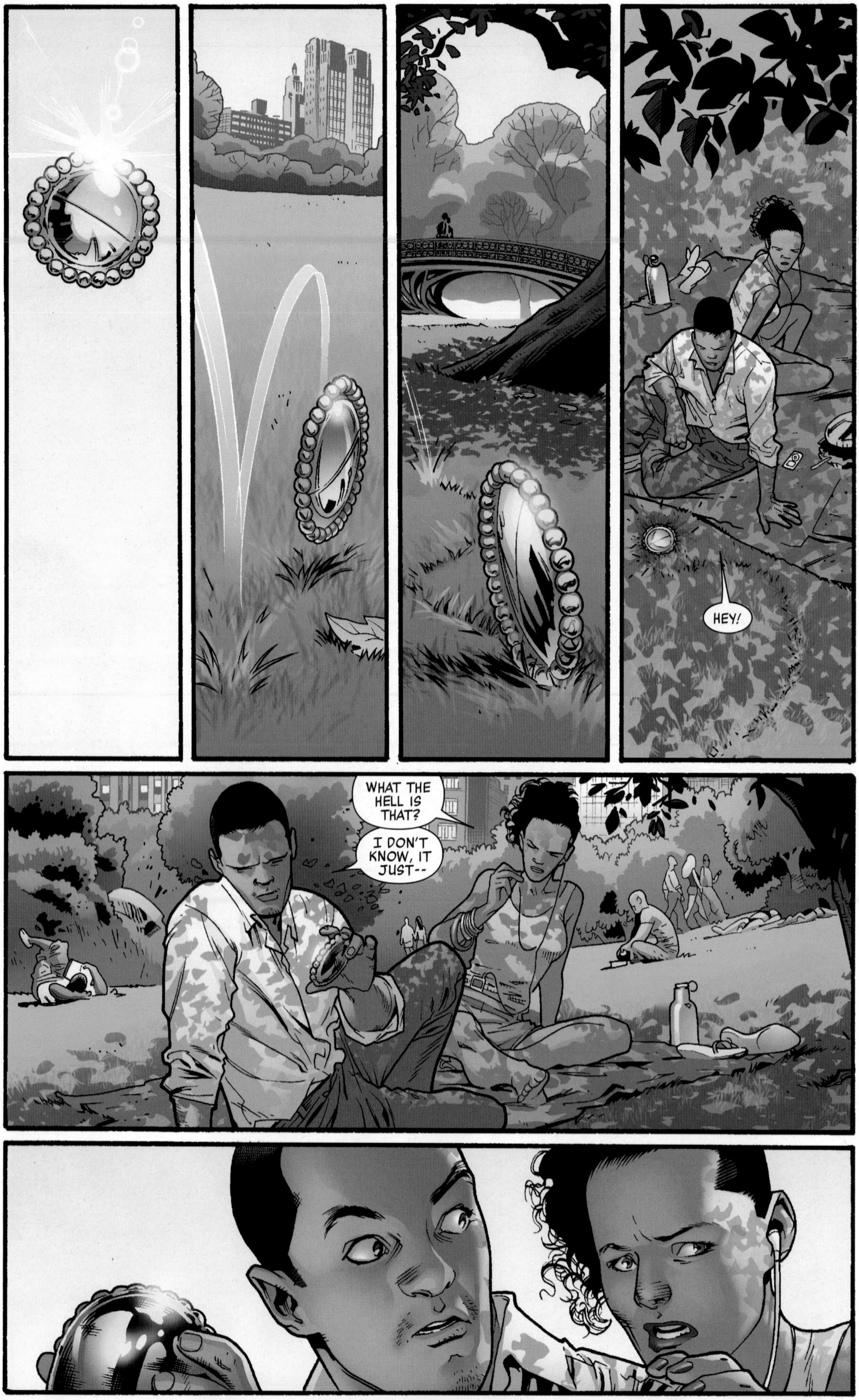
HEY!
WHAT THE HELL IS THAT?
I DON'T KNOW, IT JUST--

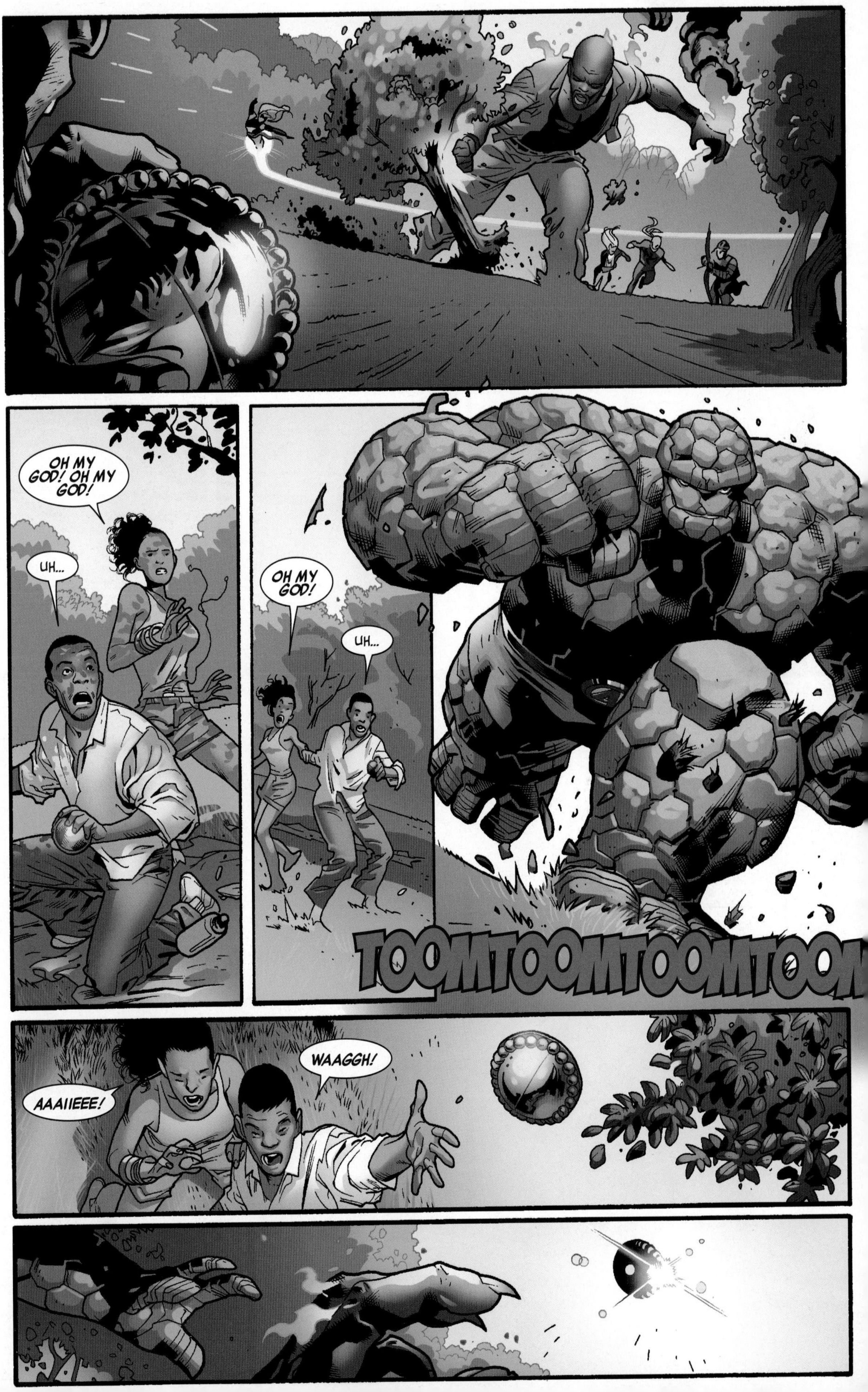
OH MY GOD! OH MY GOD!
UH...
OH MY GOD!
UH...
TOOMTOOMTOOMTOOM
AAAIIEEE!
WAAGGH!

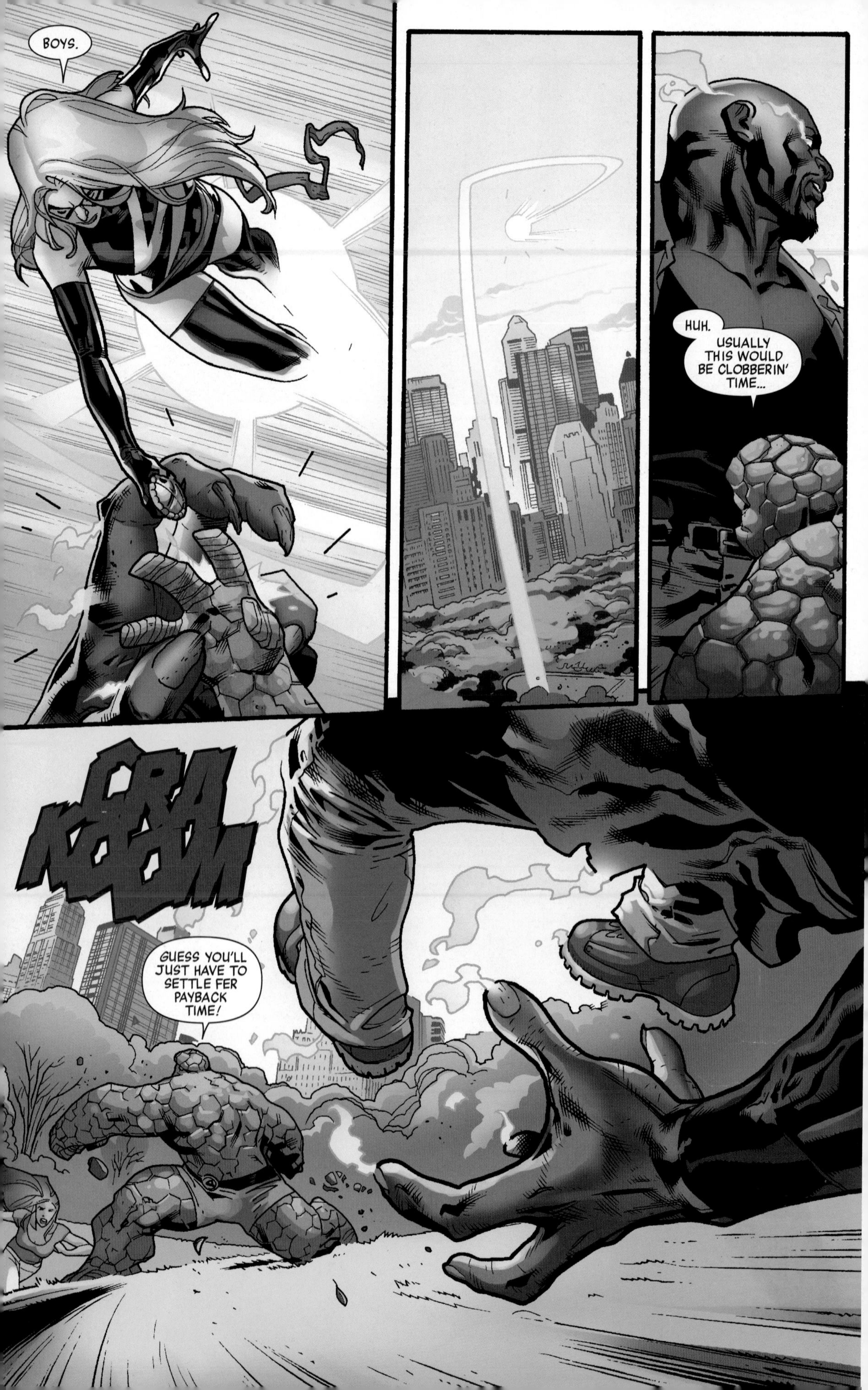
BOYS.
HUH.
USUALLY THIS WOULD BE CLOBBERIN' TIME...
CRA KOOM
GUESS YOU'LL JUST HAVE TO SETTLE FER PAYBACK TIME!

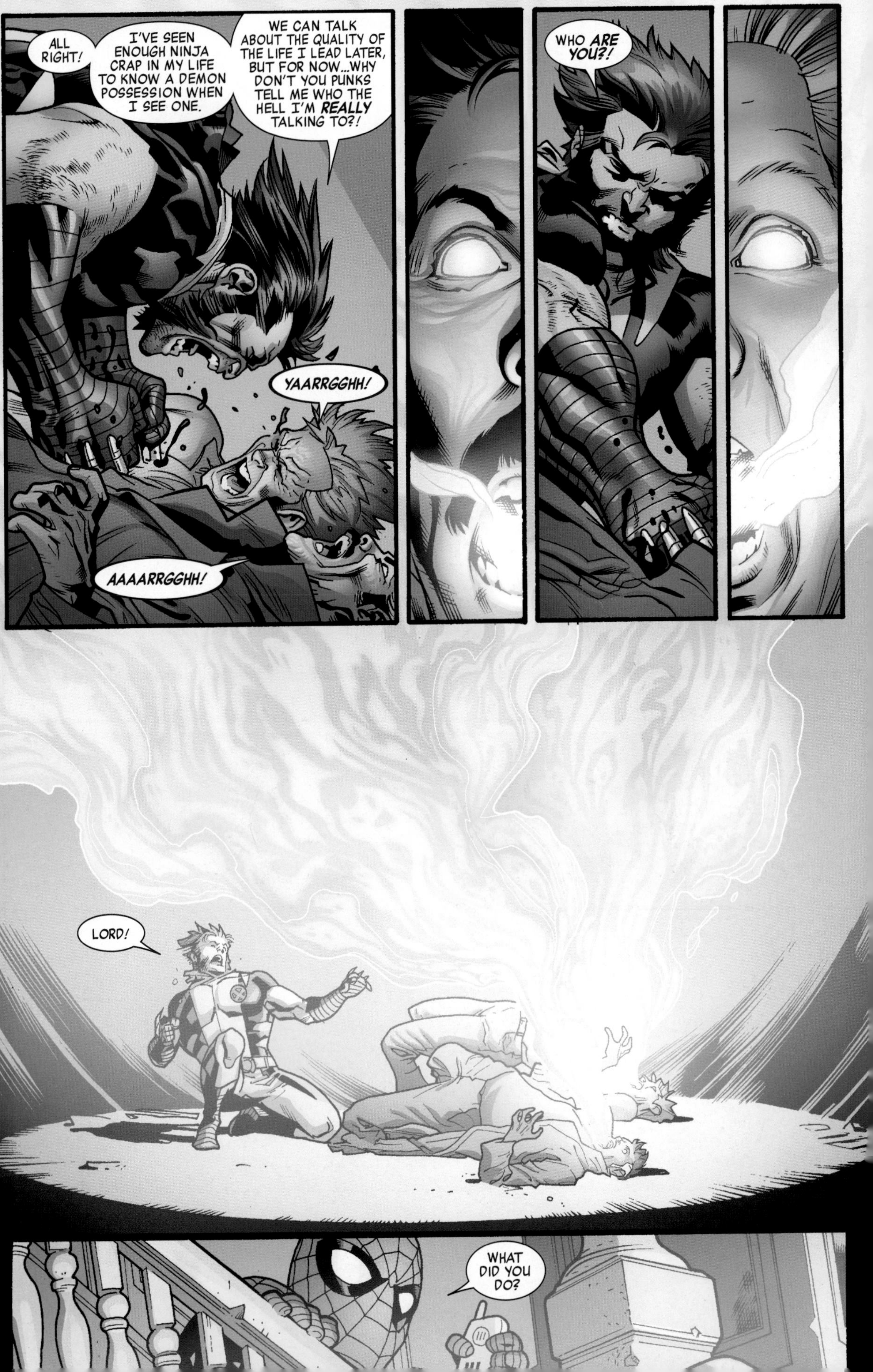
ALL RIGHT!
I'VE SEEN ENOUGH NINJA CRAP IN MY LIFE TO KNOW A DEMON POSSESSION WHEN I SEE ONE.
WE CAN TALK ABOUT THE QUALITY OF THE LIFE I LEAD LATER, BUT FOR NOW...WHY DON'T YOU PUNKS TELL ME WHO THE HELL I'M REALLY TALKING TO?!
YAARRGGHH!
AAAARRGGHH!
WHO ARE YOU?!
LORD!
WHAT DID YOU DO?

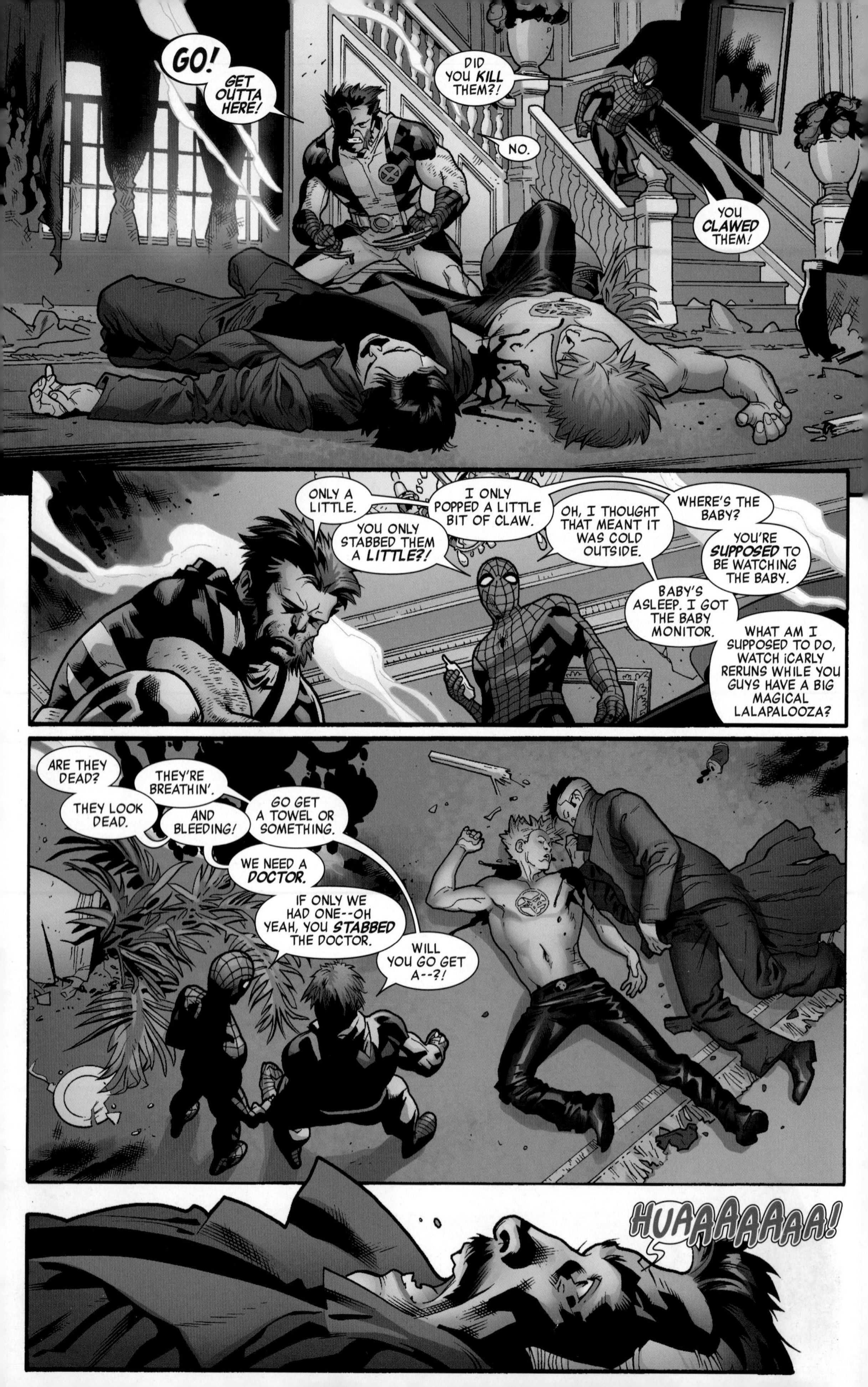
GO! GET OUTTA HERE!
DID YOU KILL THEM?!
NO.
YOU CLAWED THEM!
ONLY A LITTLE.
YOU ONLY STABBED THEM A LITTLE?!
I ONLY POPPED A LITTLE BIT OF CLAW.
OH, I THOUGHT THAT MEANT IT WAS COLD OUTSIDE.
WHERE'S THE BABY?
YOU'RE SUPPOSED TO BE WATCHING THE BABY.
BABY'S ASLEEP. I GOT THE BABY MONITOR.
WHAT AM I SUPPOSED TO DO, WATCH iCARLY RERUNS WHILE YOU GUYS HAVE A BIG MAGICAL LALAPALOOZA?
ARE THEY DEAD?
THEY LOOK DEAD.
THEY'RE BREATHIN'.
AND BLEEDING!
GO GET A TOWEL OR SOMETHING.
WE NEED A DOCTOR.
IF ONLY WE HAD ONE--OH YEAH, YOU STABBED THE DOCTOR.
WILL YOU GO GET A--?!
HUAAAAAAAA!

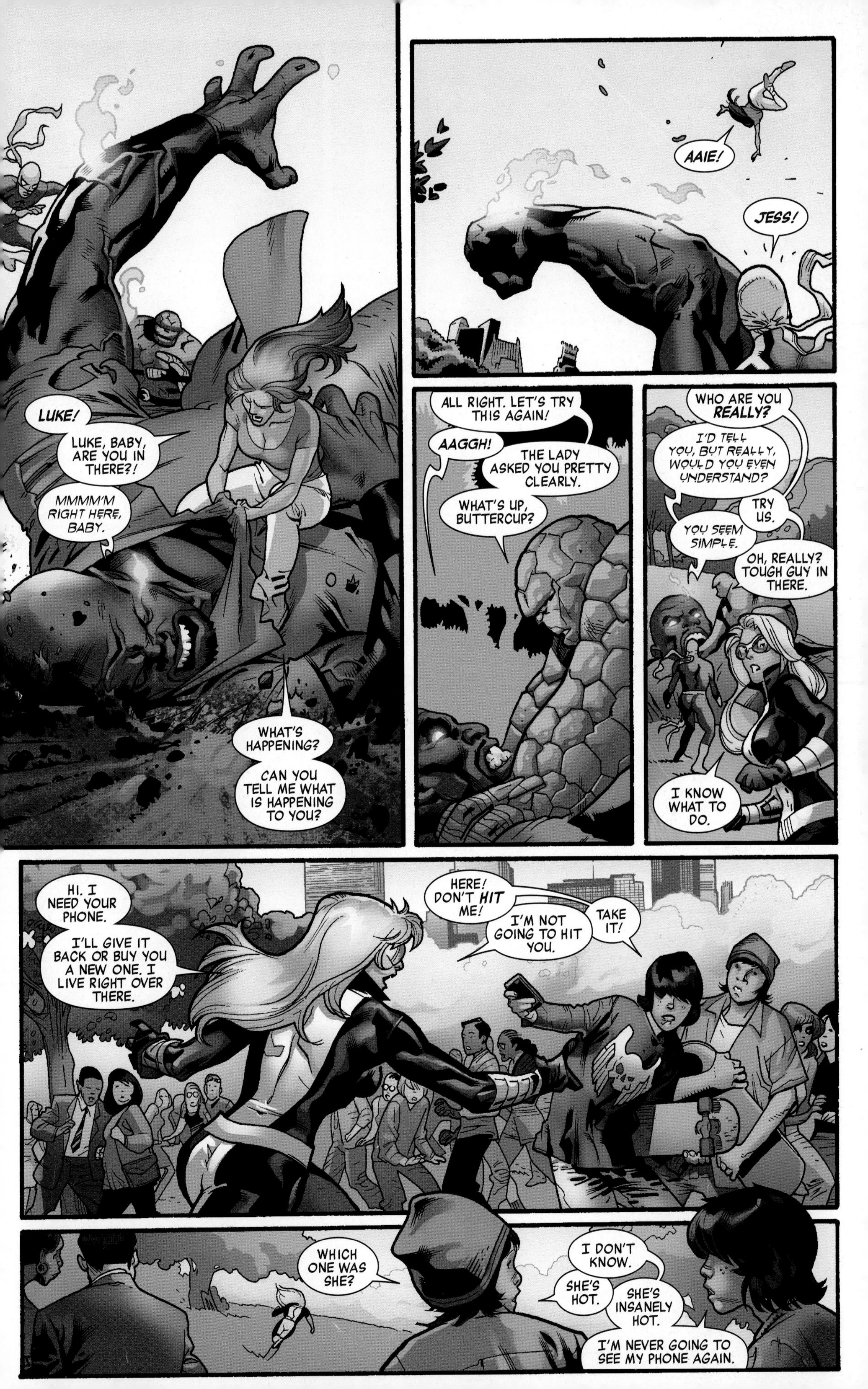
LUKE!
LUKE, BABY, ARE YOU IN THERE?!
MMMM'M RIGHT HERE, BABY.
WHAT'S HAPPENING?
CAN YOU TELL ME WHAT IS HAPPENING TO YOU?
AAIE!
JESS!
ALL RIGHT. LET'S TRY THIS AGAIN!
AAGGH!
THE LADY ASKED YOU PRETTY CLEARLY.
WHAT'S UP, BUTTERCUP?
WHO ARE YOU REALLY?
I'D TELL YOU, BUT REALLY, WOULD YOU EVEN UNDERSTAND?
TRY US.
YOU SEEM SIMPLE.
OH, REALLY? TOUGH GUY IN THERE.
I KNOW WHAT TO DO.
HI. I NEED YOUR PHONE.
I'LL GIVE IT BACK OR BUY YOU A NEW ONE. I LIVE RIGHT OVER THERE.
HERE! DON'T HIT ME!
I'M NOT GOING TO HIT YOU.
TAKE IT!
WHICH ONE WAS SHE?
I DON'T KNOW.
SHE'S HOT.
SHE'S INSANELY HOT.
I'M NEVER GOING TO SEE MY PHONE AGAIN.

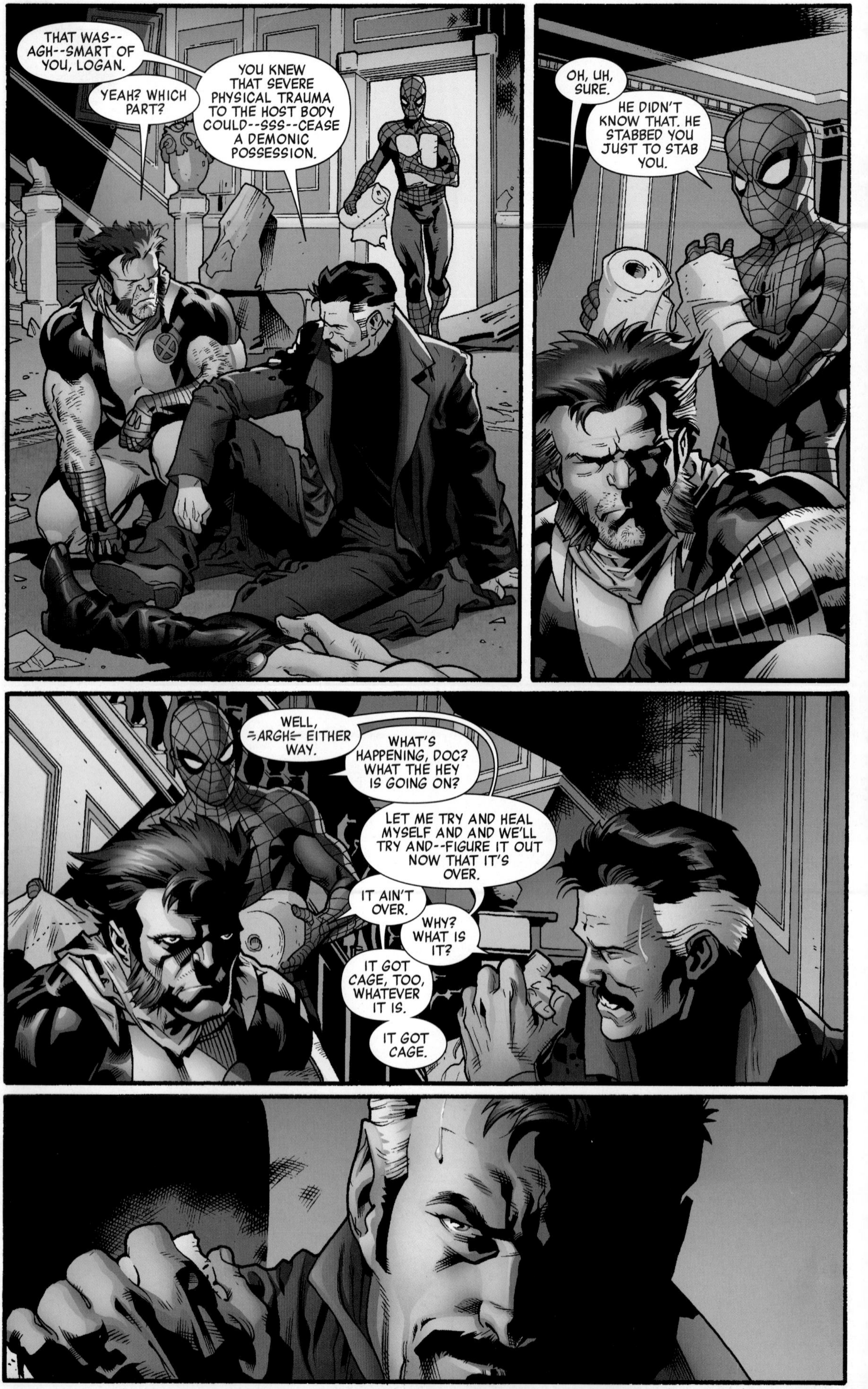
THAT WAS--AGH--SMART OF YOU, LOGAN.
YEAH? WHICH PART?
YOU KNEW THAT SEVERE PHYSICAL TRAUMA TO THE HOST BODY COULD--SSS--CEASE A DEMONIC POSSESSION.
OH, UH, SURE.
HE DIDN'T KNOW THAT. HE STABBED YOU JUST TO STAB YOU.
WELL, ARGH EITHER WAY.
WHAT'S HAPPENING, DOC? WHAT THE HEY IS GOING ON?
LET ME TRY AND HEAL MYSELF AND AND WE'LL TRY AND--FIGURE IT OUT NOW THAT IT'S OVER.
IT AIN'T OVER.
WHY? WHAT IS IT?
IT GOT CAGE, TOO, WHATEVER IT IS.
IT GOT CAGE.

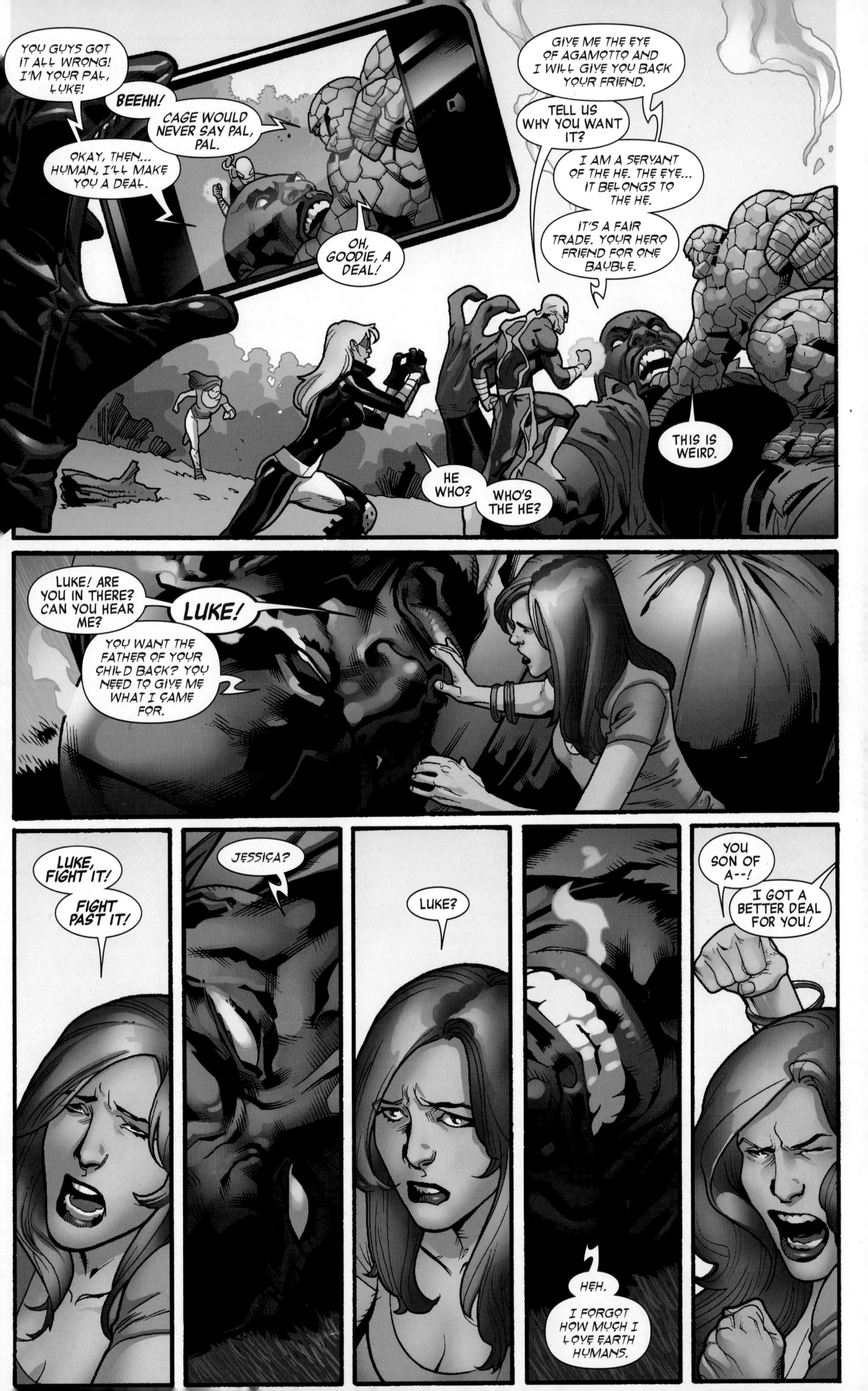
YOU GUYS GOT IT ALL WRONG! I'M YOUR PAL, LUKE!
BEEHH!
CAGE WOULD NEVER SAY PAL, PAL.
OKAY, THEN... HUMAN, I'LL MAKE YOU A DEAL.
OH, GOODIE, A DEAL!
GIVE ME THE EYE OF AGAMOTTO AND I WILL GIVE YOU BACK YOUR FRIEND.
TELL US WHY YOU WANT IT?
I AM A SERVANT OF THE HE. THE EYE... IT BELONGS TO THE HE.
IT'S A FAIR TRADE. YOUR HERO FRIEND FOR ONE BAUBLE.
THIS IS WEIRD.
HE WHO?
WHO'S THE HE?
LUKE! ARE YOU IN THERE? CAN YOU HEAR ME?
LUKE!
YOU WANT THE FATHER OF YOUR CHILD BACK? YOU NEED TO GIVE ME WHAT I CAME FOR.
LUKE, FIGHT IT!
FIGHT PAST IT!
JESSICA?
LUKE?
HEH.
I FORGOT HOW MUCH I LOVE EARTH HUMANS.
YOU SON OF A--!
I GOT A BETTER DEAL FOR YOU!

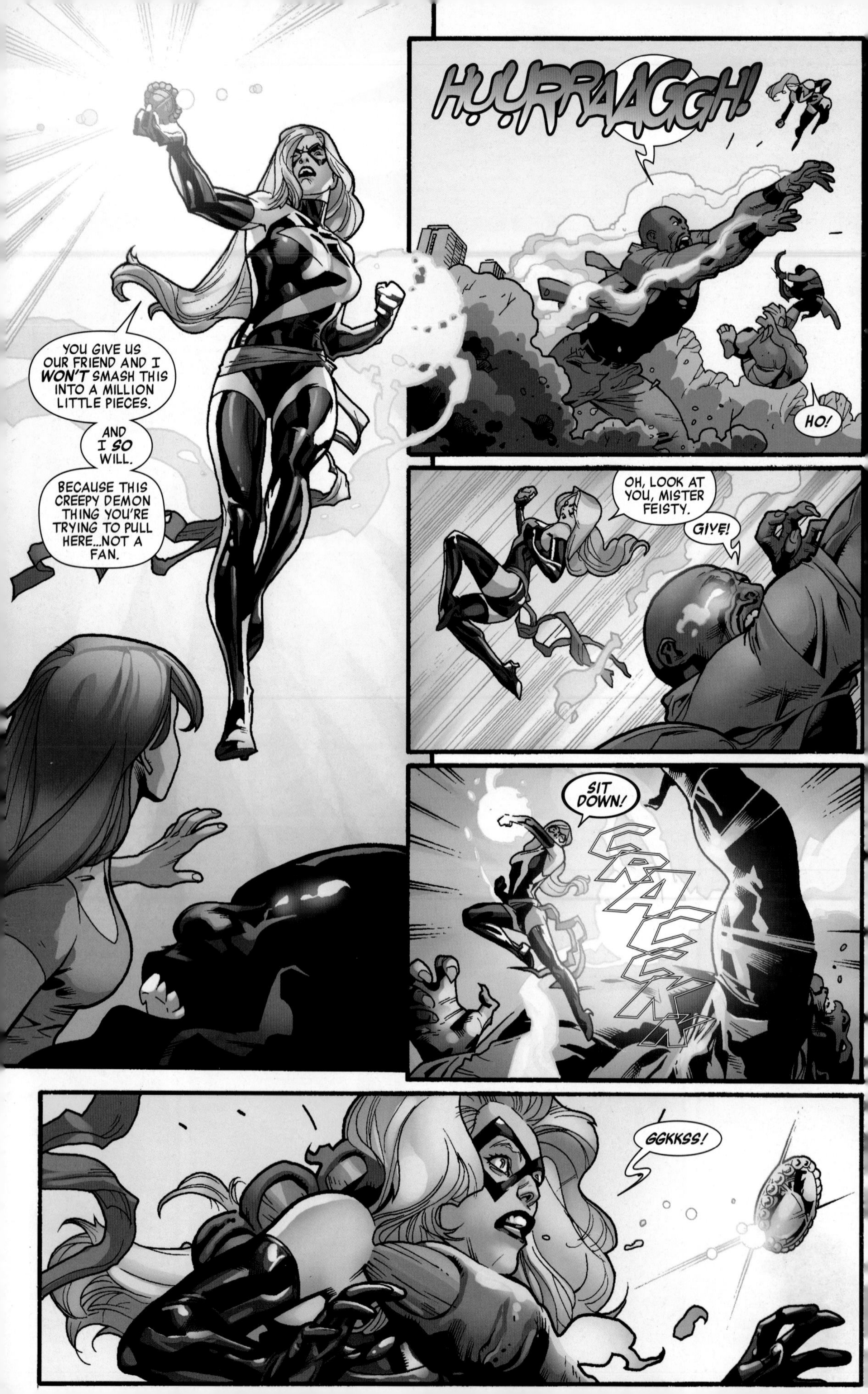
YOU GIVE US OUR FRIEND AND I WON'T SMASH THIS INTO A MILLION LITTLE PIECES.
AND I SO WILL.
BECAUSE THIS CREEPY DEMON THING YOU'RE TRYING TO PULL HERE...NOT A FAN.
HUURRAAGGH!
HO!
OH, LOOK AT YOU, MISTER FEISTY.
GIVE!
SIT DOWN!
GGKKSS!

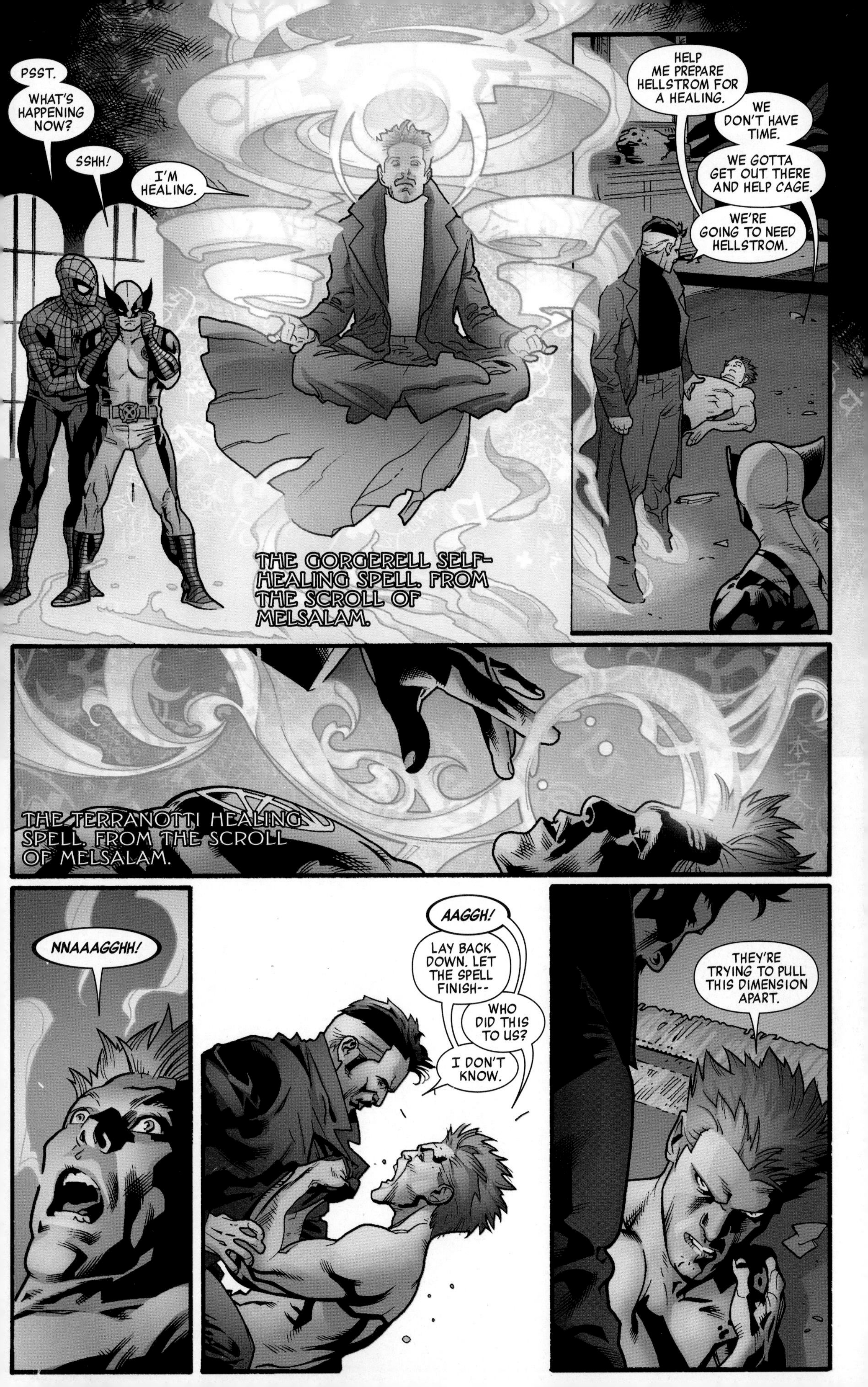
PSST.
WHAT'S HAPPENING NOW?
SSHH!
I'M HEALING.
THE GORGERELL SELF-HEALING SPELL. FROM THE SCROLL OF MELSALAM.
HELP ME PREPARE HELLSTROM FOR A HEALING.
WE DON'T HAVE TIME.
WE GOTTA GET OUT THERE AND HELP CAGE.
WE'RE GOING TO NEED HELLSTROM.
THE TERRANOTTI HEALING SPELL. FROM THE SCROLL OF MELSALAM.
NNAAAGGHH!
AAGGH!
LAY BACK DOWN. LET THE SPELL FINISH--
WHO DID THIS TO US?
I DON'T KNOW.
THEY'RE TRYING TO PULL THIS DIMENSION APART.

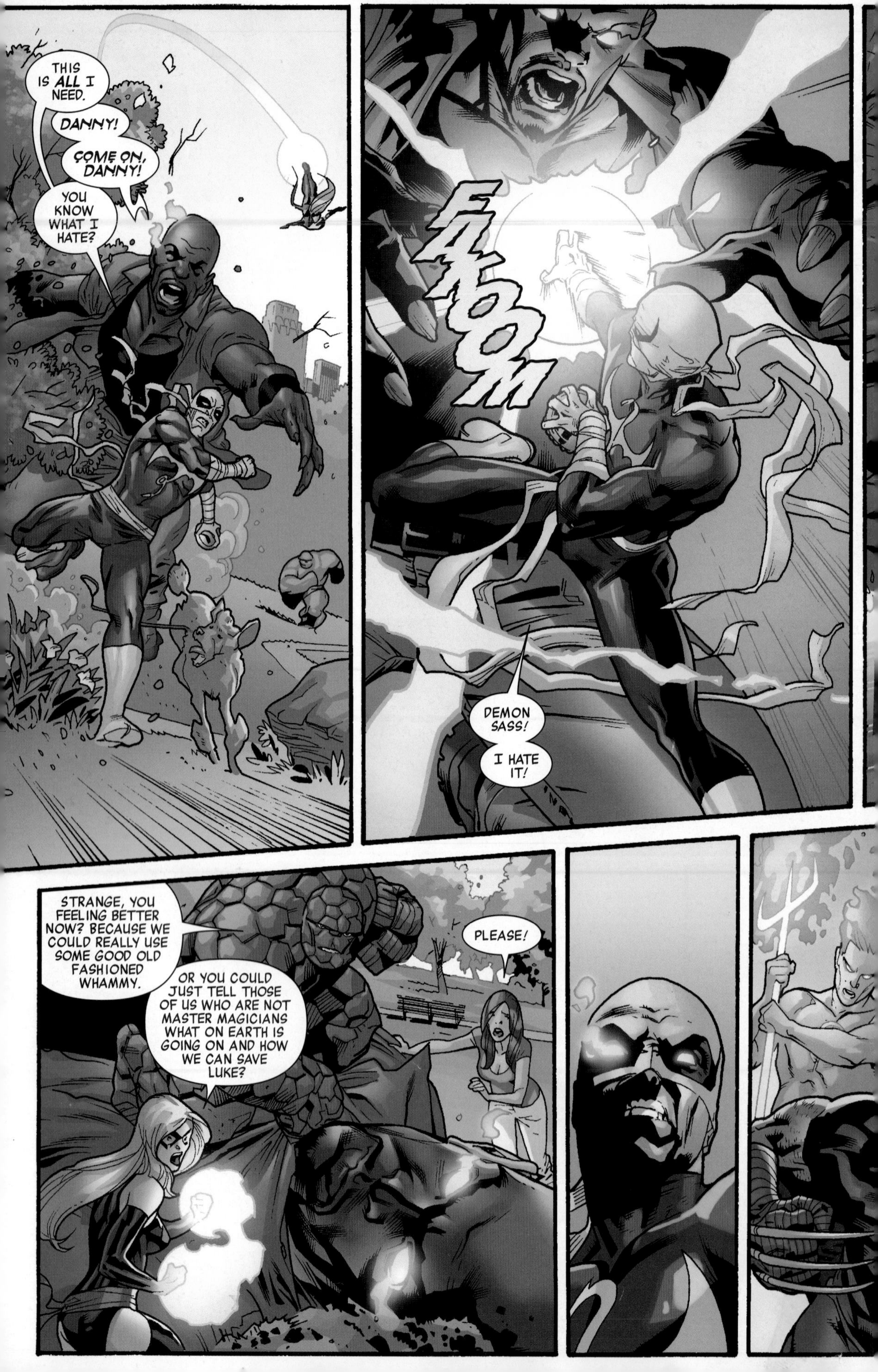
THIS IS **ALL** I NEED.
DANNY!
COME ON, DANNY!
YOU KNOW WHAT I HATE?
FAKOOM
DEMON SASS!
I HATE IT!
STRANGE, YOU FEELING BETTER NOW? BECAUSE WE COULD REALLY USE SOME GOOD OLD FASHIONED WHAMMY.
OR YOU COULD JUST TELL THOSE OF US WHO ARE NOT MASTER MAGICIANS WHAT ON EARTH IS GOING ON AND HOW WE CAN SAVE LUKE?
PLEASE!

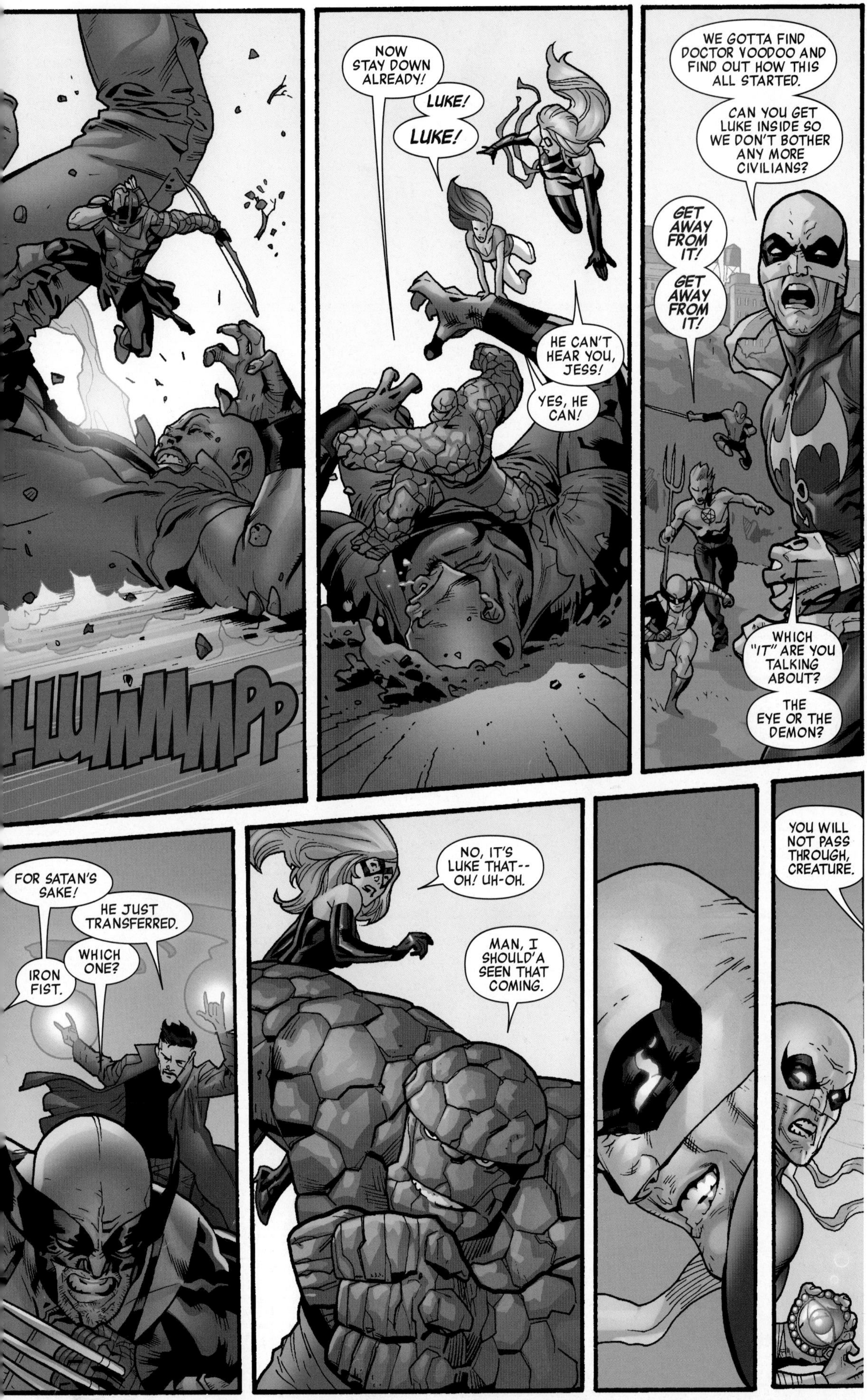

THUUMMPP
NOW STAY DOWN ALREADY!
LUKE!
LUKE!
HE CAN'T HEAR YOU, JESS!
YES, HE CAN!
WE GOTTA FIND DOCTOR VOODOO AND FIND OUT HOW THIS ALL STARTED.
CAN YOU GET LUKE INSIDE SO WE DON'T BOTHER ANY MORE CIVILIANS?
GET AWAY FROM IT!
GET AWAY FROM IT!
WHICH "IT" ARE YOU TALKING ABOUT?
THE EYE OR THE DEMON?
FOR SATAN'S SAKE!
HE JUST TRANSFERRED.
WHICH ONE?
IRON FIST.
NO, IT'S LUKE THAT-- OH! UH-OH.
MAN, I SHOULD'A SEEN THAT COMING.
YOU WILL NOT PASS THROUGH, CREATURE.

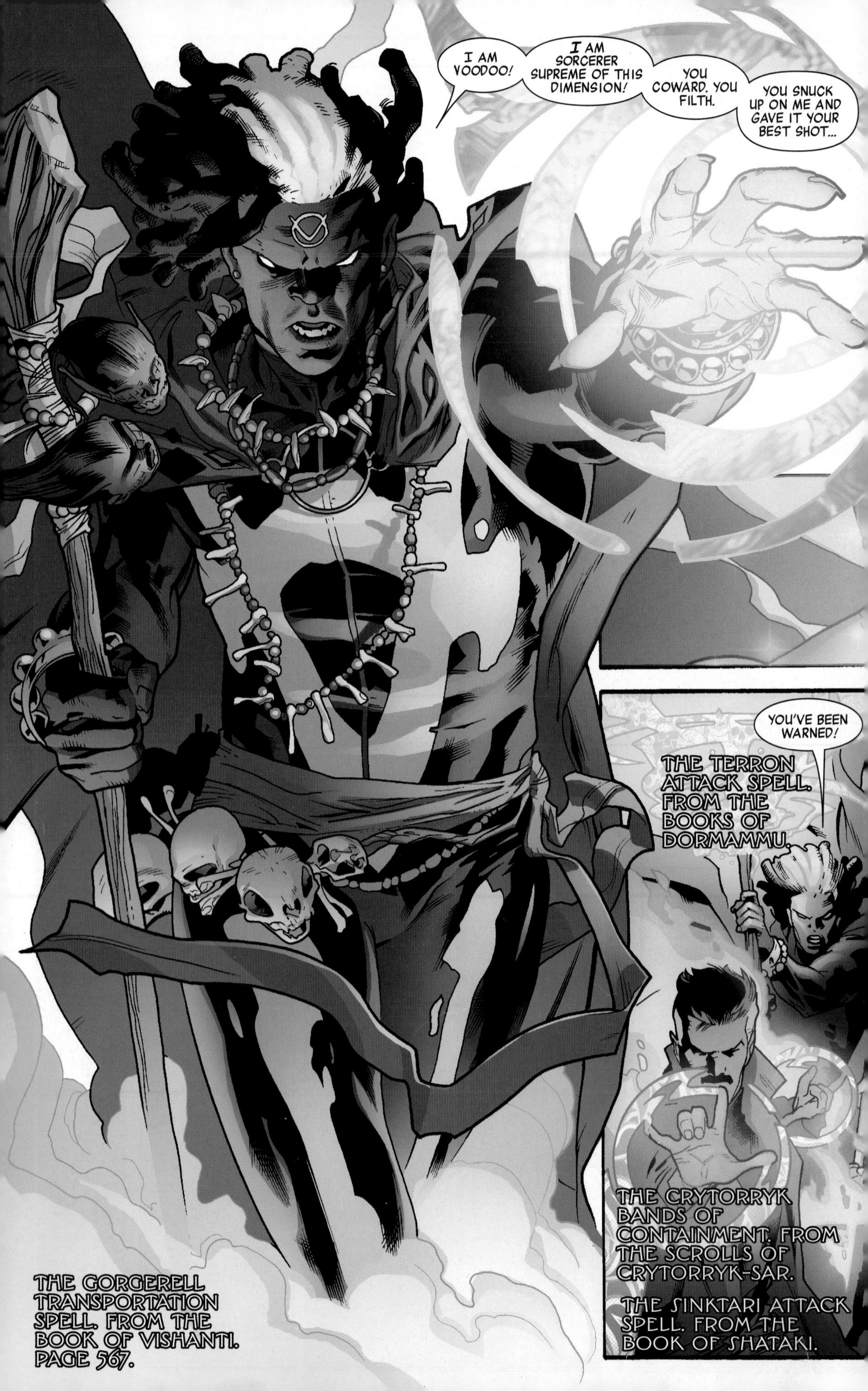
I AM VOODOO!
I AM SORCERER SUPREME OF THIS DIMENSION!
YOU COWARD. YOU FILTH.
YOU SNUCK UP ON ME AND GAVE IT YOUR BEST SHOT...
THE GORGERELL TRANSPORTATION SPELL. FROM THE BOOK OF VISHANTI. PAGE 567.
YOU'VE BEEN WARNED!
THE TERRON ATTACK SPELL. FROM THE BOOKS OF DORMAMMU.
THE CRYTORRYK BANDS OF CONTAINMENT. FROM THE SCROLLS OF CRYTORRYK-SAR.
THE SINKTARI ATTACK SPELL. FROM THE BOOK OF SHATAKI.

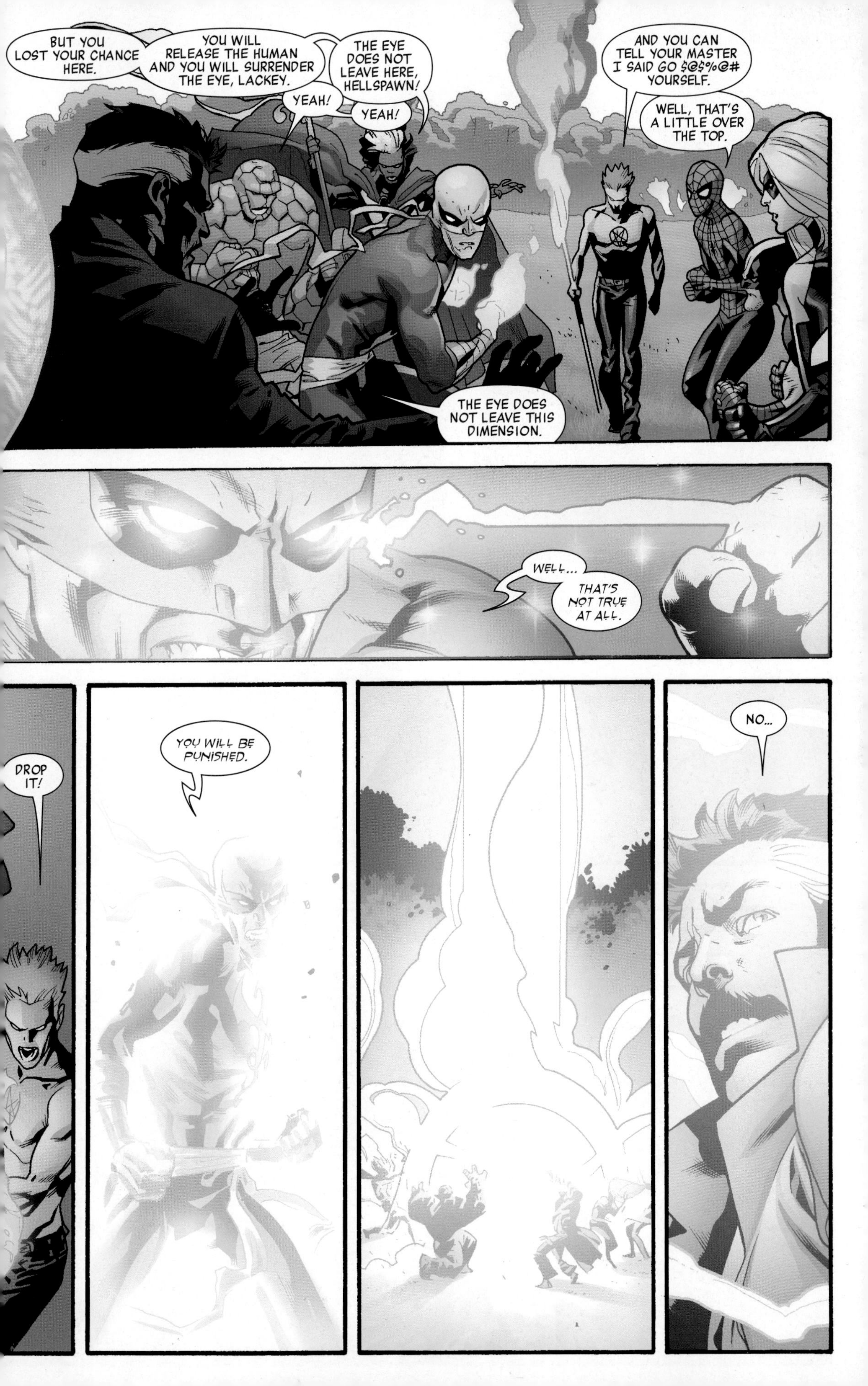

BUT YOU LOST YOUR CHANCE HERE.
YOU WILL RELEASE THE HUMAN AND YOU WILL SURRENDER THE EYE, LACKEY.
YEAH!
THE EYE DOES NOT LEAVE HERE, HELLSPAWN!
YEAH!
AND YOU CAN TELL YOUR MASTER I SAID GO $@$%@# YOURSELF.
WELL, THAT'S A LITTLE OVER THE TOP.
THE EYE DOES NOT LEAVE THIS DIMENSION.
WELL...
THAT'S NOT TRUE AT ALL.
DROP IT!
YOU WILL BE PUNISHED.
NO...

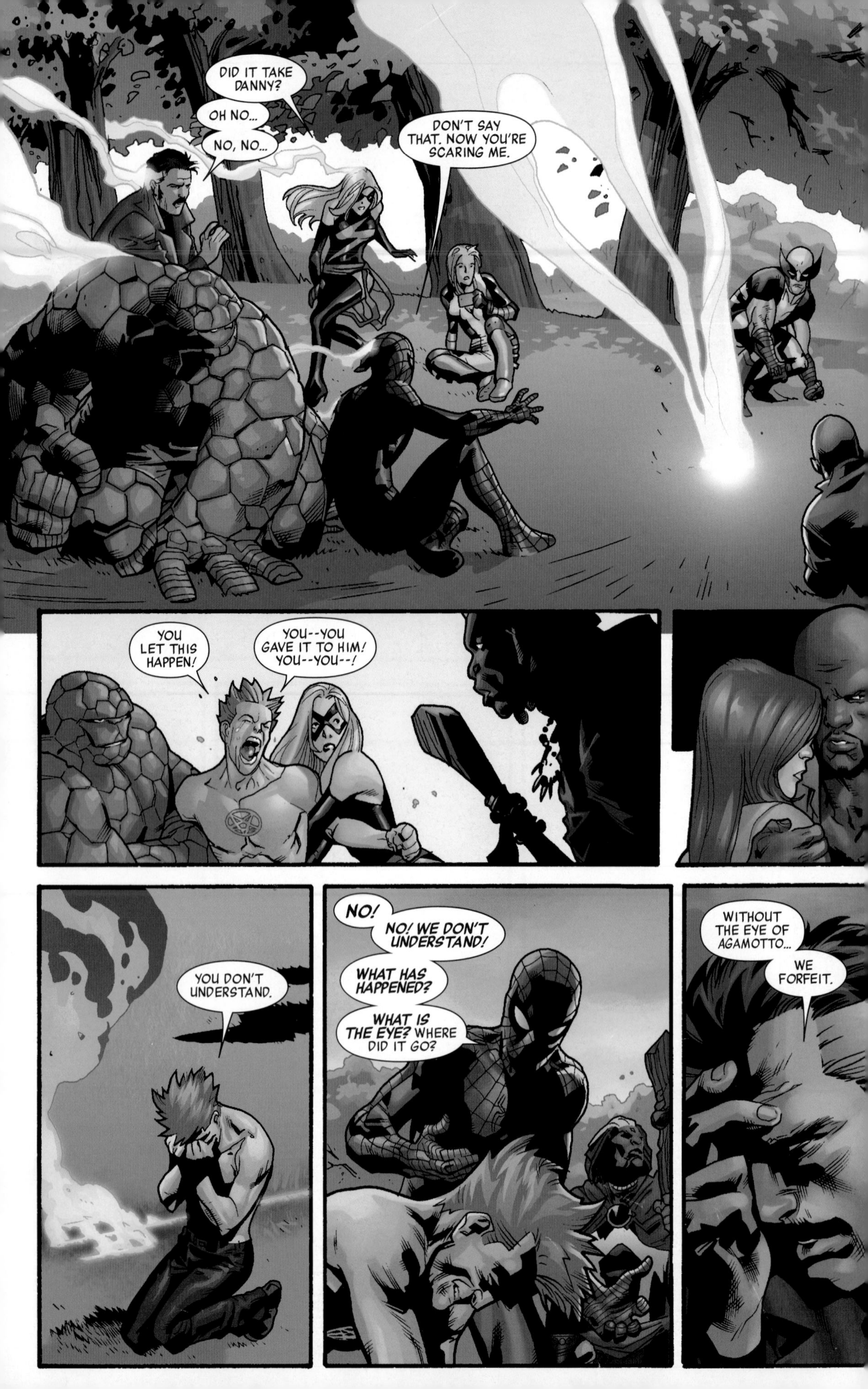
DID IT TAKE DANNY?
OH NO...
NO, NO...
DON'T SAY THAT. NOW YOU'RE SCARING ME.
YOU LET THIS HAPPEN!
YOU--YOU GAVE IT TO HIM! YOU--YOU--!
YOU DON'T UNDERSTAND.
NO!
NO! WE DON'T UNDERSTAND!
WHAT HAS HAPPENED?
WHAT IS THE EYE? WHERE DID IT GO?
WITHOUT THE EYE OF AGAMOTTO...
WE FORFEIT.

YOU BASTARD!

WHAT HAVE YOU DONE?! WHAT HAVE YOU DONE?!

WHAT HAVE I DONE?! WHAT HAVE YOU DONE?!

YOU'RE THE SORCERER SUPREME! YOU LET THIS HAPPEN!

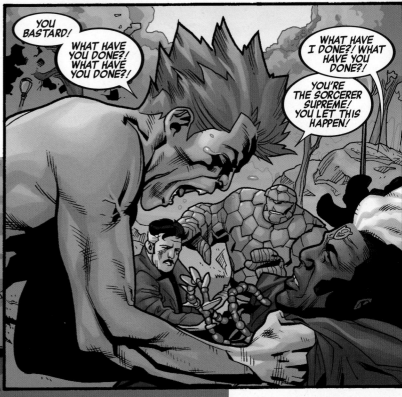

DANNY!

WHAT THE HELL?

WHAT'S GOING ON? HOW--HOW DID I GET OUT HERE?

I SHOULD KILL YOU FOR LETTING THIS HAPPEN!

WHOA! HEY!

THIS AIN'T GONNA HELP DANNY!

KILL YOU!

WE GOTTA GO GET HIM. TELL US HOW.

TELL ME WHAT TO DO.

TELL ME WHAT TO DO AND I'LL DO IT.

WHAT DO WE FORFEIT?

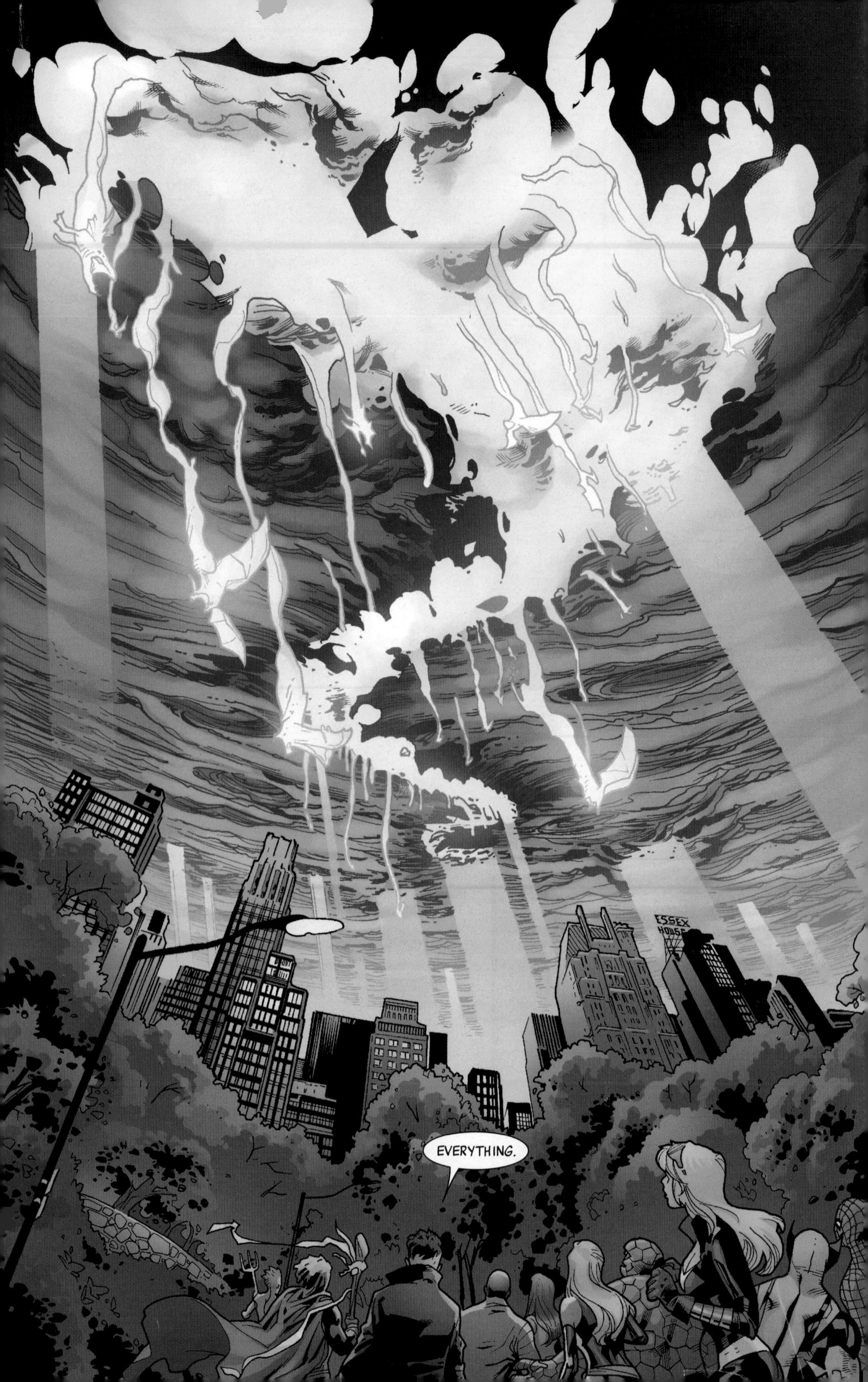
ESSEX HOUSE
EVERYTHING.

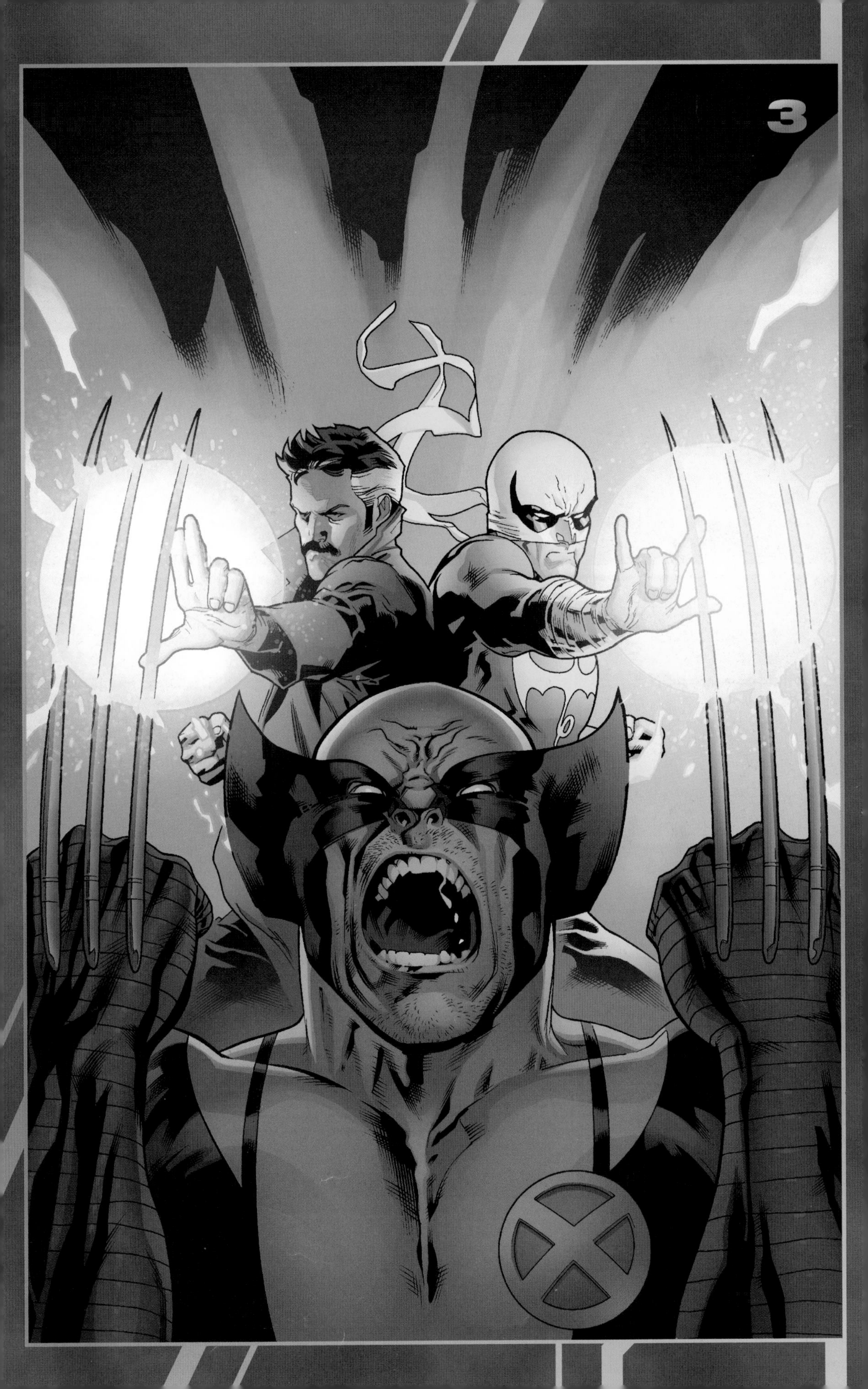
3

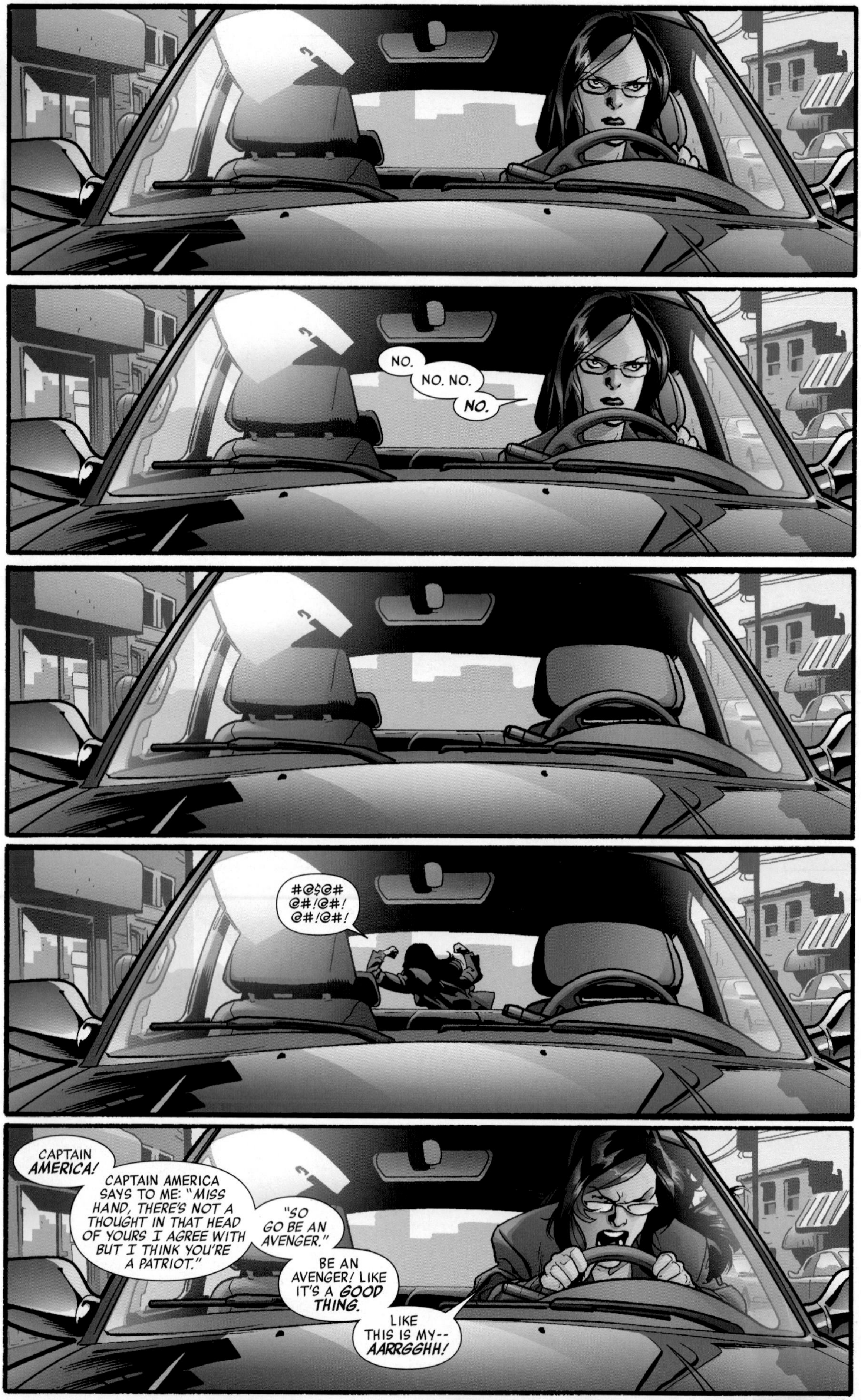
NO.
NO. NO.
NO.
#@$@# @#!@#! @#!@#!
CAPTAIN AMERICA!
CAPTAIN AMERICA SAYS TO ME: "MISS HAND, THERE'S NOT A THOUGHT IN THAT HEAD OF YOURS I AGREE WITH BUT I THINK YOU'RE A PATRIOT."
"SO GO BE AN AVENGER."
BE AN AVENGER! LIKE IT'S A GOOD THING.
LIKE THIS IS MY-- AARRGGHH!

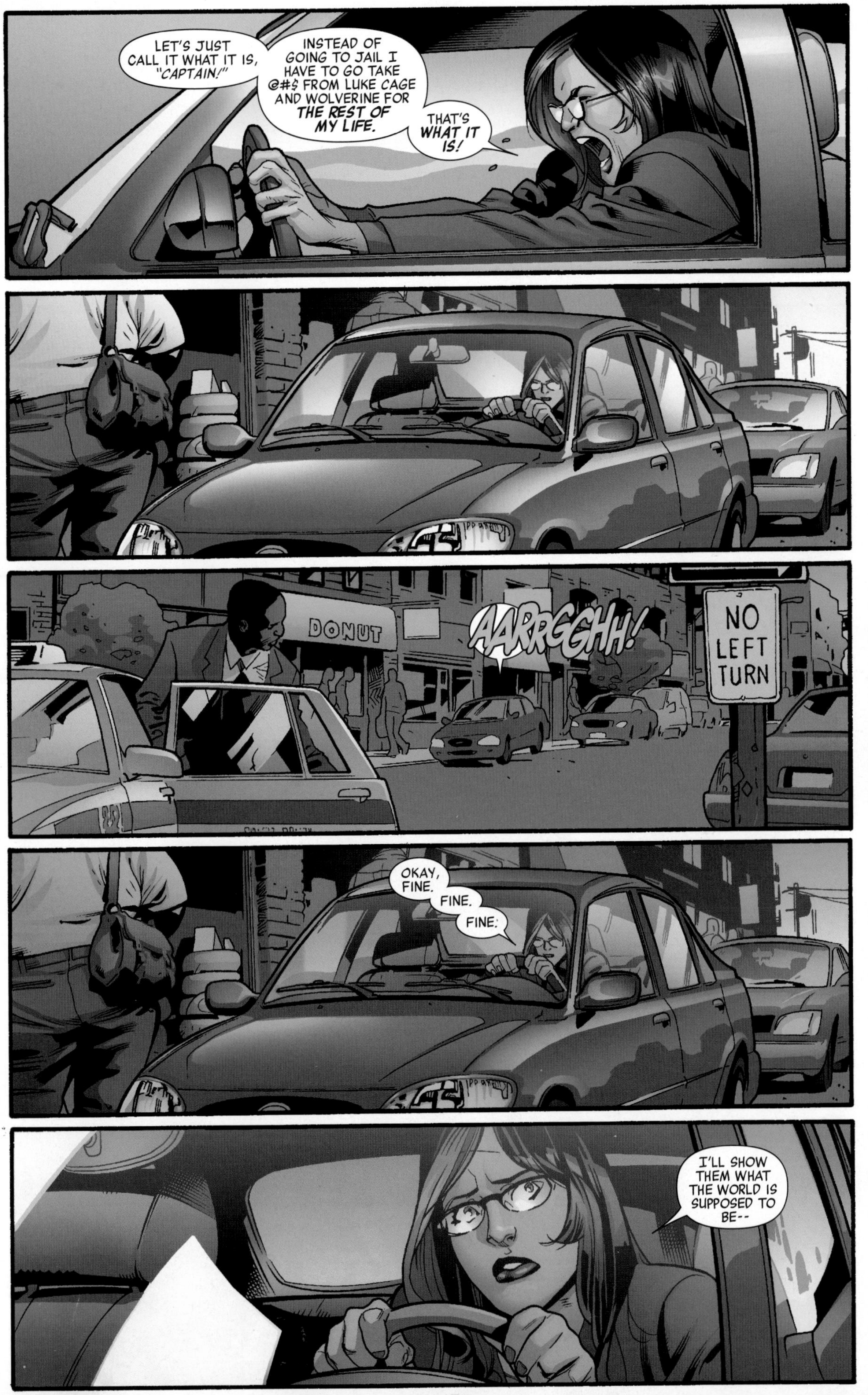
LET'S JUST CALL IT WHAT IT IS, "CAPTAIN!"
INSTEAD OF GOING TO JAIL I HAVE TO GO TAKE @#$ FROM LUKE CAGE AND WOLVERINE FOR THE REST OF MY LIFE.
THAT'S WHAT IT IS!
DONUT
AARRGGHH!
NO LEFT TURN
OKAY, FINE.
FINE.
FINE.
I'LL SHOW THEM WHAT THE WORLD IS SUPPOSED TO BE--

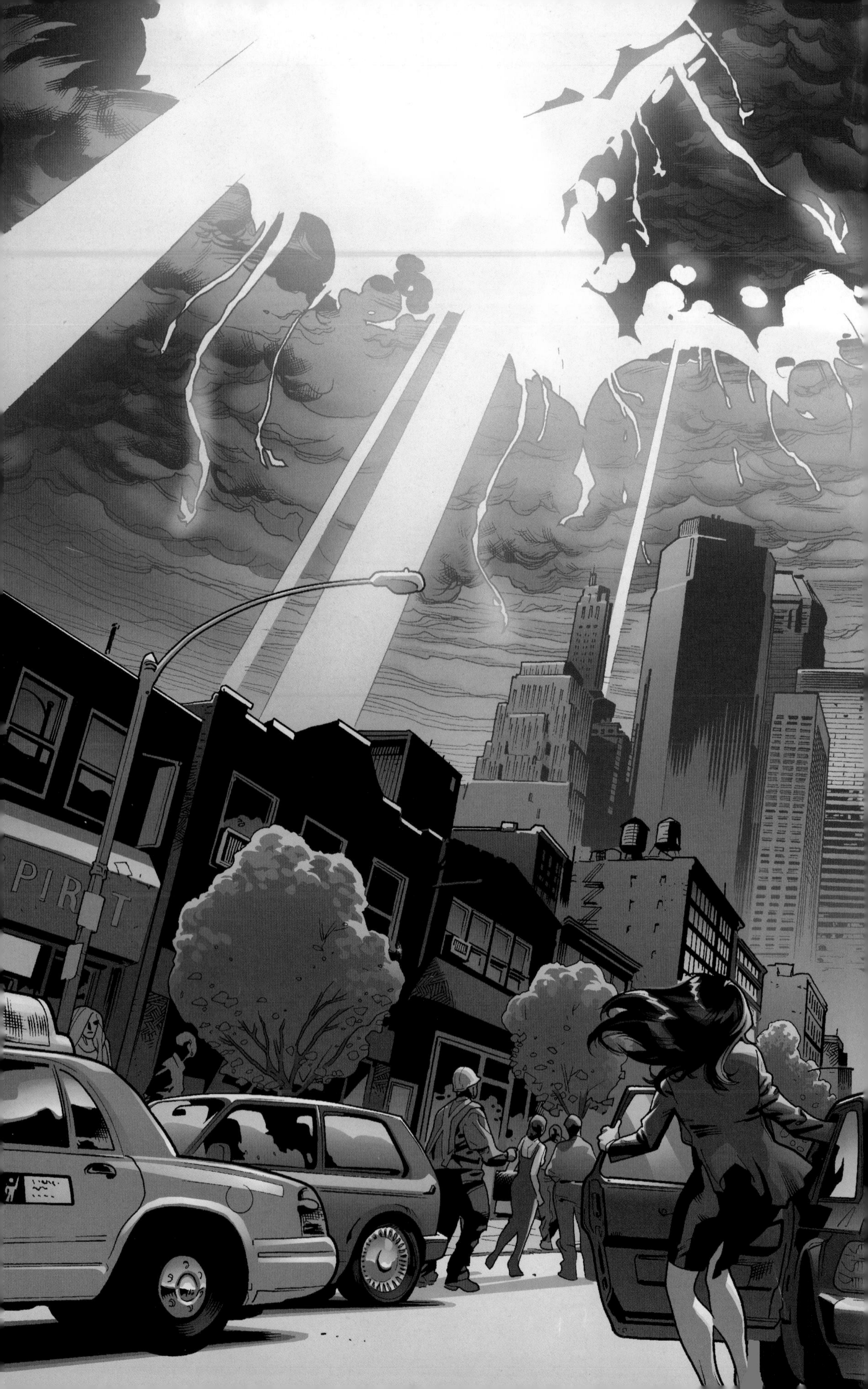

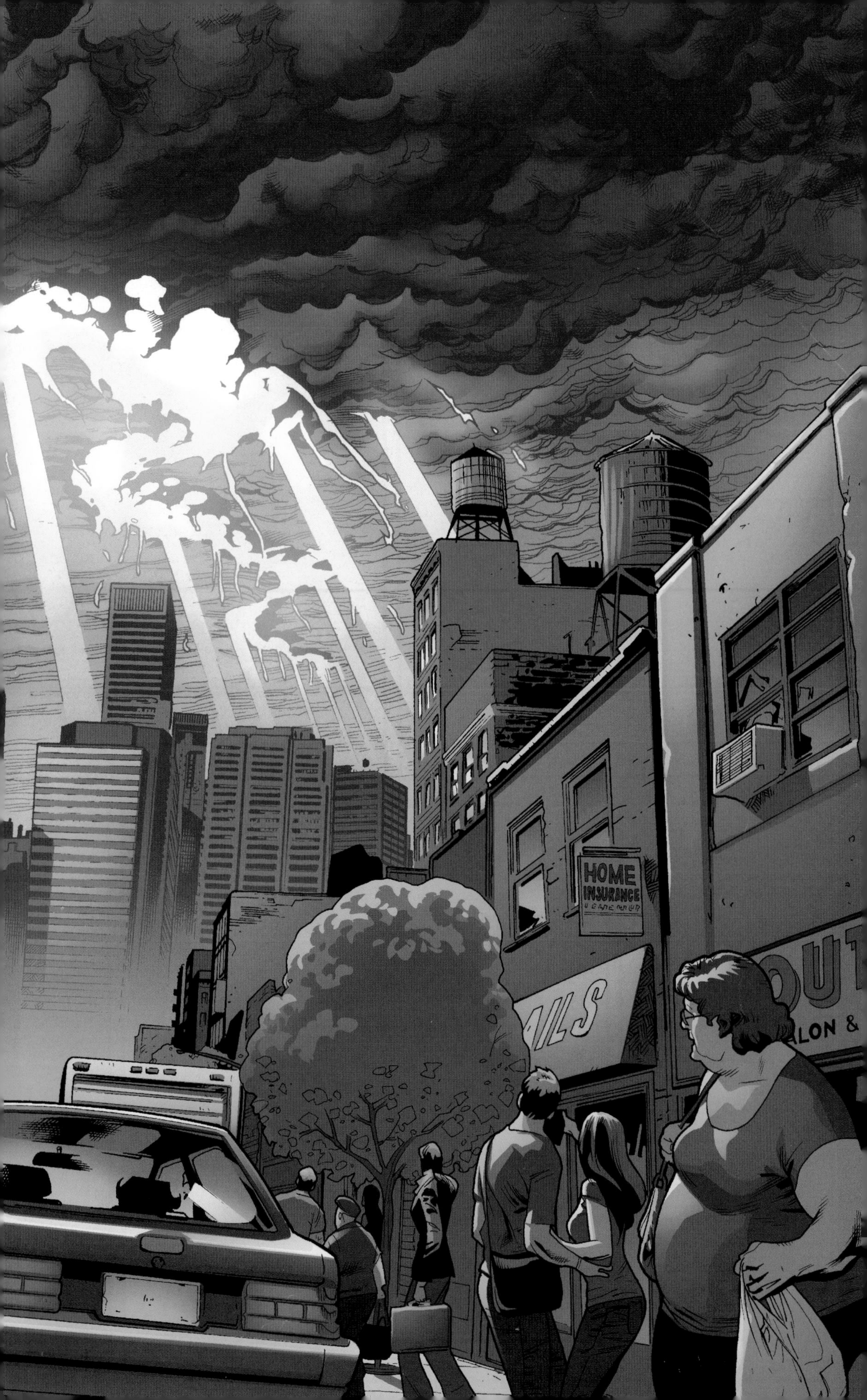
HOME INSURANCE
AILS
OUT
ALON &

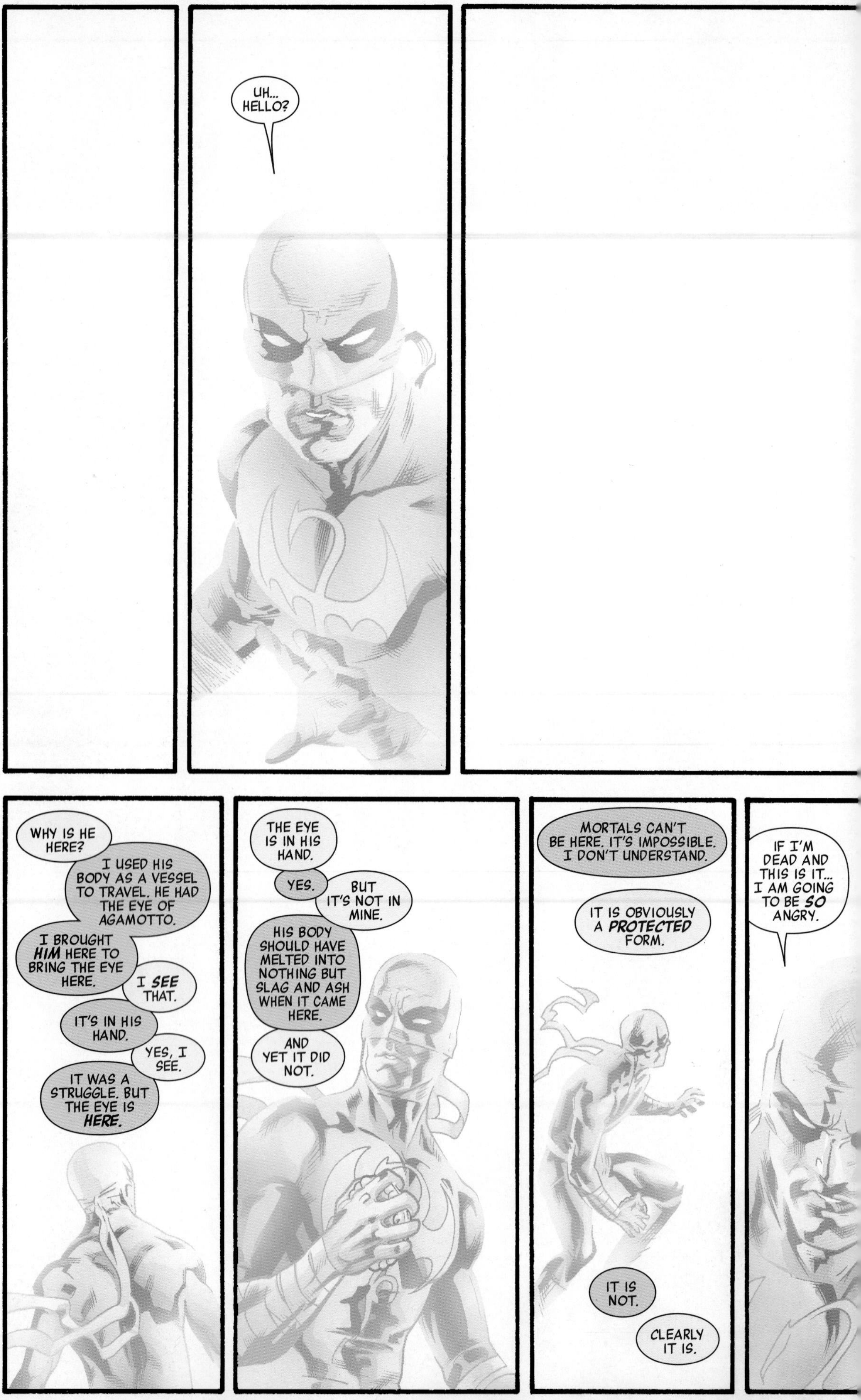
UH... HELLO?
WHY IS HE HERE?
I USED HIS BODY AS A VESSEL TO TRAVEL. HE HAD THE EYE OF AGAMOTTO.
I BROUGHT HIM HERE TO BRING THE EYE HERE.
I SEE THAT.
IT'S IN HIS HAND.
YES, I SEE.
IT WAS A STRUGGLE. BUT THE EYE IS HERE.
THE EYE IS IN HIS HAND.
YES.
BUT IT'S NOT IN MINE.
HIS BODY SHOULD HAVE MELTED INTO NOTHING BUT SLAG AND ASH WHEN IT CAME HERE.
AND YET IT DID NOT.
MORTALS CAN'T BE HERE. IT'S IMPOSSIBLE. I DON'T UNDERSTAND.
IT IS OBVIOUSLY A PROTECTED FORM.
IT IS NOT.
CLEARLY IT IS.
IF I'M DEAD AND THIS IS IT... I AM GOING TO BE SO ANGRY.

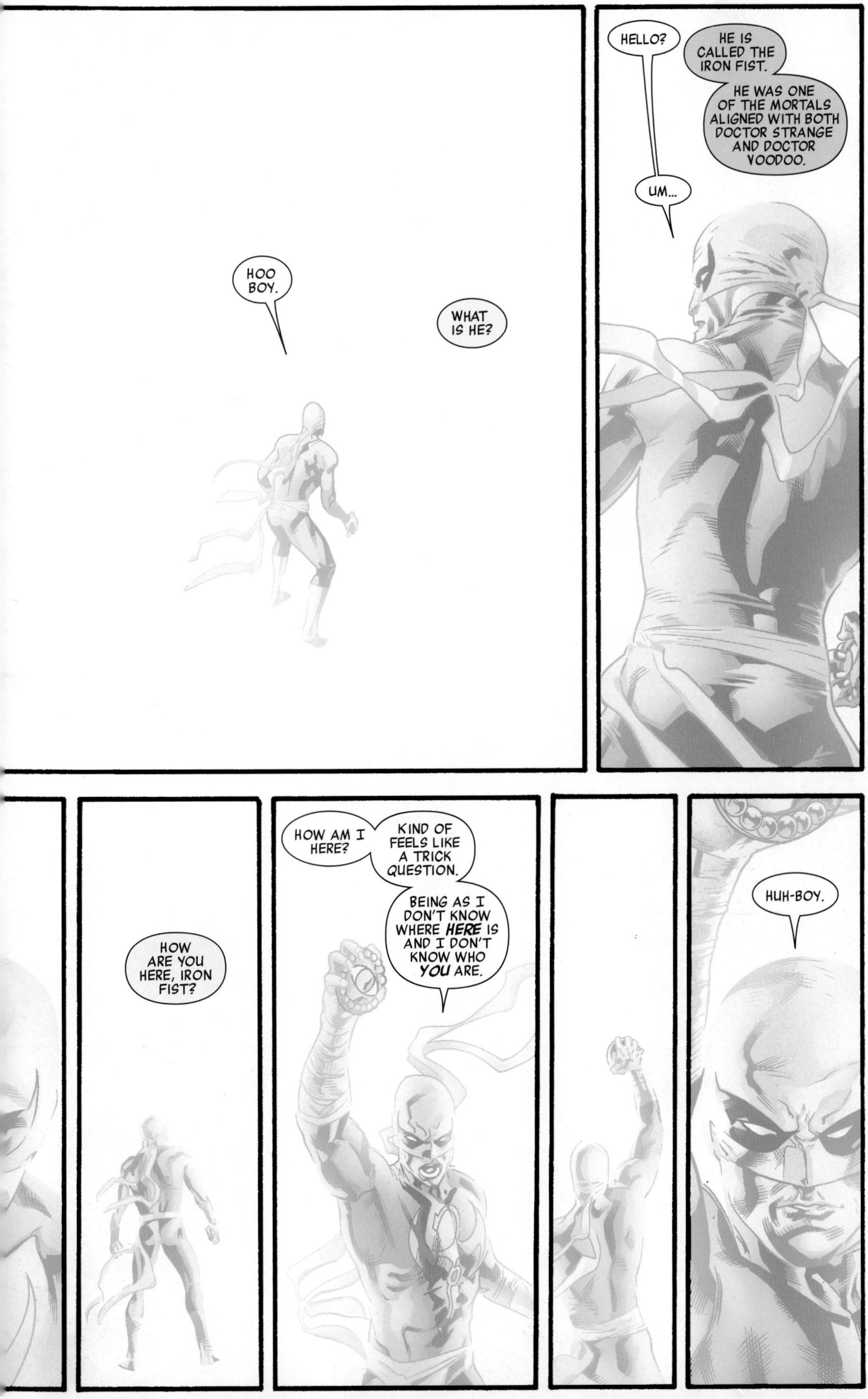
HOO BOY.
WHAT IS HE?
HELLO?
HE IS CALLED THE IRON FIST.
HE WAS ONE OF THE MORTALS ALIGNED WITH BOTH DOCTOR STRANGE AND DOCTOR VOODOO.
UM...
HOW ARE YOU HERE, IRON FIST?
HOW AM I HERE?
KIND OF FEELS LIKE A TRICK QUESTION.
BEING AS I DON'T KNOW WHERE HERE IS AND I DON'T KNOW WHO YOU ARE.
HUH-BOY.

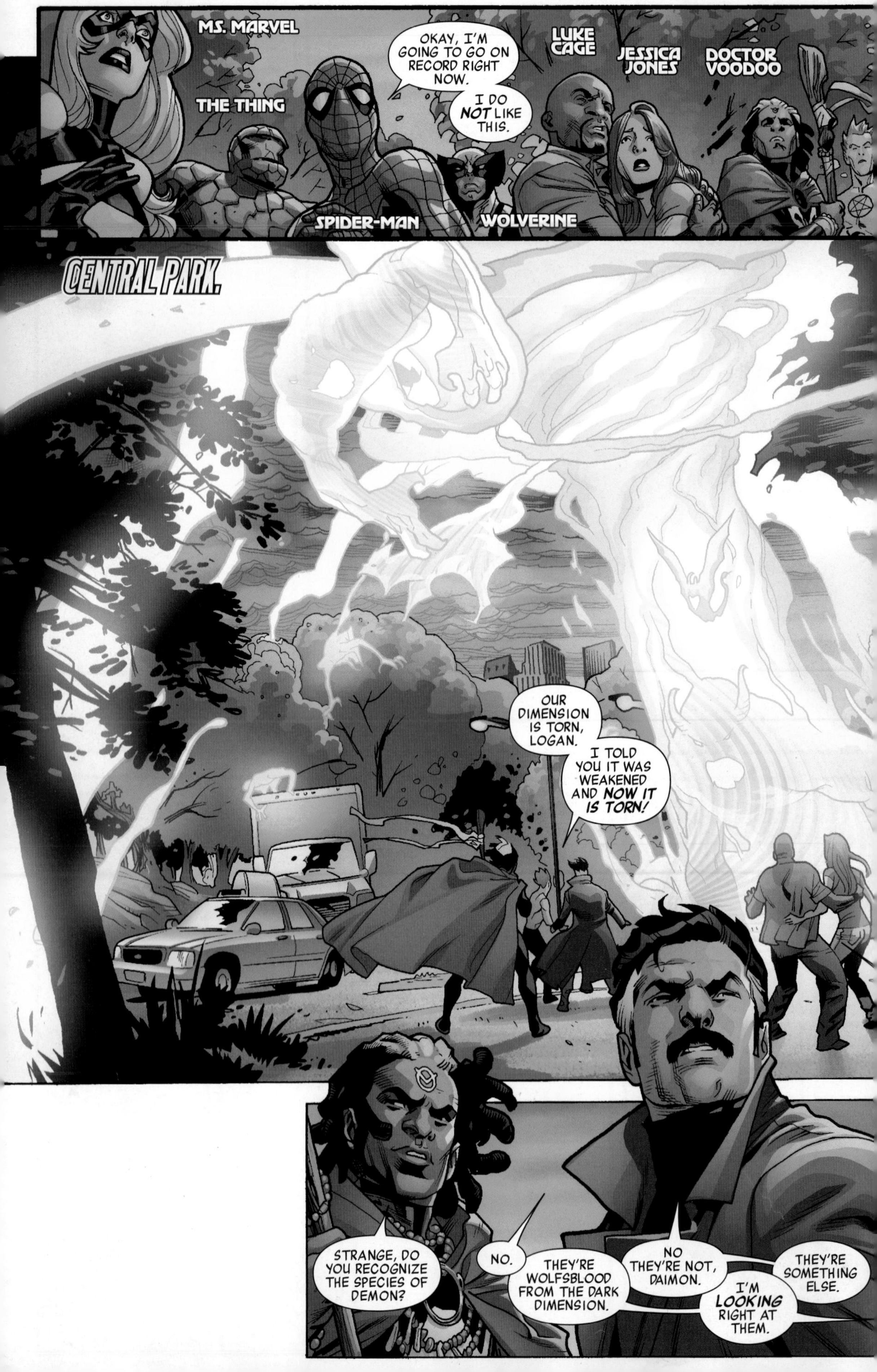
MS. MARVEL
THE THING
SPIDER-MAN
OKAY, I'M GOING TO GO ON RECORD RIGHT NOW.
I DO NOT LIKE THIS.
WOLVERINE
LUKE CAGE
JESSICA JONES
DOCTOR VOODOO
CENTRAL PARK.
OUR DIMENSION IS TORN, LOGAN.
I TOLD YOU IT WAS WEAKENED AND NOW IT IS TORN!
STRANGE, DO YOU RECOGNIZE THE SPECIES OF DEMON?
NO.
THEY'RE WOLFSBLOOD FROM THE DARK DIMENSION.
NO THEY'RE NOT, DAIMON.
I'M LOOKING RIGHT AT THEM.
THEY'RE SOMETHING ELSE.

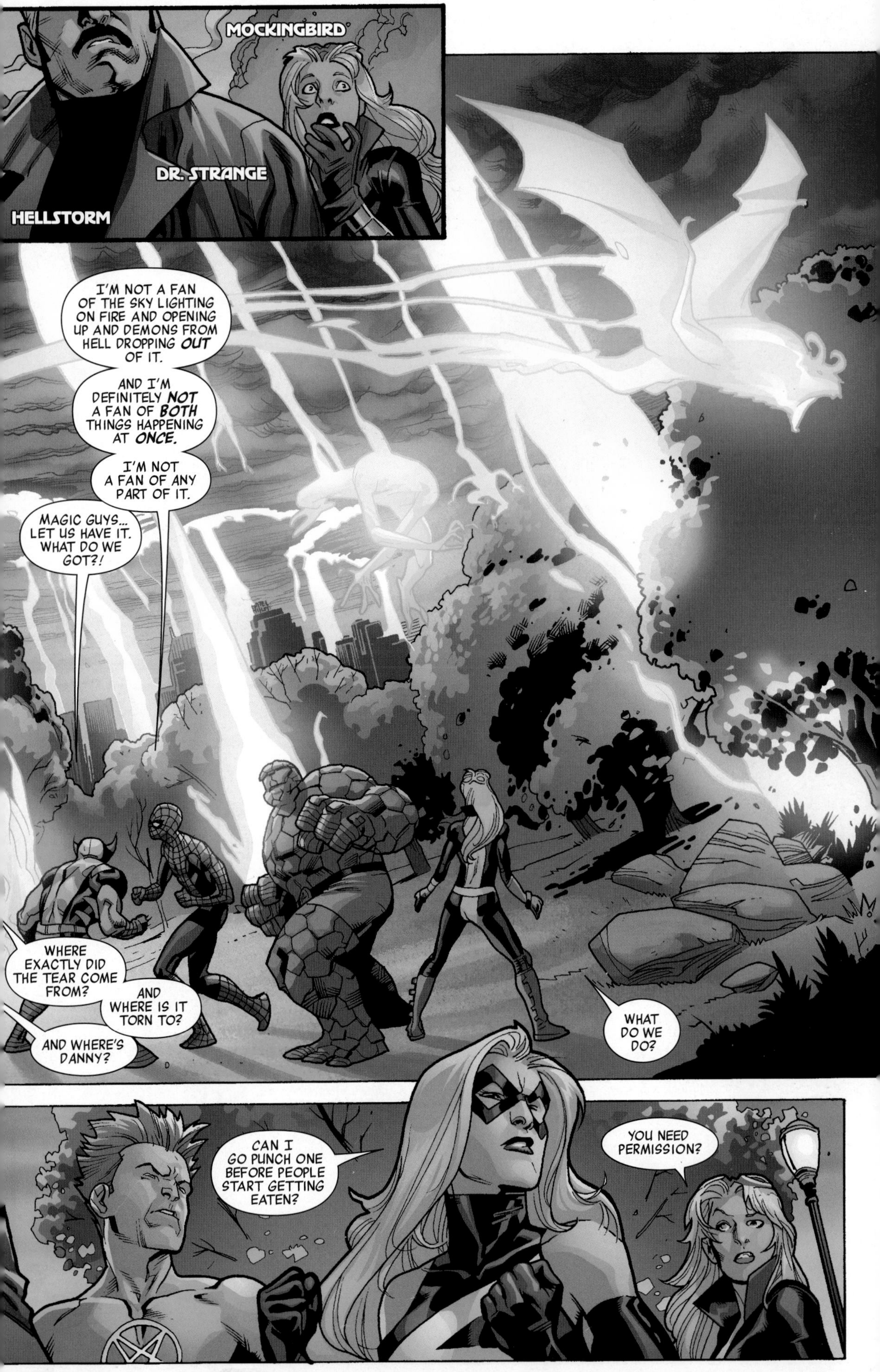
MOCKINGBIRD
DR. STRANGE
HELLSTORM
I'M NOT A FAN OF THE SKY LIGHTING ON FIRE AND OPENING UP AND DEMONS FROM HELL DROPPING OUT OF IT.
AND I'M DEFINITELY NOT A FAN OF BOTH THINGS HAPPENING AT ONCE.
I'M NOT A FAN OF ANY PART OF IT.
MAGIC GUYS... LET US HAVE IT. WHAT DO WE GOT?!
WHERE EXACTLY DID THE TEAR COME FROM?
AND WHERE IS IT TORN TO?
AND WHERE'S DANNY?
WHAT DO WE DO?
CAN I GO PUNCH ONE BEFORE PEOPLE START GETTING EATEN?
YOU NEED PERMISSION?

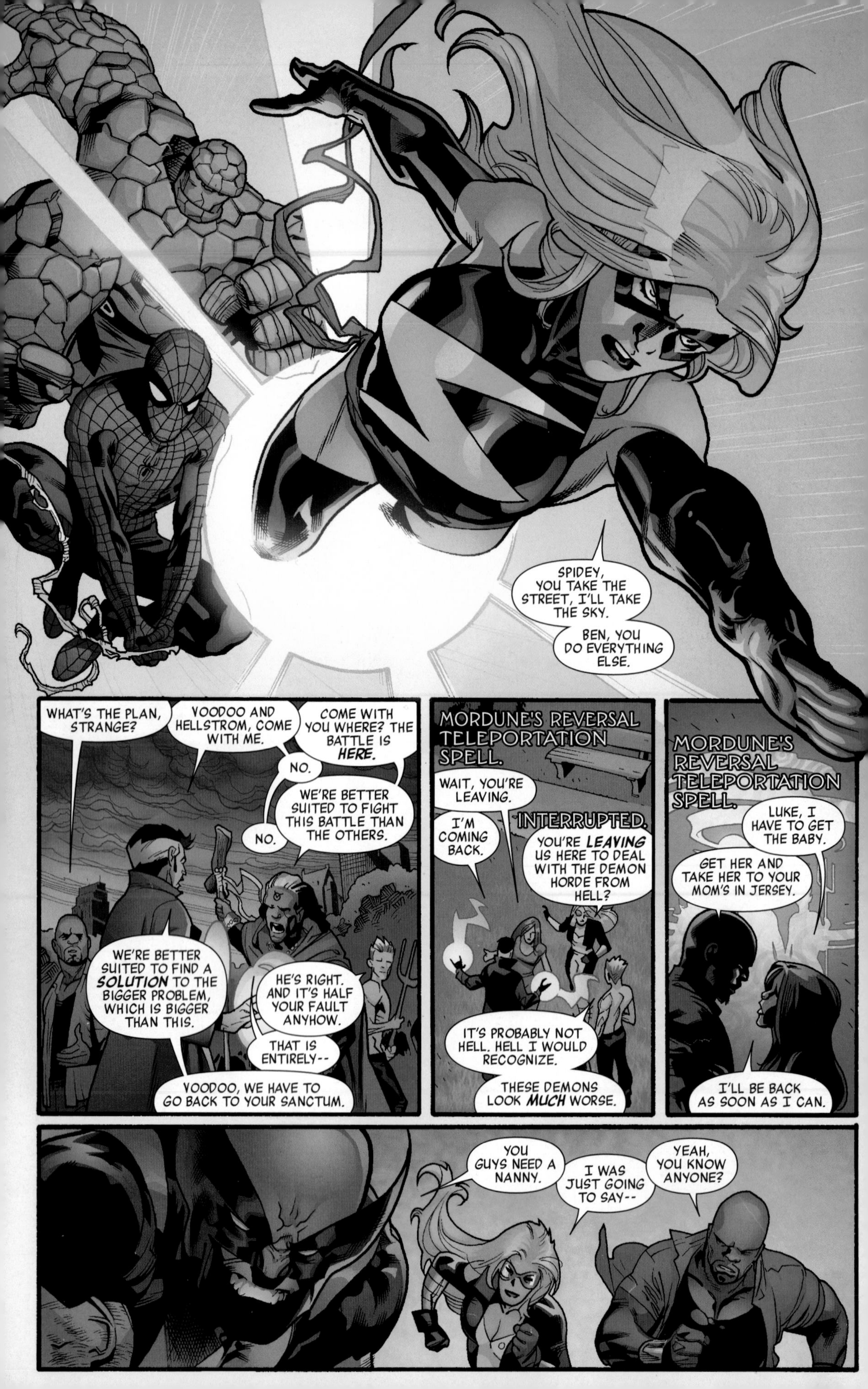
SPIDEY, YOU TAKE THE STREET, I'LL TAKE THE SKY.
BEN, YOU DO EVERYTHING ELSE.
WHAT'S THE PLAN, STRANGE?
VOODOO AND HELLSTROM, COME WITH ME.
COME WITH YOU WHERE? THE BATTLE IS HERE.
NO.
NO.
WE'RE BETTER SUITED TO FIGHT THIS BATTLE THAN THE OTHERS.
WE'RE BETTER SUITED TO FIND A SOLUTION TO THE BIGGER PROBLEM, WHICH IS BIGGER THAN THIS.
HE'S RIGHT. AND IT'S HALF YOUR FAULT ANYHOW.
THAT IS ENTIRELY--
VOODOO, WE HAVE TO GO BACK TO YOUR SANCTUM.
MORDUNE'S REVERSAL TELEPORTATION SPELL.
WAIT, YOU'RE LEAVING.
I'M COMING BACK.
INTERRUPTED.
YOU'RE LEAVING US HERE TO DEAL WITH THE DEMON HORDE FROM HELL?
IT'S PROBABLY NOT HELL. HELL I WOULD RECOGNIZE.
THESE DEMONS LOOK MUCH WORSE.
MORDUNE'S REVERSAL TELEPORTATION SPELL.
LUKE, I HAVE TO GET THE BABY.
GET HER AND TAKE HER TO YOUR MOM'S IN JERSEY.
I'LL BE BACK AS SOON AS I CAN.
YOU GUYS NEED A NANNY.
I WAS JUST GOING TO SAY--
YEAH, YOU KNOW ANYONE?

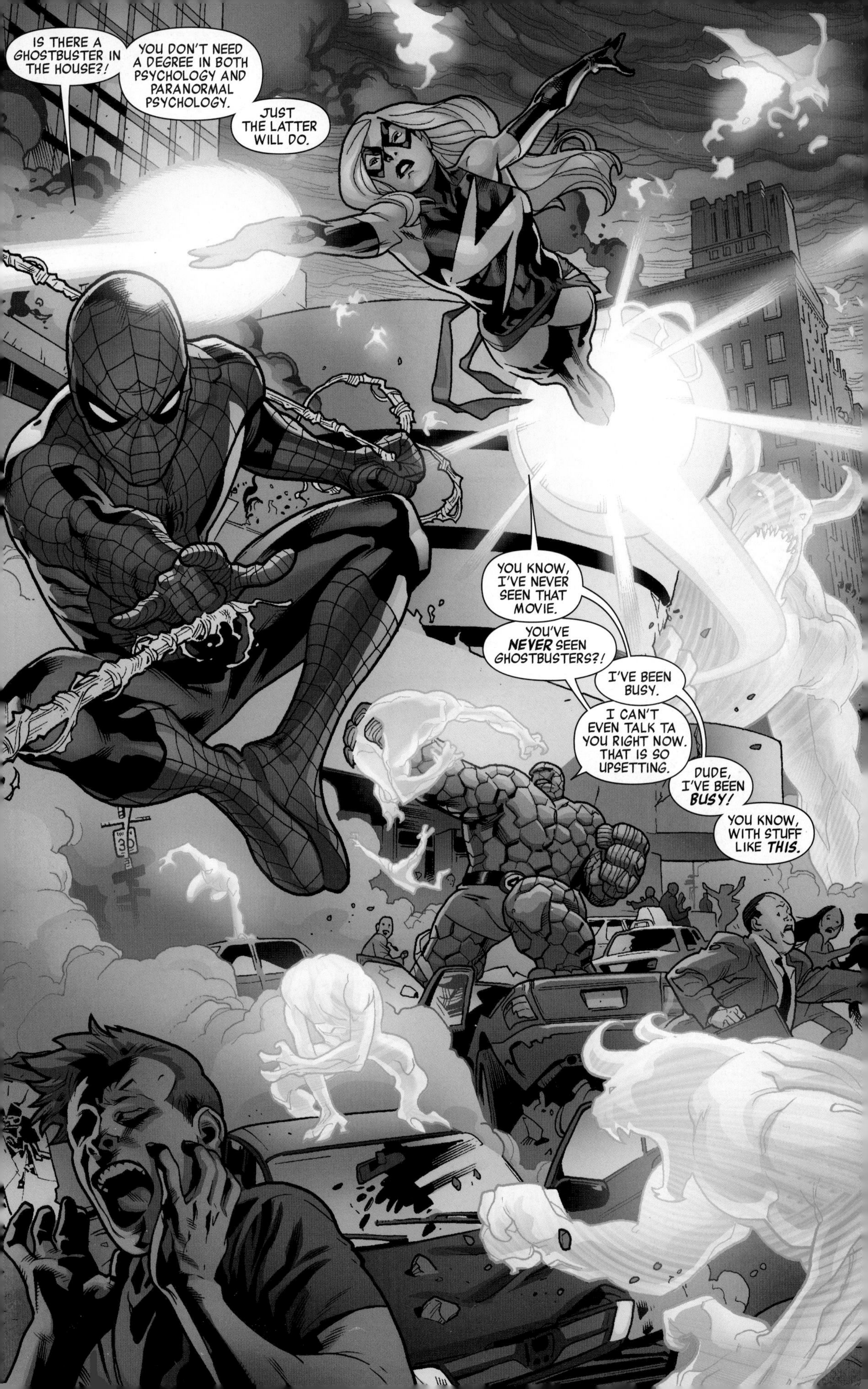
IS THERE A GHOSTBUSTER IN THE HOUSE?!
YOU DON'T NEED A DEGREE IN BOTH PSYCHOLOGY AND PARANORMAL PSYCHOLOGY.
JUST THE LATTER WILL DO.
YOU KNOW, I'VE NEVER SEEN THAT MOVIE.
YOU'VE NEVER SEEN GHOSTBUSTERS?!
I'VE BEEN BUSY.
I CAN'T EVEN TALK TA YOU RIGHT NOW. THAT IS SO UPSETTING.
DUDE, I'VE BEEN BUSY!
YOU KNOW, WITH STUFF LIKE THIS.

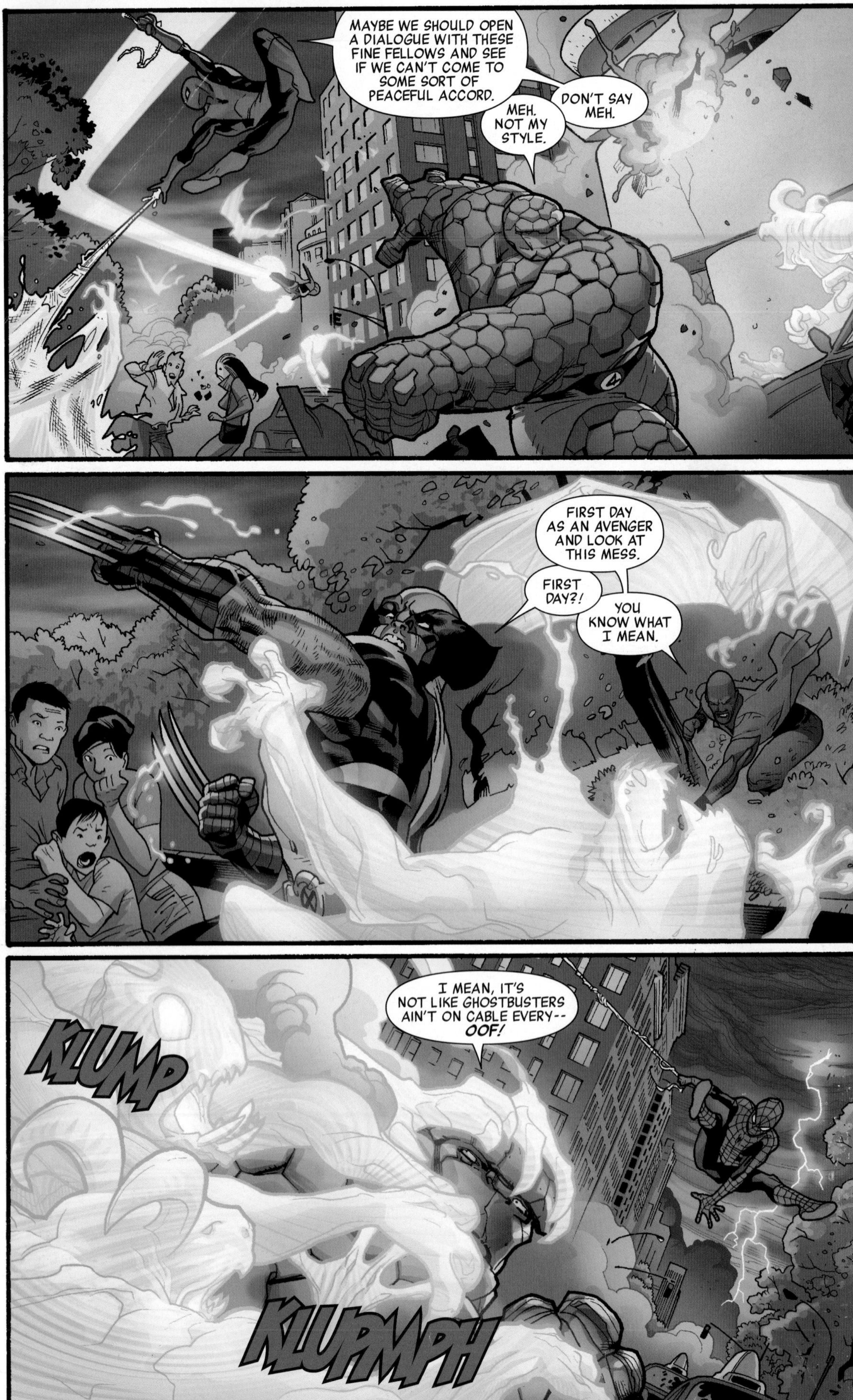
MAYBE WE SHOULD OPEN A DIALOGUE WITH THESE FINE FELLOWS AND SEE IF WE CAN'T COME TO SOME SORT OF PEACEFUL ACCORD.
MEH. NOT MY STYLE.
DON'T SAY MEH.
FIRST DAY AS AN AVENGER AND LOOK AT THIS MESS.
FIRST DAY?!
YOU KNOW WHAT I MEAN.
KLUMP
I MEAN, IT'S NOT LIKE GHOSTBUSTERS AIN'T ON CABLE EVERY-- OOF!
KLUMPH

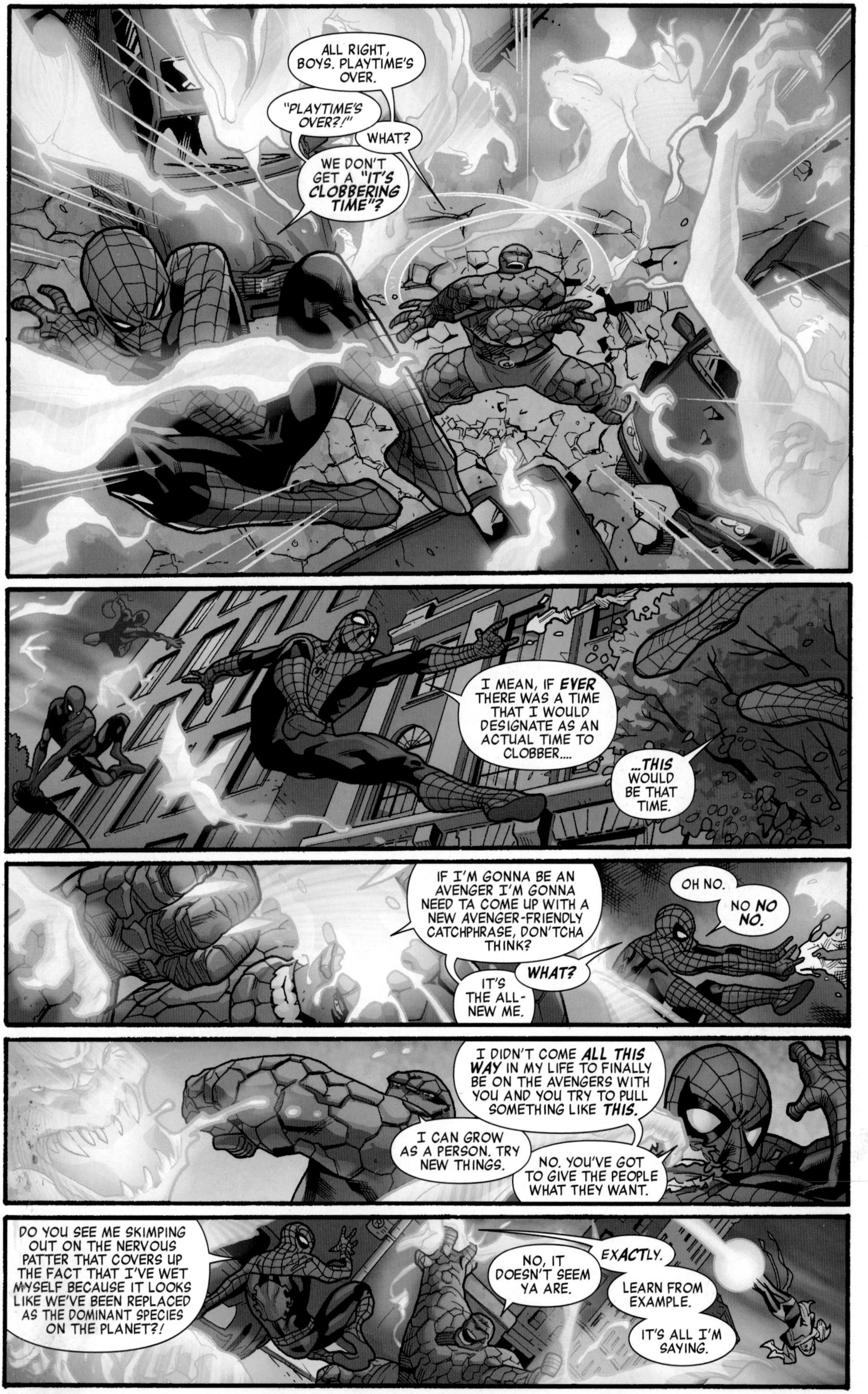
ALL RIGHT, BOYS. PLAYTIME'S OVER.
"PLAYTIME'S OVER?!"
WHAT?
WE DON'T GET A "IT'S CLOBBERING TIME"?
I MEAN, IF EVER THERE WAS A TIME THAT I WOULD DESIGNATE AS AN ACTUAL TIME TO CLOBBER....
...THIS WOULD BE THAT TIME.
IF I'M GONNA BE AN AVENGER I'M GONNA NEED TA COME UP WITH A NEW AVENGER-FRIENDLY CATCHPHRASE, DON'TCHA THINK?
WHAT?
IT'S THE ALL-NEW ME.
OH NO.
NO NO NO.
I DIDN'T COME ALL THIS WAY IN MY LIFE TO FINALLY BE ON THE AVENGERS WITH YOU AND YOU TRY TO PULL SOMETHING LIKE THIS.
I CAN GROW AS A PERSON. TRY NEW THINGS.
NO. YOU'VE GOT TO GIVE THE PEOPLE WHAT THEY WANT.
DO YOU SEE ME SKIMPING OUT ON THE NERVOUS PATTER THAT COVERS UP THE FACT THAT I'VE WET MYSELF BECAUSE IT LOOKS LIKE WE'VE BEEN REPLACED AS THE DOMINANT SPECIES ON THE PLANET?!
NO, IT DOESN'T SEEM YA ARE.
EXACTLY.
LEARN FROM EXAMPLE.
IT'S ALL I'M SAYING.

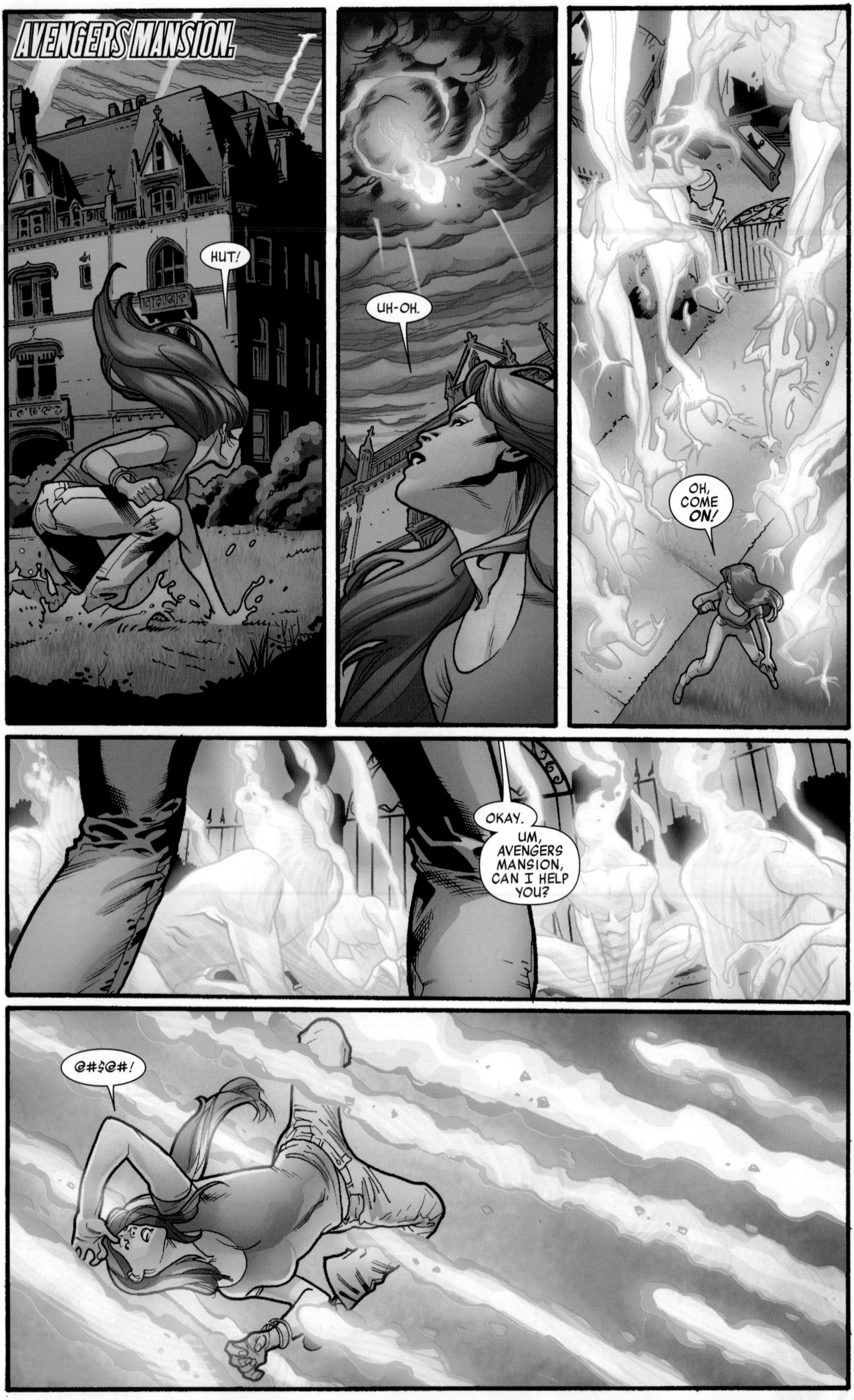
AVENGERS MANSION.
HUT!
UH-OH.
OH, COME ON!
OKAY.
UM, AVENGERS MANSION, CAN I HELP YOU?
@#$@#!

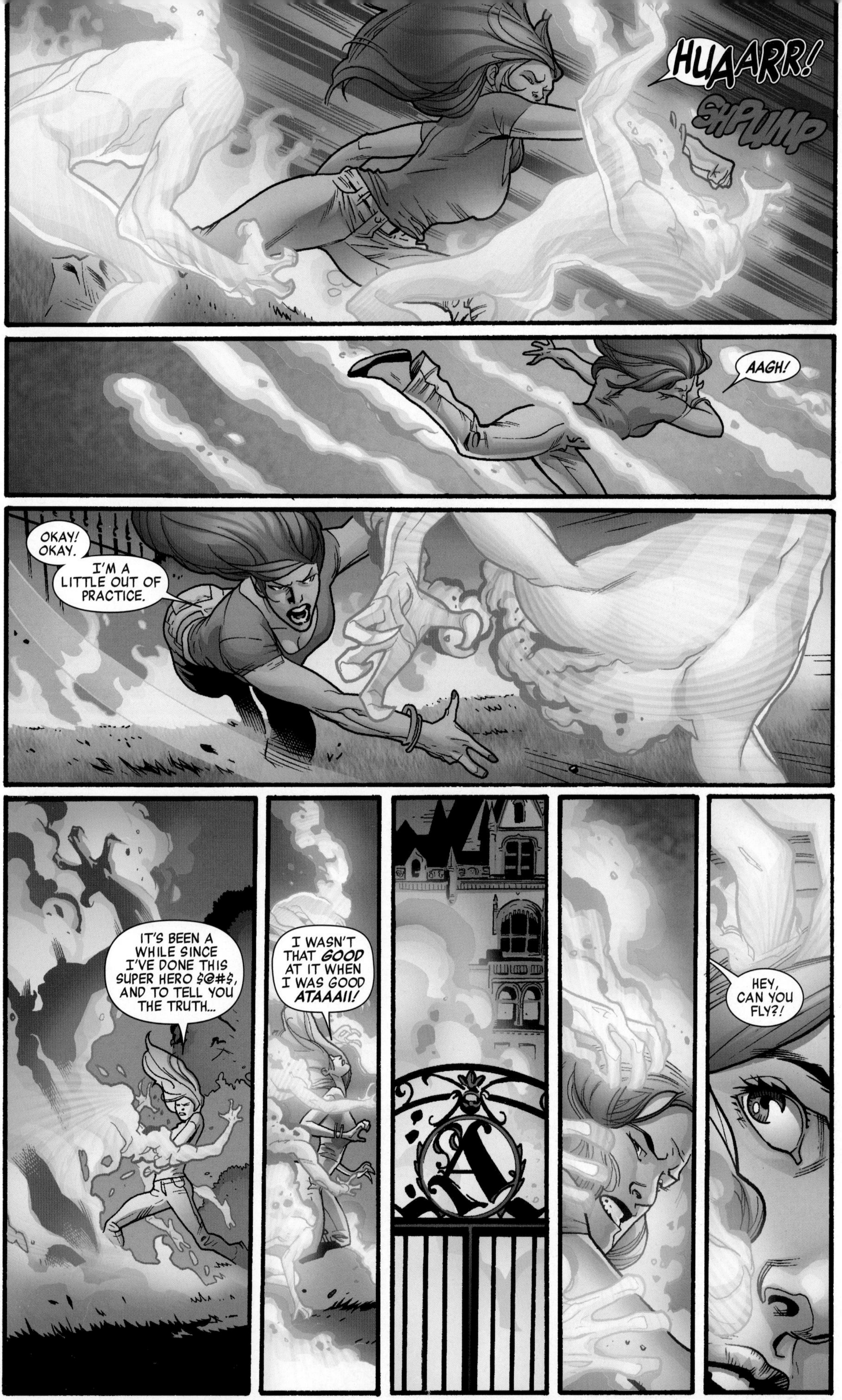
HUAARR!
SHPLUMP
AAGH!
OKAY! OKAY.
I'M A LITTLE OUT OF PRACTICE.
IT'S BEEN A WHILE SINCE I'VE DONE THIS SUPER HERO $@#$, AND TO TELL YOU THE TRUTH...
I WASN'T THAT GOOD AT IT WHEN I WAS GOOD ATAAAII!
HEY, CAN YOU FLY?!

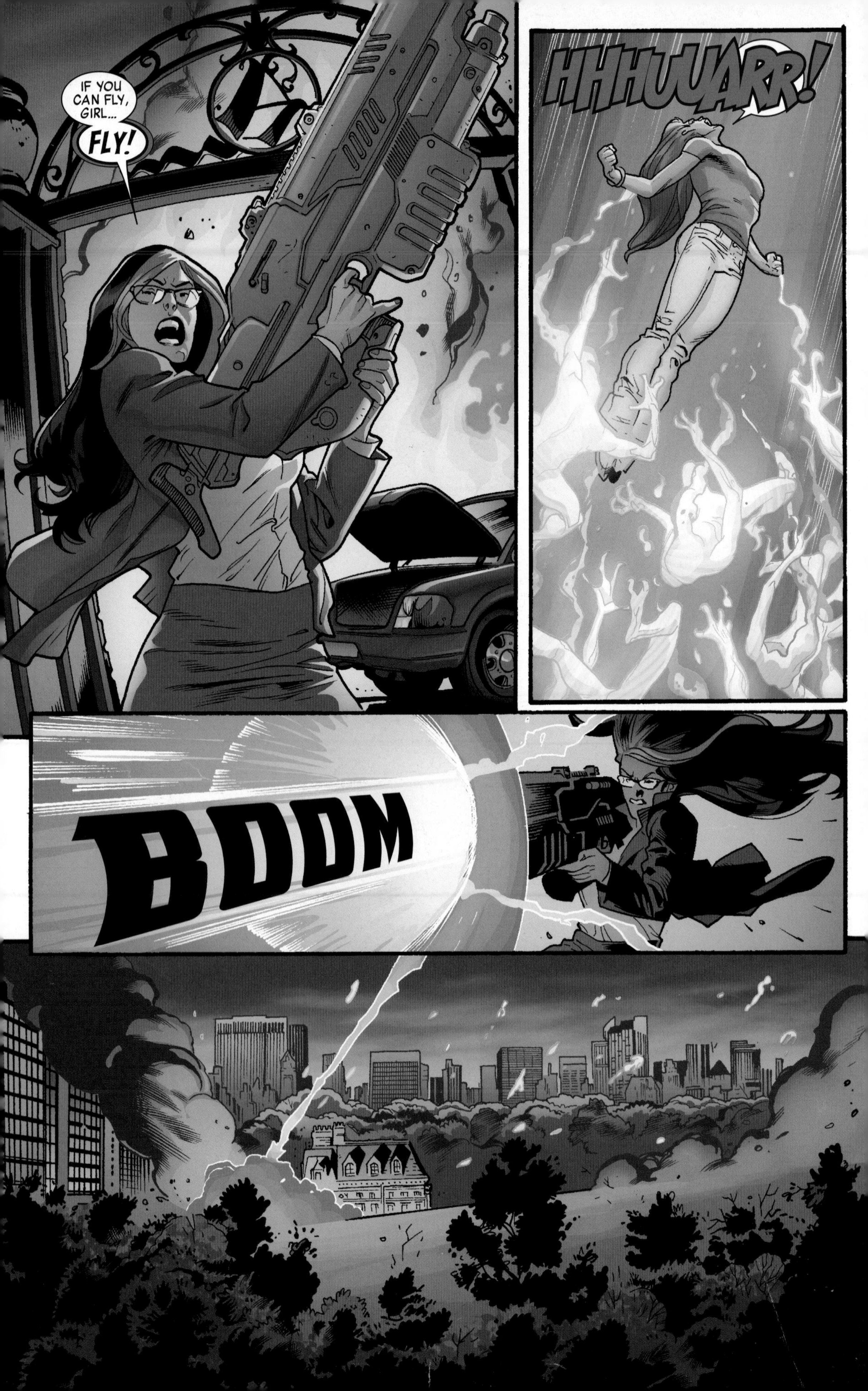
IF YOU CAN FLY, GIRL...
FLY!
HHHUUARR!
BOOM

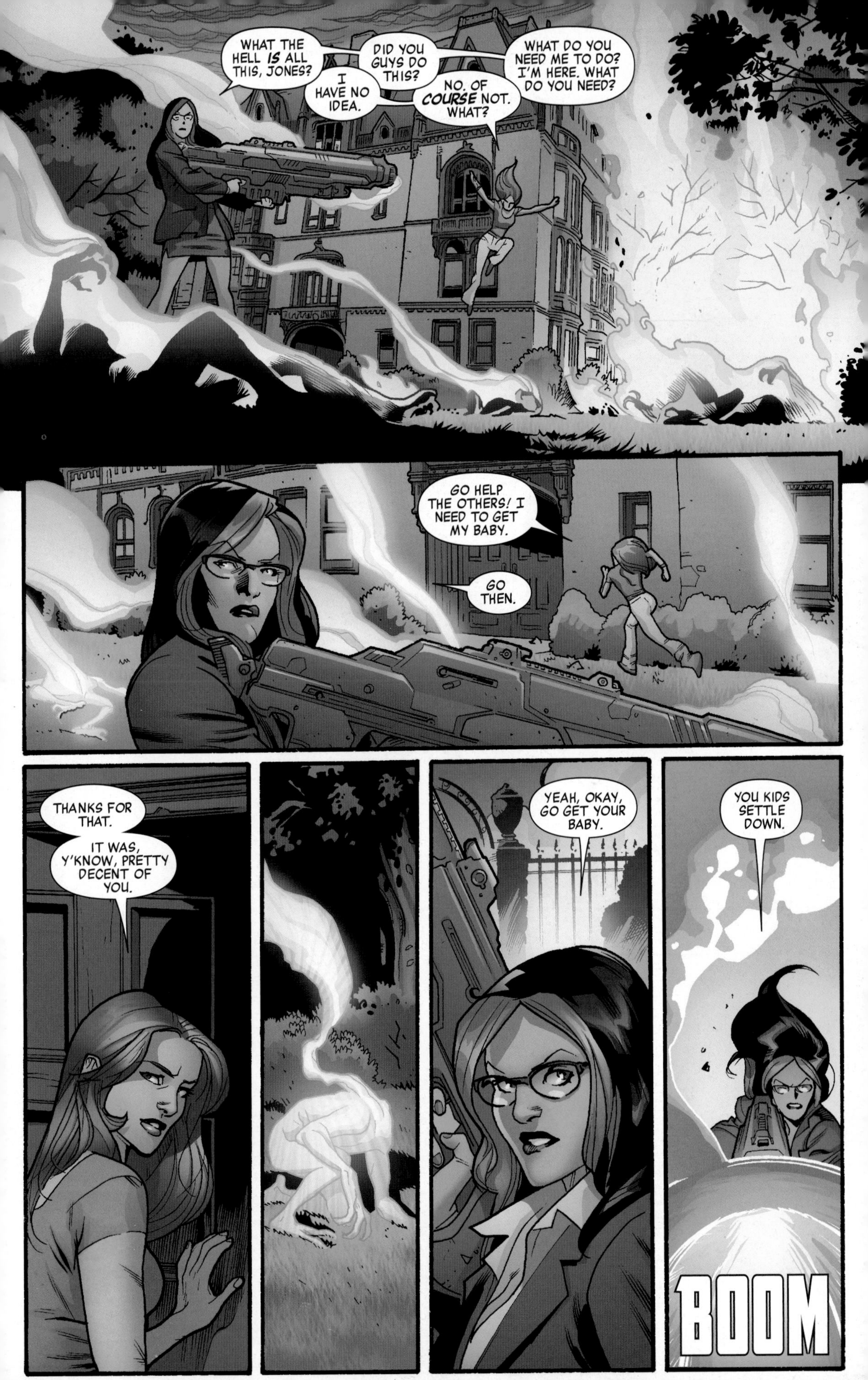
WHAT THE HELL *IS* ALL THIS, JONES?
DID YOU GUYS DO THIS?
I HAVE NO IDEA.
NO. OF *COURSE* NOT. WHAT?
WHAT DO YOU NEED ME TO DO? I'M HERE. WHAT DO YOU NEED?
GO HELP THE OTHERS! I NEED TO GET MY BABY.
GO THEN.
THANKS FOR THAT.
IT WAS, Y'KNOW, PRETTY DECENT OF YOU.
YEAH, OKAY, GO GET YOUR BABY.
YOU KIDS SETTLE DOWN.
BOOM

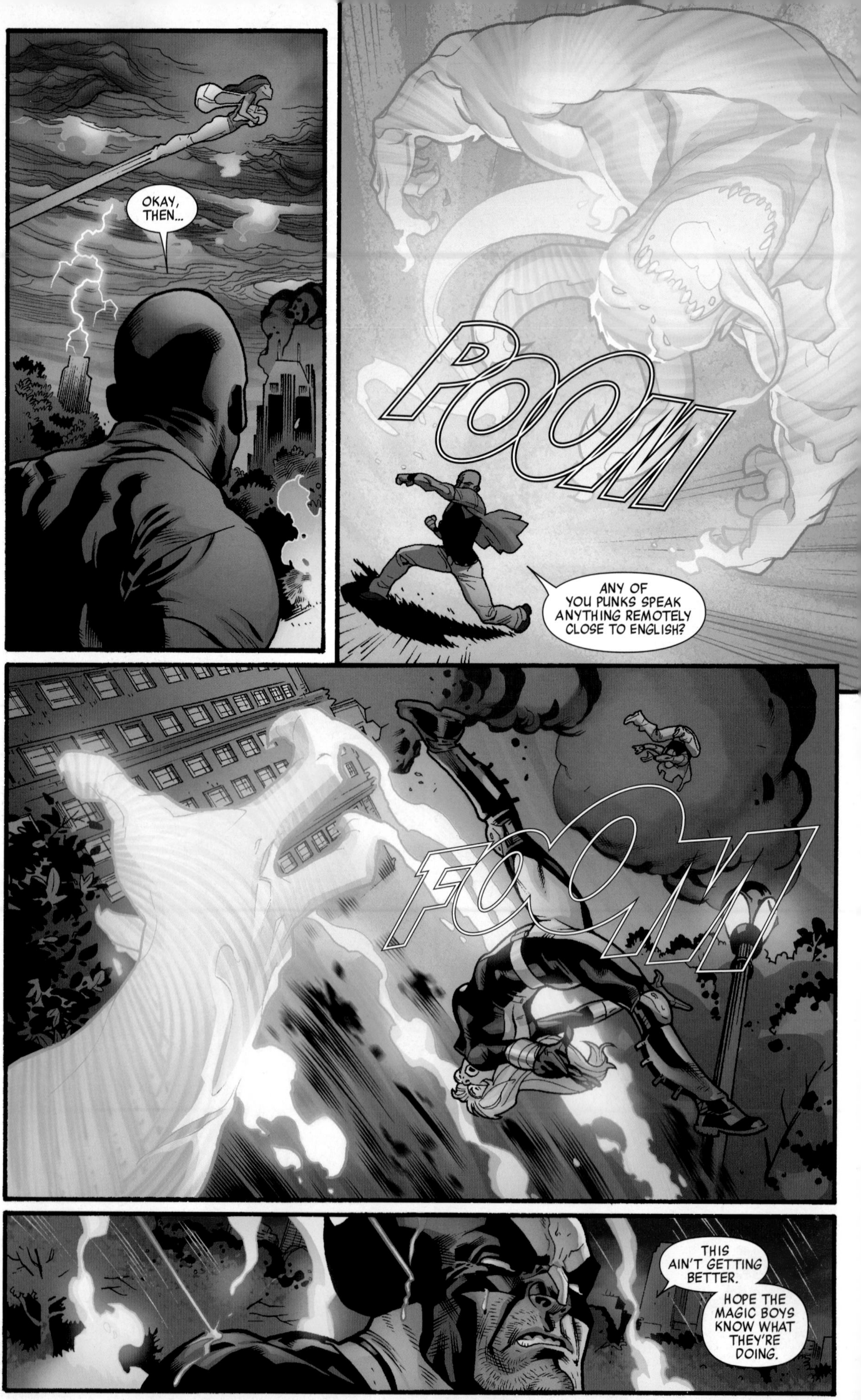
OKAY, THEN...
POOM
ANY OF YOU PUNKS SPEAK ANYTHING REMOTELY CLOSE TO ENGLISH?
FOOM
THIS AIN'T GETTING BETTER.
HOPE THE MAGIC BOYS KNOW WHAT THEY'RE DOING.

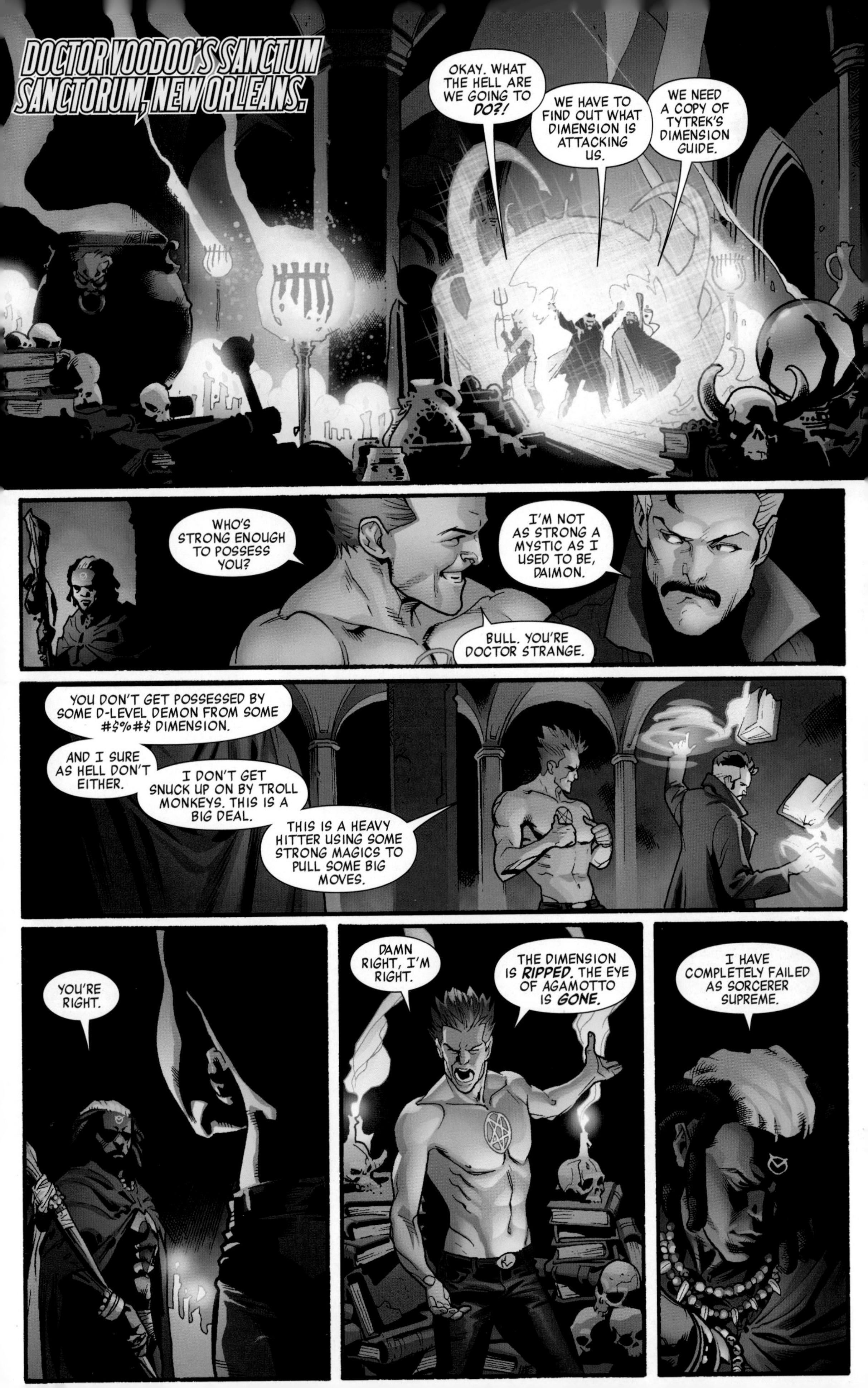
DOCTOR VOODOO'S SANCTUM SANCTORUM, NEW ORLEANS.
OKAY. WHAT THE HELL ARE WE GOING TO DO?!
WE HAVE TO FIND OUT WHAT DIMENSION IS ATTACKING US.
WE NEED A COPY OF TYTREK'S DIMENSION GUIDE.
WHO'S STRONG ENOUGH TO POSSESS YOU?
I'M NOT AS STRONG A MYSTIC AS I USED TO BE, DAIMON.
BULL. YOU'RE DOCTOR STRANGE.
YOU DON'T GET POSSESSED BY SOME D-LEVEL DEMON FROM SOME #$%#$ DIMENSION.
AND I SURE AS HELL DON'T EITHER.
I DON'T GET SNUCK UP ON BY TROLL MONKEYS. THIS IS A BIG DEAL.
THIS IS A HEAVY HITTER USING SOME STRONG MAGICS TO PULL SOME BIG MOVES.
YOU'RE RIGHT.
DAMN RIGHT, I'M RIGHT.
THE DIMENSION IS RIPPED. THE EYE OF AGAMOTTO IS GONE.
I HAVE COMPLETELY FAILED AS SORCERER SUPREME.

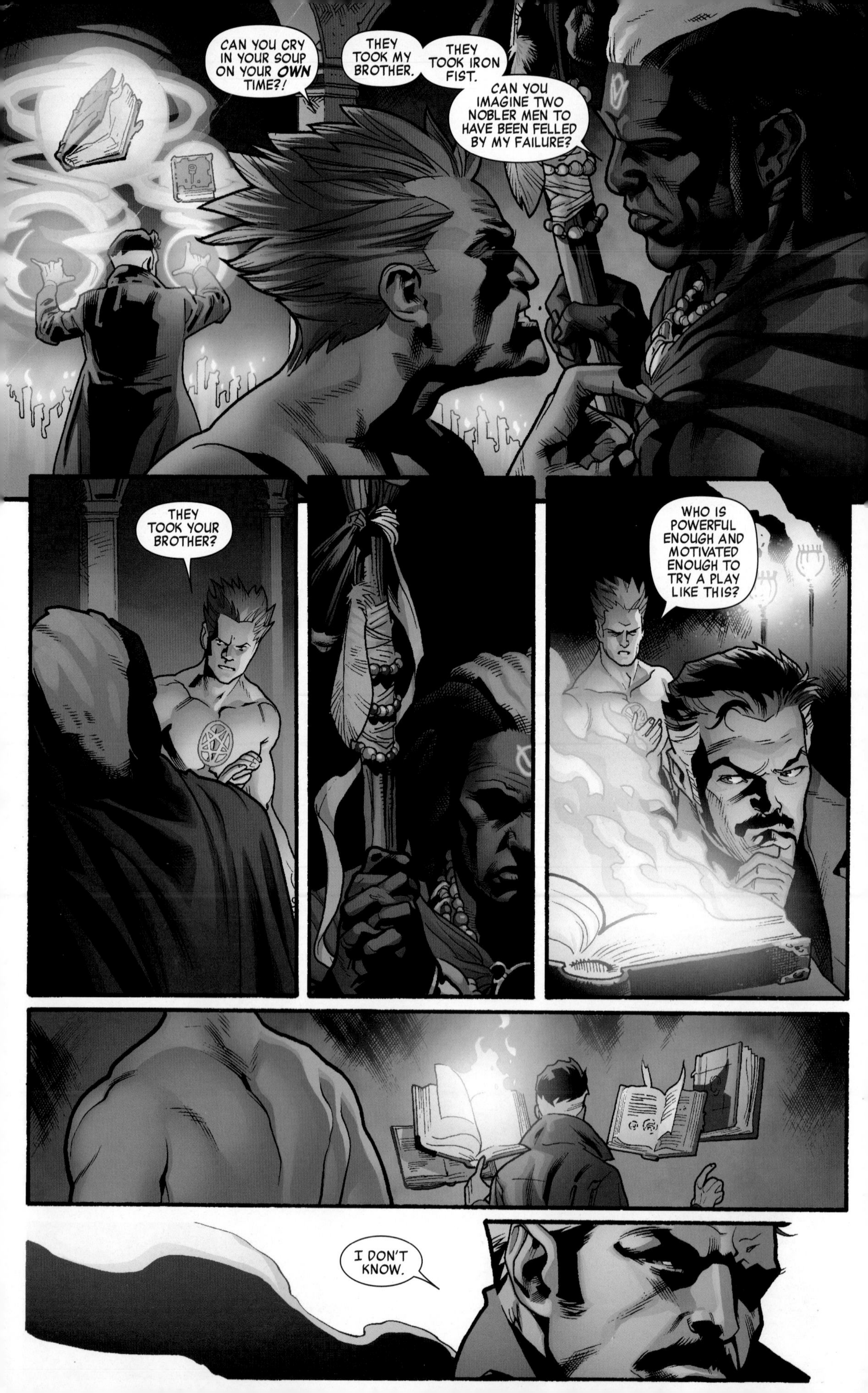
CAN YOU CRY IN YOUR SOUP ON YOUR OWN TIME?!
THEY TOOK MY BROTHER.
THEY TOOK IRON FIST.
CAN YOU IMAGINE TWO NOBLER MEN TO HAVE BEEN FELLED BY MY FAILURE?
THEY TOOK YOUR BROTHER?
WHO IS POWERFUL ENOUGH AND MOTIVATED ENOUGH TO TRY A PLAY LIKE THIS?
I DON'T KNOW.

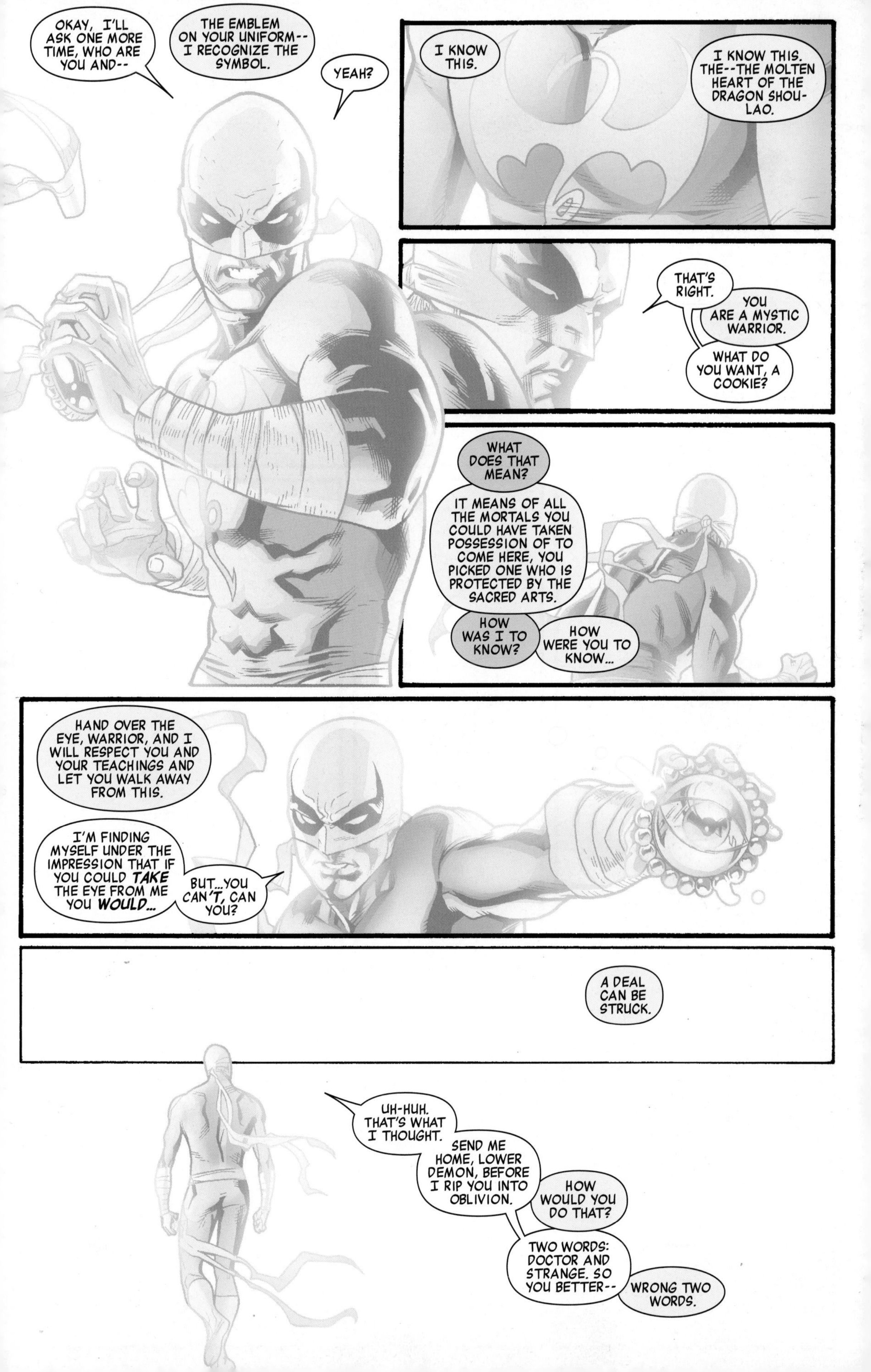
OKAY, I'LL ASK ONE MORE TIME, WHO ARE YOU AND--
THE EMBLEM ON YOUR UNIFORM--I RECOGNIZE THE SYMBOL.
YEAH?
I KNOW THIS.
I KNOW THIS. THE--THE MOLTEN HEART OF THE DRAGON SHOU-LAO.
THAT'S RIGHT.
YOU ARE A MYSTIC WARRIOR.
WHAT DO YOU WANT, A COOKIE?
WHAT DOES THAT MEAN?
IT MEANS OF ALL THE MORTALS YOU COULD HAVE TAKEN POSSESSION OF TO COME HERE, YOU PICKED ONE WHO IS PROTECTED BY THE SACRED ARTS.
HOW WAS I TO KNOW?
HOW WERE YOU TO KNOW...
HAND OVER THE EYE, WARRIOR, AND I WILL RESPECT YOU AND YOUR TEACHINGS AND LET YOU WALK AWAY FROM THIS.
I'M FINDING MYSELF UNDER THE IMPRESSION THAT IF YOU COULD *TAKE* THE EYE FROM ME YOU *WOULD...*
BUT...YOU CAN'*T,* CAN YOU?
A DEAL CAN BE STRUCK.
UH-HUH. THAT'S WHAT I THOUGHT.
SEND ME HOME, LOWER DEMON, BEFORE I RIP YOU INTO OBLIVION.
HOW WOULD YOU DO THAT?
TWO WORDS: DOCTOR AND STRANGE. SO YOU BETTER--
WRONG TWO WORDS.

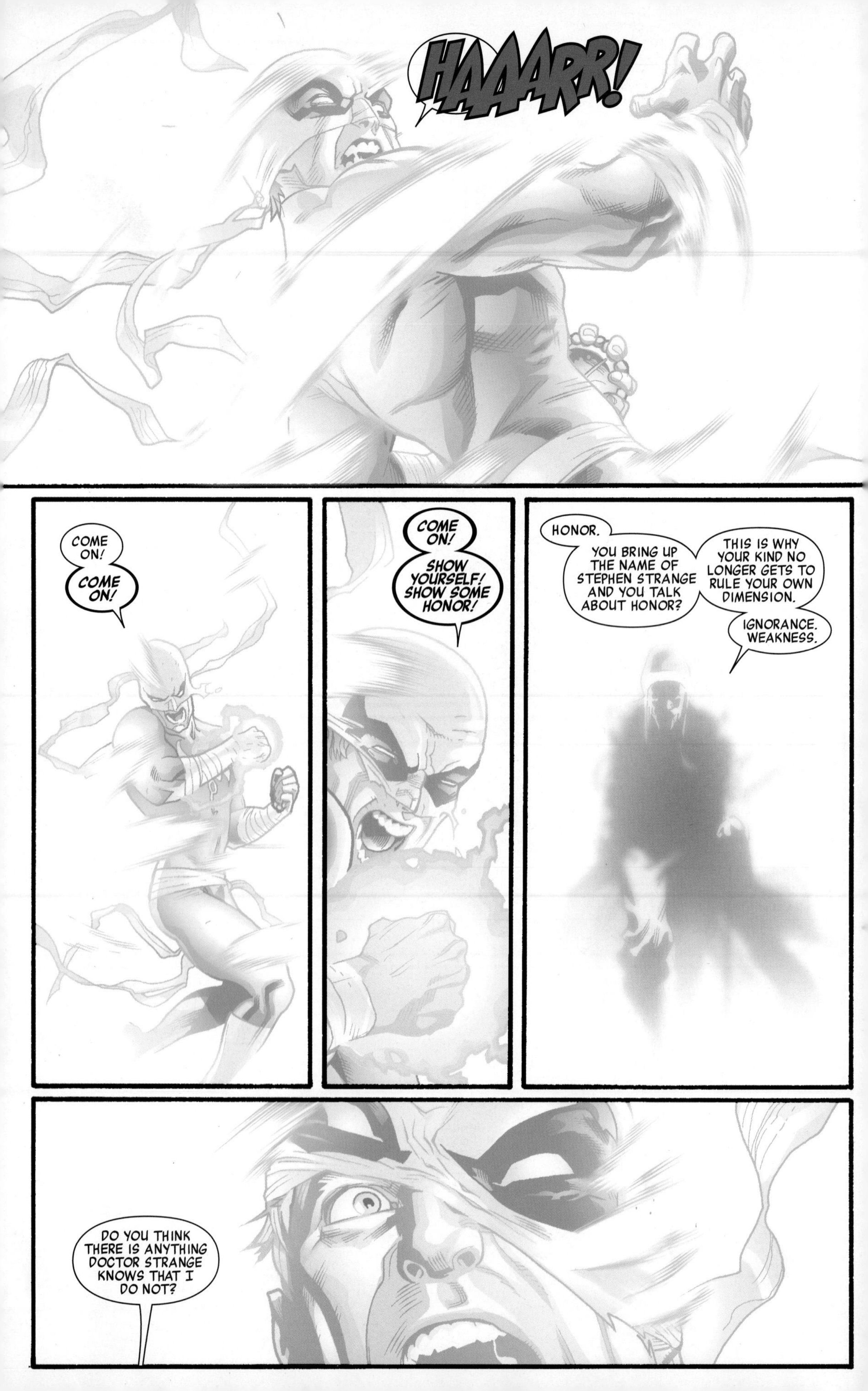
HAAARR!
COME ON!
COME ON!
COME ON!
SHOW YOURSELF! SHOW SOME HONOR!
HONOR.
YOU BRING UP THE NAME OF STEPHEN STRANGE AND YOU TALK ABOUT HONOR?
THIS IS WHY YOUR KIND NO LONGER GETS TO RULE YOUR OWN DIMENSION.
IGNORANCE. WEAKNESS.
DO YOU THINK THERE IS ANYTHING DOCTOR STRANGE KNOWS THAT I DO NOT?

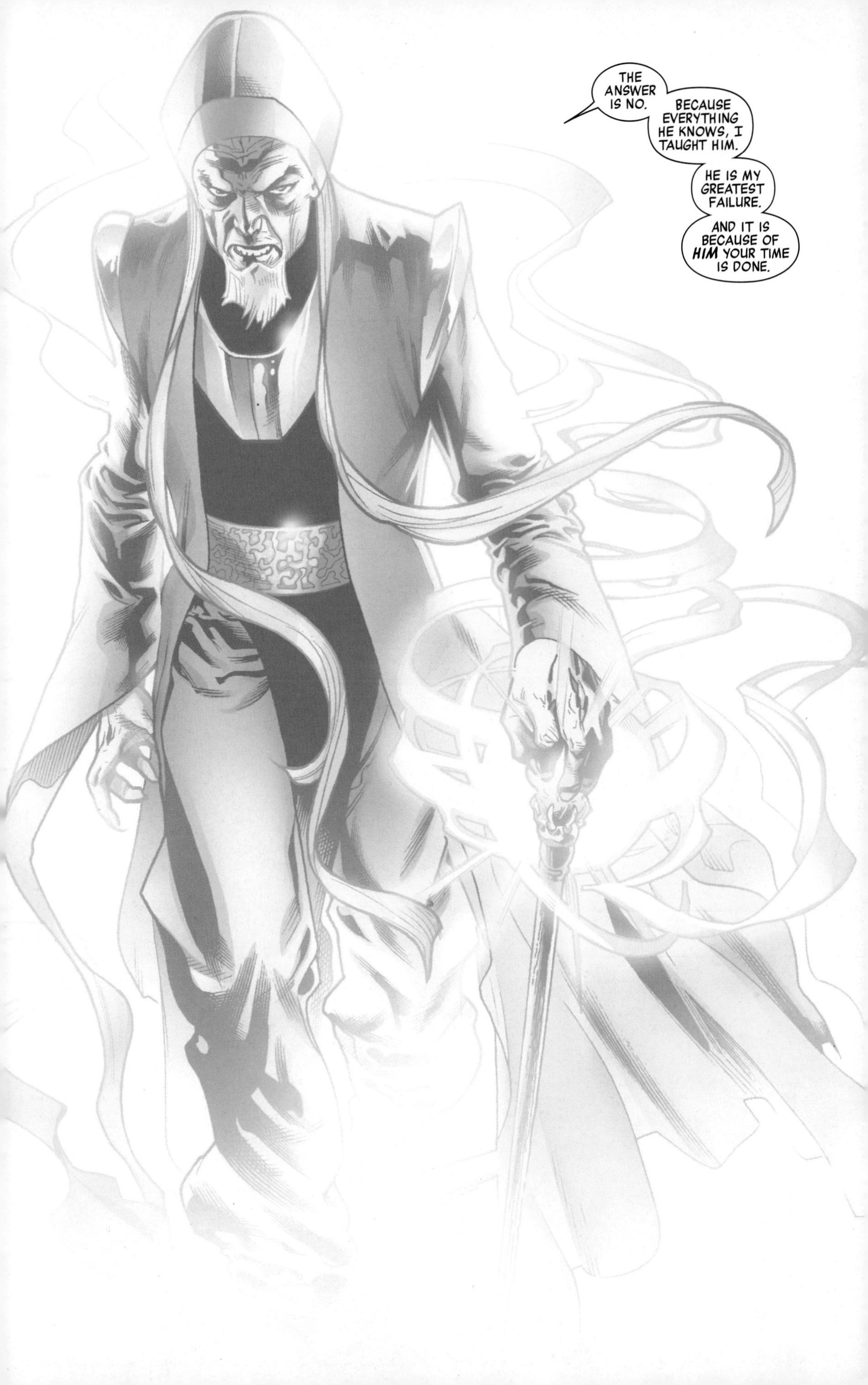
THE ANSWER IS NO.
BECAUSE EVERYTHING HE KNOWS, I TAUGHT HIM.
HE IS MY GREATEST FAILURE.
AND IT IS BECAUSE OF *HIM* YOUR TIME IS DONE.

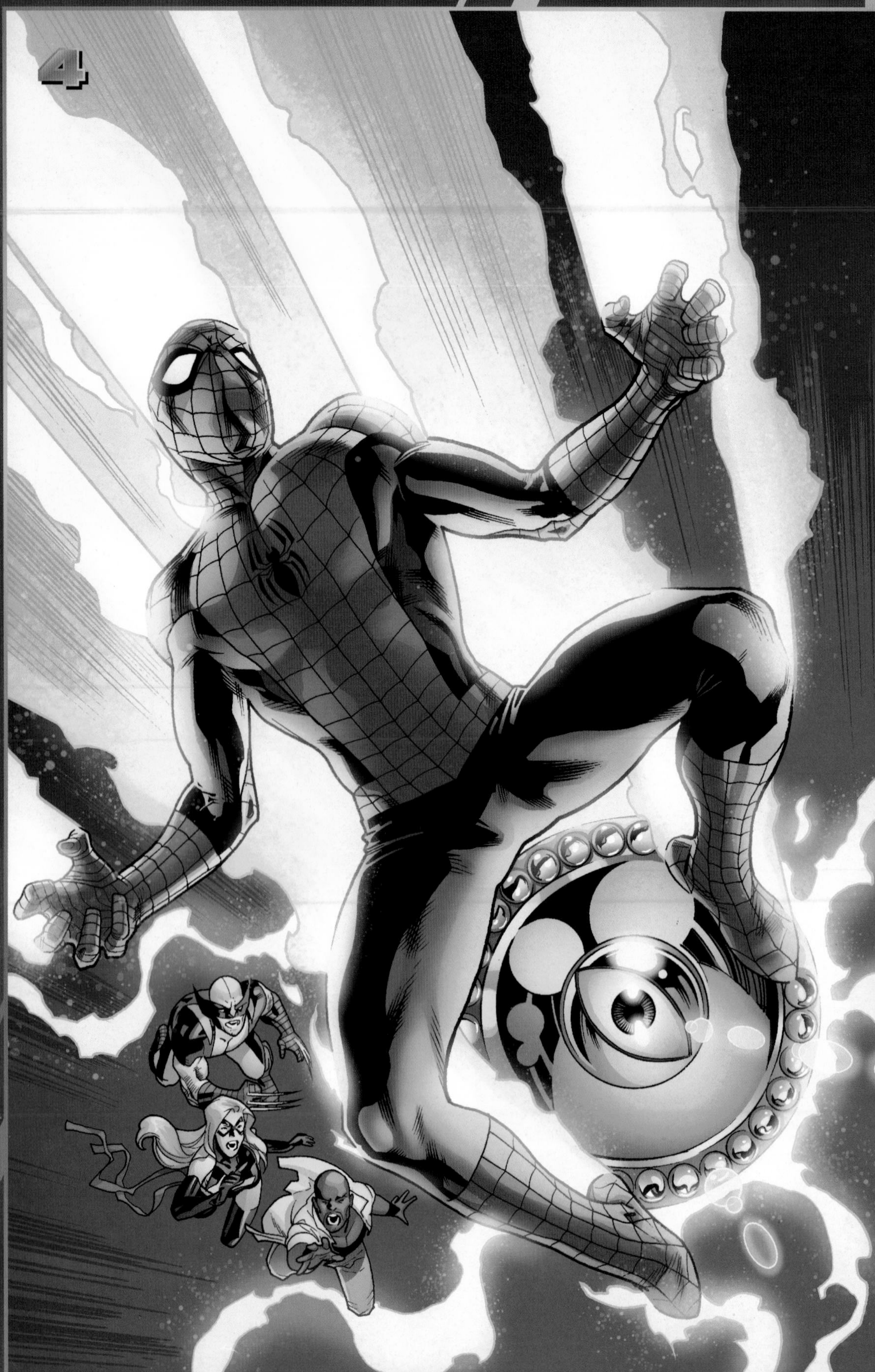
4

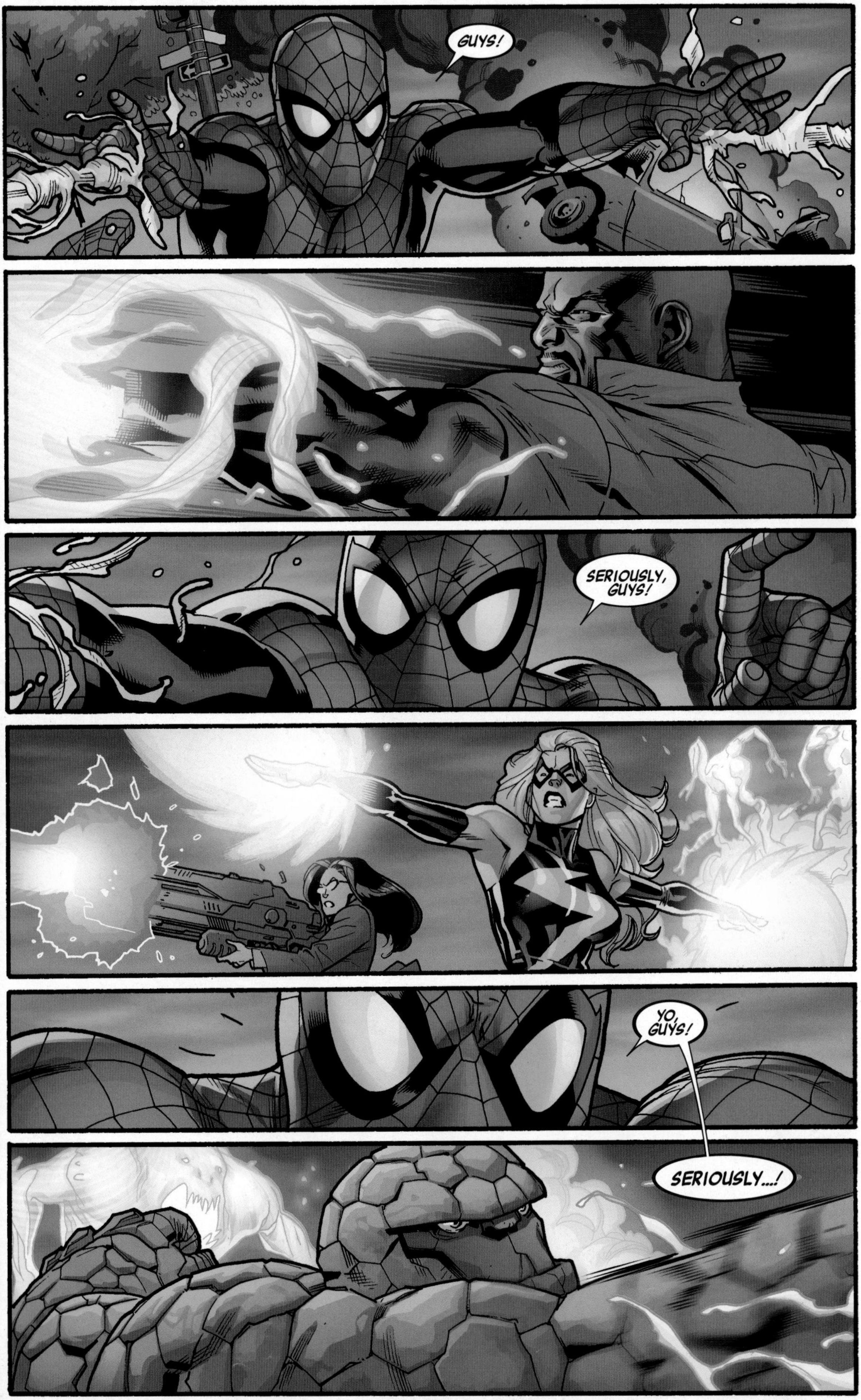
GUYS!
SERIOUSLY, GUYS!
YO, GUYS!
SERIOUSLY...!

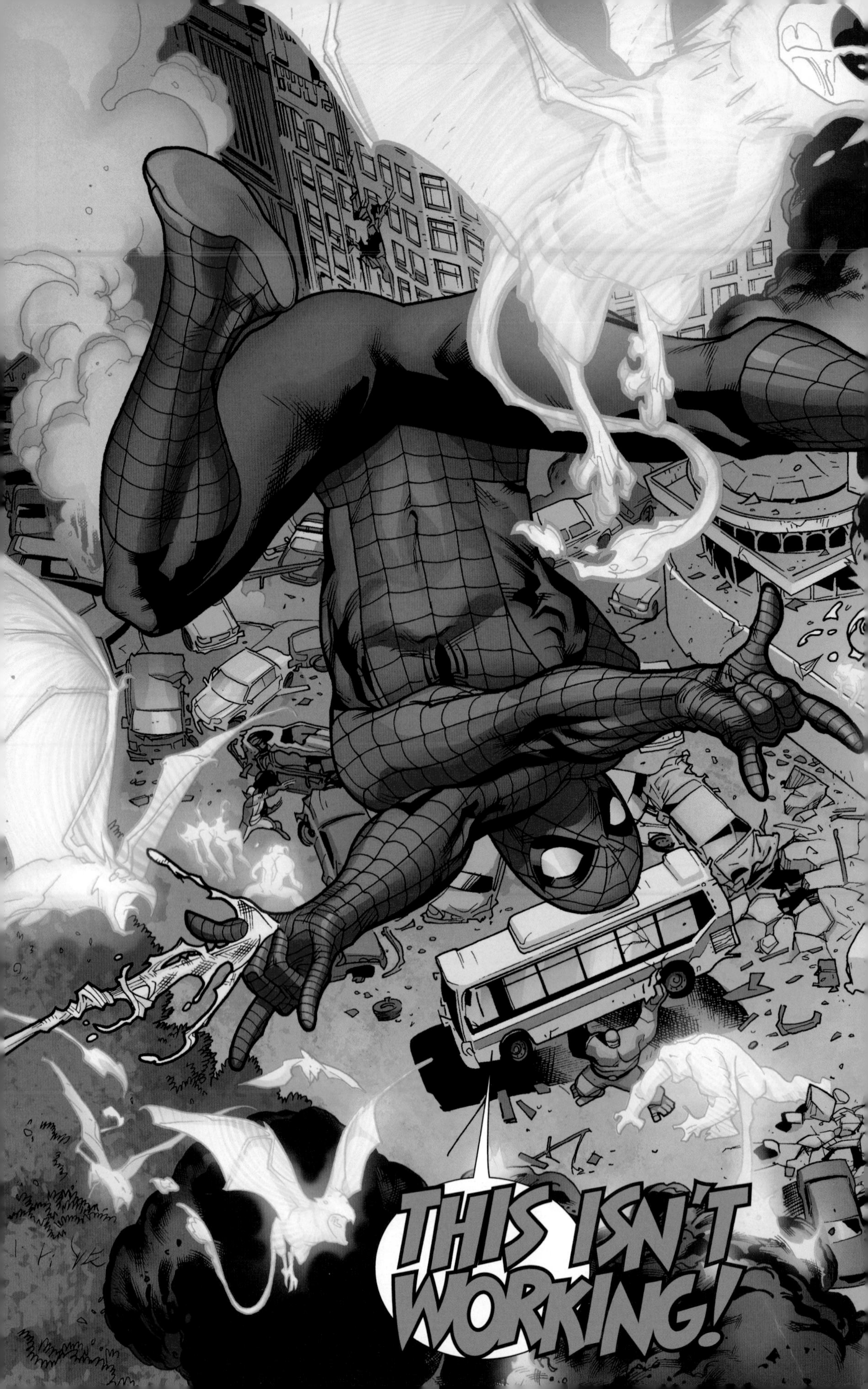
THIS ISN'T WORKING!

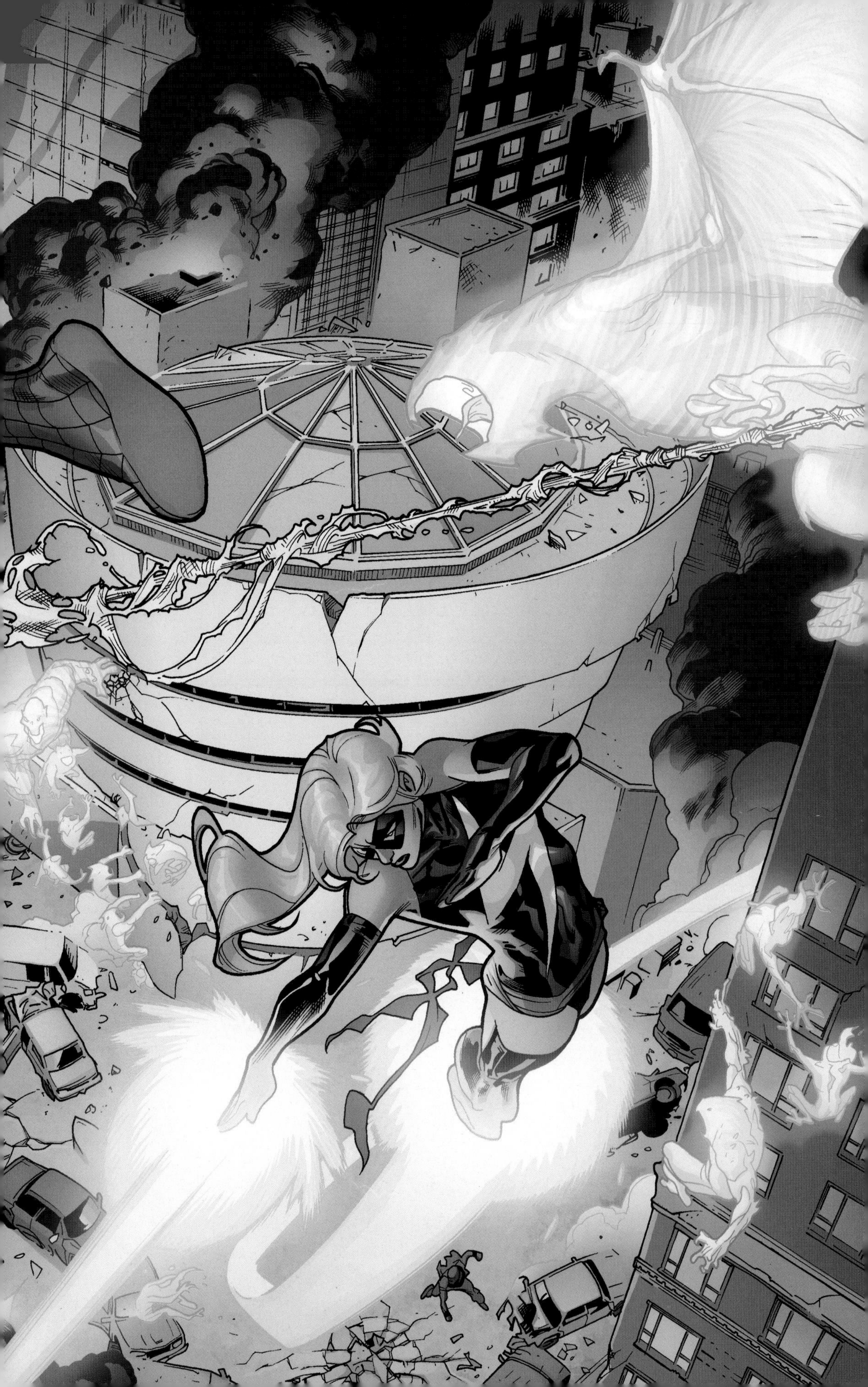

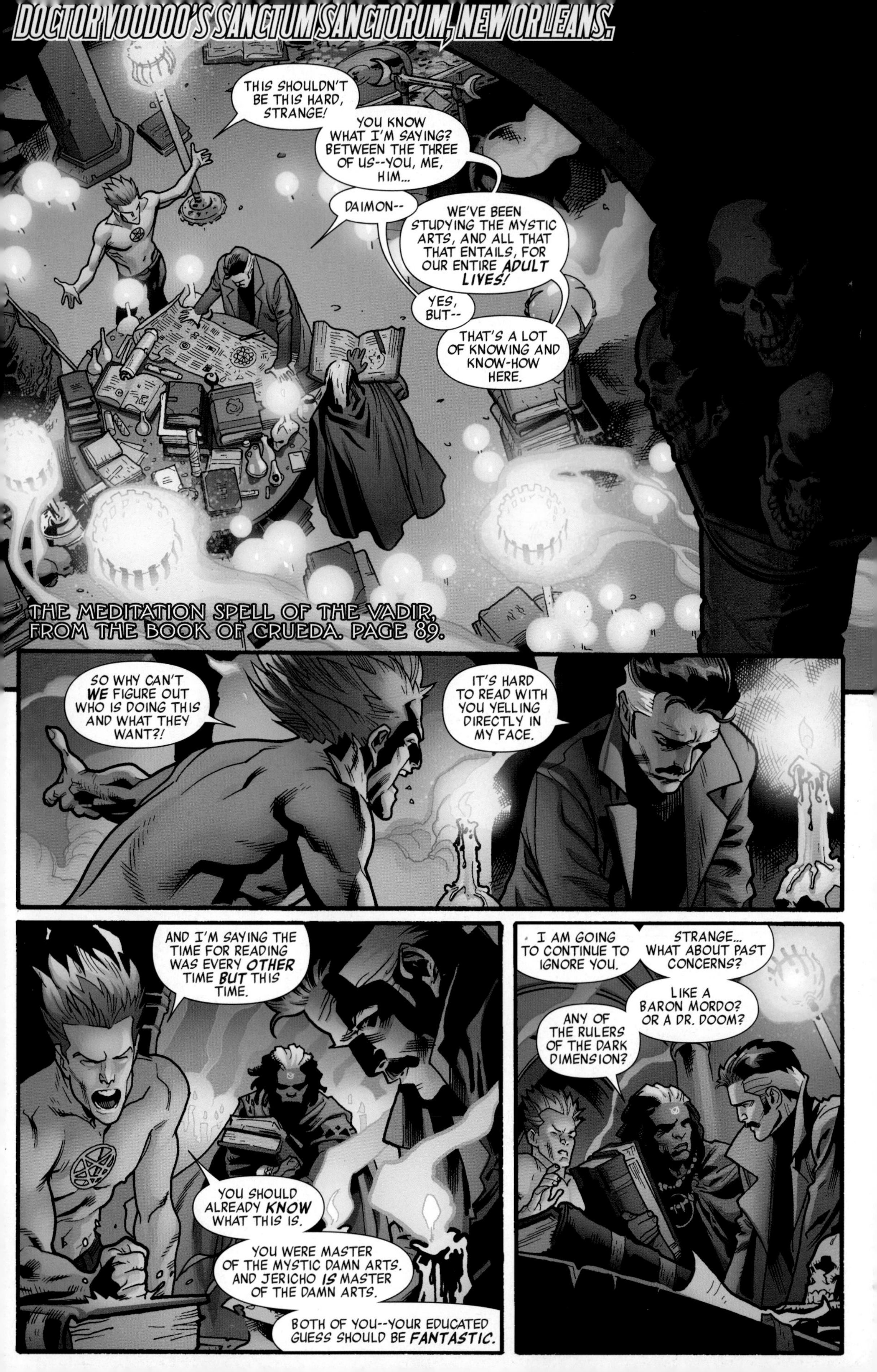
DOCTOR VOODOO'S SANCTUM SANCTORUM, NEW ORLEANS.
THIS SHOULDN'T BE THIS HARD, STRANGE!
YOU KNOW WHAT I'M SAYING? BETWEEN THE THREE OF US--YOU, ME, HIM...
DAIMON--
WE'VE BEEN STUDYING THE MYSTIC ARTS, AND ALL THAT THAT ENTAILS, FOR OUR ENTIRE ADULT LIVES!
YES, BUT--
THAT'S A LOT OF KNOWING AND KNOW-HOW HERE.
THE MEDITATION SPELL OF THE VADIR, FROM THE BOOK OF CRUEDA. PAGE 89.
SO WHY CAN'T WE FIGURE OUT WHO IS DOING THIS AND WHAT THEY WANT?!
IT'S HARD TO READ WITH YOU YELLING DIRECTLY IN MY FACE.
AND I'M SAYING THE TIME FOR READING WAS EVERY OTHER TIME BUT THIS TIME.
YOU SHOULD ALREADY KNOW WHAT THIS IS.
YOU WERE MASTER OF THE MYSTIC DAMN ARTS. AND JERICHO IS MASTER OF THE DAMN ARTS.
BOTH OF YOU--YOUR EDUCATED GUESS SHOULD BE FANTASTIC.
I AM GOING TO CONTINUE TO IGNORE YOU.
STRANGE... WHAT ABOUT PAST CONCERNS?
LIKE A BARON MORDO? OR A DR. DOOM?
ANY OF THE RULERS OF THE DARK DIMENSION?

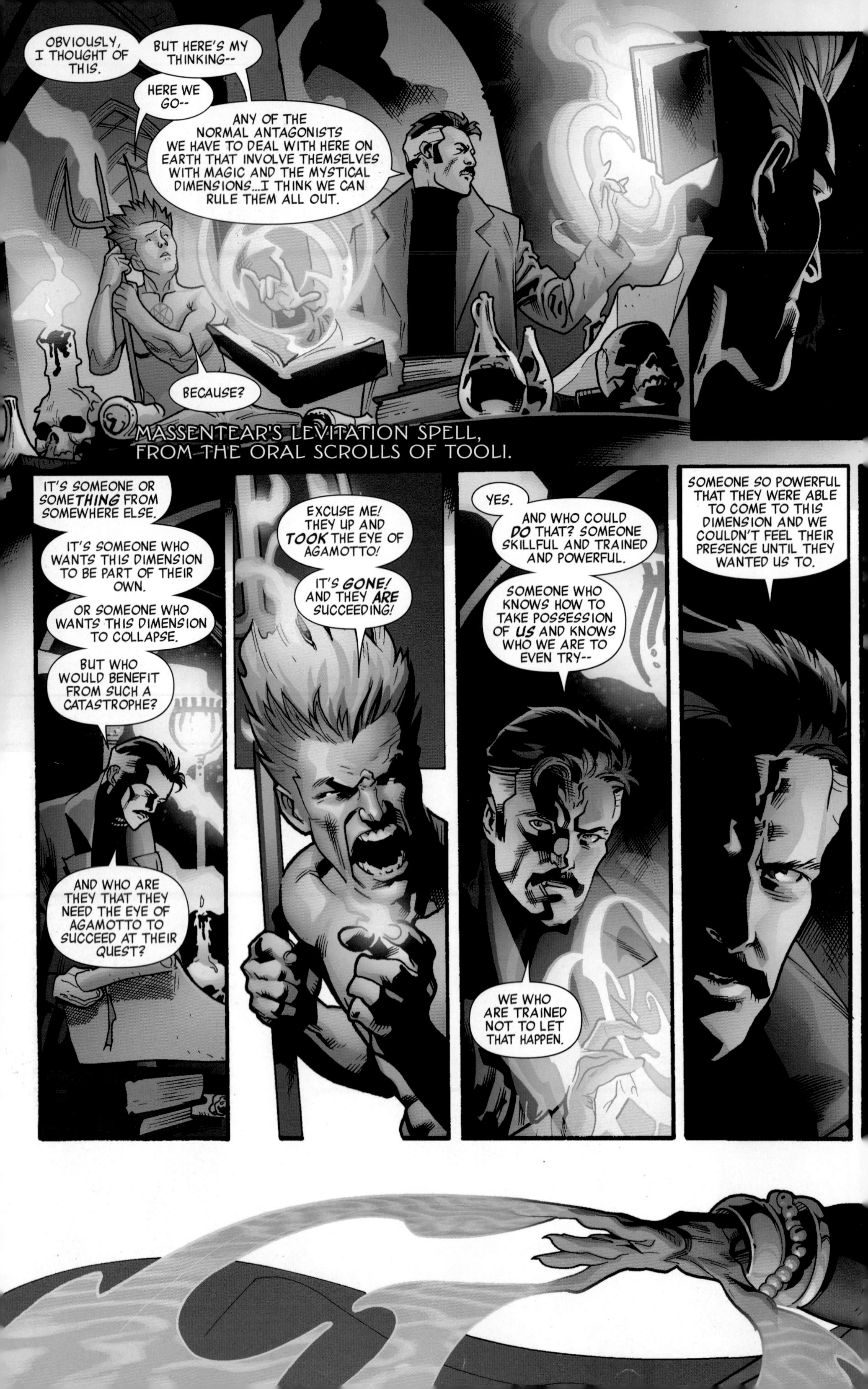
OBVIOUSLY, I THOUGHT OF THIS.
BUT HERE'S MY THINKING--
HERE WE GO--
ANY OF THE NORMAL ANTAGONISTS WE HAVE TO DEAL WITH HERE ON EARTH THAT INVOLVE THEMSELVES WITH MAGIC AND THE MYSTICAL DIMENSIONS...I THINK WE CAN RULE THEM ALL OUT.
BECAUSE?
MASSENTEAR'S LEVITATION SPELL, FROM THE ORAL SCROLLS OF TOOLI.
IT'S SOMEONE OR SOMETHING FROM SOMEWHERE ELSE.
IT'S SOMEONE WHO WANTS THIS DIMENSION TO BE PART OF THEIR OWN.
OR SOMEONE WHO WANTS THIS DIMENSION TO COLLAPSE.
BUT WHO WOULD BENEFIT FROM SUCH A CATASTROPHE?
AND WHO ARE THEY THAT THEY NEED THE EYE OF AGAMOTTO TO SUCCEED AT THEIR QUEST?
EXCUSE ME! THEY UP AND TOOK THE EYE OF AGAMOTTO!
IT'S GONE! AND THEY ARE SUCCEEDING!
YES.
AND WHO COULD DO THAT? SOMEONE SKILLFUL AND TRAINED AND POWERFUL.
SOMEONE WHO KNOWS HOW TO TAKE POSSESSION OF US AND KNOWS WHO WE ARE TO EVEN TRY--
WE WHO ARE TRAINED NOT TO LET THAT HAPPEN.
SOMEONE SO POWERFUL THAT THEY WERE ABLE TO COME TO THIS DIMENSION AND WE COULDN'T FEEL THEIR PRESENCE UNTIL THEY WANTED US TO.

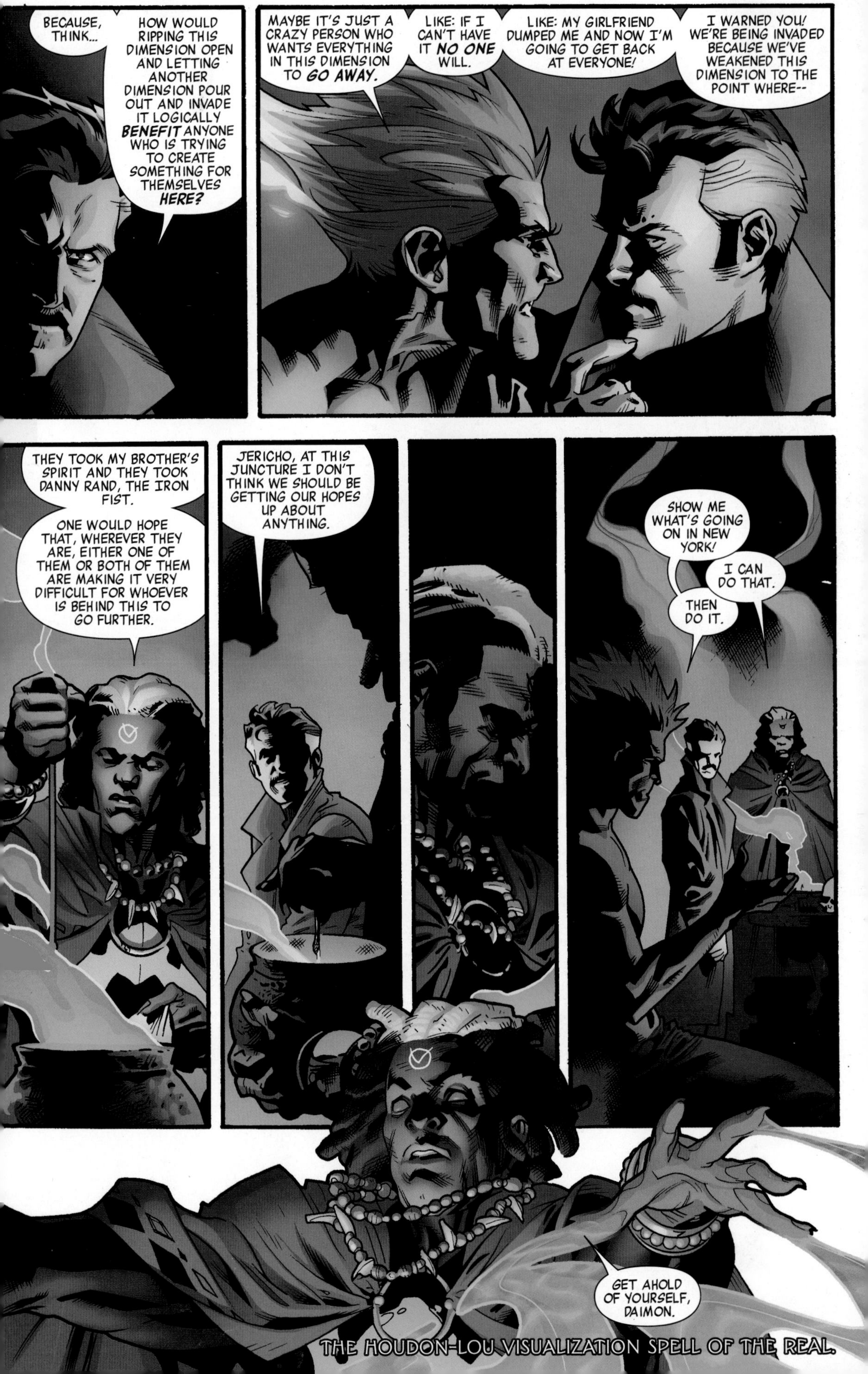
BECAUSE, THINK...
HOW WOULD RIPPING THIS DIMENSION OPEN AND LETTING ANOTHER DIMENSION POUR OUT AND INVADE IT LOGICALLY **BENEFIT** ANYONE WHO IS TRYING TO CREATE SOMETHING FOR THEMSELVES **HERE?**
MAYBE IT'S JUST A CRAZY PERSON WHO WANTS EVERYTHING IN THIS DIMENSION TO **GO AWAY.**
LIKE: IF I CAN'T HAVE IT **NO ONE** WILL.
LIKE: MY GIRLFRIEND DUMPED ME AND NOW I'M GOING TO GET BACK AT EVERYONE!
I WARNED YOU! WE'RE BEING INVADED BECAUSE WE'VE WEAKENED THIS DIMENSION TO THE POINT WHERE--
THEY TOOK MY BROTHER'S SPIRIT AND THEY TOOK DANNY RAND, THE IRON FIST.
ONE WOULD HOPE THAT, WHEREVER THEY ARE, EITHER ONE OF THEM OR BOTH OF THEM ARE MAKING IT VERY DIFFICULT FOR WHOEVER IS BEHIND THIS TO GO FURTHER.
JERICHO, AT THIS JUNCTURE I DON'T THINK WE SHOULD BE GETTING OUR HOPES UP ABOUT ANYTHING.
SHOW ME WHAT'S GOING ON IN NEW YORK!
I CAN DO THAT.
THEN DO IT.
GET AHOLD OF YOURSELF, DAIMON.
THE HOUDON-LOU VISUALIZATION SPELL OF THE REAL.

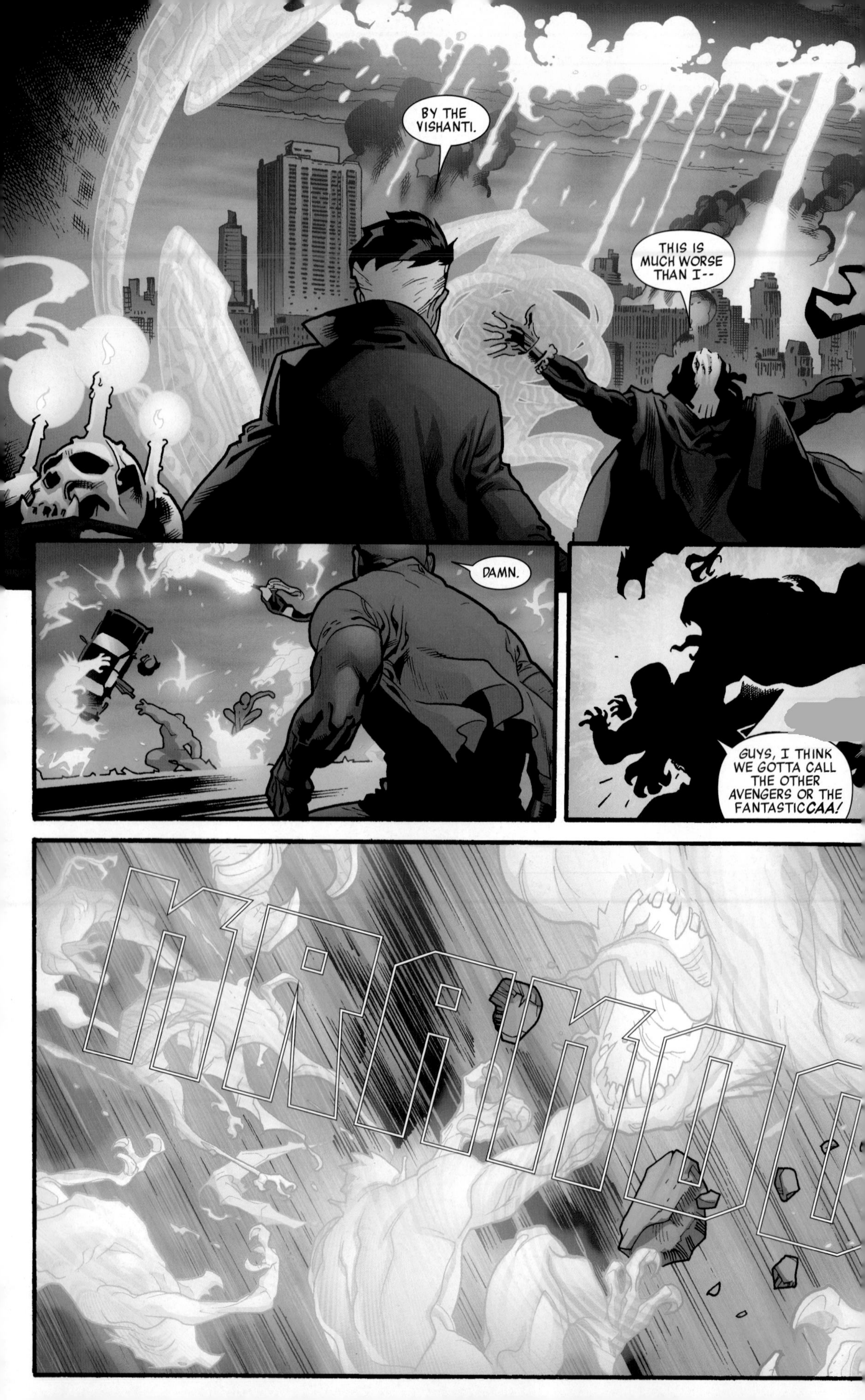
BY THE VISHANTI.
THIS IS MUCH WORSE THAN I--
DAMN.
GUYS, I THINK WE GOTTA CALL THE OTHER AVENGERS OR THE FANTASTIC CAA!

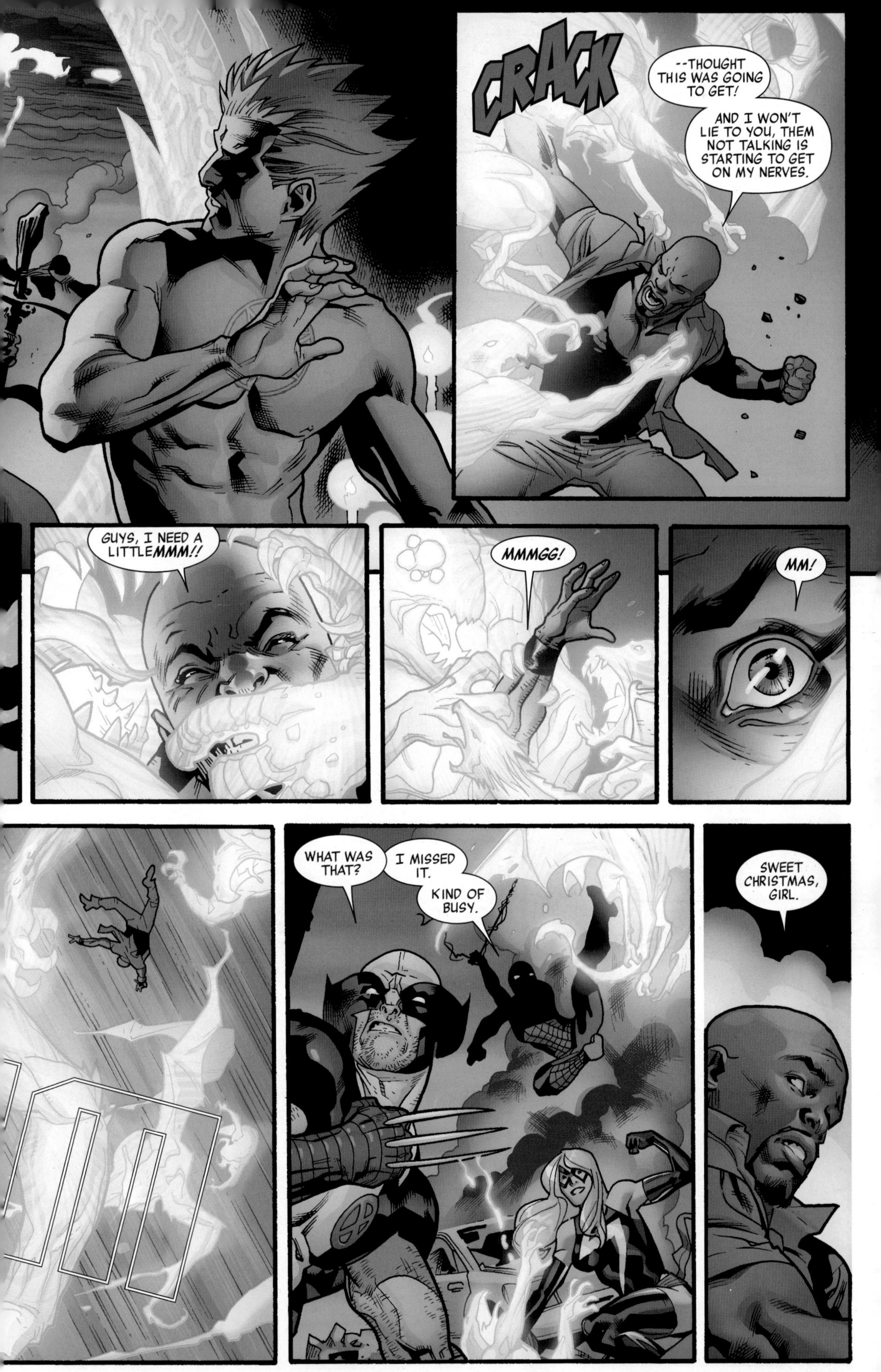
CRACK
--THOUGHT THIS WAS GOING TO GET!
AND I WON'T LIE TO YOU, THEM NOT TALKING IS STARTING TO GET ON MY NERVES.
GUYS, I NEED A LITTLEMMM!!
MMMGG!
MM!
WHAT WAS THAT?
I MISSED IT.
KIND OF BUSY.
SWEET CHRISTMAS, GIRL.

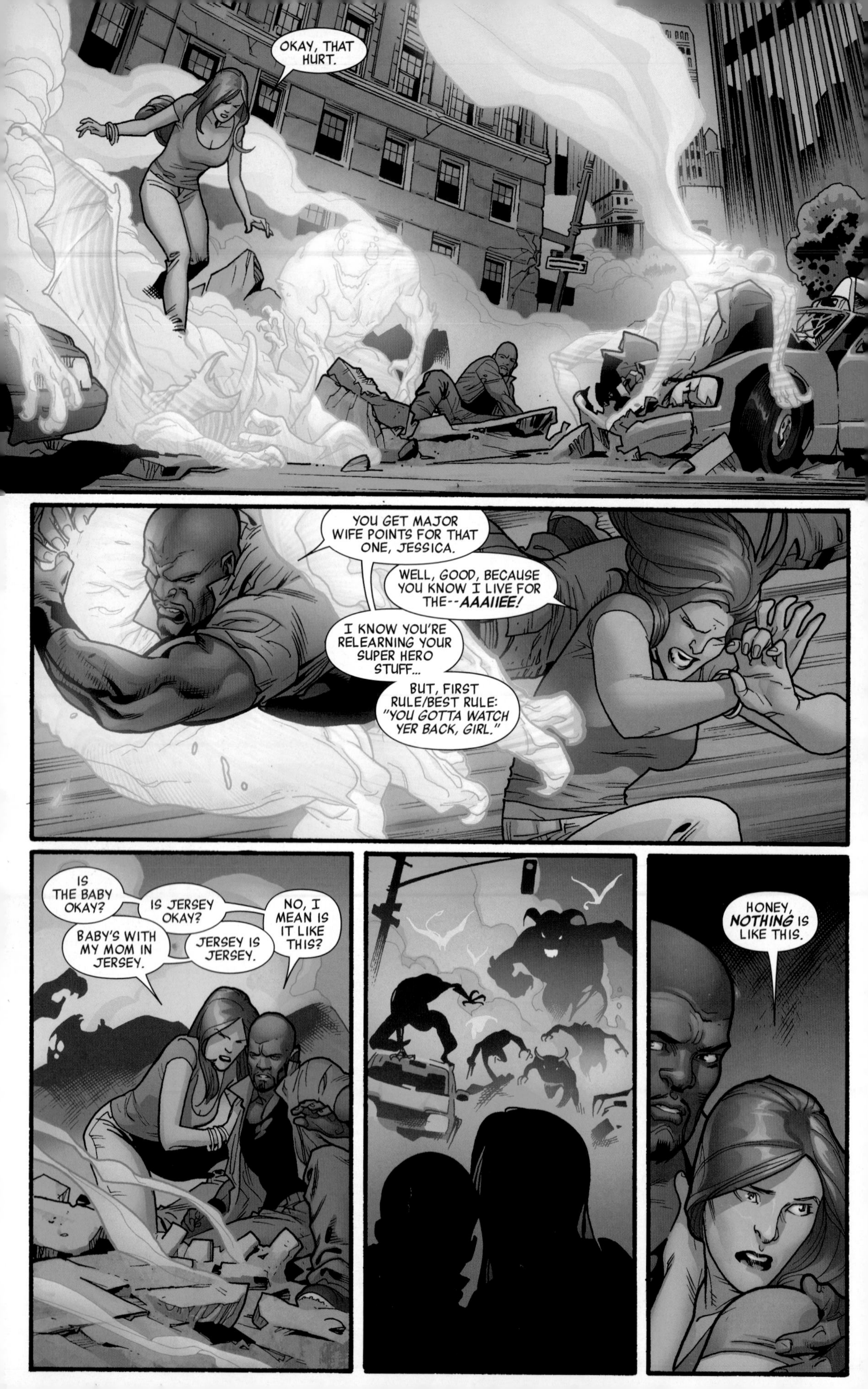
OKAY, THAT HURT.
YOU GET MAJOR WIFE POINTS FOR THAT ONE, JESSICA.
WELL, GOOD, BECAUSE YOU KNOW I LIVE FOR THE--AAAIIEE!
I KNOW YOU'RE RELEARNING YOUR SUPER HERO STUFF...
BUT, FIRST RULE/BEST RULE: "YOU GOTTA WATCH YER BACK, GIRL."
IS THE BABY OKAY?
BABY'S WITH MY MOM IN JERSEY.
IS JERSEY OKAY?
JERSEY IS JERSEY.
NO, I MEAN IS IT LIKE THIS?
HONEY, NOTHING IS LIKE THIS.

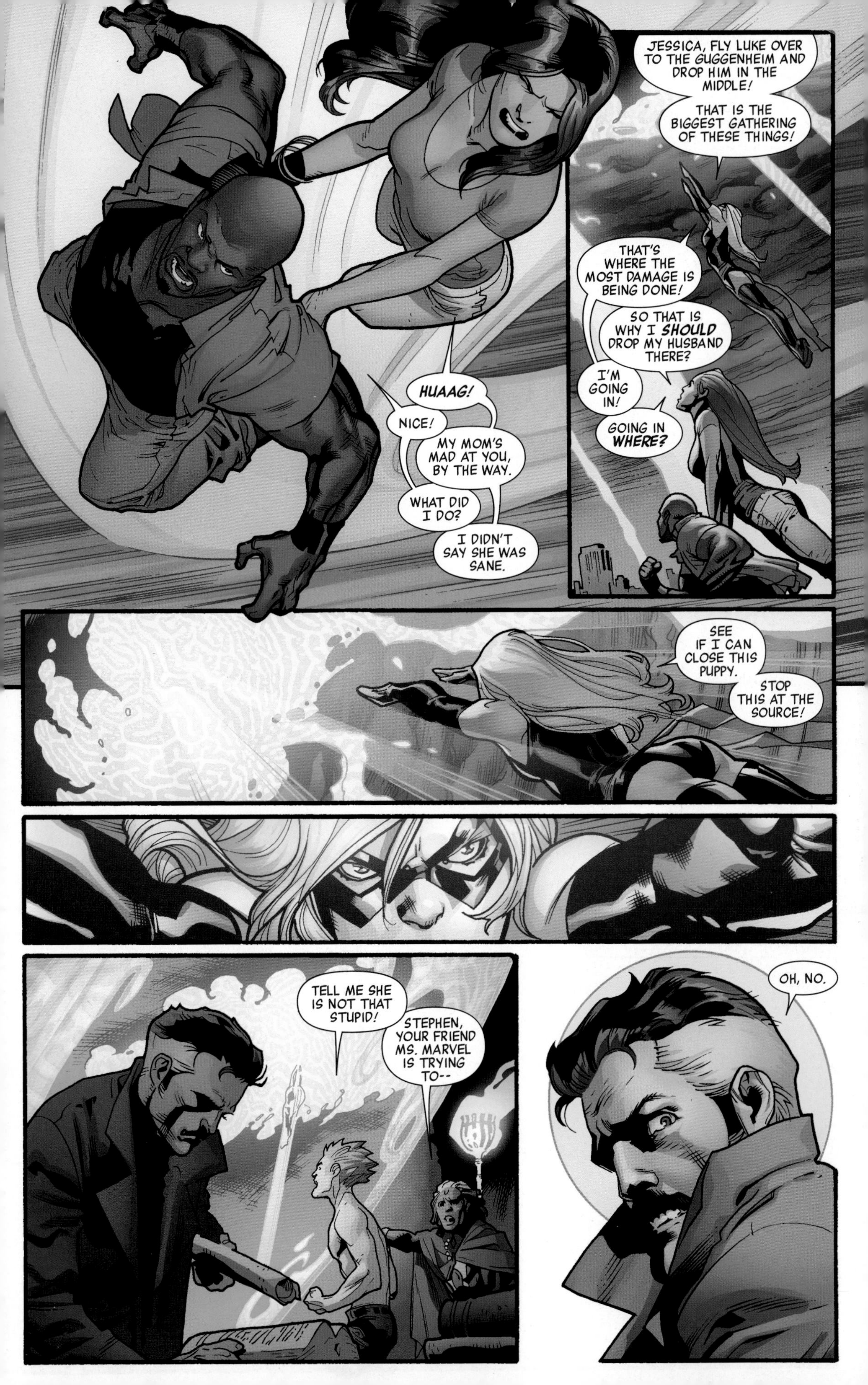
HUAAG!
NICE!
MY MOM'S MAD AT YOU, BY THE WAY.
WHAT DID I DO?
I DIDN'T SAY SHE WAS SANE.
JESSICA, FLY LUKE OVER TO THE GUGGENHEIM AND DROP HIM IN THE MIDDLE!
THAT IS THE BIGGEST GATHERING OF THESE THINGS!
THAT'S WHERE THE MOST DAMAGE IS BEING DONE!
SO THAT IS WHY I SHOULD DROP MY HUSBAND THERE?
I'M GOING IN!
GOING IN WHERE?
SEE IF I CAN CLOSE THIS PUPPY.
STOP THIS AT THE SOURCE!
TELL ME SHE IS NOT THAT STUPID!
STEPHEN, YOUR FRIEND MS. MARVEL IS TRYING TO--
OH, NO.

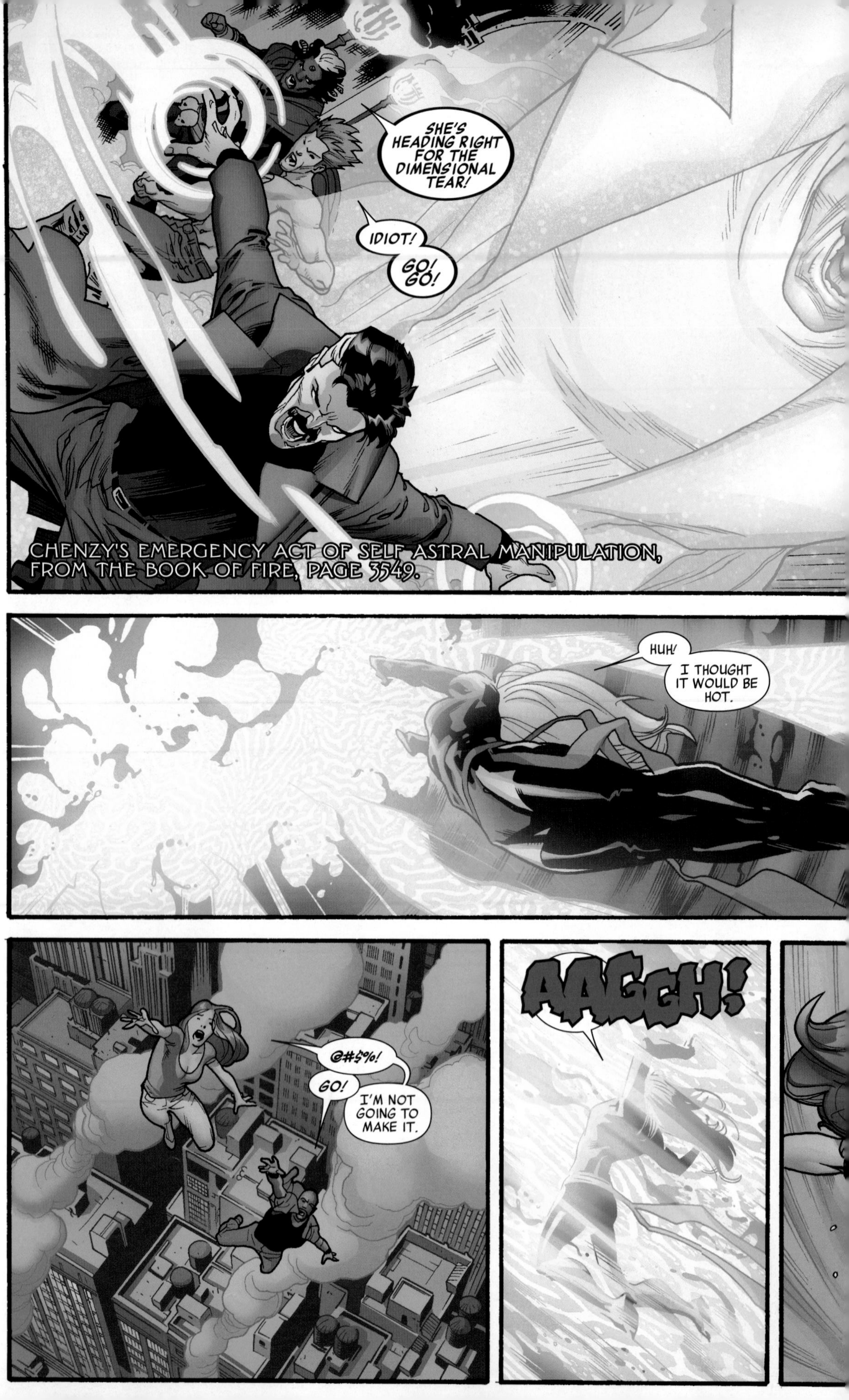
SHE'S HEADING RIGHT FOR THE DIMENSIONAL TEAR!
IDIOT!
GO! GO!
CHENZY'S EMERGENCY ACT OF SELF ASTRAL MANIPULATION, FROM THE BOOK OF FIRE, PAGE 3549.
HUH!
I THOUGHT IT WOULD BE HOT.
@#$%!
GO!
I'M NOT GOING TO MAKE IT.
AAGGH!

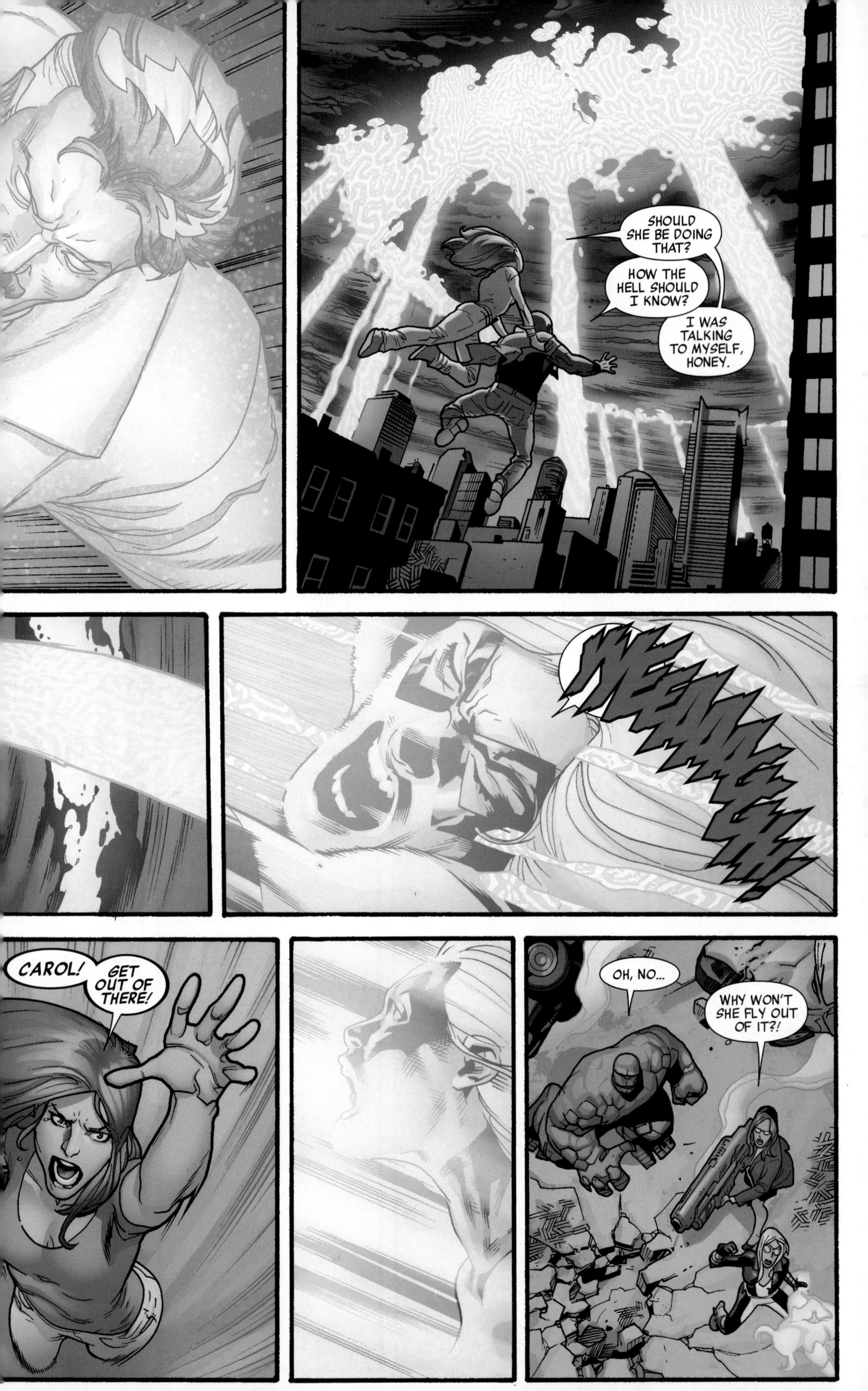

SHOULD SHE BE DOING THAT?
HOW THE HELL SHOULD I KNOW?
I WAS TALKING TO MYSELF, HONEY.
CAROL!
GET OUT OF THERE!
OH, NO...
WHY WON'T SHE FLY OUT OF IT?!

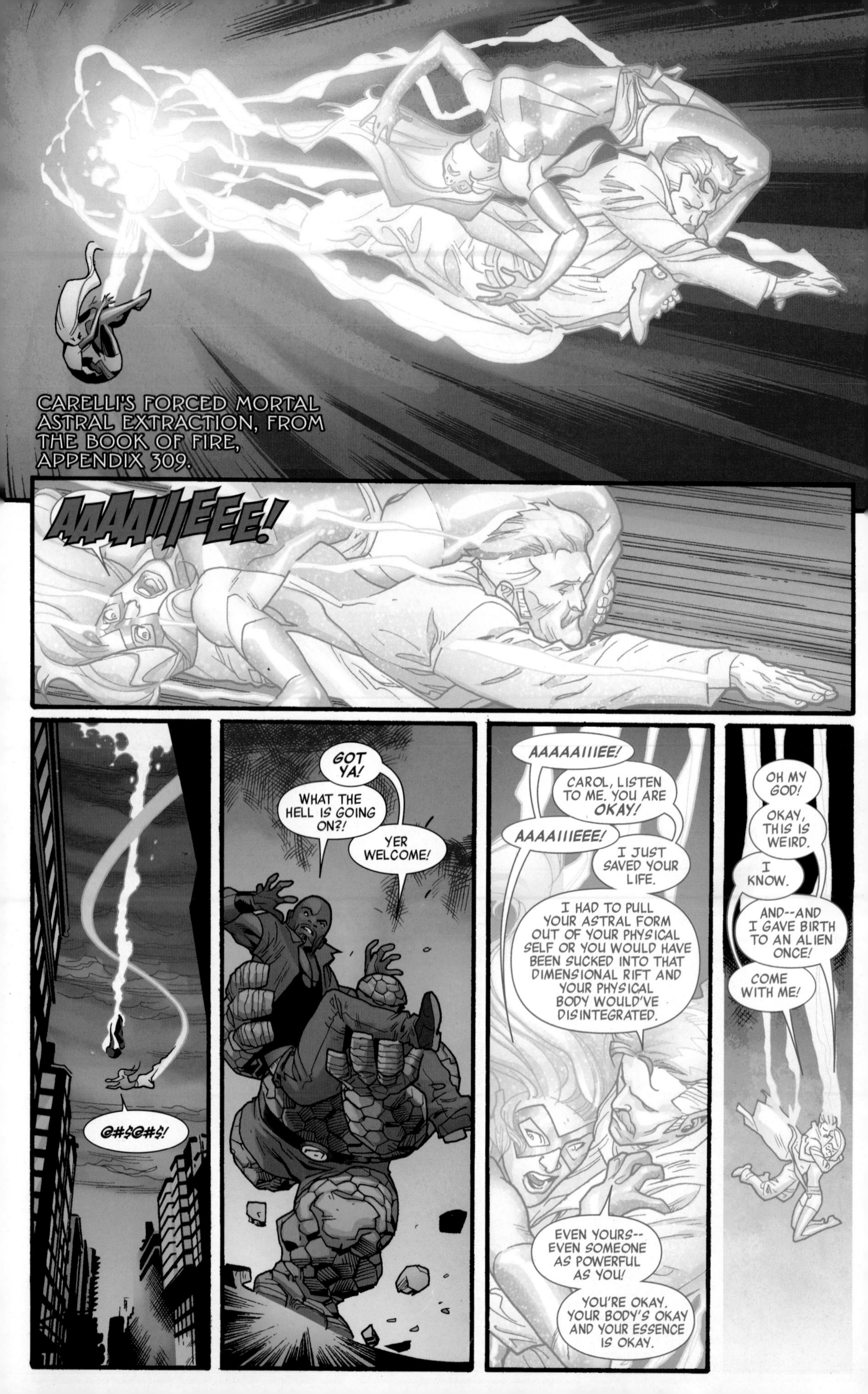
CARELLI'S FORCED MORTAL ASTRAL EXTRACTION, FROM THE BOOK OF FIRE, APPENDIX 309.
AAAAIIIEEE!
GOT YA!
WHAT THE HELL IS GOING ON?!
YER WELCOME!
@#$@#$!
AAAAAIIIEE!
CAROL, LISTEN TO ME. YOU ARE OKAY!
AAAAIIIEEE!
I JUST SAVED YOUR LIFE.
I HAD TO PULL YOUR ASTRAL FORM OUT OF YOUR PHYSICAL SELF OR YOU WOULD HAVE BEEN SUCKED INTO THAT DIMENSIONAL RIFT AND YOUR PHYSICAL BODY WOULD'VE DISINTEGRATED.
EVEN YOURS-- EVEN SOMEONE AS POWERFUL AS YOU!
YOU'RE OKAY. YOUR BODY'S OKAY AND YOUR ESSENCE IS OKAY.
OH MY GOD!
OKAY, THIS IS WEIRD.
I KNOW.
AND--AND I GAVE BIRTH TO AN ALIEN ONCE!
COME WITH ME!

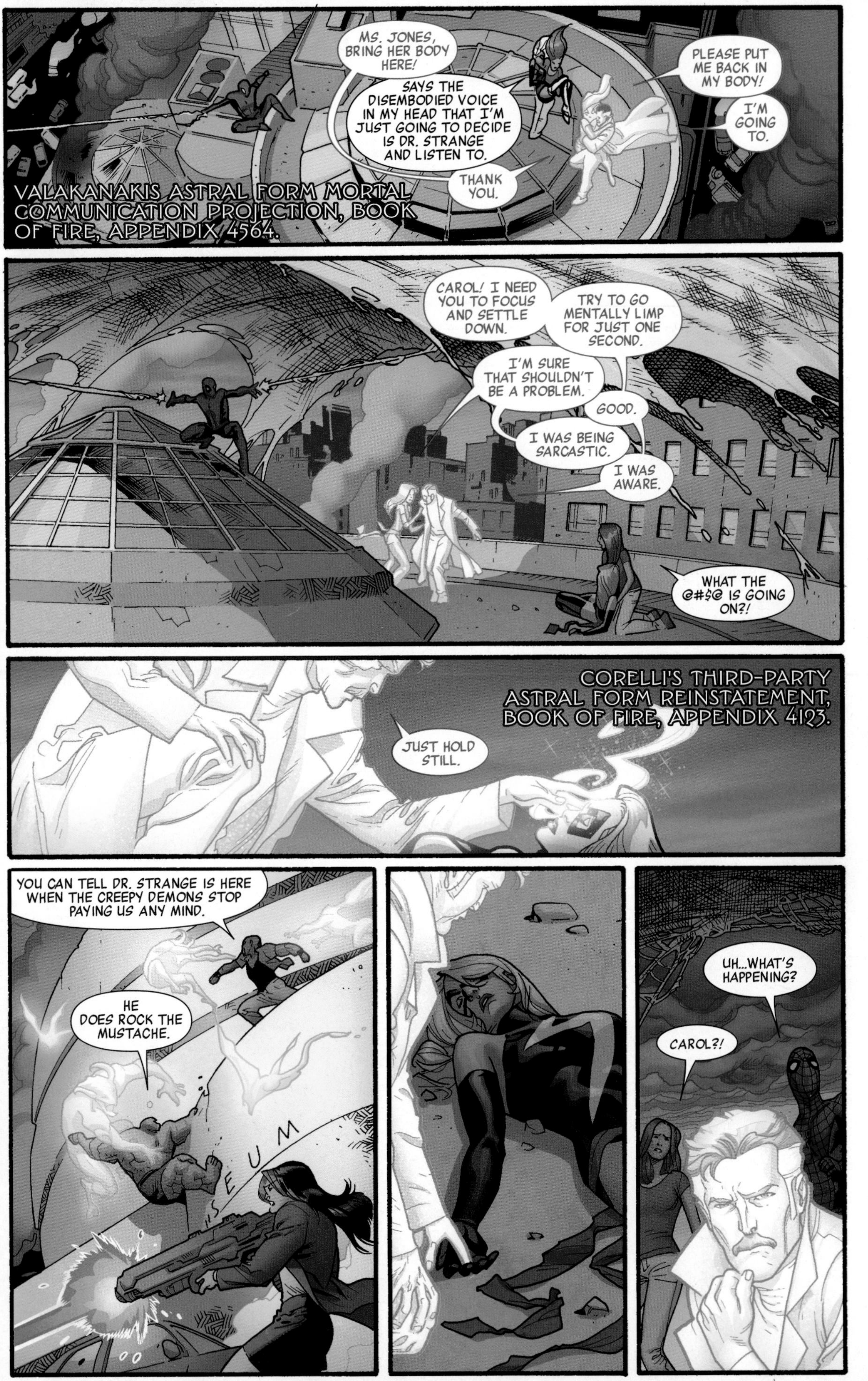
MS. JONES, BRING HER BODY HERE!
SAYS THE DISEMBODIED VOICE IN MY HEAD THAT I'M JUST GOING TO DECIDE IS DR. STRANGE AND LISTEN TO.
THANK YOU.
PLEASE PUT ME BACK IN MY BODY!
I'M GOING TO.
VALAKANAKIS ASTRAL FORM MORTAL COMMUNICATION PROJECTION, BOOK OF FIRE, APPENDIX 4564.
CAROL! I NEED YOU TO FOCUS AND SETTLE DOWN.
TRY TO GO MENTALLY LIMP FOR JUST ONE SECOND.
I'M SURE THAT SHOULDN'T BE A PROBLEM.
GOOD.
I WAS BEING SARCASTIC.
I WAS AWARE.
WHAT THE @#$@ IS GOING ON?!
CORELLI'S THIRD-PARTY ASTRAL FORM REINSTATEMENT, BOOK OF FIRE, APPENDIX 4123.
JUST HOLD STILL.
YOU CAN TELL DR. STRANGE IS HERE WHEN THE CREEPY DEMONS STOP PAYING US ANY MIND.
HE DOES ROCK THE MUSTACHE.
SEUM
UH...WHAT'S HAPPENING?
CAROL?!

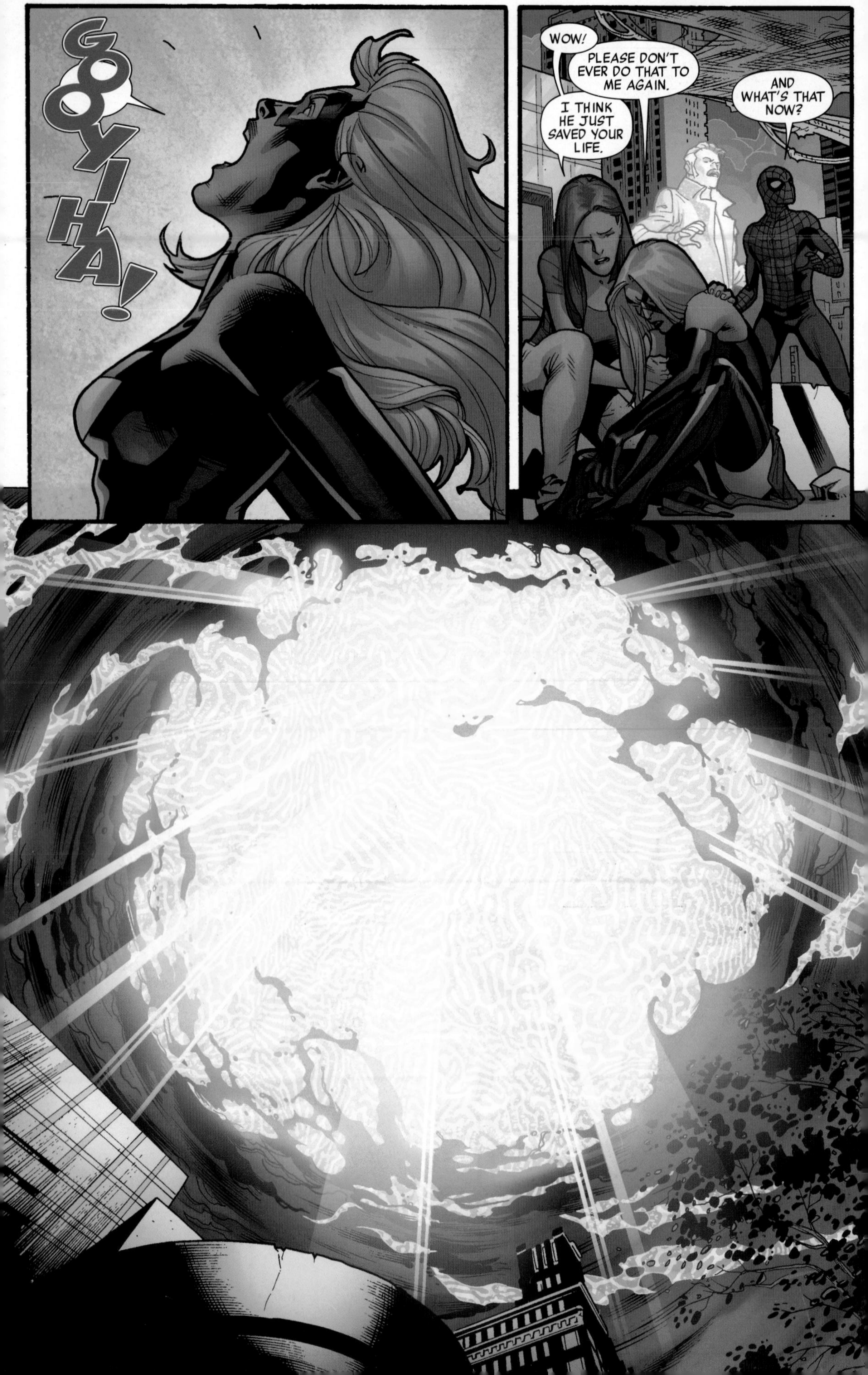
GOOYIHA!
WOW!
I THINK HE JUST SAVED YOUR LIFE.
PLEASE DON'T EVER DO THAT TO ME AGAIN.
AND WHAT'S THAT NOW?

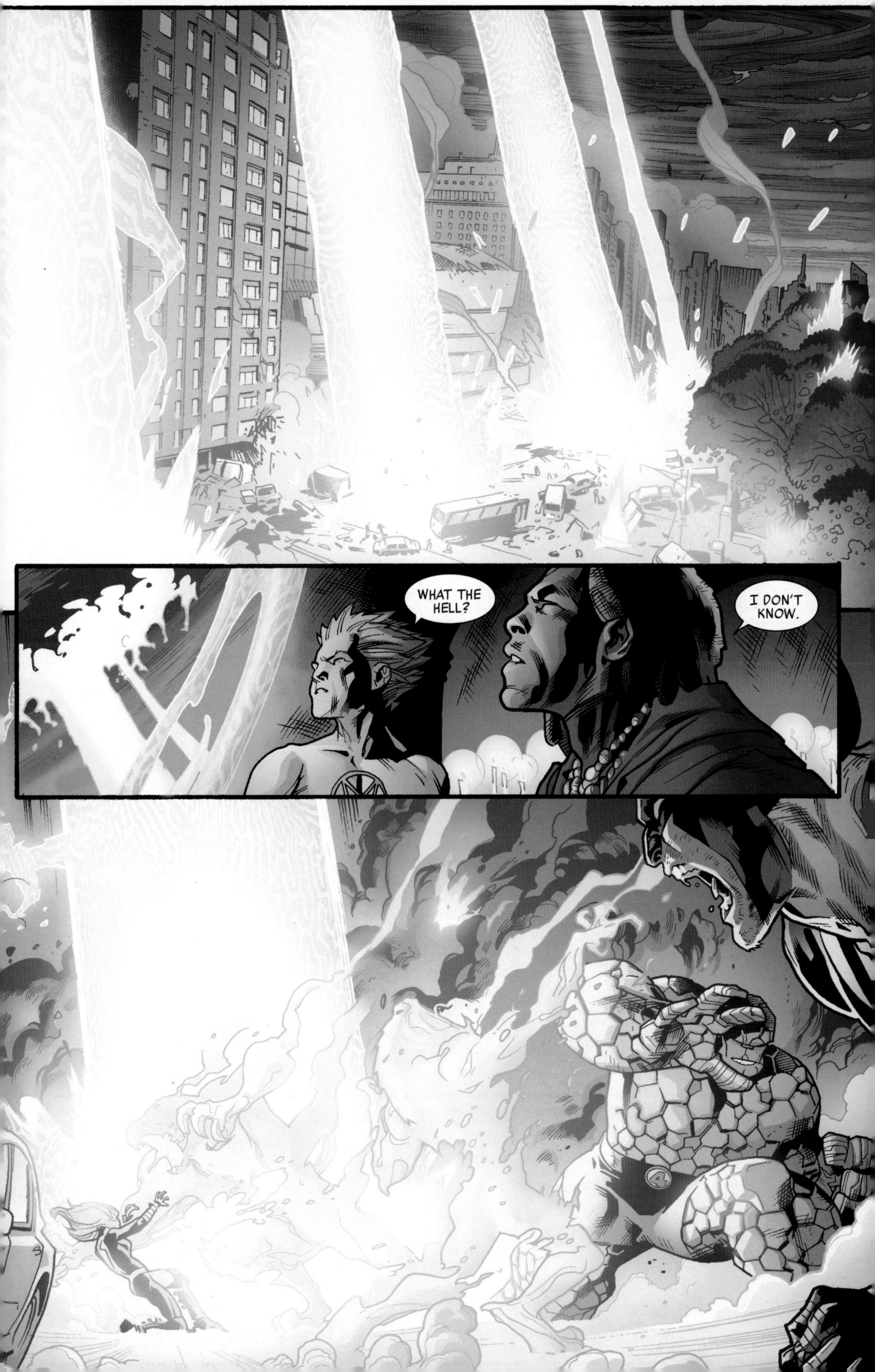
WHAT THE HELL?
I DON'T KNOW.

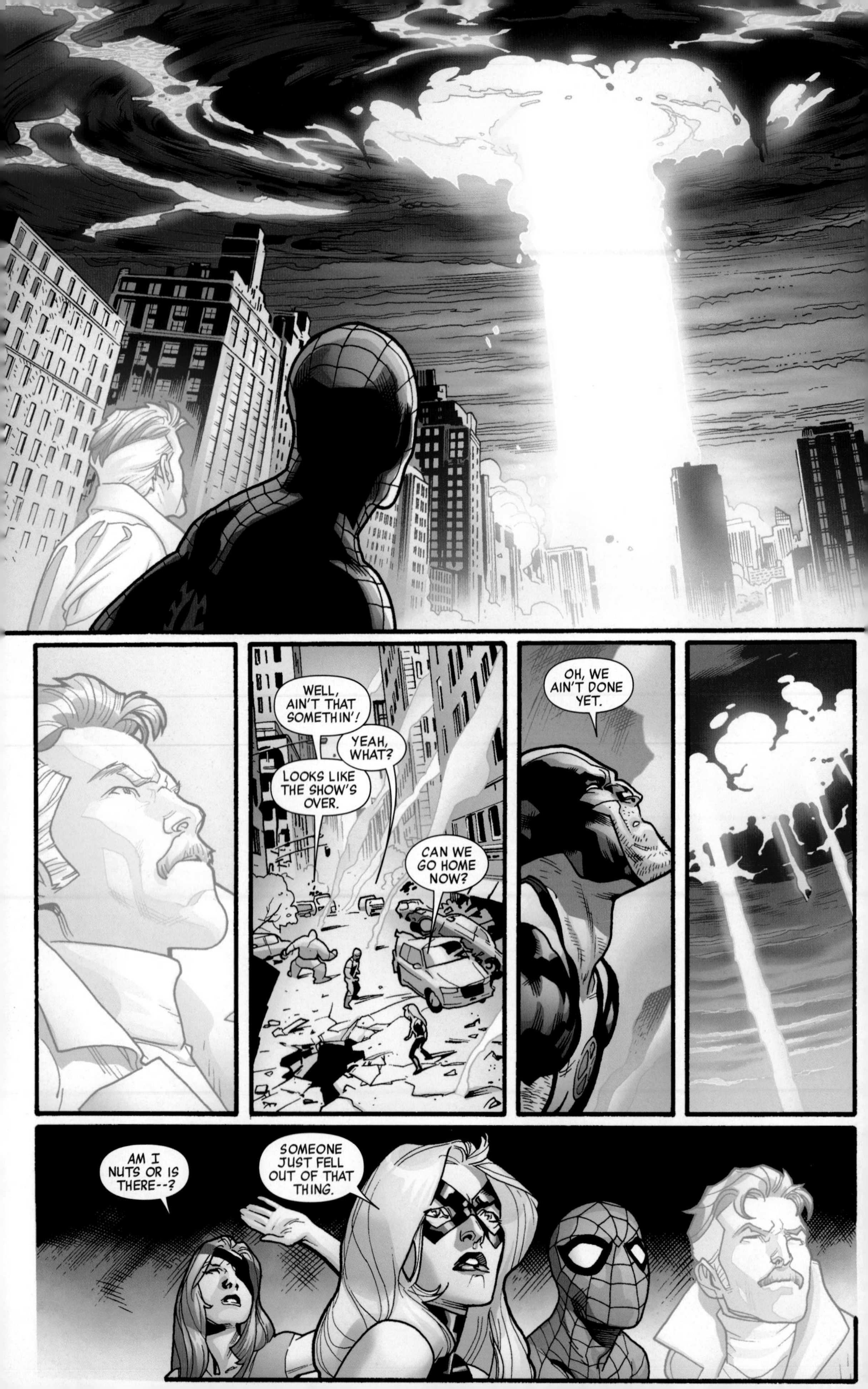
WELL, AIN'T THAT SOMETHIN'!
YEAH, WHAT?
LOOKS LIKE THE SHOW'S OVER.
CAN WE GO HOME NOW?
OH, WE AIN'T DONE YET.
AM I NUTS OR IS THERE--?
SOMEONE JUST FELL OUT OF THAT THING.

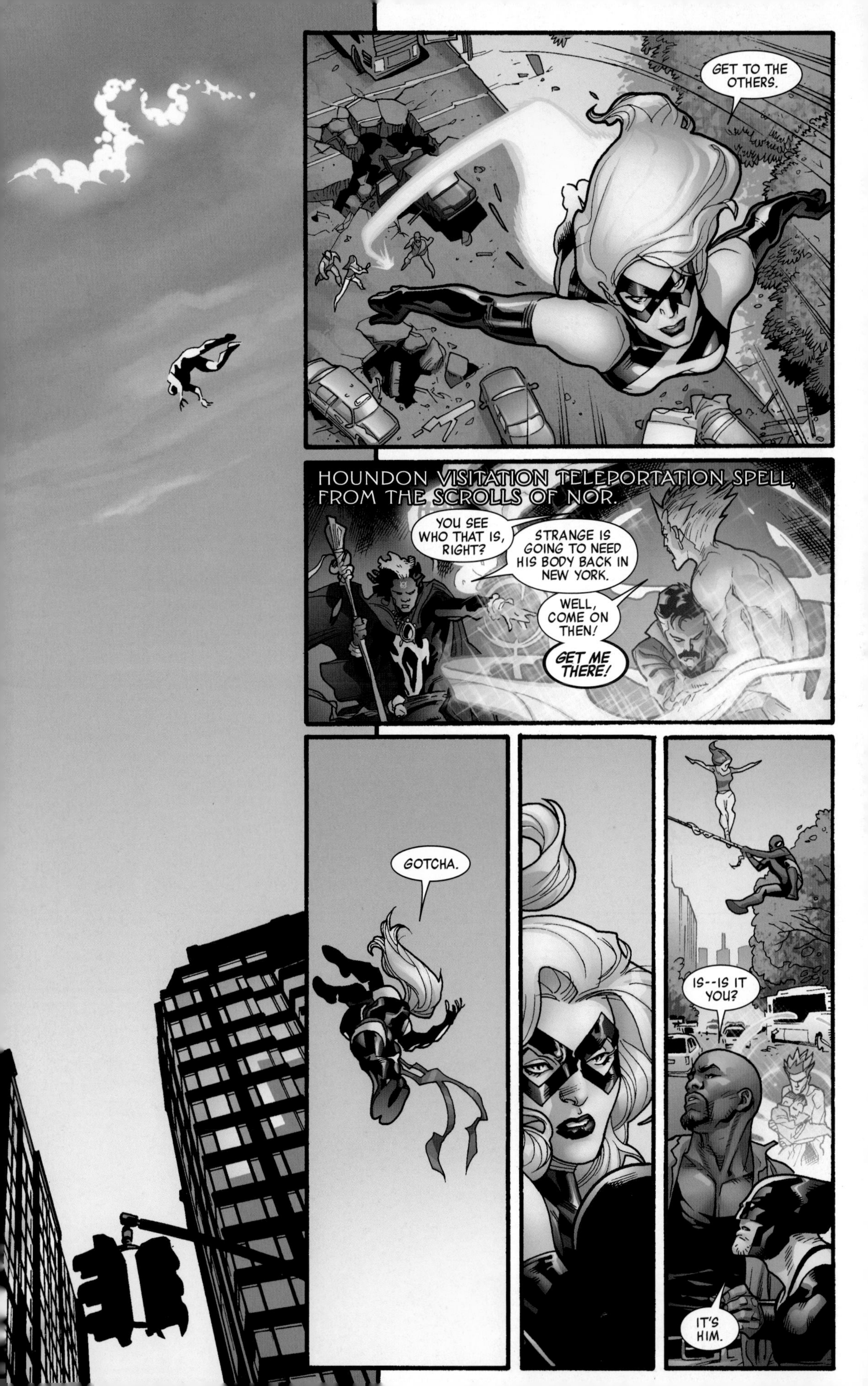
GET TO THE OTHERS.
HOUNDON VISITATION TELEPORTATION SPELL, FROM THE SCROLLS OF NOR.
YOU SEE WHO THAT IS, RIGHT?
STRANGE IS GOING TO NEED HIS BODY BACK IN NEW YORK.
WELL, COME ON THEN!
GET ME THERE!
GOTCHA.
IS--IS IT YOU?
IT'S HIM.

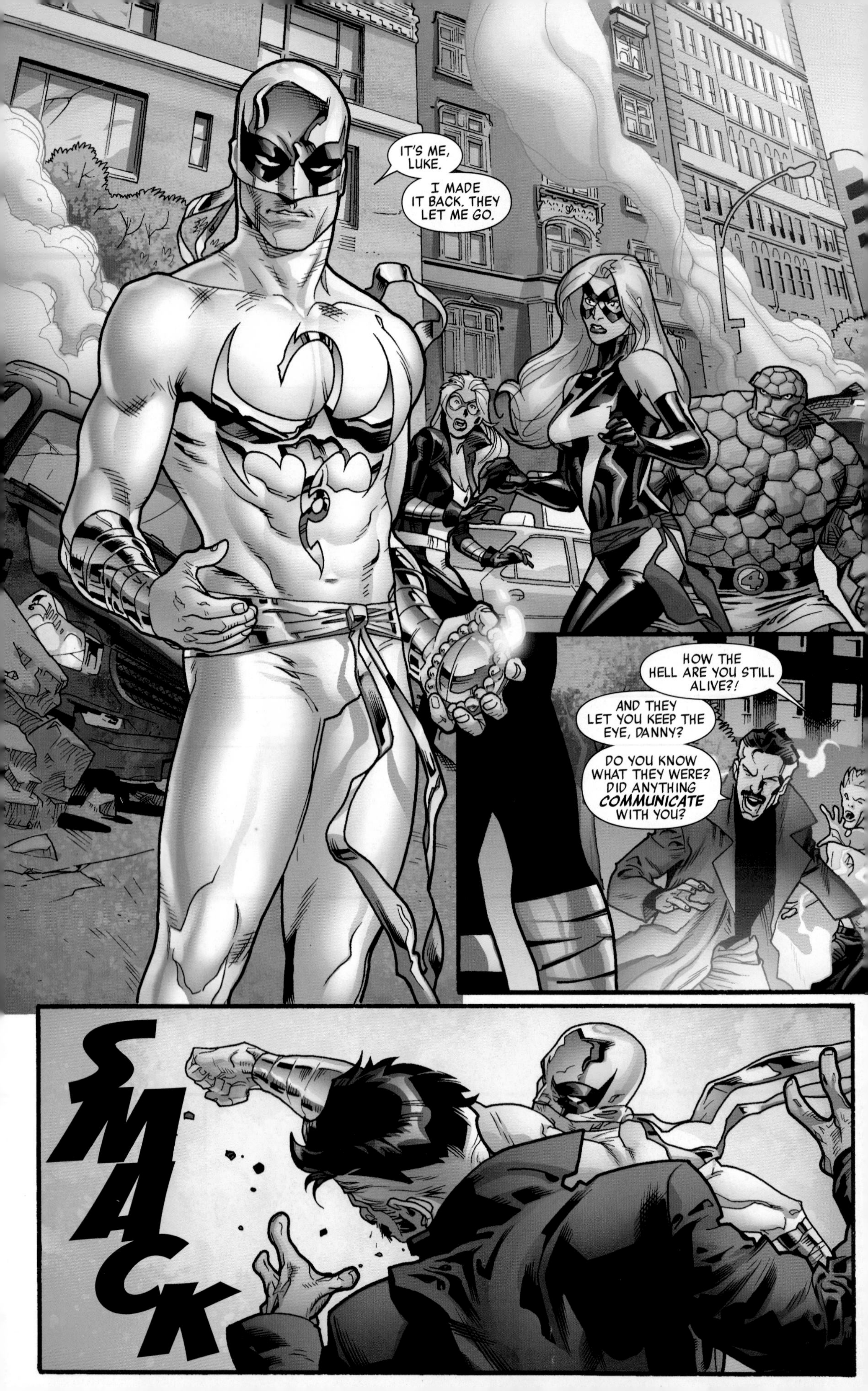
IT'S ME, LUKE.
I MADE IT BACK. THEY LET ME GO.
HOW THE HELL ARE YOU STILL ALIVE?!
AND THEY LET YOU KEEP THE EYE, DANNY?
DO YOU KNOW WHAT THEY WERE? DID ANYTHING **COMMUNICATE** WITH YOU?
SMACK

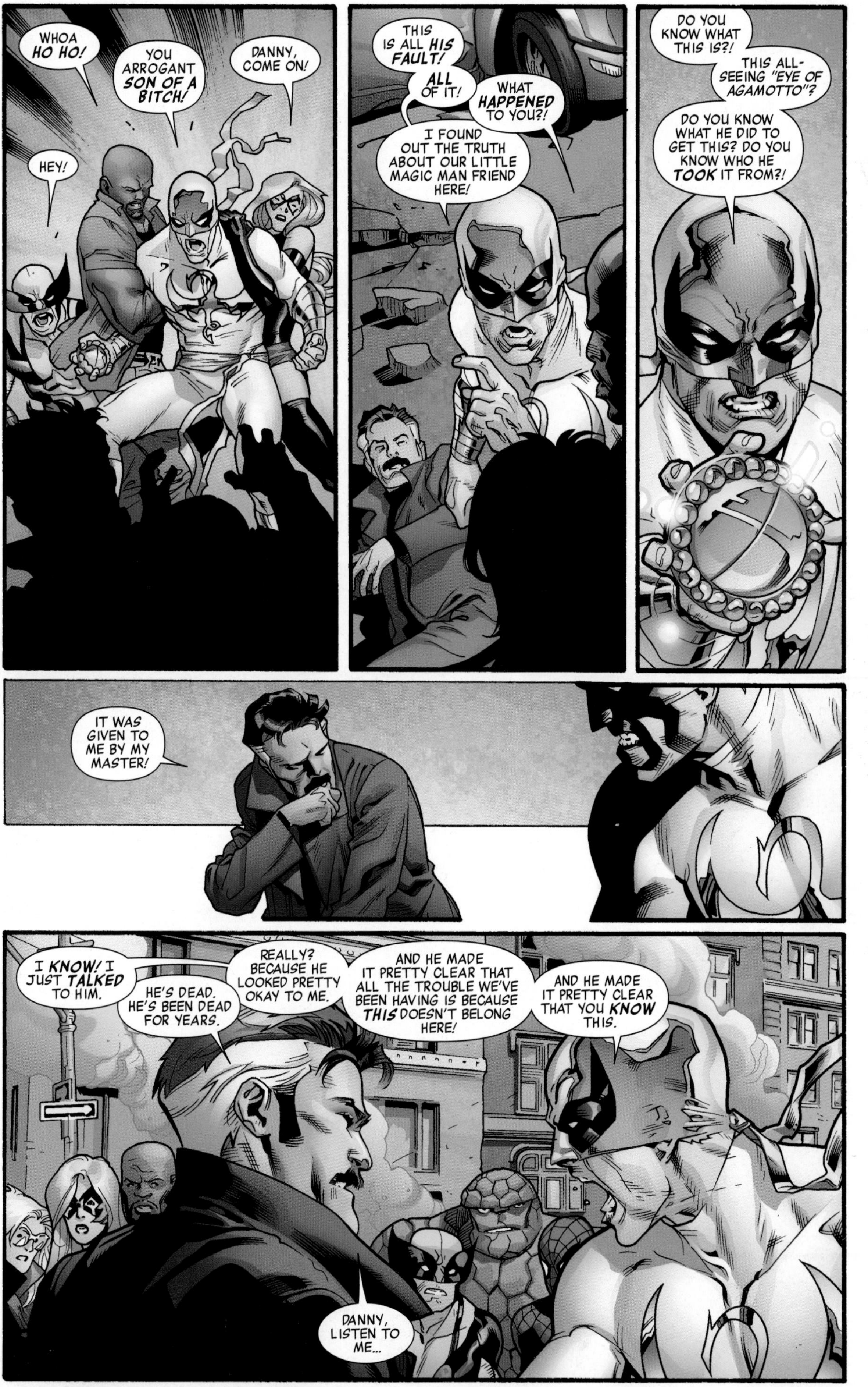
WHOA HO HO!
YOU ARROGANT SON OF A BITCH!
DANNY, COME ON!
HEY!
THIS IS ALL HIS FAULT!
ALL OF IT!
WHAT HAPPENED TO YOU?!
I FOUND OUT THE TRUTH ABOUT OUR LITTLE MAGIC MAN FRIEND HERE!
DO YOU KNOW WHAT THIS IS?!
THIS ALL-SEEING "EYE OF AGAMOTTO"?
DO YOU KNOW WHAT HE DID TO GET THIS? DO YOU KNOW WHO HE TOOK IT FROM?!
IT WAS GIVEN TO ME BY MY MASTER!
HE'S DEAD. HE'S BEEN DEAD FOR YEARS.
I KNOW! I JUST TALKED TO HIM.
REALLY? BECAUSE HE LOOKED PRETTY OKAY TO ME.
AND HE MADE IT PRETTY CLEAR THAT ALL THE TROUBLE WE'VE BEEN HAVING IS BECAUSE THIS DOESN'T BELONG HERE!
AND HE MADE IT PRETTY CLEAR THAT YOU KNOW THIS.
DANNY, LISTEN TO ME...

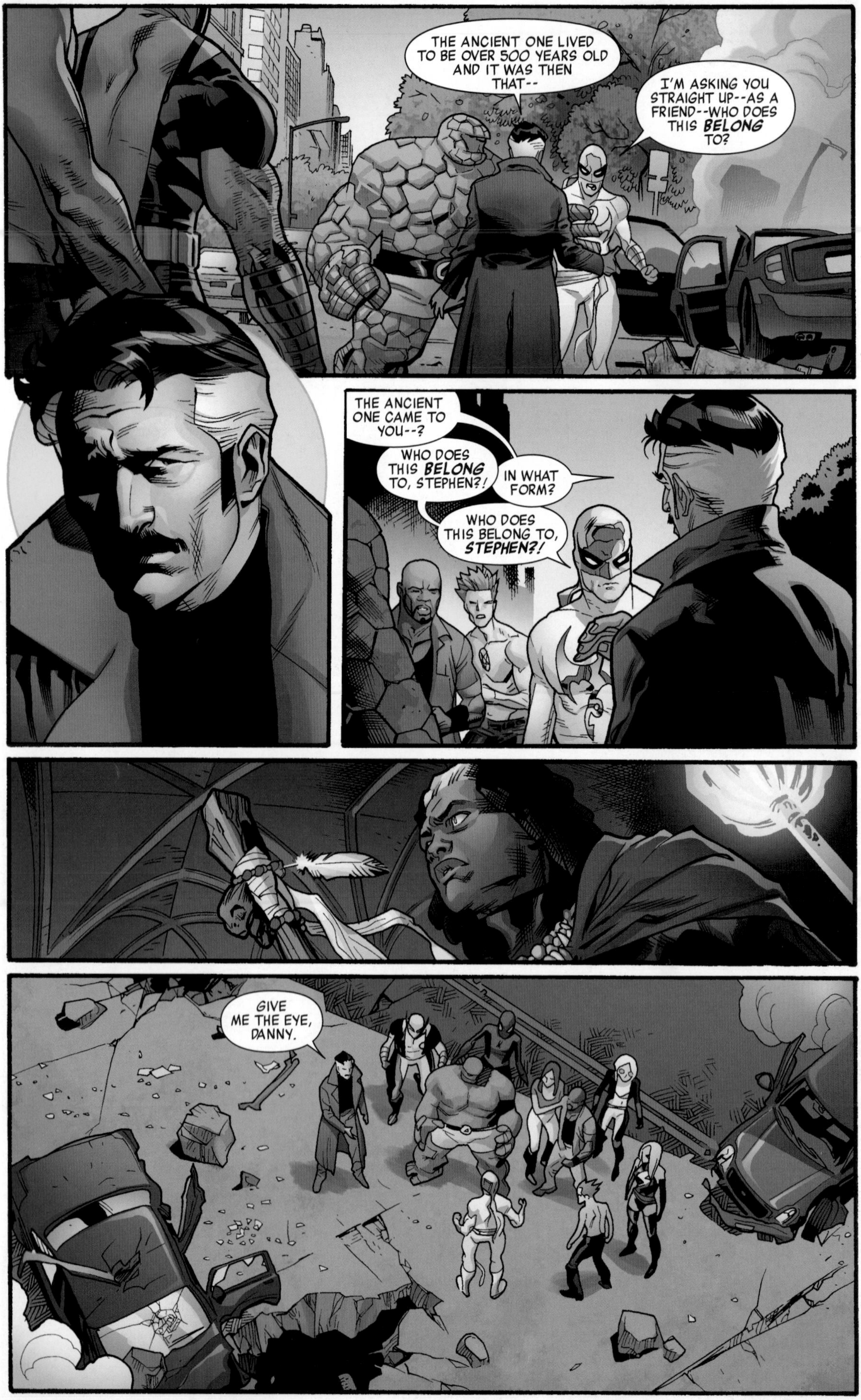
THE ANCIENT ONE LIVED TO BE OVER 500 YEARS OLD AND IT WAS THEN THAT--
I'M ASKING YOU STRAIGHT UP--AS A FRIEND--WHO DOES THIS BELONG TO?
THE ANCIENT ONE CAME TO YOU--?
WHO DOES THIS BELONG TO, STEPHEN?!
IN WHAT FORM?
WHO DOES THIS BELONG TO, STEPHEN?!
GIVE ME THE EYE, DANNY.

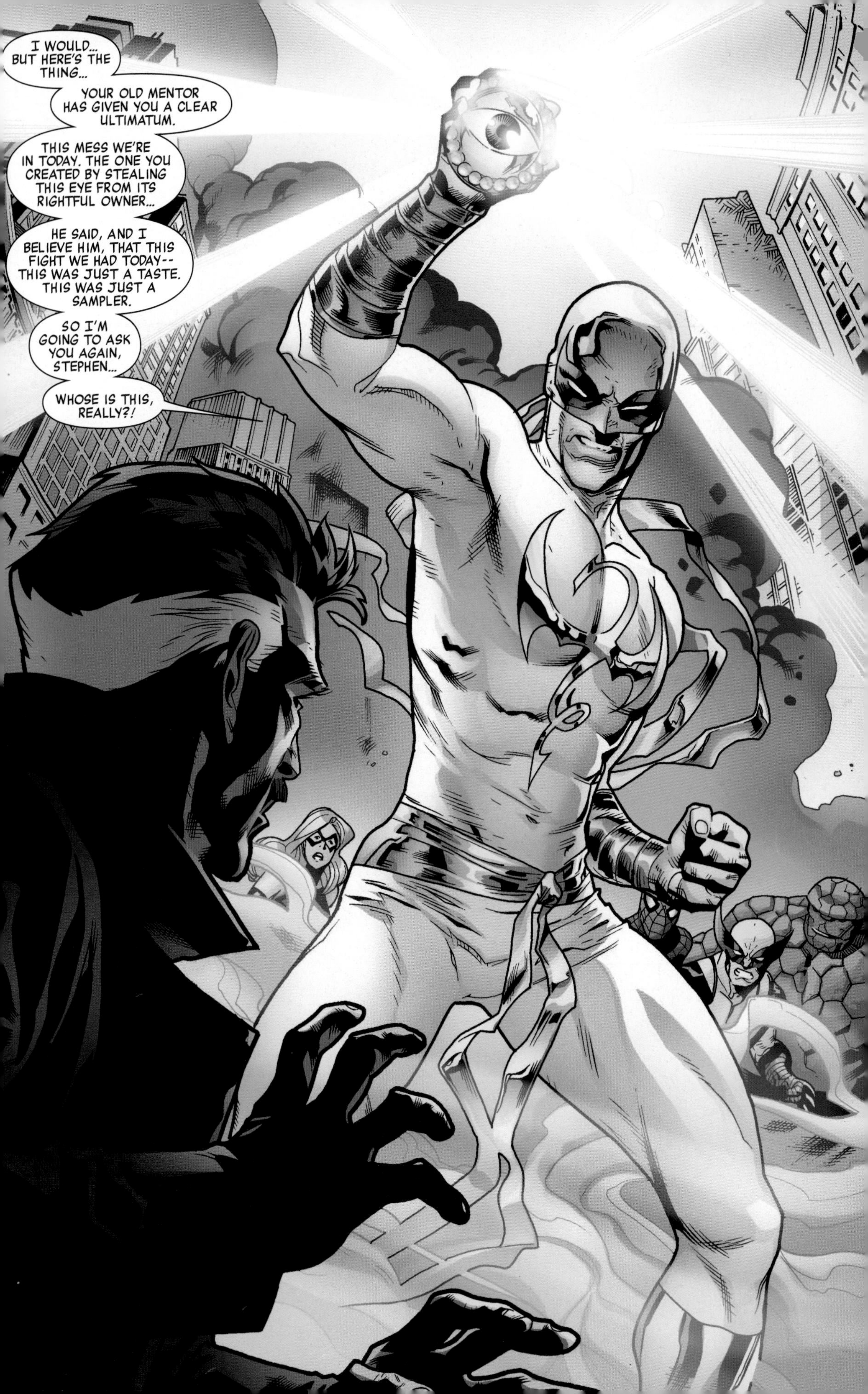

I WOULD... BUT HERE'S THE THING...
YOUR OLD MENTOR HAS GIVEN YOU A CLEAR ULTIMATUM.
THIS MESS WE'RE IN TODAY. THE ONE YOU CREATED BY STEALING THIS EYE FROM ITS RIGHTFUL OWNER...
HE SAID, AND I BELIEVE HIM, THAT THIS FIGHT WE HAD TODAY-- THIS WAS JUST A TASTE. THIS WAS JUST A SAMPLER.
SO I'M GOING TO ASK YOU AGAIN, STEPHEN...
WHOSE IS THIS, REALLY?!

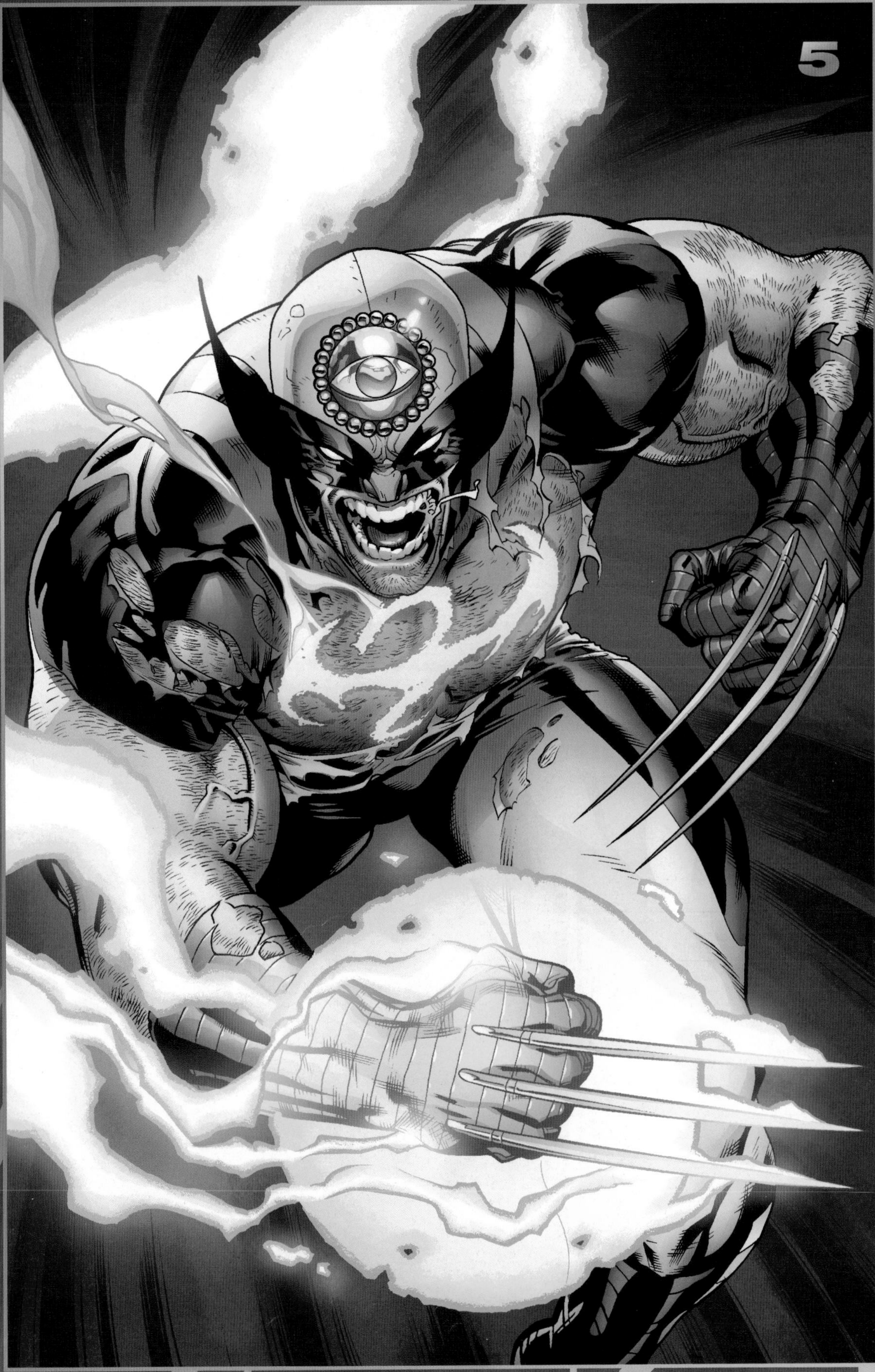
5

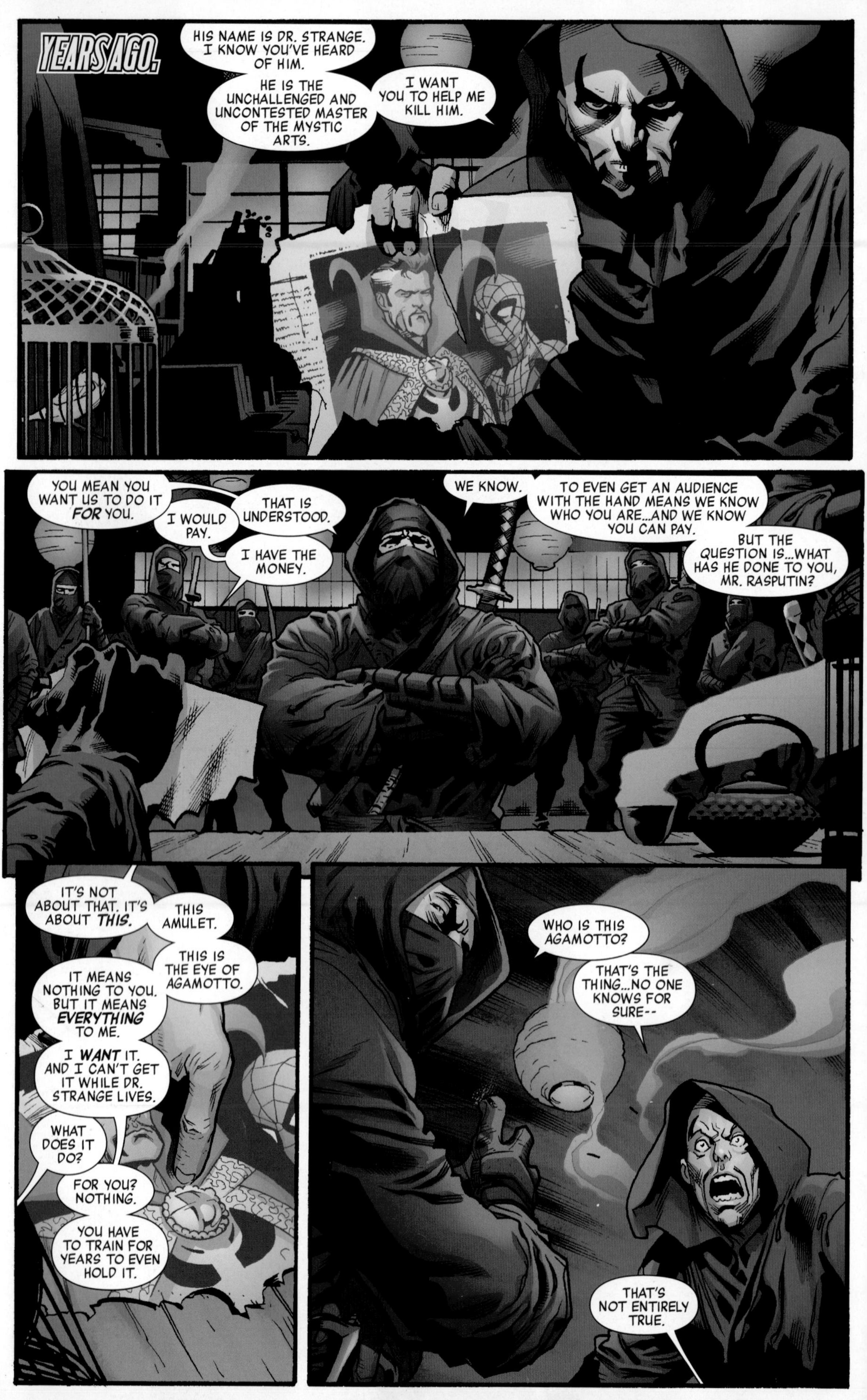

YEARS AGO.
HIS NAME IS DR. STRANGE. I KNOW YOU'VE HEARD OF HIM.
HE IS THE UNCHALLENGED AND UNCONTESTED MASTER OF THE MYSTIC ARTS.
I WANT YOU TO HELP ME KILL HIM.
YOU MEAN YOU WANT US TO DO IT FOR YOU.
I WOULD PAY.
THAT IS UNDERSTOOD.
I HAVE THE MONEY.
WE KNOW.
TO EVEN GET AN AUDIENCE WITH THE HAND MEANS WE KNOW WHO YOU ARE...AND WE KNOW YOU CAN PAY.
BUT THE QUESTION IS...WHAT HAS HE DONE TO YOU, MR. RASPUTIN?
IT'S NOT ABOUT THAT. IT'S ABOUT THIS.
THIS AMULET.
THIS IS THE EYE OF AGAMOTTO.
IT MEANS NOTHING TO YOU. BUT IT MEANS EVERYTHING TO ME.
I WANT IT. AND I CAN'T GET IT WHILE DR. STRANGE LIVES.
WHAT DOES IT DO?
FOR YOU? NOTHING.
YOU HAVE TO TRAIN FOR YEARS TO EVEN HOLD IT.
WHO IS THIS AGAMOTTO?
THAT'S THE THING...NO ONE KNOWS FOR SURE--
THAT'S NOT ENTIRELY TRUE.

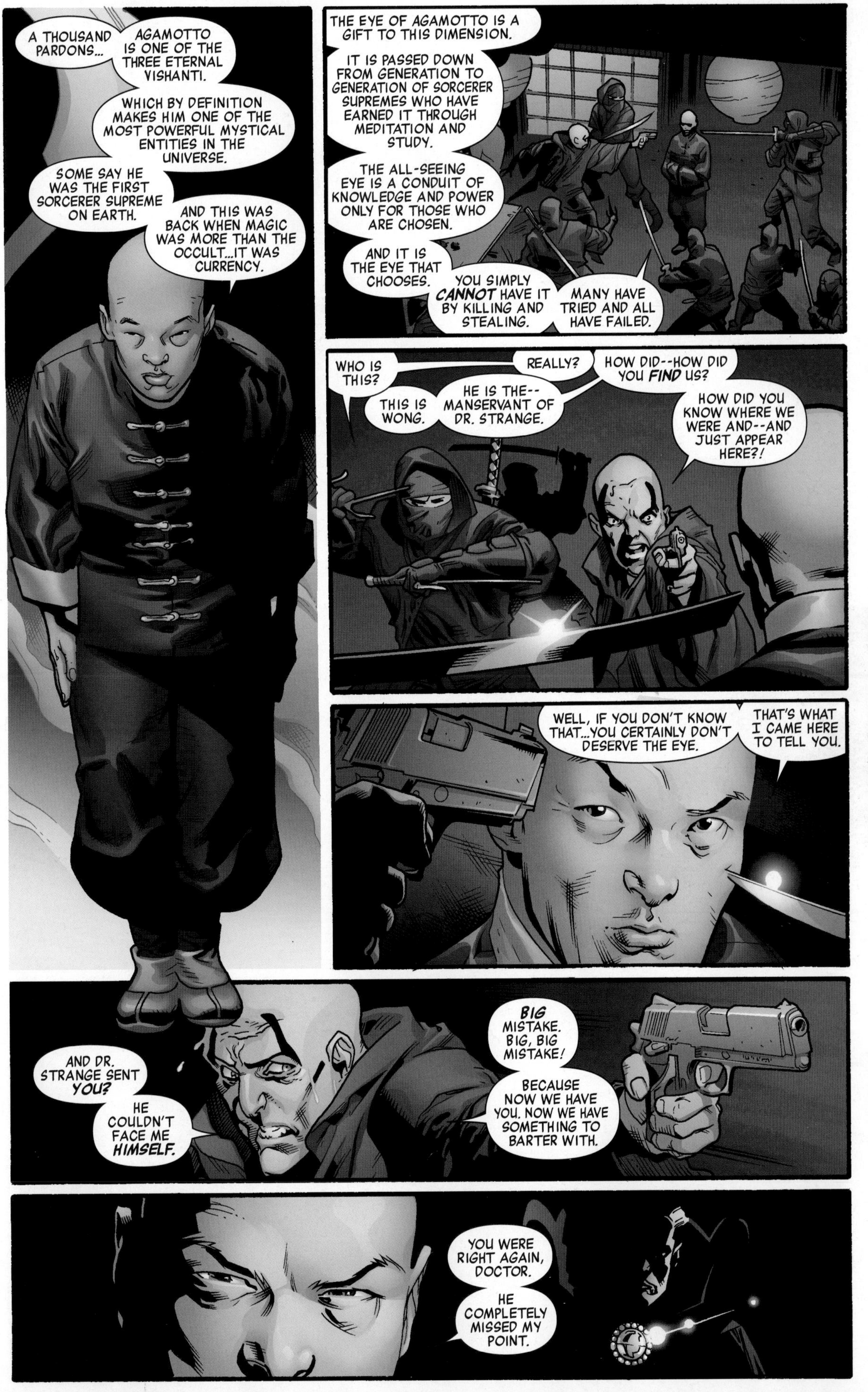

A THOUSAND PARDONS...
AGAMOTTO IS ONE OF THE THREE ETERNAL VISHANTI.
WHICH BY DEFINITION MAKES HIM ONE OF THE MOST POWERFUL MYSTICAL ENTITIES IN THE UNIVERSE.
SOME SAY HE WAS THE FIRST SORCERER SUPREME ON EARTH.
AND THIS WAS BACK WHEN MAGIC WAS MORE THAN THE OCCULT...IT WAS CURRENCY.
THE EYE OF AGAMOTTO IS A GIFT TO THIS DIMENSION.
IT IS PASSED DOWN FROM GENERATION TO GENERATION OF SORCERER SUPREMES WHO HAVE EARNED IT THROUGH MEDITATION AND STUDY.
THE ALL-SEEING EYE IS A CONDUIT OF KNOWLEDGE AND POWER ONLY FOR THOSE WHO ARE CHOSEN.
AND IT IS THE EYE THAT CHOOSES.
YOU SIMPLY CANNOT HAVE IT BY KILLING AND STEALING.
MANY HAVE TRIED AND ALL HAVE FAILED.
WHO IS THIS?
REALLY?
THIS IS WONG.
HE IS THE--MANSERVANT OF DR. STRANGE.
HOW DID--HOW DID YOU FIND US?
HOW DID YOU KNOW WHERE WE WERE AND--AND JUST APPEAR HERE?!
WELL, IF YOU DON'T KNOW THAT...YOU CERTAINLY DON'T DESERVE THE EYE.
THAT'S WHAT I CAME HERE TO TELL YOU.
AND DR. STRANGE SENT YOU?
HE COULDN'T FACE ME HIMSELF.
BIG MISTAKE. BIG, BIG MISTAKE!
BECAUSE NOW WE HAVE YOU. NOW WE HAVE SOMETHING TO BARTER WITH.
YOU WERE RIGHT AGAIN, DOCTOR.
HE COMPLETELY MISSED MY POINT.

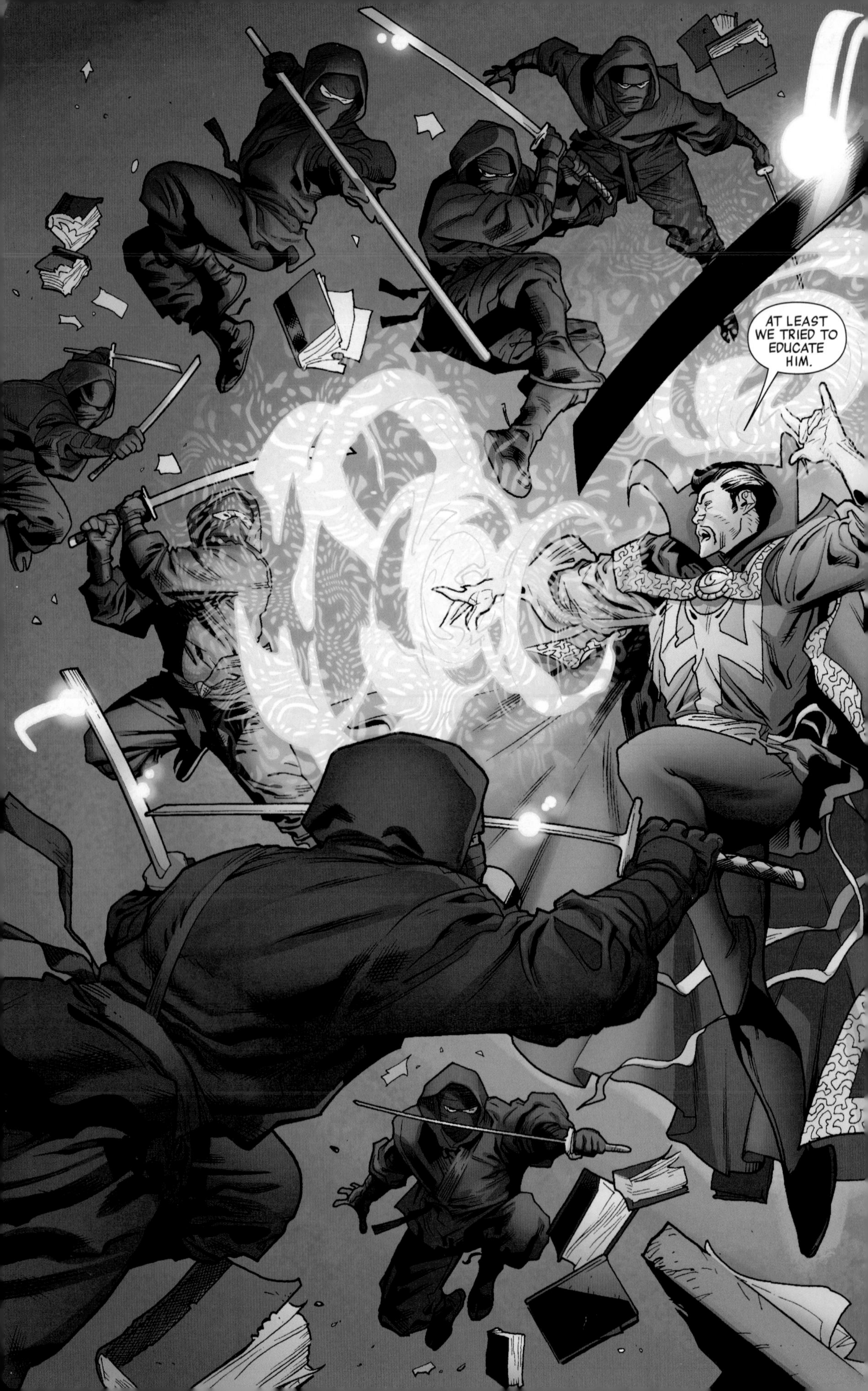
AT LEAST WE TRIED TO EDUCATE HIM.

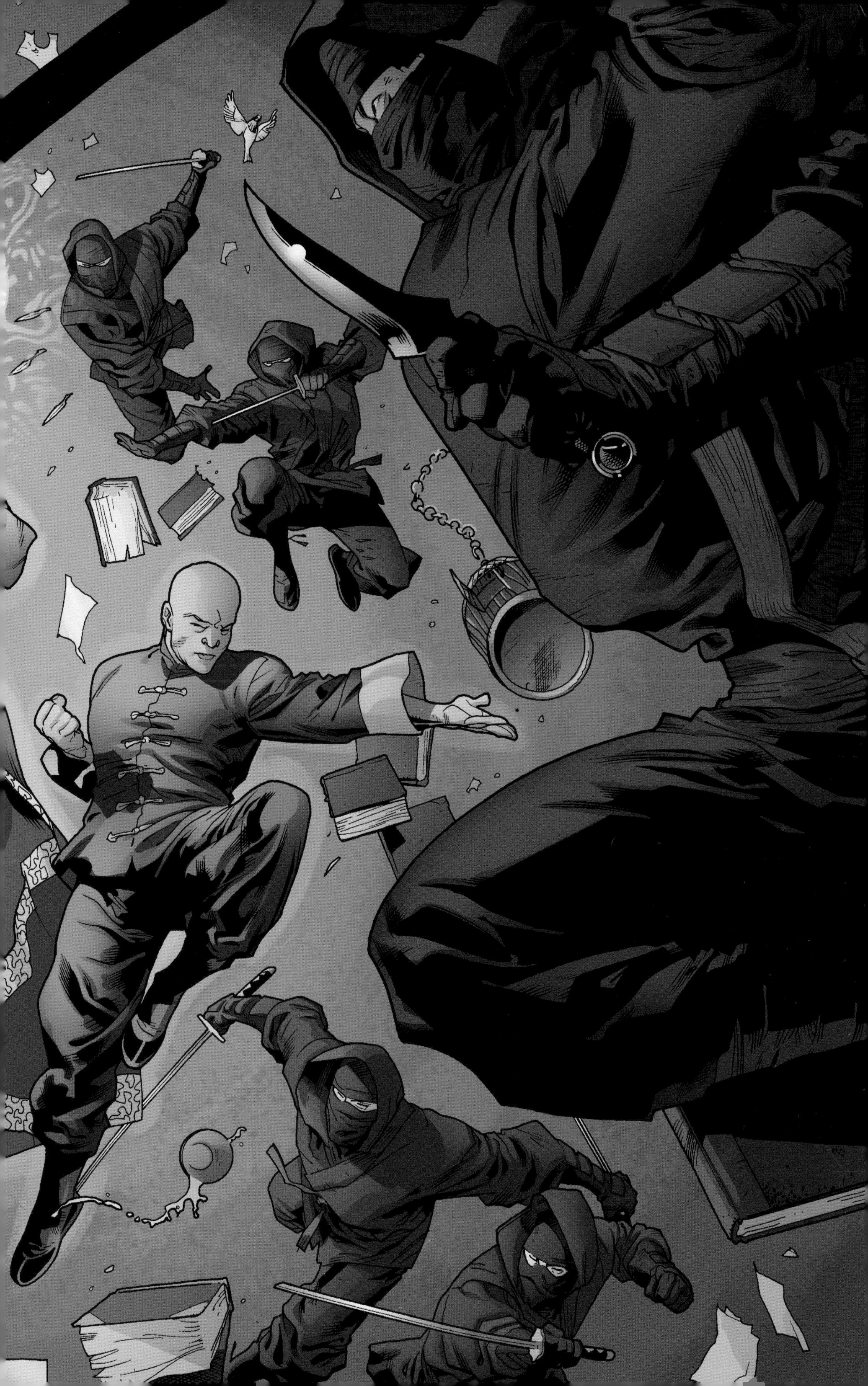

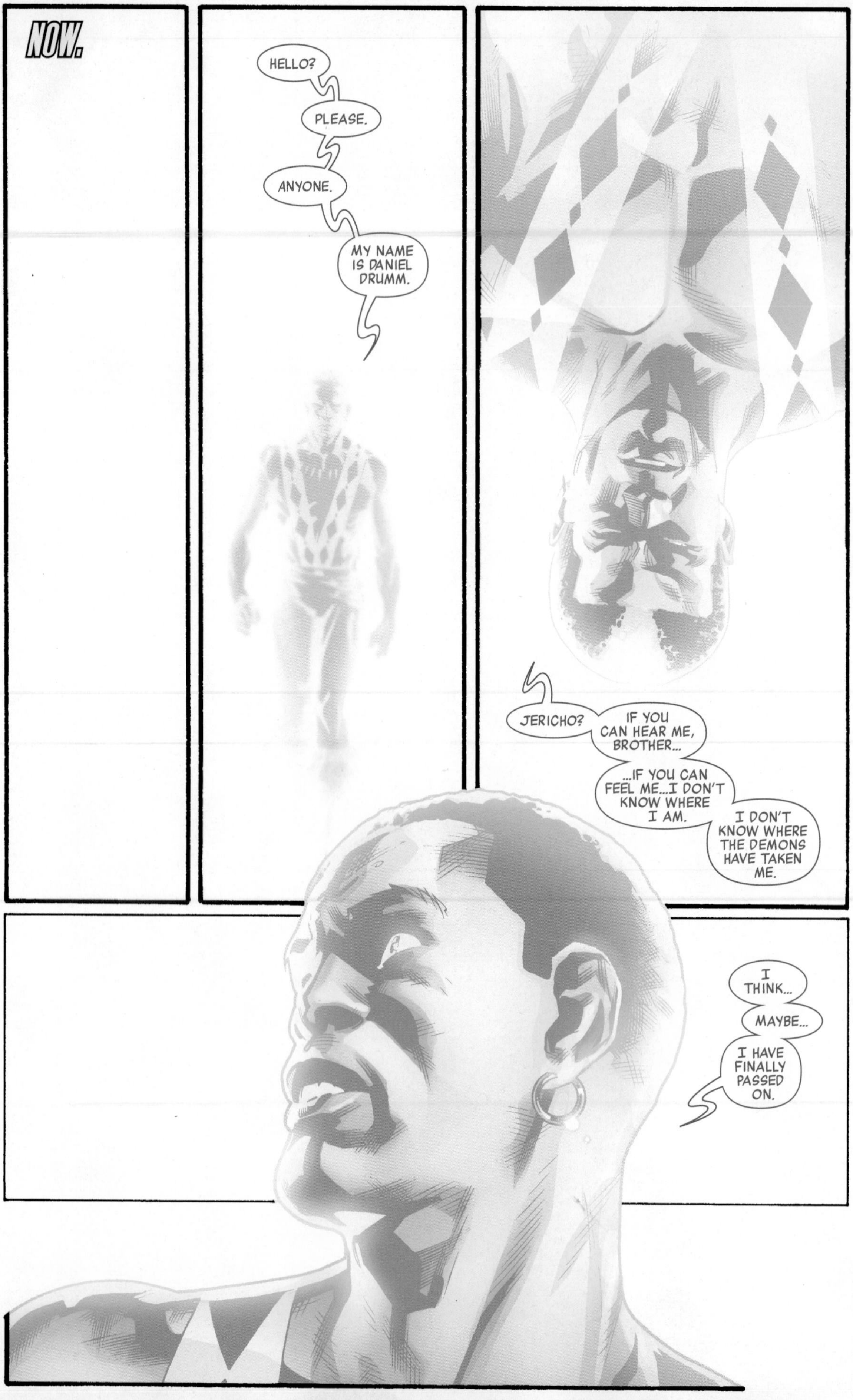
NOW.
HELLO?
PLEASE.
ANYONE.
MY NAME IS DANIEL DRUMM.
JERICHO?
IF YOU CAN HEAR ME, BROTHER...
...IF YOU CAN FEEL ME...I DON'T KNOW WHERE I AM.
I DON'T KNOW WHERE THE DEMONS HAVE TAKEN ME.
I THINK...
MAYBE...
I HAVE FINALLY PASSED ON.

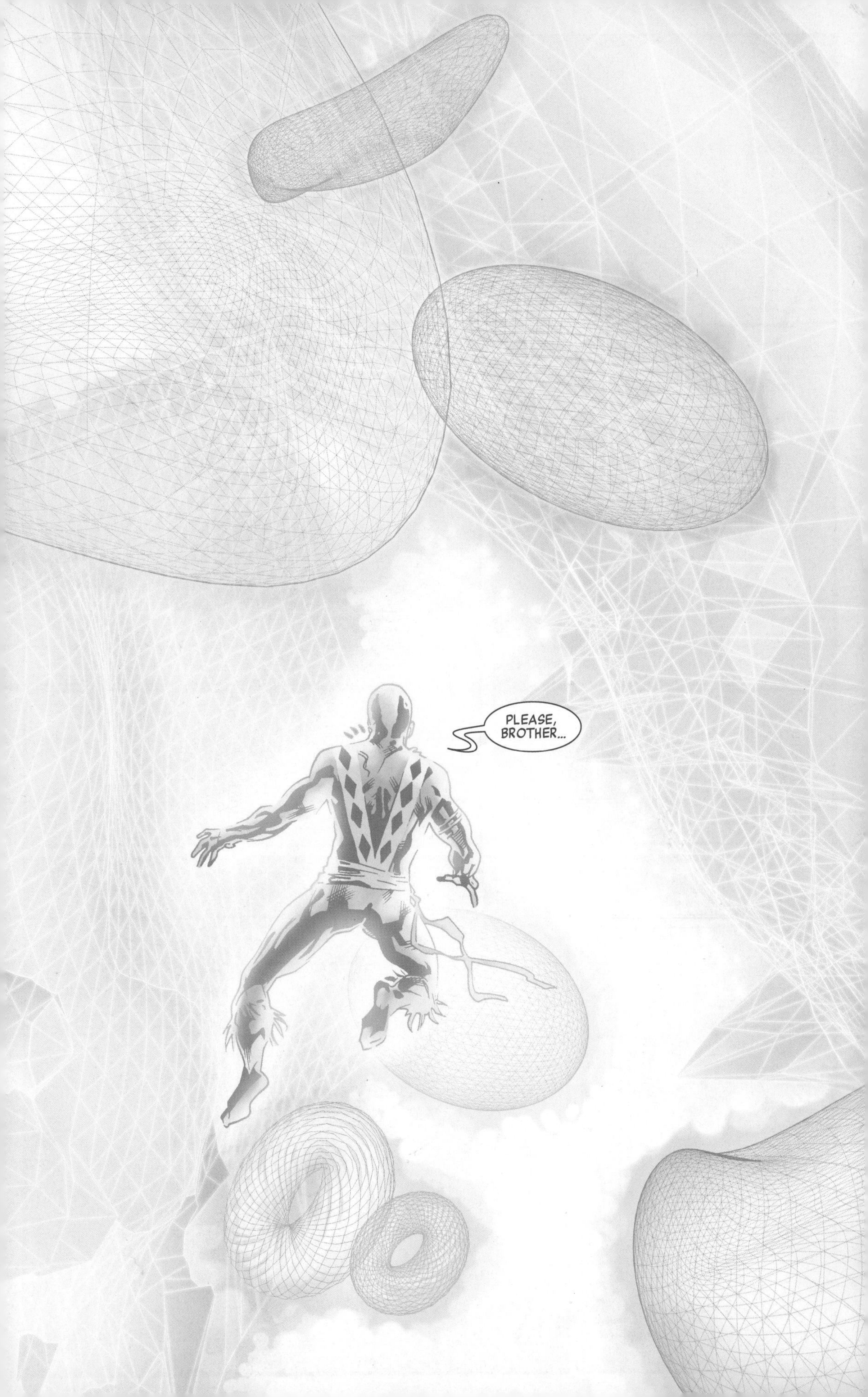
PLEASE, BROTHER...

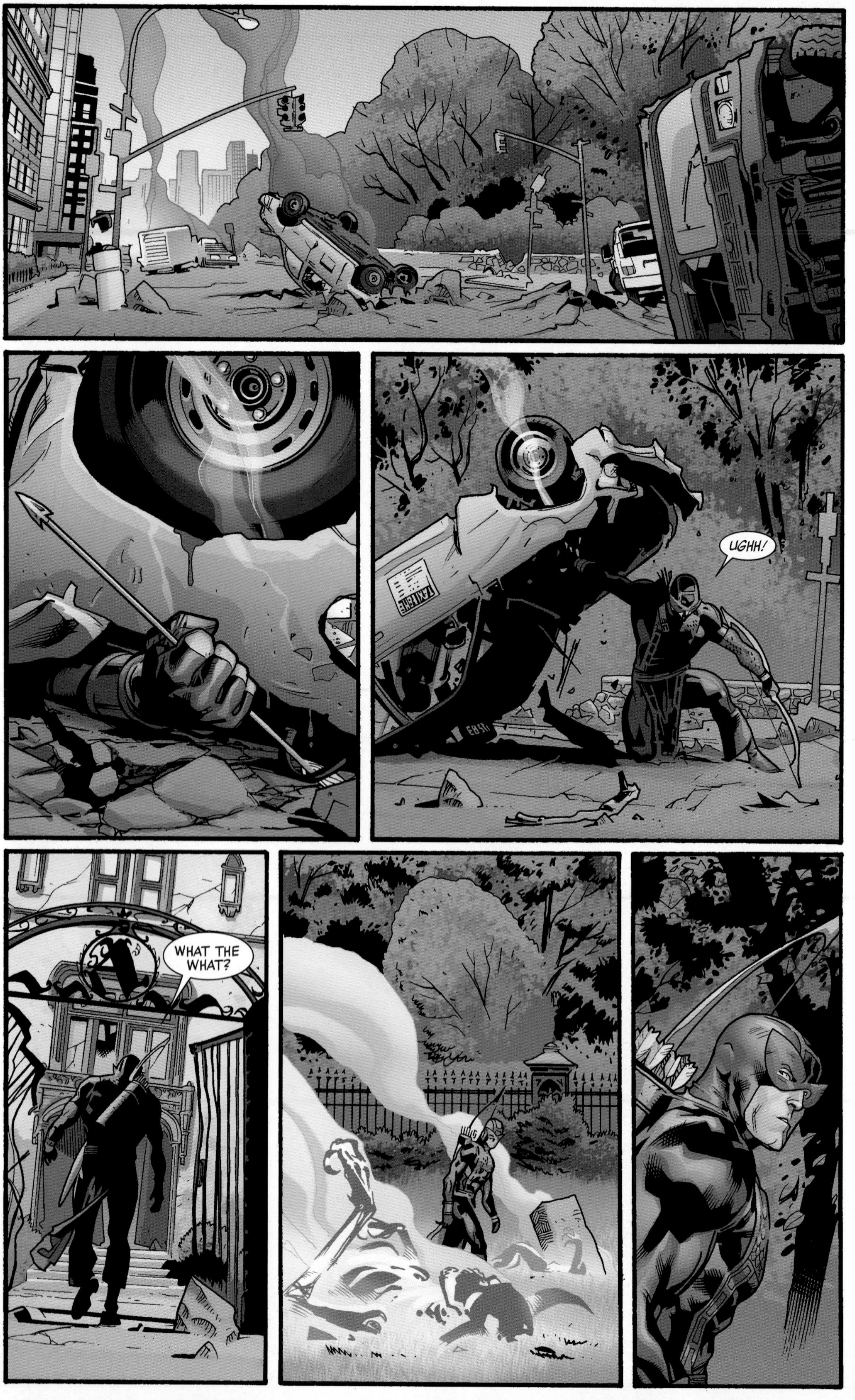
UGHH!
WHAT THE WHAT?

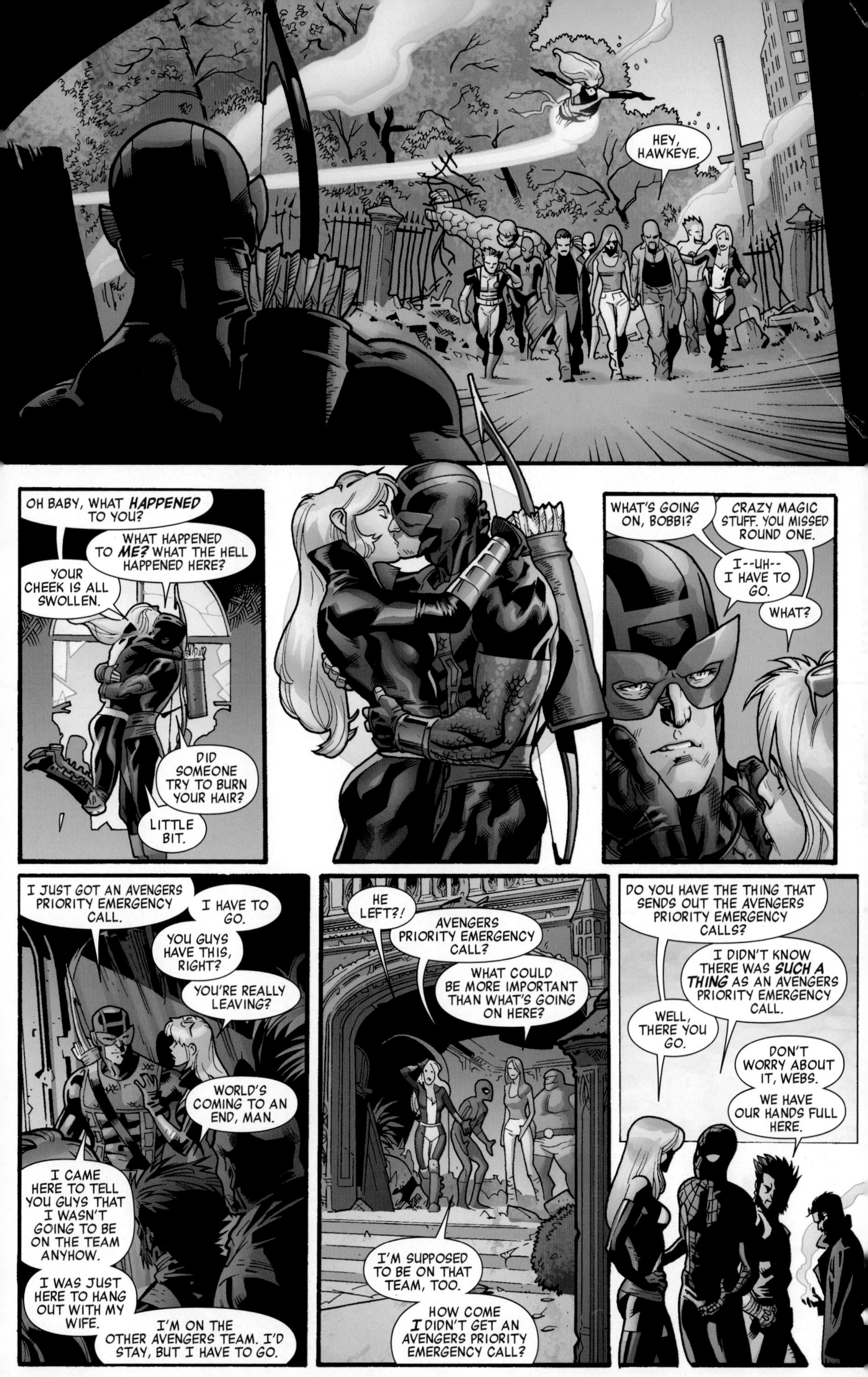
HEY, HAWKEYE.
OH BABY, WHAT HAPPENED TO YOU?
WHAT HAPPENED TO ME? WHAT THE HELL HAPPENED HERE?
YOUR CHEEK IS ALL SWOLLEN.
DID SOMEONE TRY TO BURN YOUR HAIR?
LITTLE BIT.
WHAT'S GOING ON, BOBBI?
CRAZY MAGIC STUFF. YOU MISSED ROUND ONE.
I--UH-- I HAVE TO GO.
WHAT?
I JUST GOT AN AVENGERS PRIORITY EMERGENCY CALL.
I HAVE TO GO.
YOU GUYS HAVE THIS, RIGHT?
YOU'RE REALLY LEAVING?
WORLD'S COMING TO AN END, MAN.
I CAME HERE TO TELL YOU GUYS THAT I WASN'T GOING TO BE ON THE TEAM ANYHOW.
I WAS JUST HERE TO HANG OUT WITH MY WIFE.
I'M ON THE OTHER AVENGERS TEAM. I'D STAY, BUT I HAVE TO GO.
HE LEFT?!
AVENGERS PRIORITY EMERGENCY CALL?
WHAT COULD BE MORE IMPORTANT THAN WHAT'S GOING ON HERE?
I'M SUPPOSED TO BE ON THAT TEAM, TOO.
HOW COME I DIDN'T GET AN AVENGERS PRIORITY EMERGENCY CALL?
DO YOU HAVE THE THING THAT SENDS OUT THE AVENGERS PRIORITY EMERGENCY CALLS?
I DIDN'T KNOW THERE WAS SUCH A THING AS AN AVENGERS PRIORITY EMERGENCY CALL.
WELL, THERE YOU GO.
DON'T WORRY ABOUT IT, WEBS.
WE HAVE OUR HANDS FULL HERE.

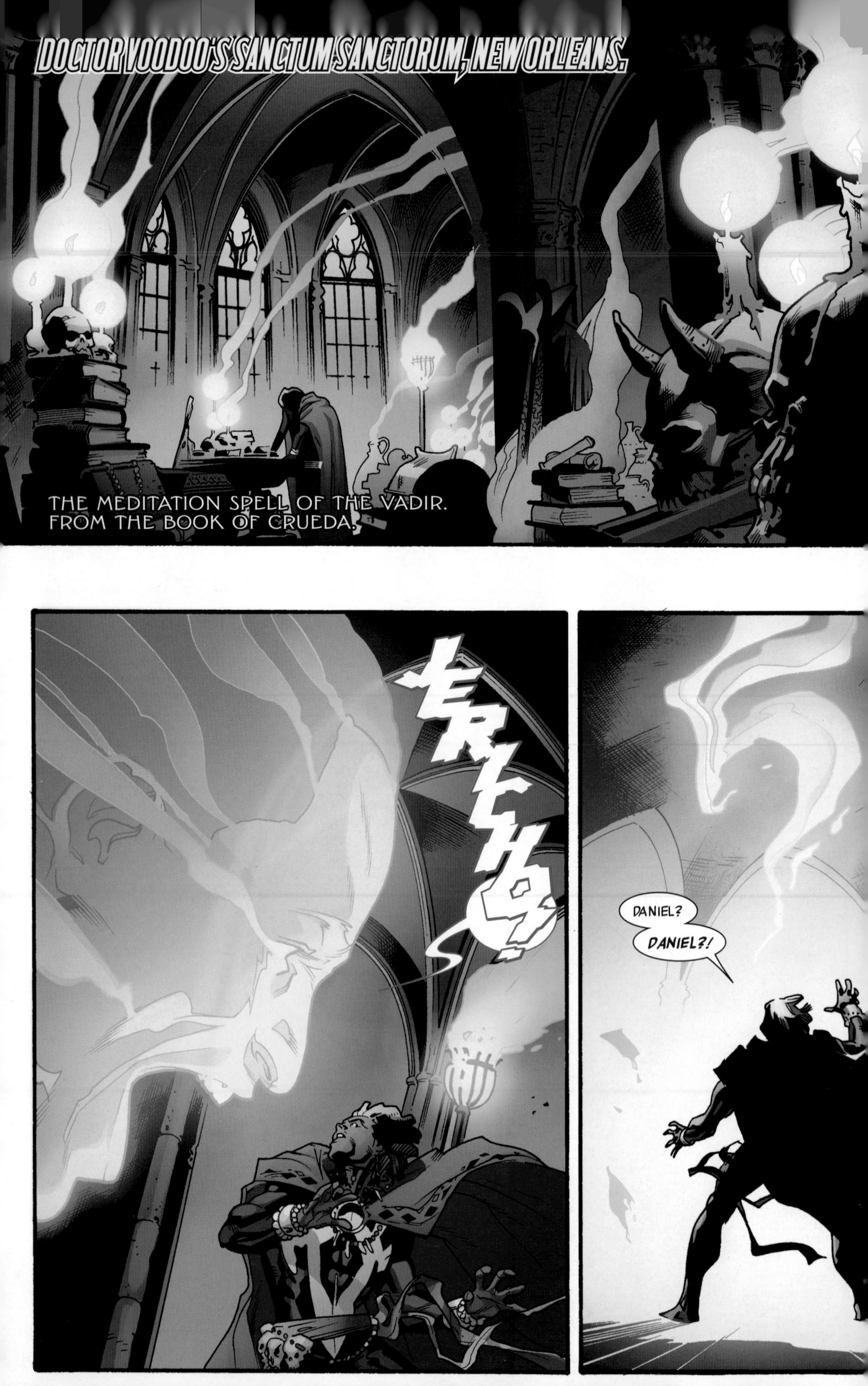
DOCTOR VOODOO'S SANCTUM SANCTORUM, NEW ORLEANS.
THE MEDITATION SPELL OF THE VADIR. FROM THE BOOK OF CRUEDA.
DANIEL?
DANIEL?!

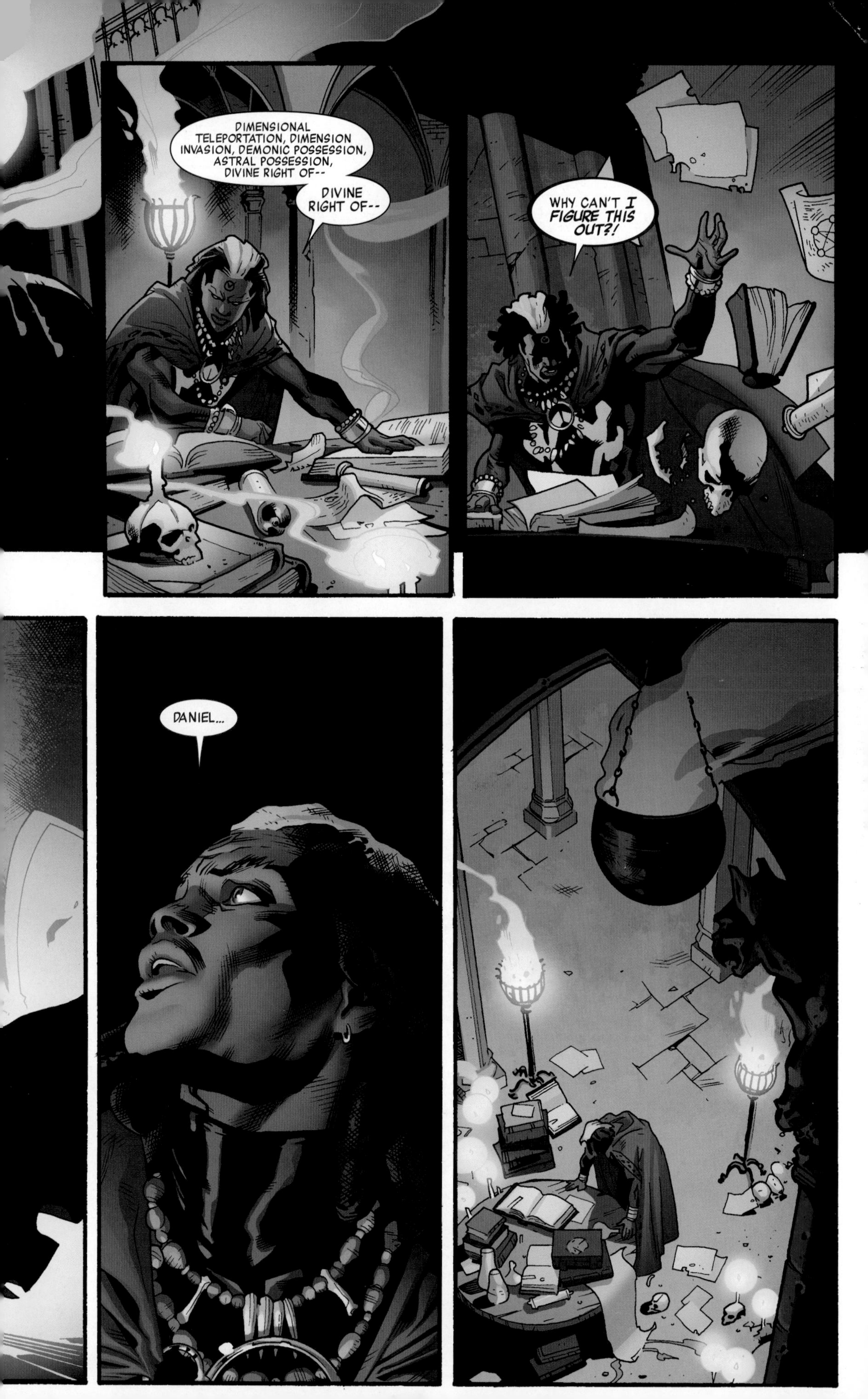
DIMENSIONAL TELEPORTATION, DIMENSION INVASION, DEMONIC POSSESSION, ASTRAL POSSESSION, DIVINE RIGHT OF--
DIVINE RIGHT OF--
WHY CAN'T I FIGURE THIS OUT?!
DANIEL...

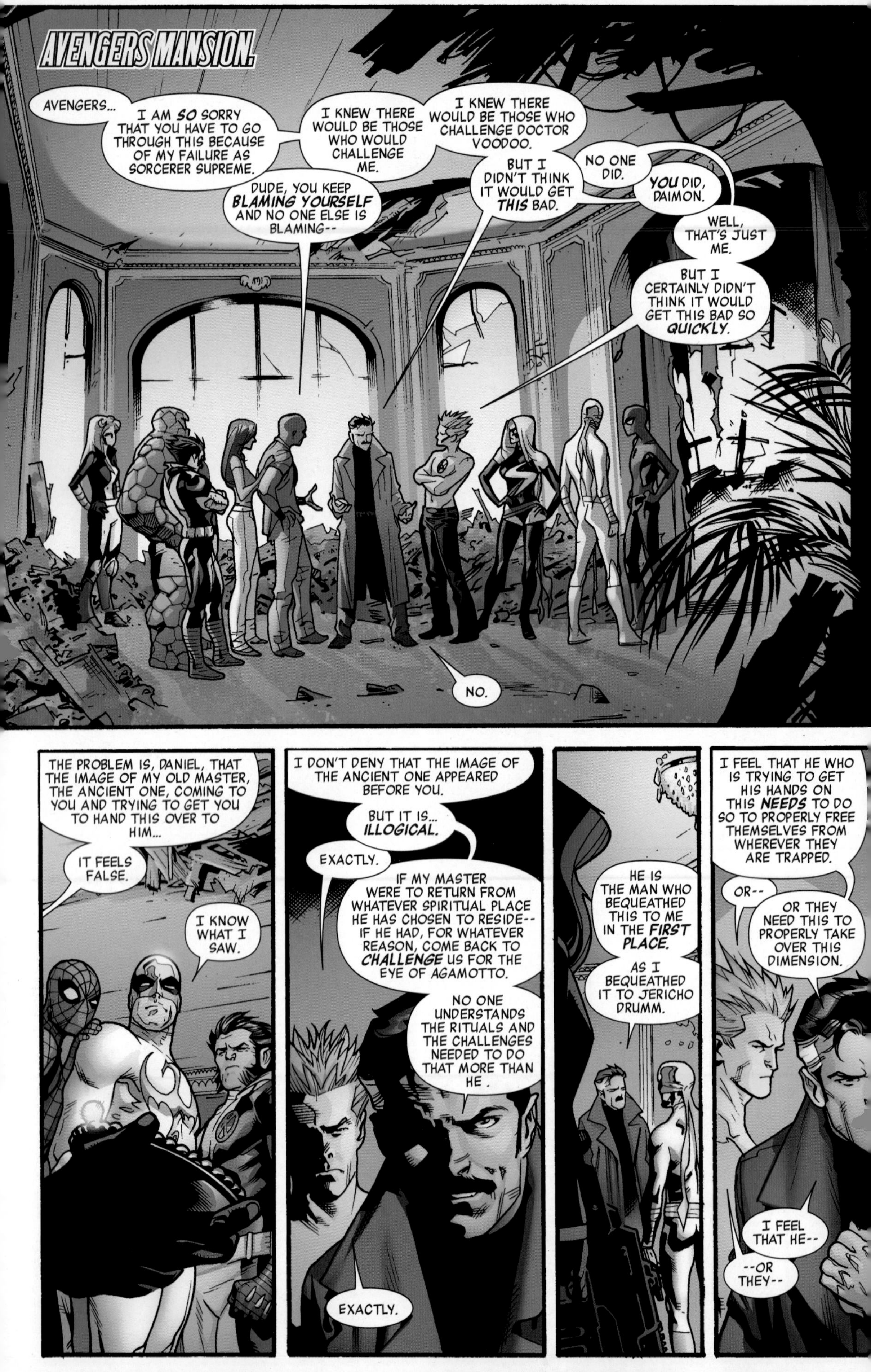
AVENGERS MANSION.
AVENGERS...
I AM SO SORRY THAT YOU HAVE TO GO THROUGH THIS BECAUSE OF MY FAILURE AS SORCERER SUPREME.
I KNEW THERE WOULD BE THOSE WHO WOULD CHALLENGE ME.
I KNEW THERE WOULD BE THOSE WHO CHALLENGE DOCTOR VOODOO.
DUDE, YOU KEEP BLAMING YOURSELF AND NO ONE ELSE IS BLAMING--
BUT I DIDN'T THINK IT WOULD GET THIS BAD.
NO ONE DID.
YOU DID, DAIMON.
WELL, THAT'S JUST ME.
BUT I CERTAINLY DIDN'T THINK IT WOULD GET THIS BAD SO QUICKLY.
NO.
THE PROBLEM IS, DANIEL, THAT THE IMAGE OF MY OLD MASTER, THE ANCIENT ONE, COMING TO YOU AND TRYING TO GET YOU TO HAND THIS OVER TO HIM...
IT FEELS FALSE.
I KNOW WHAT I SAW.
I DON'T DENY THAT THE IMAGE OF THE ANCIENT ONE APPEARED BEFORE YOU.
BUT IT IS... ILLOGICAL.
EXACTLY.
IF MY MASTER WERE TO RETURN FROM WHATEVER SPIRITUAL PLACE HE HAS CHOSEN TO RESIDE--IF HE HAD, FOR WHATEVER REASON, COME BACK TO CHALLENGE US FOR THE EYE OF AGAMOTTO.
NO ONE UNDERSTANDS THE RITUALS AND THE CHALLENGES NEEDED TO DO THAT MORE THAN HE .
EXACTLY.
HE IS THE MAN WHO BEQUEATHED THIS TO ME IN THE FIRST PLACE.
AS I BEQUEATHED IT TO JERICHO DRUMM.
I FEEL THAT HE WHO IS TRYING TO GET HIS HANDS ON THIS NEEDS TO DO SO TO PROPERLY FREE THEMSELVES FROM WHEREVER THEY ARE TRAPPED.
OR--
OR THEY NEED THIS TO PROPERLY TAKE OVER THIS DIMENSION.
I FEEL THAT HE--
--OR THEY--

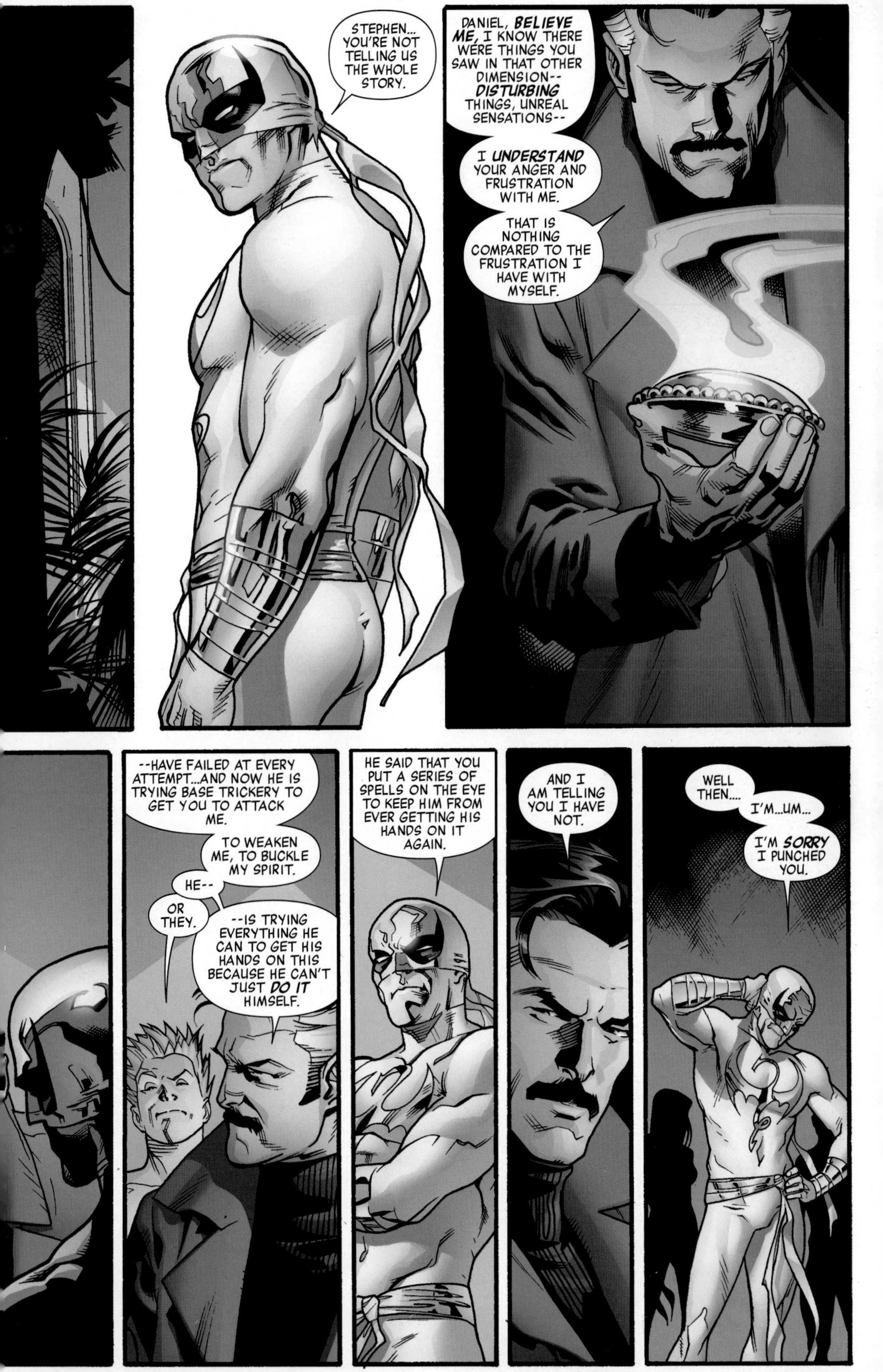
STEPHEN... YOU'RE NOT TELLING US THE WHOLE STORY.
DANIEL, BELIEVE ME, I KNOW THERE WERE THINGS YOU SAW IN THAT OTHER DIMENSION-- DISTURBING THINGS, UNREAL SENSATIONS--
I UNDERSTAND YOUR ANGER AND FRUSTRATION WITH ME.
THAT IS NOTHING COMPARED TO THE FRUSTRATION I HAVE WITH MYSELF.
--HAVE FAILED AT EVERY ATTEMPT...AND NOW HE IS TRYING BASE TRICKERY TO GET YOU TO ATTACK ME.
TO WEAKEN ME, TO BUCKLE MY SPIRIT.
HE--
OR THEY.
--IS TRYING EVERYTHING HE CAN TO GET HIS HANDS ON THIS BECAUSE HE CAN'T JUST DO IT HIMSELF.
HE SAID THAT YOU PUT A SERIES OF SPELLS ON THE EYE TO KEEP HIM FROM EVER GETTING HIS HANDS ON IT AGAIN.
AND I AM TELLING YOU I HAVE NOT.
WELL THEN....
I'M...UM...
I'M SORRY I PUNCHED YOU.

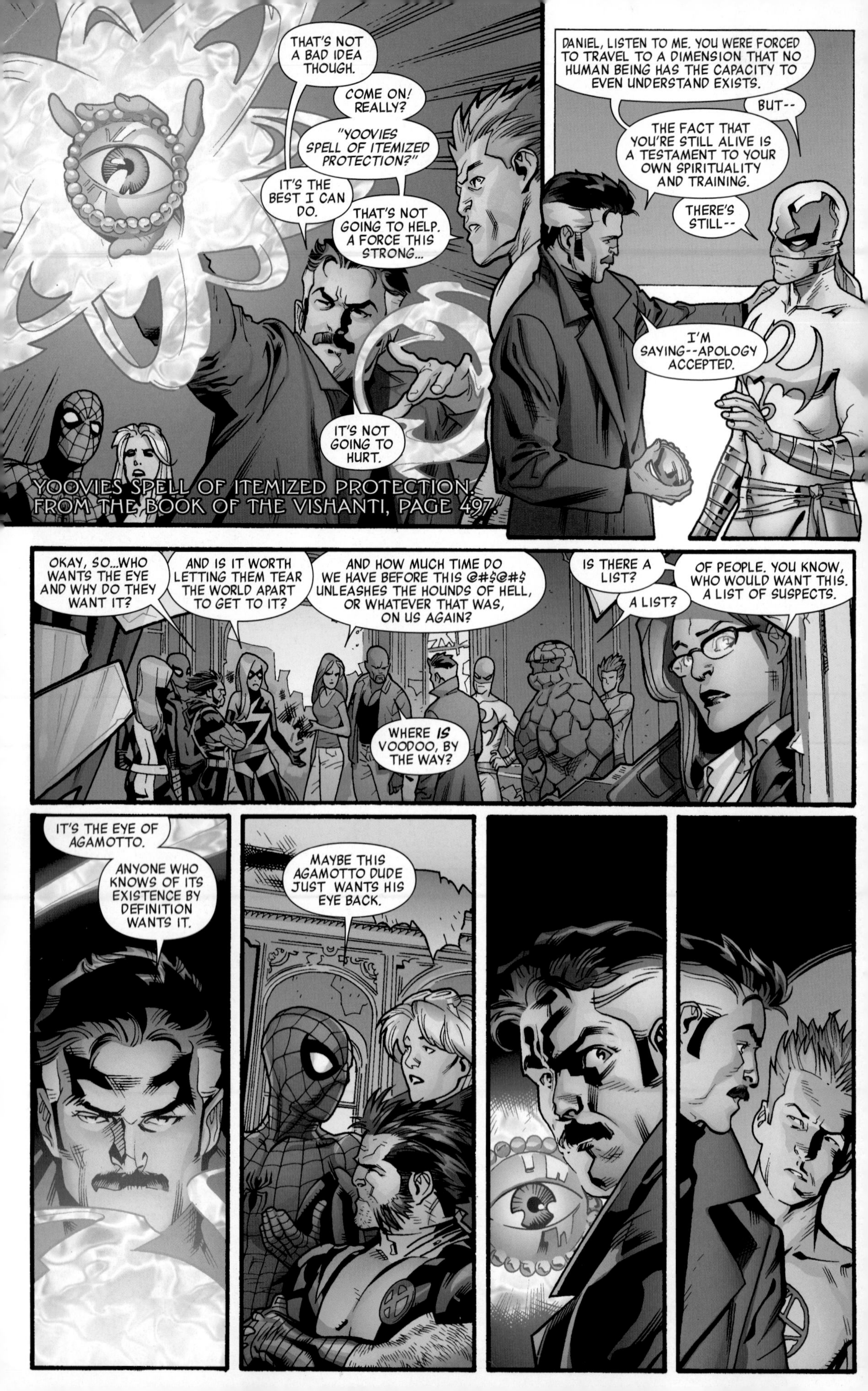
THAT'S NOT A BAD IDEA THOUGH.
COME ON! REALLY?
"YOOVIES SPELL OF ITEMIZED PROTECTION?"
IT'S THE BEST I CAN DO.
THAT'S NOT GOING TO HELP. A FORCE THIS STRONG...
IT'S NOT GOING TO HURT.
YOOVIES SPELL OF ITEMIZED PROTECTION. FROM THE BOOK OF THE VISHANTI, PAGE 497.
DANIEL, LISTEN TO ME. YOU WERE FORCED TO TRAVEL TO A DIMENSION THAT NO HUMAN BEING HAS THE CAPACITY TO EVEN UNDERSTAND EXISTS.
BUT--
THE FACT THAT YOU'RE STILL ALIVE IS A TESTAMENT TO YOUR OWN SPIRITUALITY AND TRAINING.
THERE'S STILL--
I'M SAYING--APOLOGY ACCEPTED.
OKAY, SO...WHO WANTS THE EYE AND WHY DO THEY WANT IT?
AND IS IT WORTH LETTING THEM TEAR THE WORLD APART TO GET TO IT?
AND HOW MUCH TIME DO WE HAVE BEFORE THIS @#$@#$ UNLEASHES THE HOUNDS OF HELL, OR WHATEVER THAT WAS, ON US AGAIN?
WHERE IS VOODOO, BY THE WAY?
IS THERE A LIST?
A LIST?
OF PEOPLE. YOU KNOW, WHO WOULD WANT THIS. A LIST OF SUSPECTS.
IT'S THE EYE OF AGAMOTTO.
ANYONE WHO KNOWS OF ITS EXISTENCE BY DEFINITION WANTS IT.
MAYBE THIS AGAMOTTO DUDE JUST WANTS HIS EYE BACK.

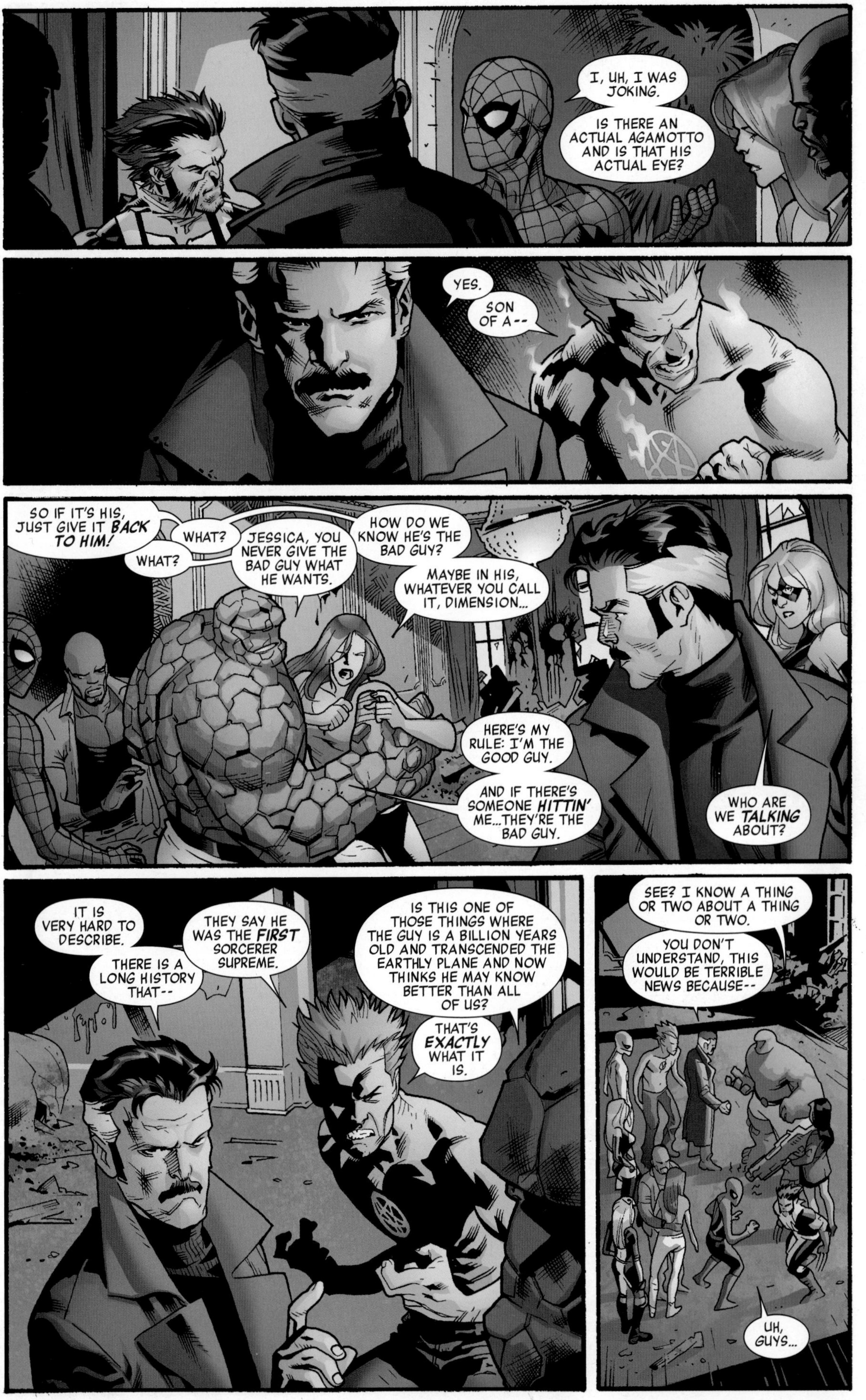
I, UH, I WAS JOKING.
IS THERE AN ACTUAL AGAMOTTO AND IS THAT HIS ACTUAL EYE?
YES.
SON OF A--
SO IF IT'S HIS, JUST GIVE IT BACK TO HIM!
WHAT?
WHAT?
JESSICA, YOU NEVER GIVE THE BAD GUY WHAT HE WANTS.
HOW DO WE KNOW HE'S THE BAD GUY?
MAYBE IN HIS, WHATEVER YOU CALL IT, DIMENSION...
HERE'S MY RULE: I'M THE GOOD GUY.
AND IF THERE'S SOMEONE HITTIN' ME...THEY'RE THE BAD GUY.
WHO ARE WE TALKING ABOUT?
IT IS VERY HARD TO DESCRIBE.
THERE IS A LONG HISTORY THAT--
THEY SAY HE WAS THE FIRST SORCERER SUPREME.
IS THIS ONE OF THOSE THINGS WHERE THE GUY IS A BILLION YEARS OLD AND TRANSCENDED THE EARTHLY PLANE AND NOW THINKS HE MAY KNOW BETTER THAN ALL OF US?
THAT'S EXACTLY WHAT IT IS.
SEE? I KNOW A THING OR TWO ABOUT A THING OR TWO.
YOU DON'T UNDERSTAND, THIS WOULD BE TERRIBLE NEWS BECAUSE--
UH, GUYS...

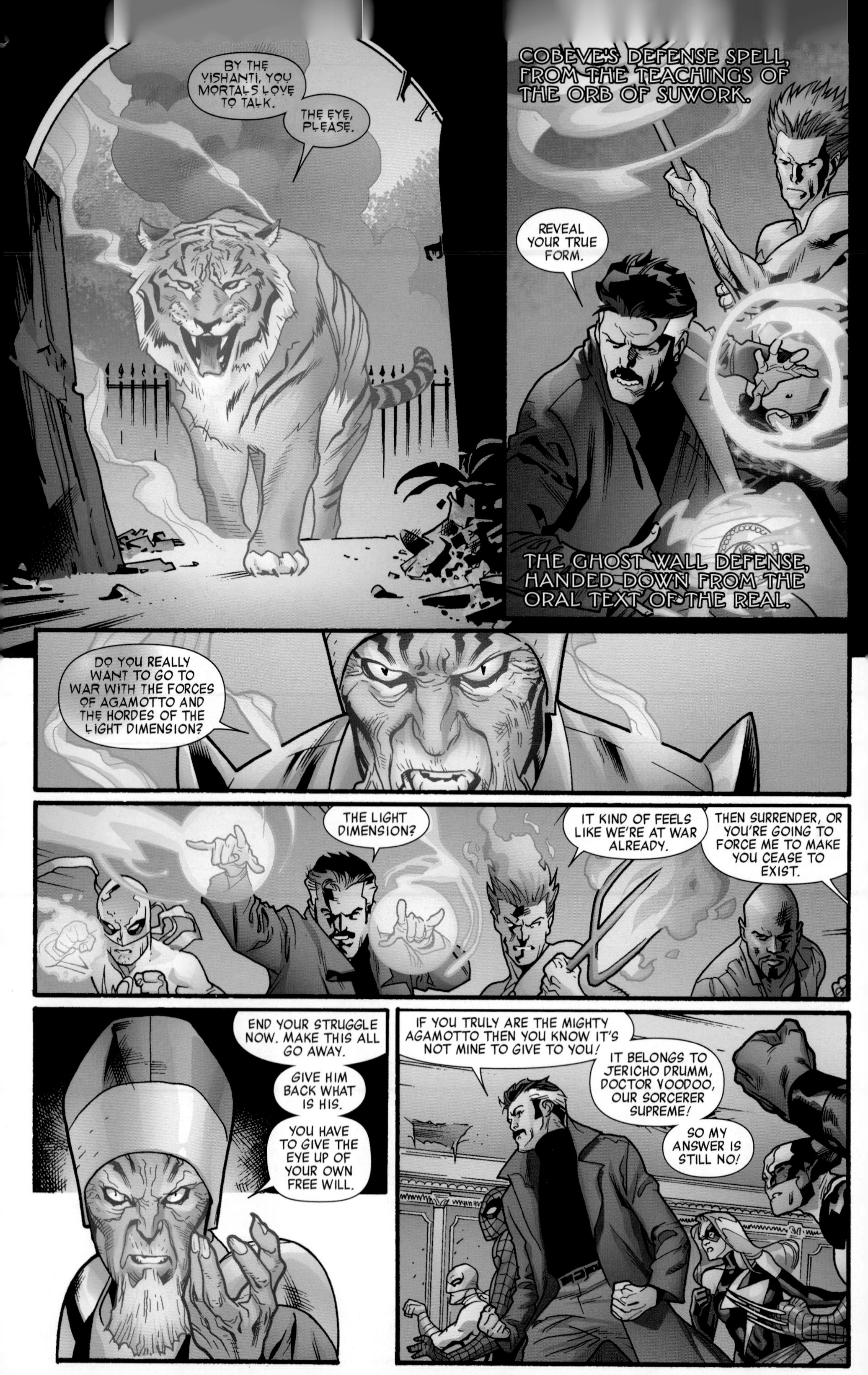

BY THE VISHANTI, YOU MORTALS LOVE TO TALK.
THE EYE, PLEASE.
COBEVE'S DEFENSE SPELL, FROM THE TEACHINGS OF THE ORB OF SUWORK.
REVEAL YOUR TRUE FORM.
THE GHOST WALL DEFENSE, HANDED DOWN FROM THE ORAL TEXT OF THE REAL.
DO YOU REALLY WANT TO GO TO WAR WITH THE FORCES OF AGAMOTTO AND THE HORDES OF THE LIGHT DIMENSION?
THE LIGHT DIMENSION?
IT KIND OF FEELS LIKE WE'RE AT WAR ALREADY.
THEN SURRENDER, OR YOU'RE GOING TO FORCE ME TO MAKE YOU CEASE TO EXIST.
END YOUR STRUGGLE NOW. MAKE THIS ALL GO AWAY.
GIVE HIM BACK WHAT IS HIS.
YOU HAVE TO GIVE THE EYE UP OF YOUR OWN FREE WILL.
IF YOU TRULY ARE THE MIGHTY AGAMOTTO THEN YOU KNOW IT'S NOT MINE TO GIVE TO YOU!
IT BELONGS TO JERICHO DRUMM, DOCTOR VOODOO, OUR SORCERER SUPREME!
SO MY ANSWER IS STILL NO!

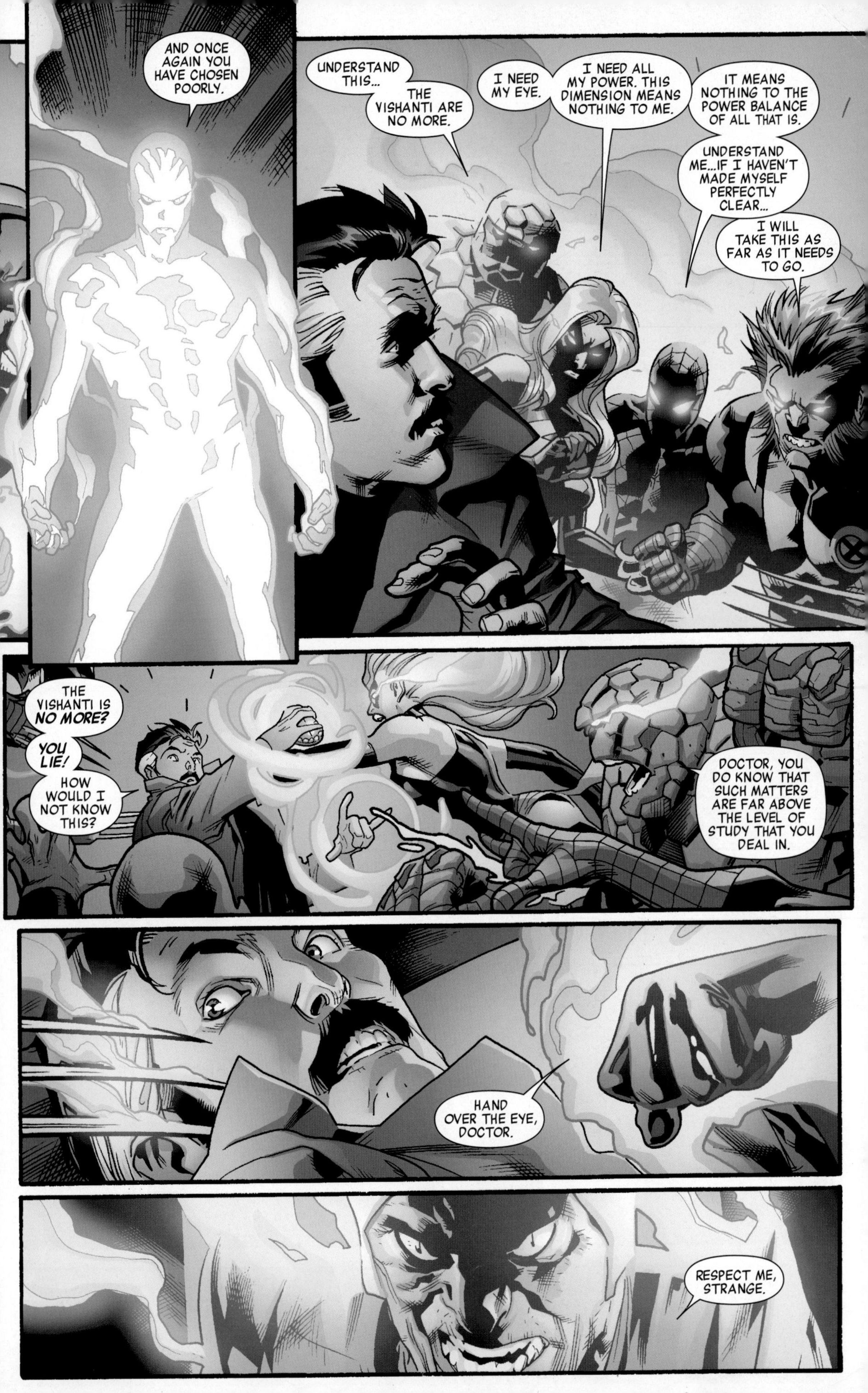
AND ONCE AGAIN YOU HAVE CHOSEN POORLY.
UNDERSTAND THIS...
THE VISHANTI ARE NO MORE.
I NEED MY EYE.
I NEED ALL MY POWER. THIS DIMENSION MEANS NOTHING TO ME.
IT MEANS NOTHING TO THE POWER BALANCE OF ALL THAT IS.
UNDERSTAND ME...IF I HAVEN'T MADE MYSELF PERFECTLY CLEAR...
I WILL TAKE THIS AS FAR AS IT NEEDS TO GO.
THE VISHANTI IS NO MORE?
YOU LIE!
HOW WOULD I NOT KNOW THIS?
DOCTOR, YOU DO KNOW THAT SUCH MATTERS ARE FAR ABOVE THE LEVEL OF STUDY THAT YOU DEAL IN.
HAND OVER THE EYE, DOCTOR.
RESPECT ME, STRANGE.

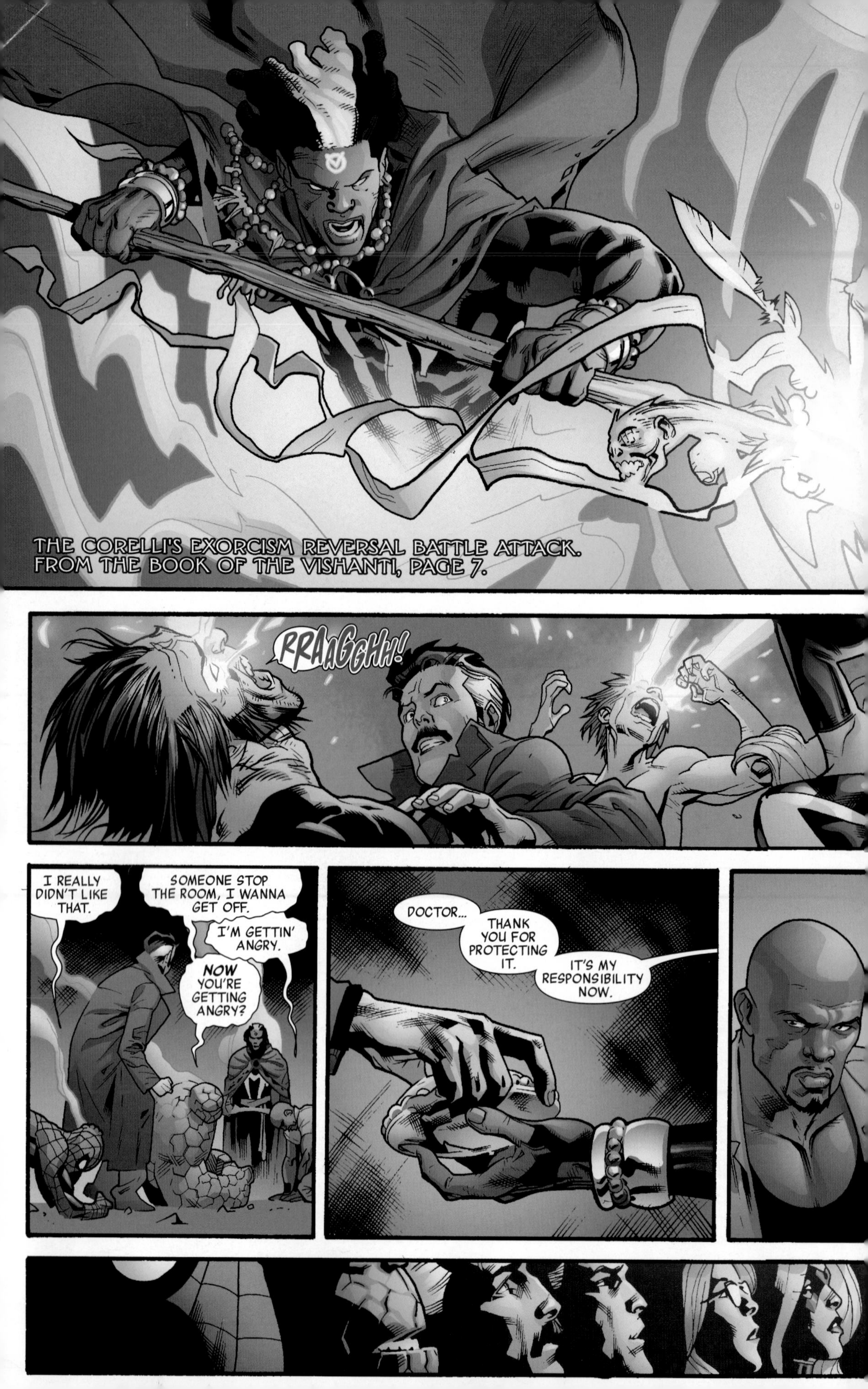
THE CORELLI'S EXORCISM REVERSAL BATTLE ATTACK. FROM THE BOOK OF THE VISHANTI, PAGE 7.
RRAAGGHH!
I REALLY DIDN'T LIKE THAT.
SOMEONE STOP THE ROOM, I WANNA GET OFF.
I'M GETTIN' ANGRY.
NOW YOU'RE GETTING ANGRY?
DOCTOR...
THANK YOU FOR PROTECTING IT.
IT'S MY RESPONSIBILITY NOW.

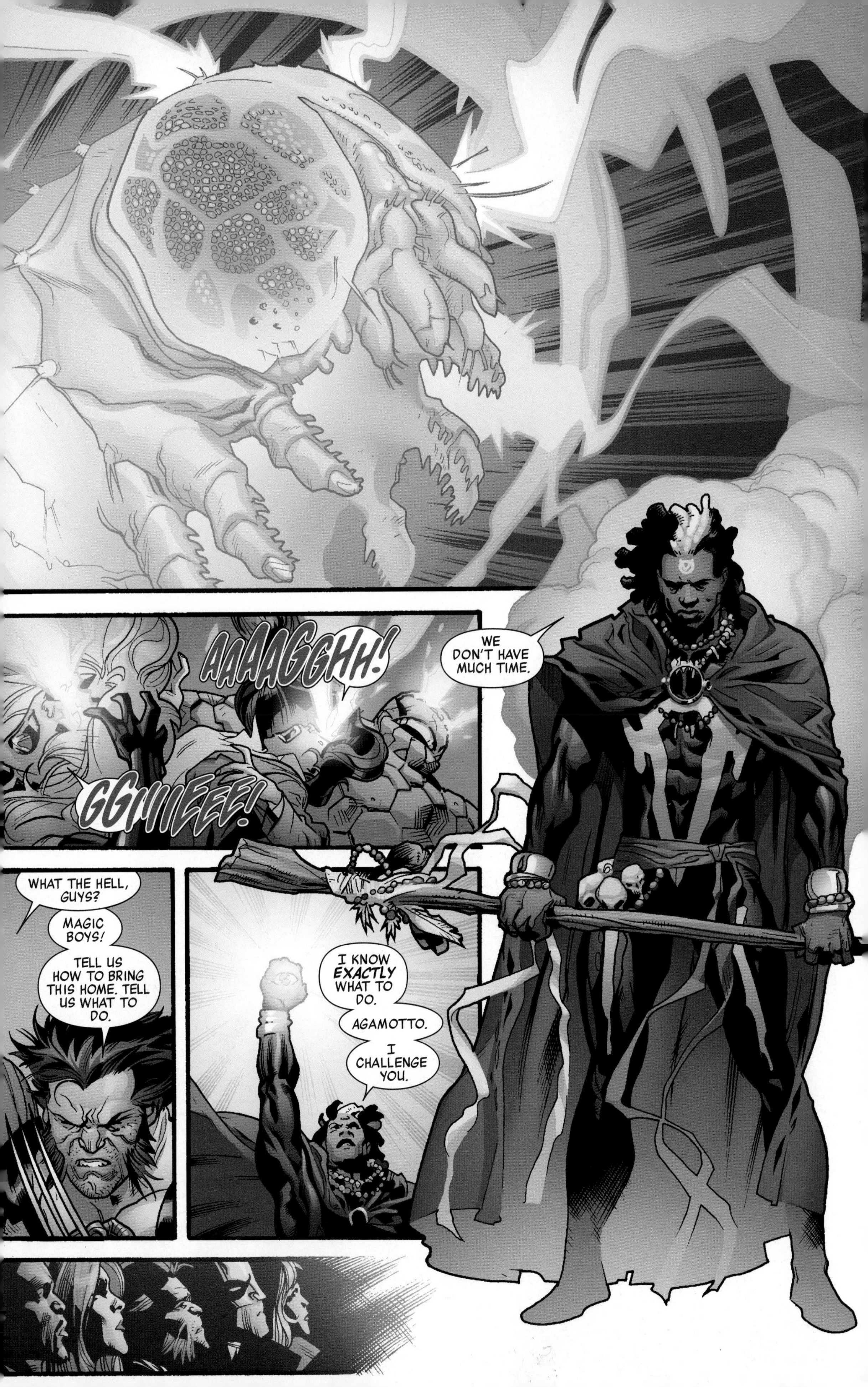
WE DON'T HAVE MUCH TIME.
AAAAAGGHH!
GGIIIIEEE!
WHAT THE HELL, GUYS?
MAGIC BOYS!
TELL US HOW TO BRING THIS HOME. TELL US WHAT TO DO.
I KNOW EXACTLY WHAT TO DO.
AGAMOTTO.
I CHALLENGE YOU.

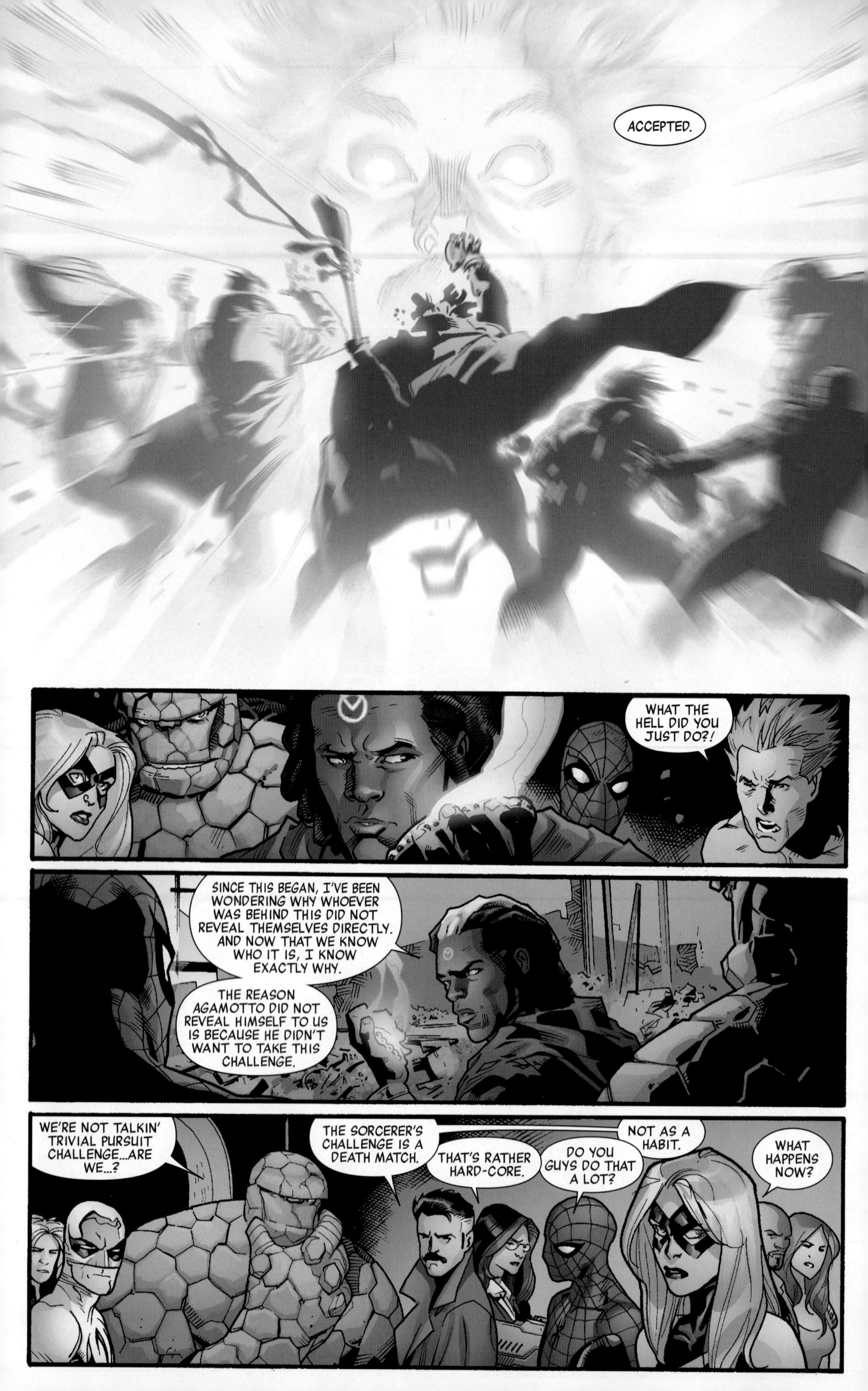
ACCEPTED.
WHAT THE HELL DID YOU JUST DO?!
SINCE THIS BEGAN, I'VE BEEN WONDERING WHY WHOEVER WAS BEHIND THIS DID NOT REVEAL THEMSELVES DIRECTLY. AND NOW THAT WE KNOW WHO IT IS, I KNOW EXACTLY WHY.
THE REASON AGAMOTTO DID NOT REVEAL HIMSELF TO US IS BECAUSE HE DIDN'T WANT TO TAKE THIS CHALLENGE.
WE'RE NOT TALKIN' TRIVIAL PURSUIT CHALLENGE...ARE WE...?
THE SORCERER'S CHALLENGE IS A DEATH MATCH.
NOT AS A HABIT.
THAT'S RATHER HARD-CORE.
DO YOU GUYS DO THAT A LOT?
WHAT HAPPENS NOW?

I FIND HIM AND DO BATTLE WITH HIM.

YOU ARE OUT *OF YOUR MIND!*

YOU'RE A VERY *NICE* GUY, JERICHO, BUT YOU ARE IN *NO WAY* CAPABLE OF DOING MYSTICAL BATTLE WITH AN IMMORTAL TRANSCENDED SORCERER SUPREME!

YOU DON'T EVEN KNOW WHERE HE IS, JERICHO.

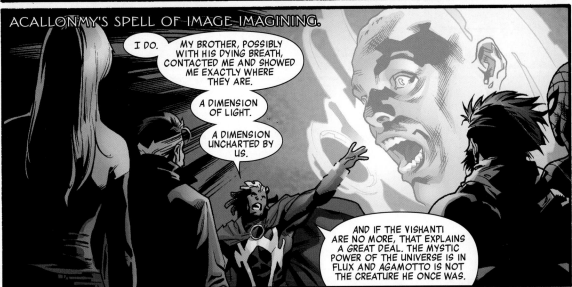

ACALLONMY'S SPELL OF IMAGE IMAGINING.

I DO.

MY BROTHER, POSSIBLY WITH HIS DYING BREATH, CONTACTED ME AND SHOWED ME EXACTLY WHERE THEY ARE.

A DIMENSION OF LIGHT.

A DIMENSION UNCHARTED BY US.

AND IF THE VISHANTI ARE NO MORE, THAT EXPLAINS A GREAT DEAL. THE MYSTIC POWER OF THE UNIVERSE IS IN FLUX AND AGAMOTTO IS NOT THE CREATURE HE ONCE WAS.

MAYBE.

WE WILL FIND OUT SHORTLY.

WHY DON'T YOU JUST GO STAND IN FRONT OF A *BUS.* SAME END RESULT.

CAN WE HELP?

ACTUALLY, *ALL OF YOU* ARE GOING TO HELP.

I THOUGHT THIS WAS A ONE-ON-ONE KIND OF RUMBLE IN THE BRONX.

IT IS.

ONE VESSEL AGAINST ONE VESSEL.

VESSEL? WHAT ARE YOU THINKING?

THE MACOLDINE SPELL OF BINDING.

HUH.

WELL, IT'S NOT AGAINST THE RULES.

WHAT RULES?

THERE IS A CODE IN THE MYSTIC WORLD. THERE ARE RULES. WE *FOLLOW* THE RULES.

BUT WE CHALLENGE OURSELVES TO FIND CREATIVE WAYS *AROUND* THOSE RULES.

I THINK OUR SORCERER SUPREME JUST FOUND ONE.

EVERYTHING AGAMOTTO'S DONE TO US IS "*AGAINST THE RULES*" AND NOW WE HAVE TO FOLLOW THE RULES?

AS OUR FRIEND BEN JUST SAID...*THAT'S* HOW WE KNOW WHO THE GOOD GUYS ARE.

UUGGH!

THE MACOLDINE SPELL OF BINDING WOULD GATHER ALL OF THE POWERS AND ABILITIES OF OUR GROUP...INTO ONE VESSEL.

THAT VESSEL WILL ENTER THE CHALLENGE.

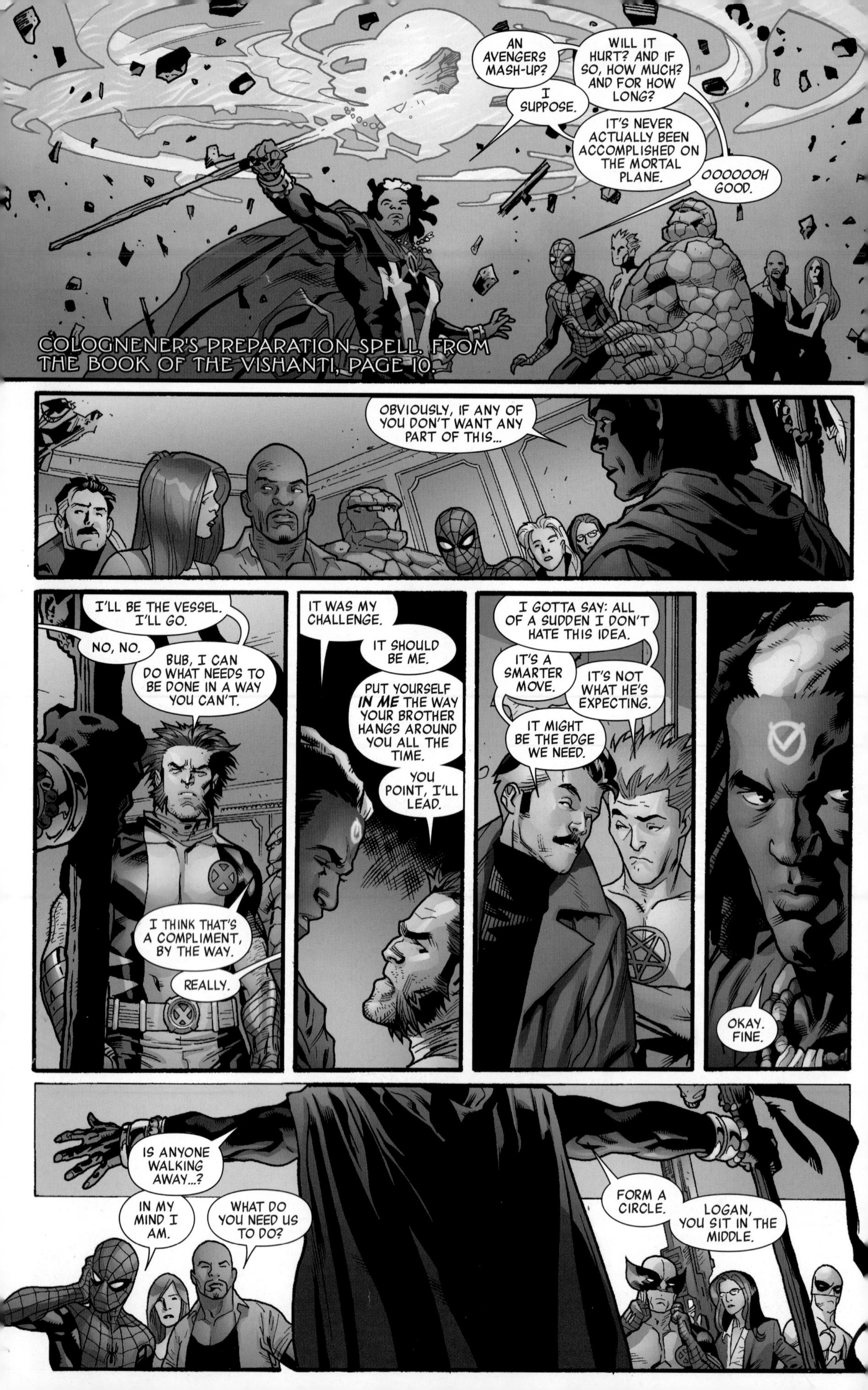
AN AVENGERS MASH-UP?
WILL IT HURT? AND IF SO, HOW MUCH? AND FOR HOW LONG?
I SUPPOSE.
IT'S NEVER ACTUALLY BEEN ACCOMPLISHED ON THE MORTAL PLANE.
OOOOOOH GOOD.
COLOGNENER'S PREPARATION SPELL. FROM THE BOOK OF THE VISHANTI, PAGE 10.
OBVIOUSLY, IF ANY OF YOU DON'T WANT ANY PART OF THIS...
I'LL BE THE VESSEL. I'LL GO.
NO, NO.
BUB, I CAN DO WHAT NEEDS TO BE DONE IN A WAY YOU CAN'T.
I THINK THAT'S A COMPLIMENT, BY THE WAY.
REALLY.
IT WAS MY CHALLENGE.
IT SHOULD BE ME.
PUT YOURSELF IN ME THE WAY YOUR BROTHER HANGS AROUND YOU ALL THE TIME.
YOU POINT, I'LL LEAD.
I GOTTA SAY: ALL OF A SUDDEN I DON'T HATE THIS IDEA.
IT'S A SMARTER MOVE.
IT'S NOT WHAT HE'S EXPECTING.
IT MIGHT BE THE EDGE WE NEED.
OKAY. FINE.
IS ANYONE WALKING AWAY...?
IN MY MIND I AM.
WHAT DO YOU NEED US TO DO?
FORM A CIRCLE.
LOGAN, YOU SIT IN THE MIDDLE.

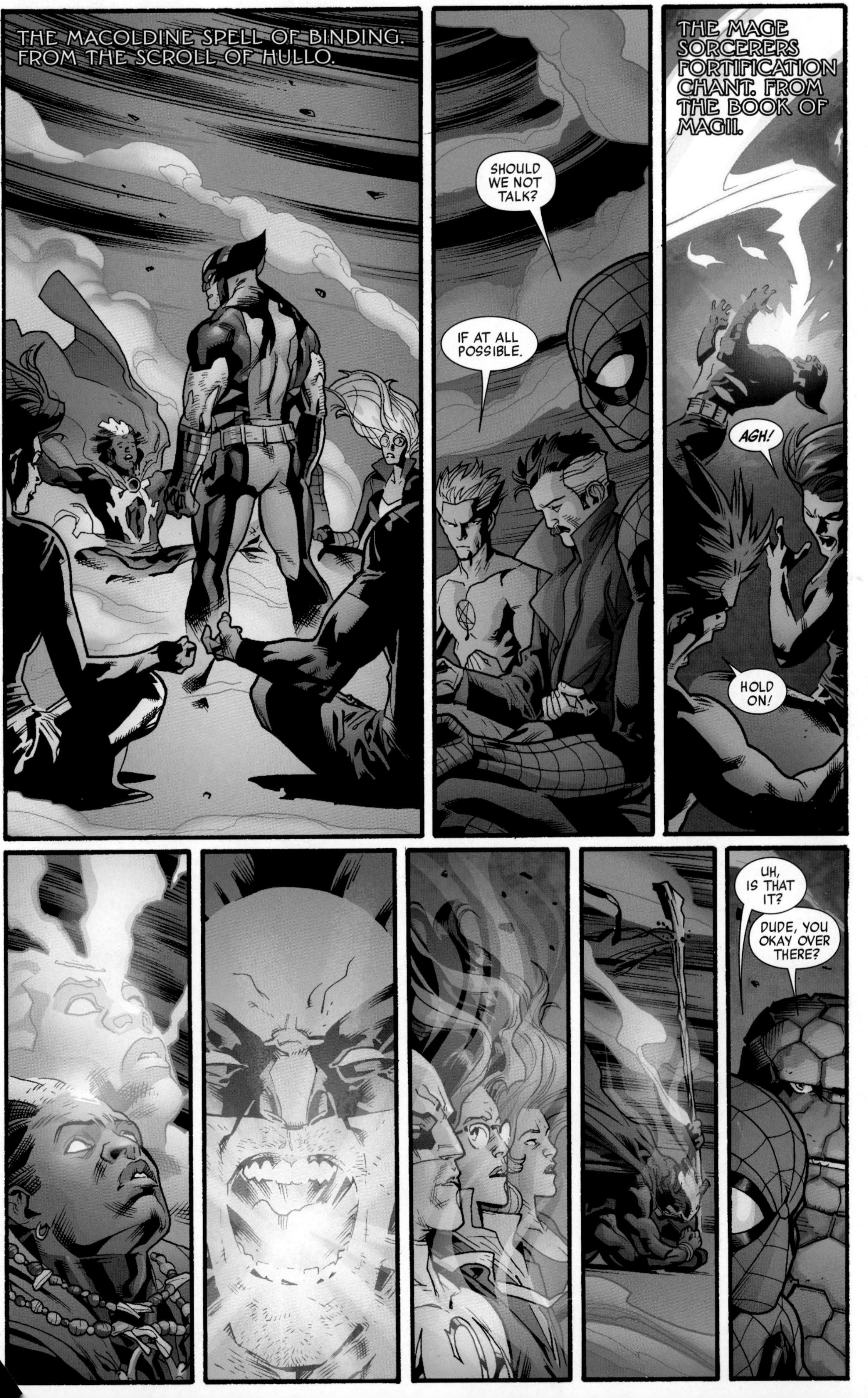
THE MACOLDINE SPELL OF BINDING. FROM THE SCROLL OF HULLO.
SHOULD WE NOT TALK?
IF AT ALL POSSIBLE.
THE MAGE SORCERERS FORTIFICATION CHANT. FROM THE BOOK OF MAGII.
AGH!
HOLD ON!
UH, IS THAT IT?
DUDE, YOU OKAY OVER THERE?

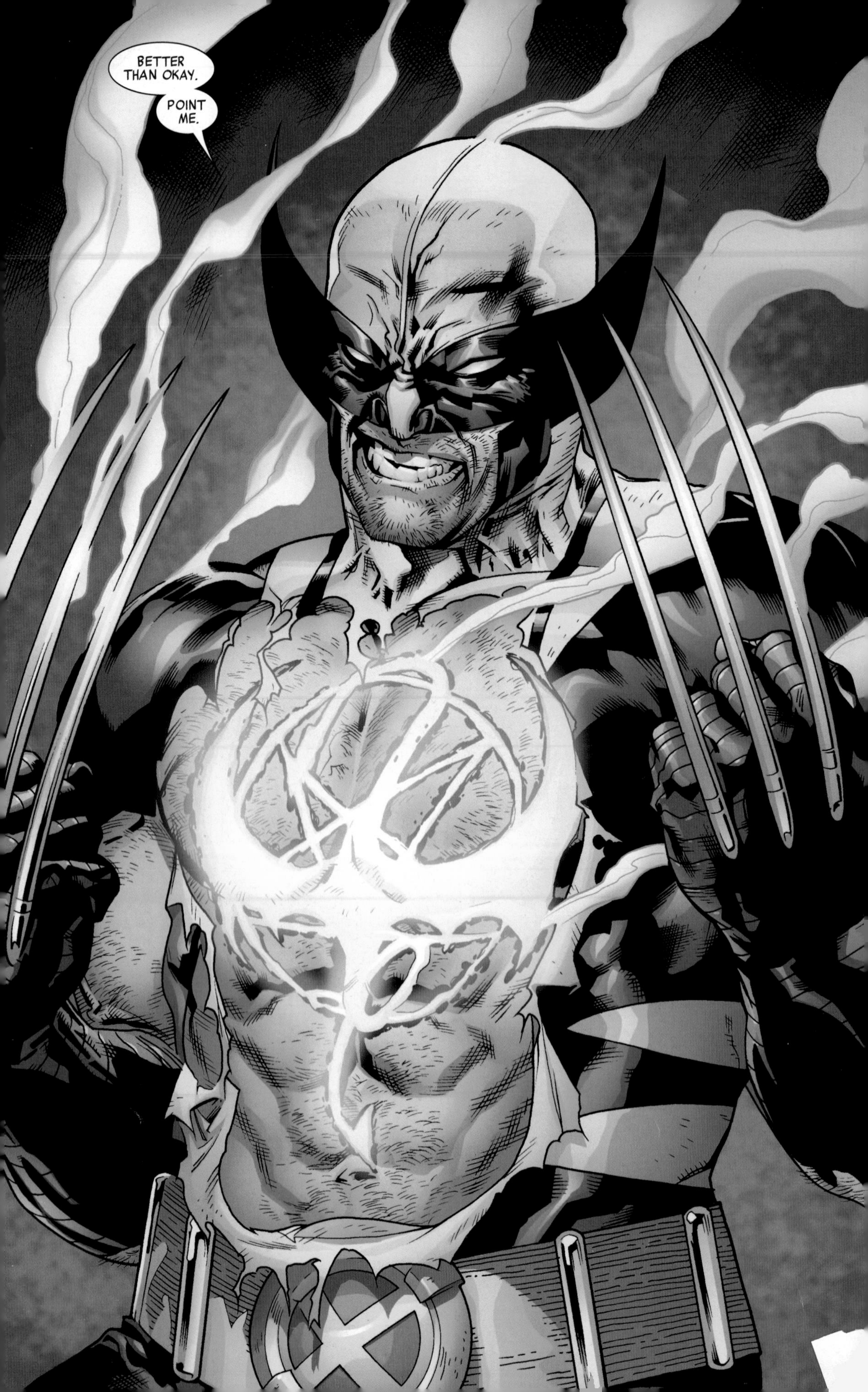
BETTER THAN OKAY.
POINT ME.

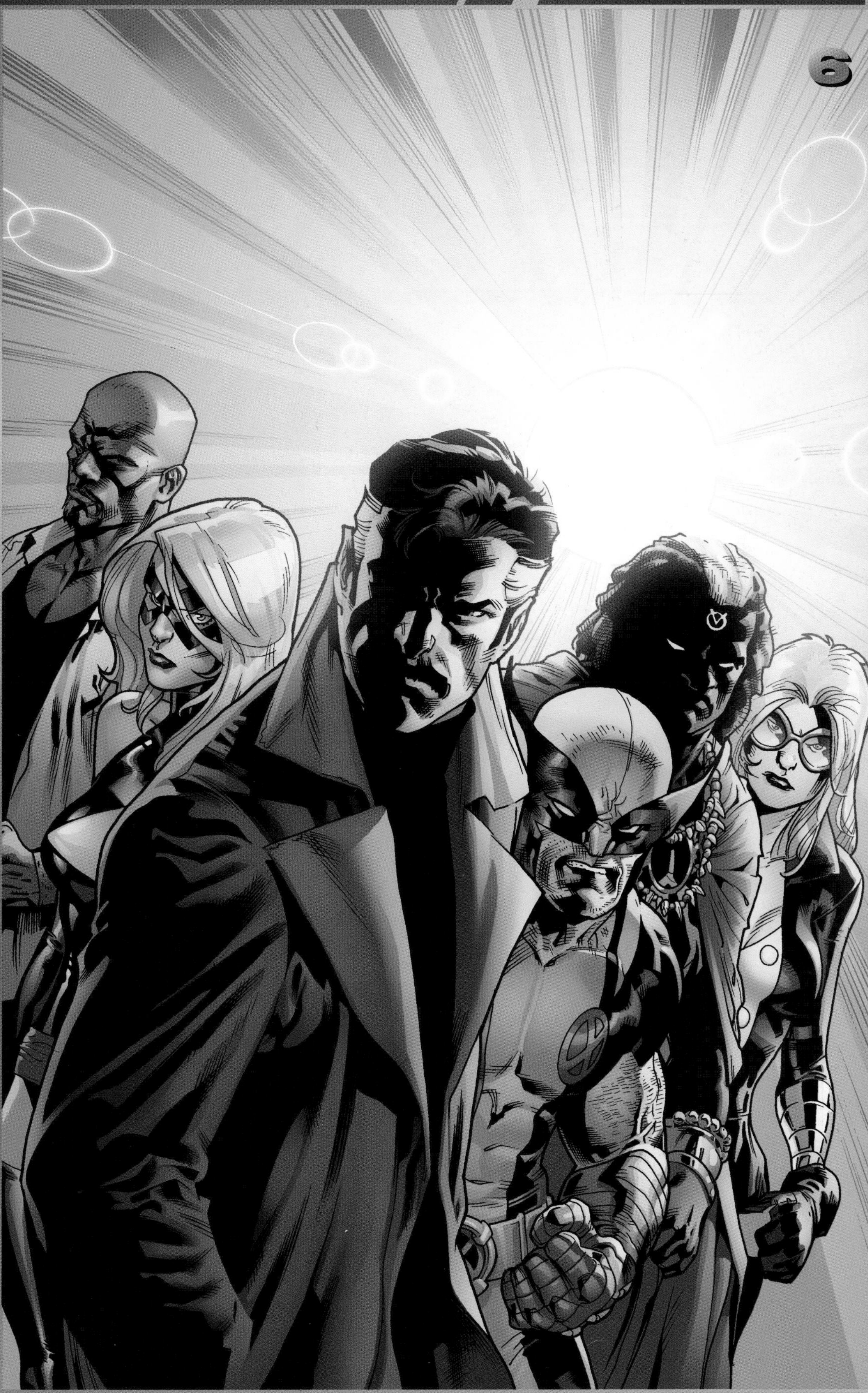
6

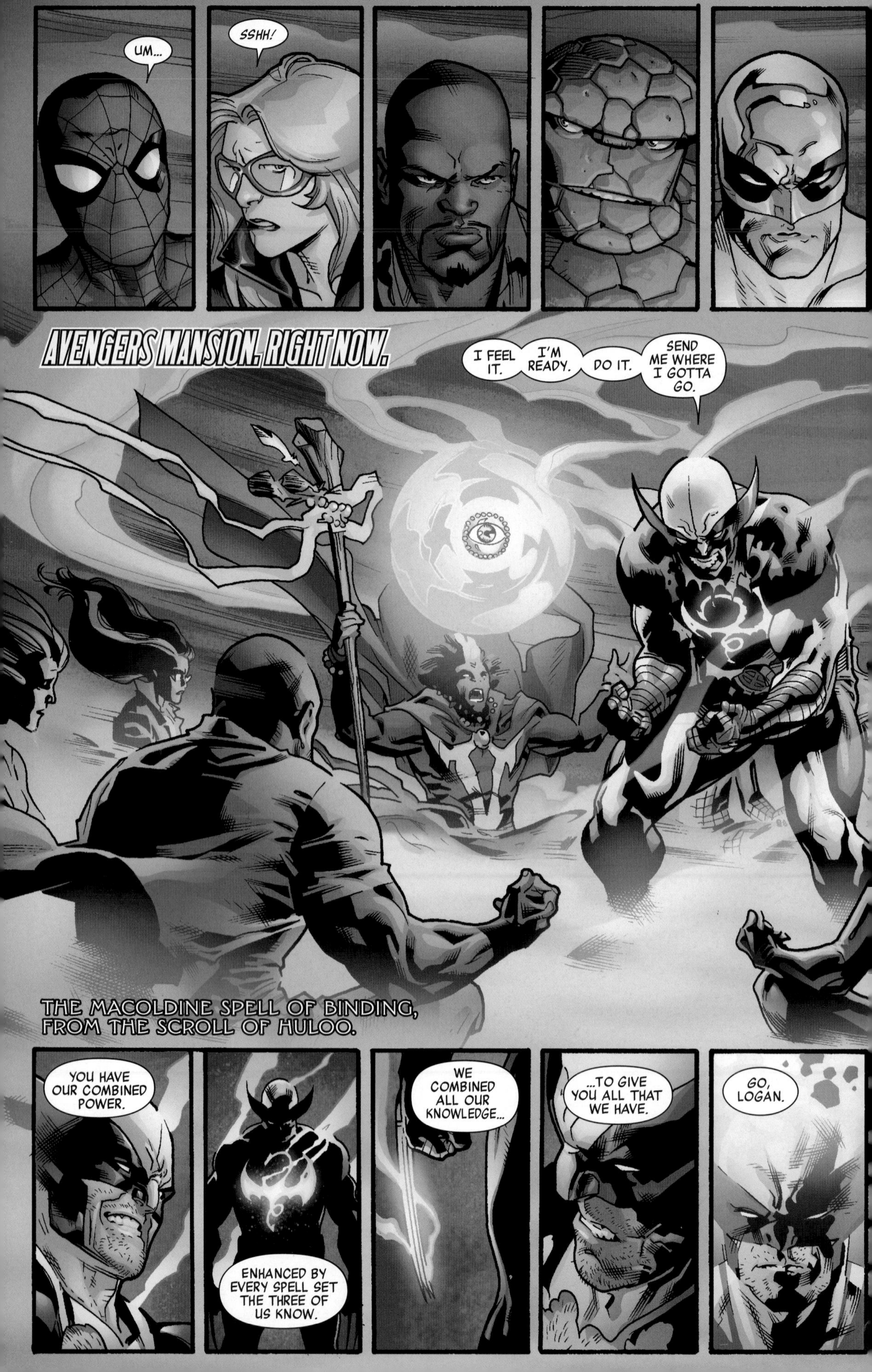
UM...
SSHH!
AVENGERS MANSION. RIGHT NOW.
I FEEL IT.
I'M READY.
DO IT.
SEND ME WHERE I GOTTA GO.
THE MACOLDINE SPELL OF BINDING, FROM THE SCROLL OF HULOO.
YOU HAVE OUR COMBINED POWER.
ENHANCED BY EVERY SPELL SET THE THREE OF US KNOW.
WE COMBINED ALL OUR KNOWLEDGE...
...TO GIVE YOU ALL THAT WE HAVE.
GO, LOGAN.

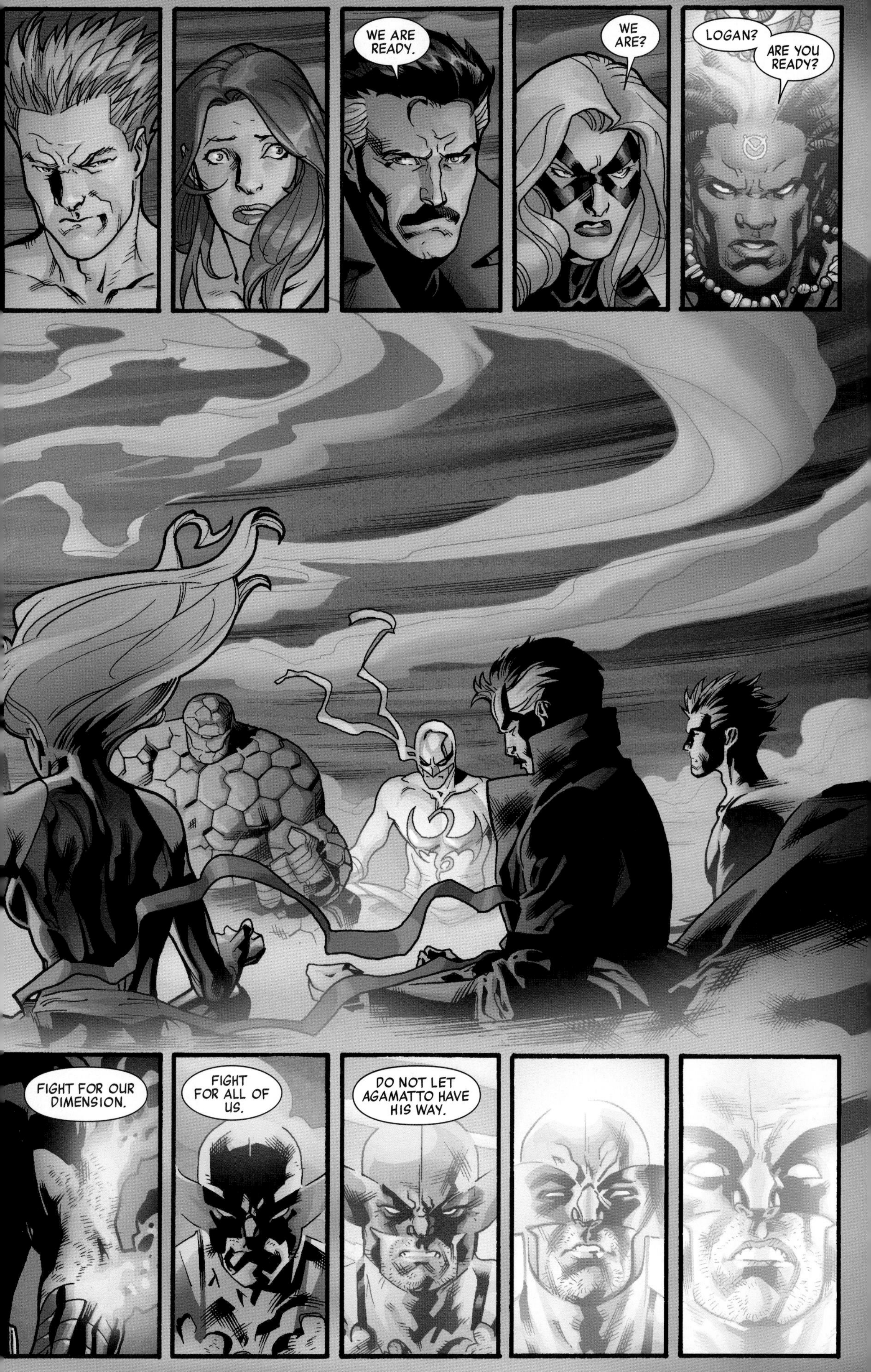
WE ARE READY.
WE ARE?
LOGAN?
ARE YOU READY?
FIGHT FOR OUR DIMENSION.
FIGHT FOR ALL OF US.
DO NOT LET AGAMATTO HAVE HIS WAY.

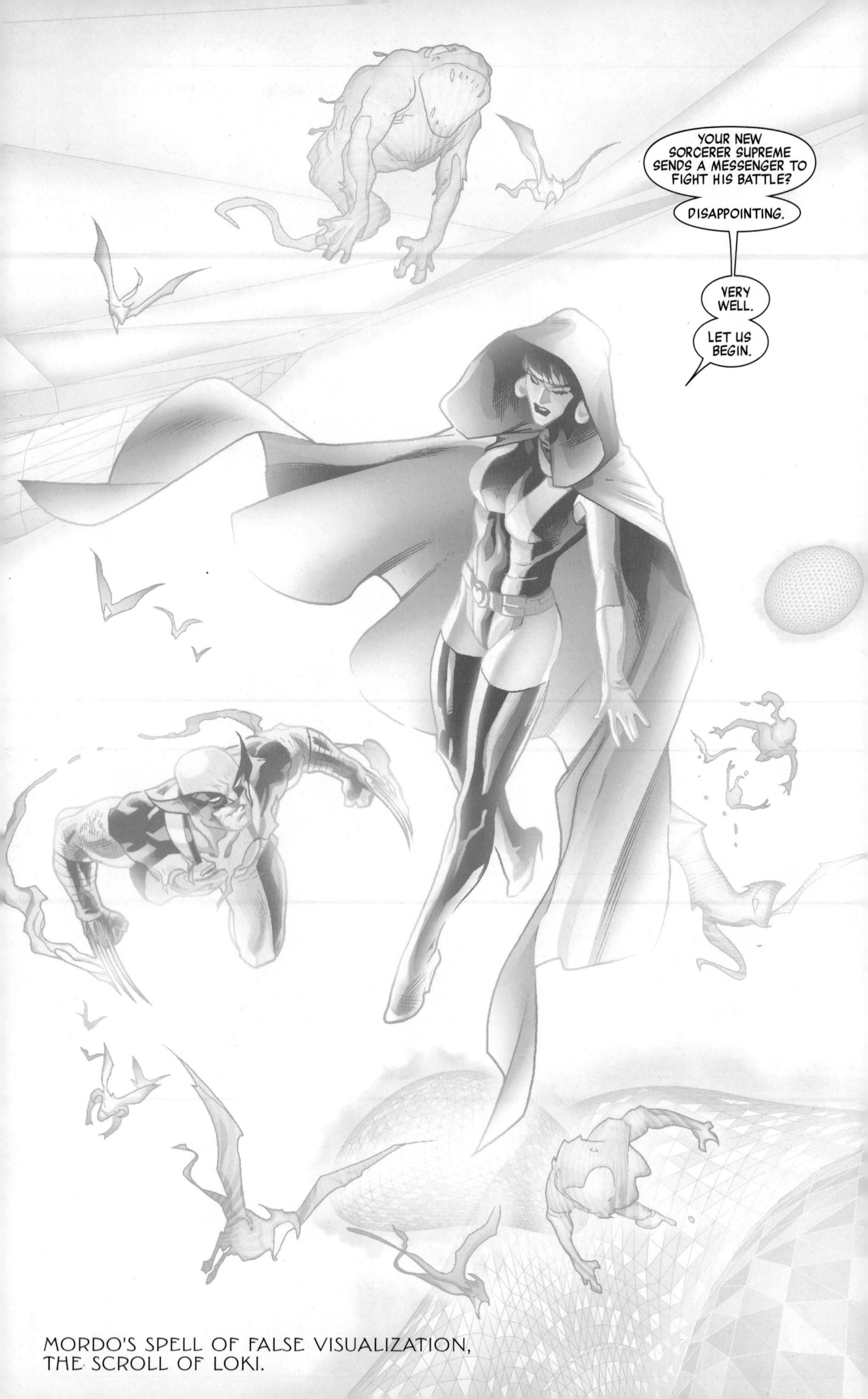
YOUR NEW SORCERER SUPREME SENDS A MESSENGER TO FIGHT HIS BATTLE?
DISAPPOINTING.
VERY WELL.
LET US BEGIN.
MORDO'S SPELL OF FALSE VISUALIZATION, THE SCROLL OF LOKI.

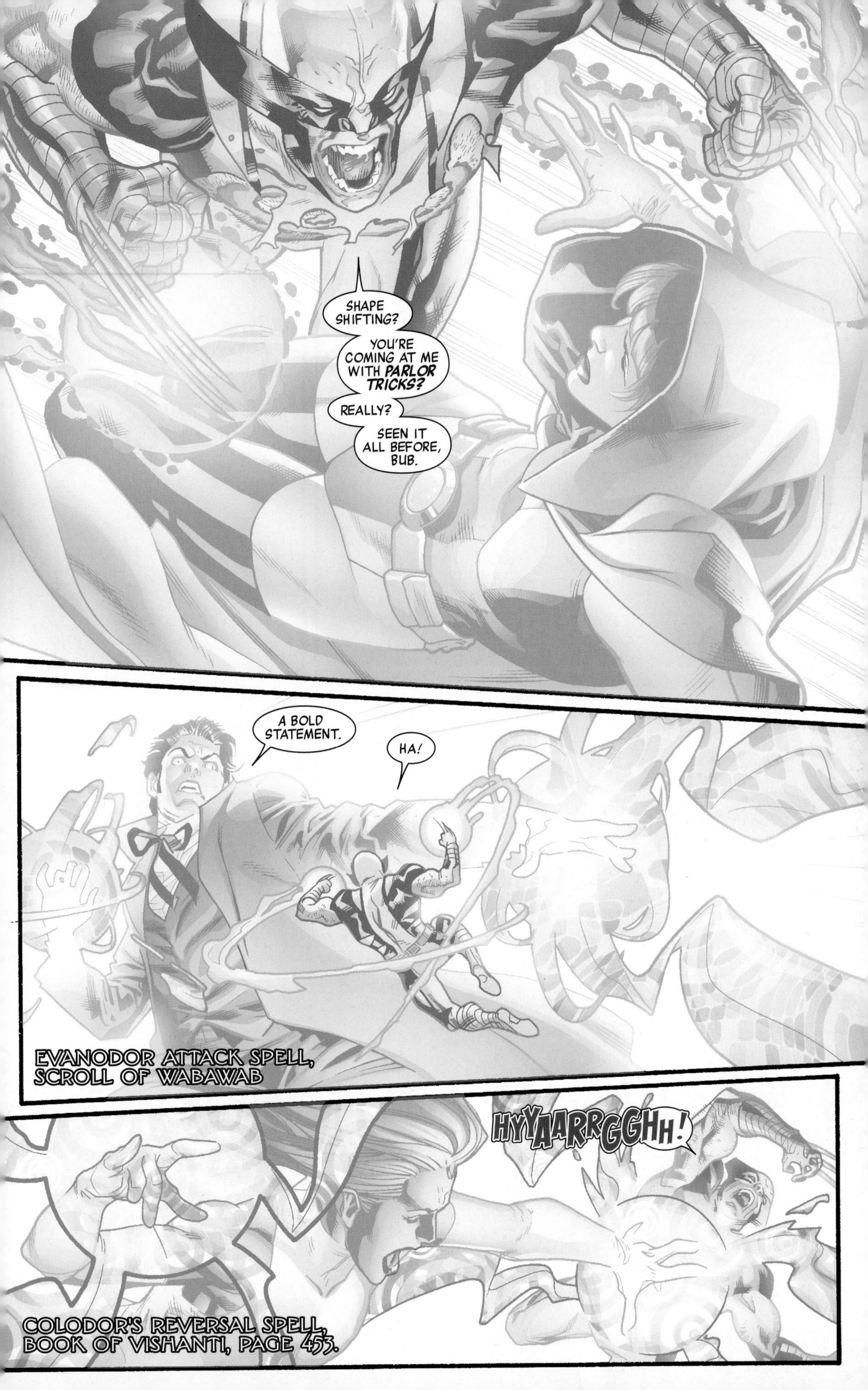
SHAPE SHIFTING?
YOU'RE COMING AT ME WITH PARLOR TRICKS?
REALLY?
SEEN IT ALL BEFORE, BUB.
A BOLD STATEMENT.
HA!
EVANODOR ATTACK SPELL, SCROLL OF WABAWAB
HYYAARRGGHH!
COLODOR'S REVERSAL SPELL, BOOK OF VISHANTI, PAGE 453.

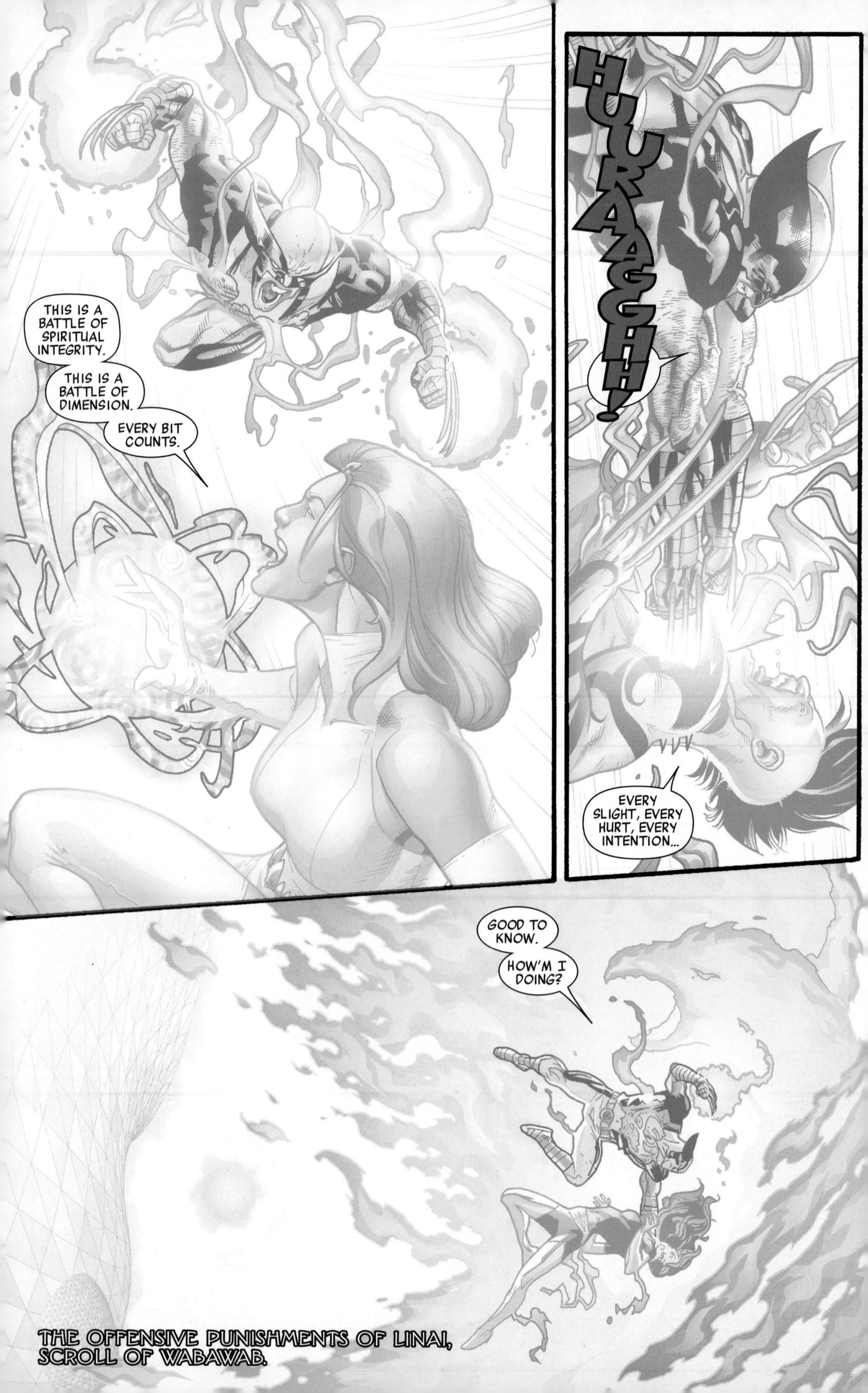
THIS IS A BATTLE OF SPIRITUAL INTEGRITY.
THIS IS A BATTLE OF DIMENSION.
EVERY BIT COUNTS.
HUURAAAGGHHH!
EVERY SLIGHT, EVERY HURT, EVERY INTENTION...
GOOD TO KNOW.
HOW'M I DOING?
THE OFFENSIVE PUNISHMENTS OF LINAI, SCROLL OF WABAWAB.

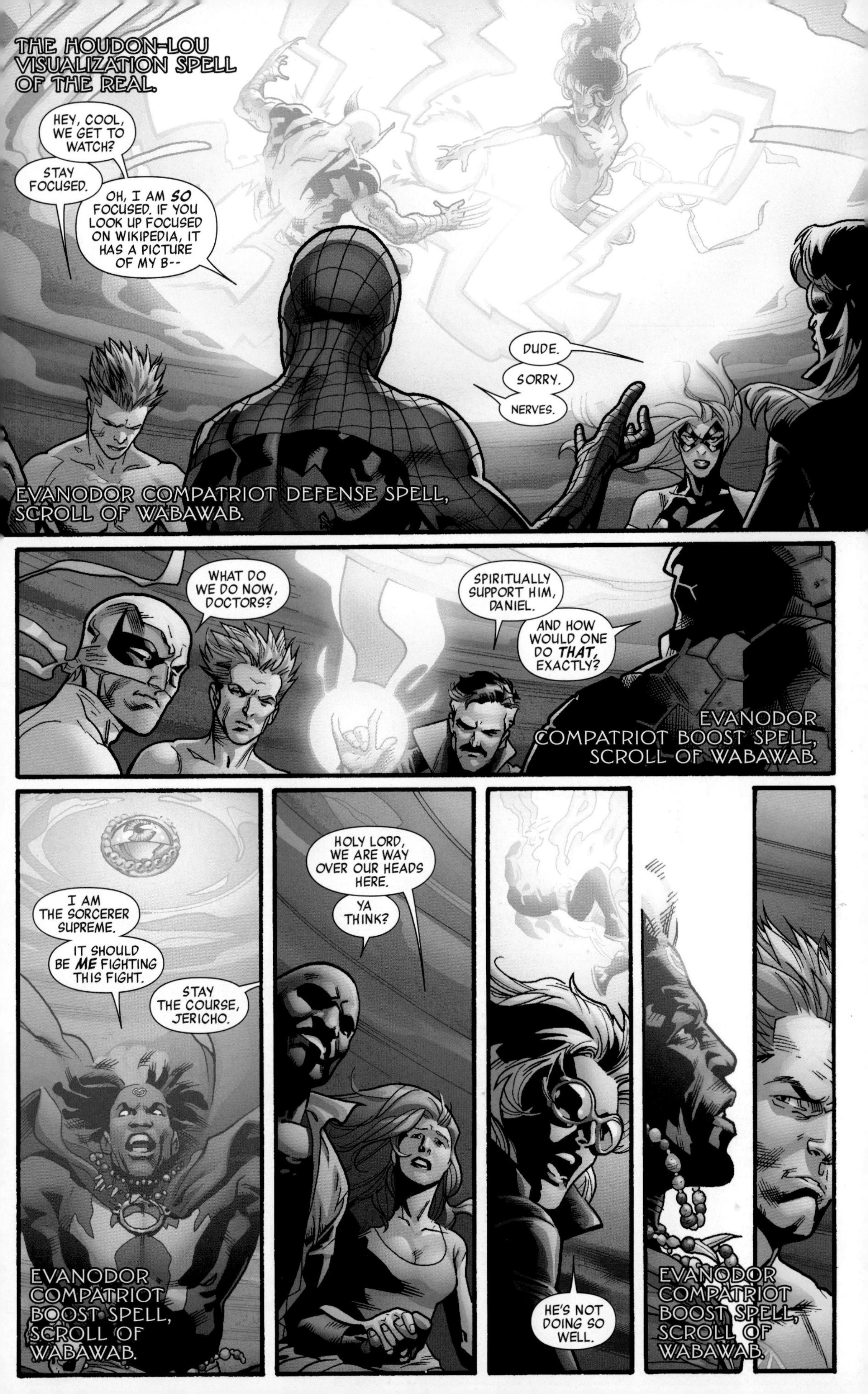
THE HOUDON-LOU VISUALIZATION SPELL OF THE REAL.
HEY, COOL, WE GET TO WATCH?
STAY FOCUSED.
OH, I AM SO FOCUSED. IF YOU LOOK UP FOCUSED ON WIKIPEDIA, IT HAS A PICTURE OF MY B--
DUDE.
SORRY.
NERVES.
EVANODOR COMPATRIOT DEFENSE SPELL, SCROLL OF WABAWAB.
WHAT DO WE DO NOW, DOCTORS?
SPIRITUALLY SUPPORT HIM, DANIEL.
AND HOW WOULD ONE DO THAT, EXACTLY?
EVANODOR COMPATRIOT BOOST SPELL, SCROLL OF WABAWAB.
I AM THE SORCERER SUPREME.
IT SHOULD BE ME FIGHTING THIS FIGHT.
STAY THE COURSE, JERICHO.
EVANODOR COMPATRIOT BOOST SPELL, SCROLL OF WABAWAB.
HOLY LORD, WE ARE WAY OVER OUR HEADS HERE.
YA THINK?
HE'S NOT DOING SO WELL.
EVANODOR COMPATRIOT BOOST SPELL, SCROLL OF WABAWAB.

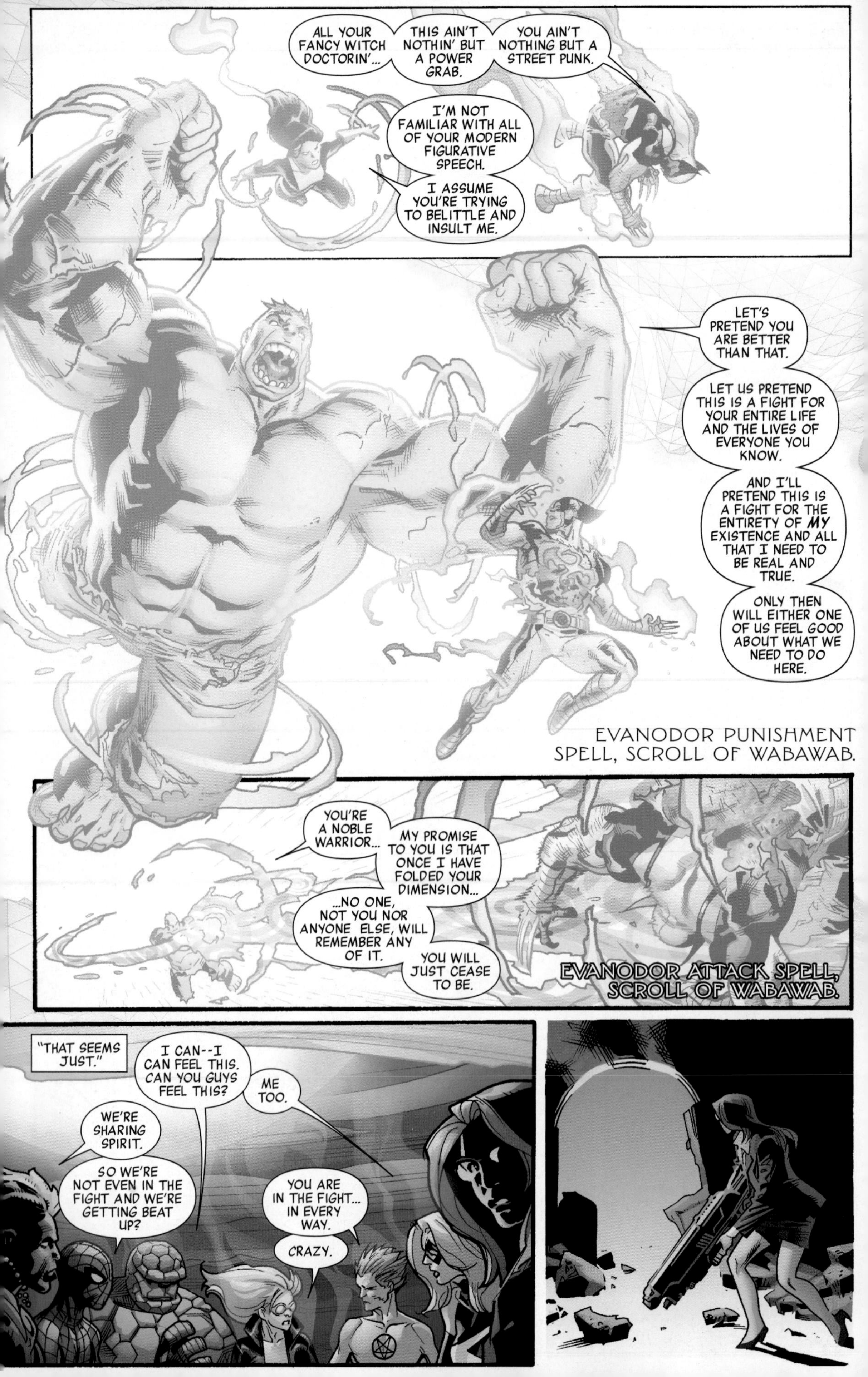

ALL YOUR FANCY WITCH DOCTORIN'...
THIS AIN'T NOTHIN' BUT A POWER GRAB.
YOU AIN'T NOTHING BUT A STREET PUNK.
I'M NOT FAMILIAR WITH ALL OF YOUR MODERN FIGURATIVE SPEECH.
I ASSUME YOU'RE TRYING TO BELITTLE AND INSULT ME.
LET'S PRETEND YOU ARE BETTER THAN THAT.
LET US PRETEND THIS IS A FIGHT FOR YOUR ENTIRE LIFE AND THE LIVES OF EVERYONE YOU KNOW.
AND I'LL PRETEND THIS IS A FIGHT FOR THE ENTIRETY OF *MY* EXISTENCE AND ALL THAT I NEED TO BE REAL AND TRUE.
ONLY THEN WILL EITHER ONE OF US FEEL GOOD ABOUT WHAT WE NEED TO DO HERE.
EVANODOR PUNISHMENT SPELL, SCROLL OF WABAWAB.
YOU'RE A NOBLE WARRIOR...
MY PROMISE TO YOU IS THAT ONCE I HAVE FOLDED YOUR DIMENSION...
...NO ONE, NOT YOU NOR ANYONE ELSE, WILL REMEMBER ANY OF IT.
YOU WILL JUST CEASE TO BE.
EVANODOR ATTACK SPELL, SCROLL OF WABAWAB.
"THAT SEEMS JUST."
I CAN--I CAN FEEL THIS. CAN YOU GUYS FEEL THIS?
ME TOO.
WE'RE SHARING SPIRIT.
SO WE'RE NOT EVEN IN THE FIGHT AND WE'RE GETTING BEAT UP?
YOU ARE IN THE FIGHT... IN EVERY WAY.
CRAZY.

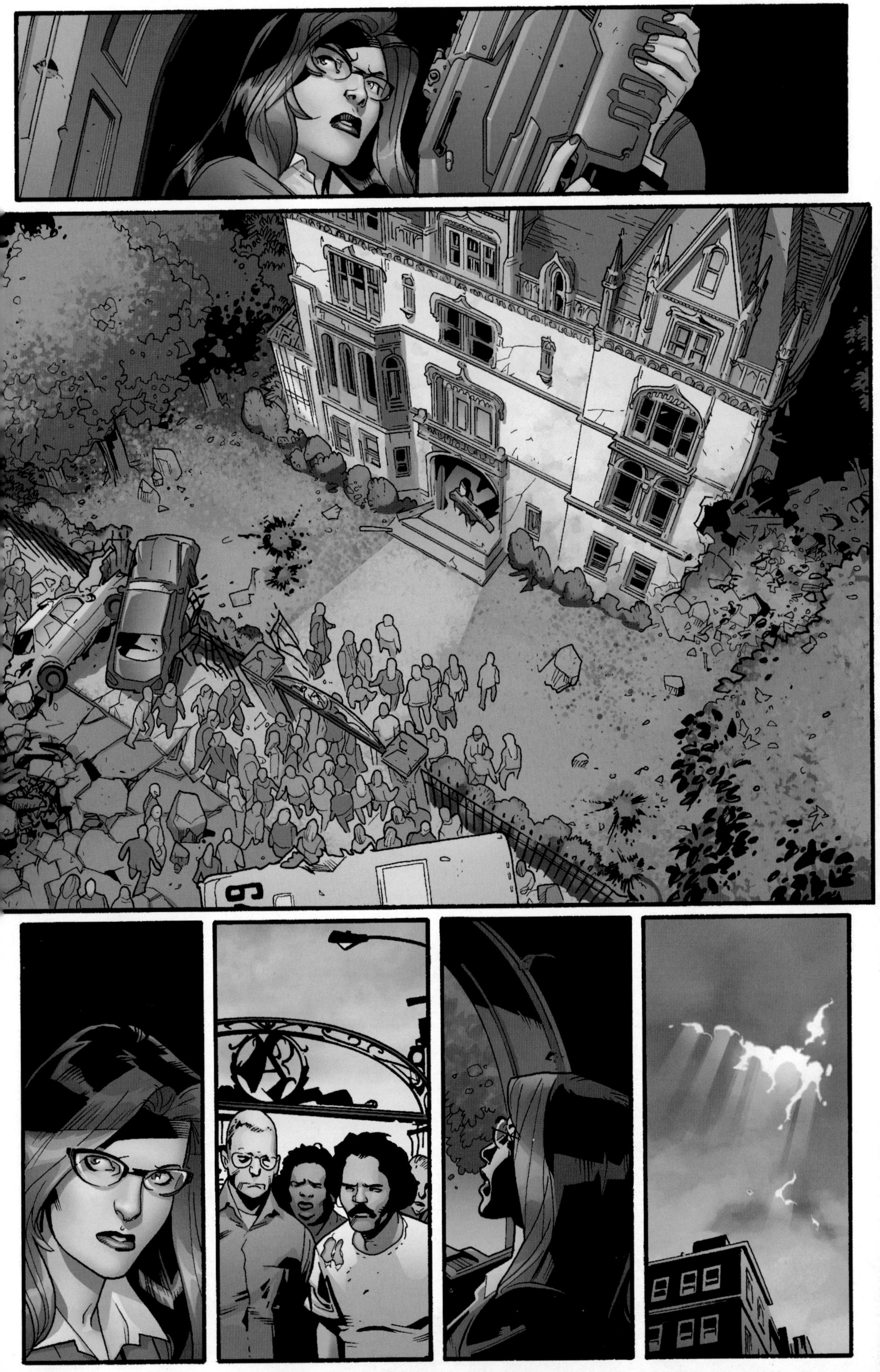

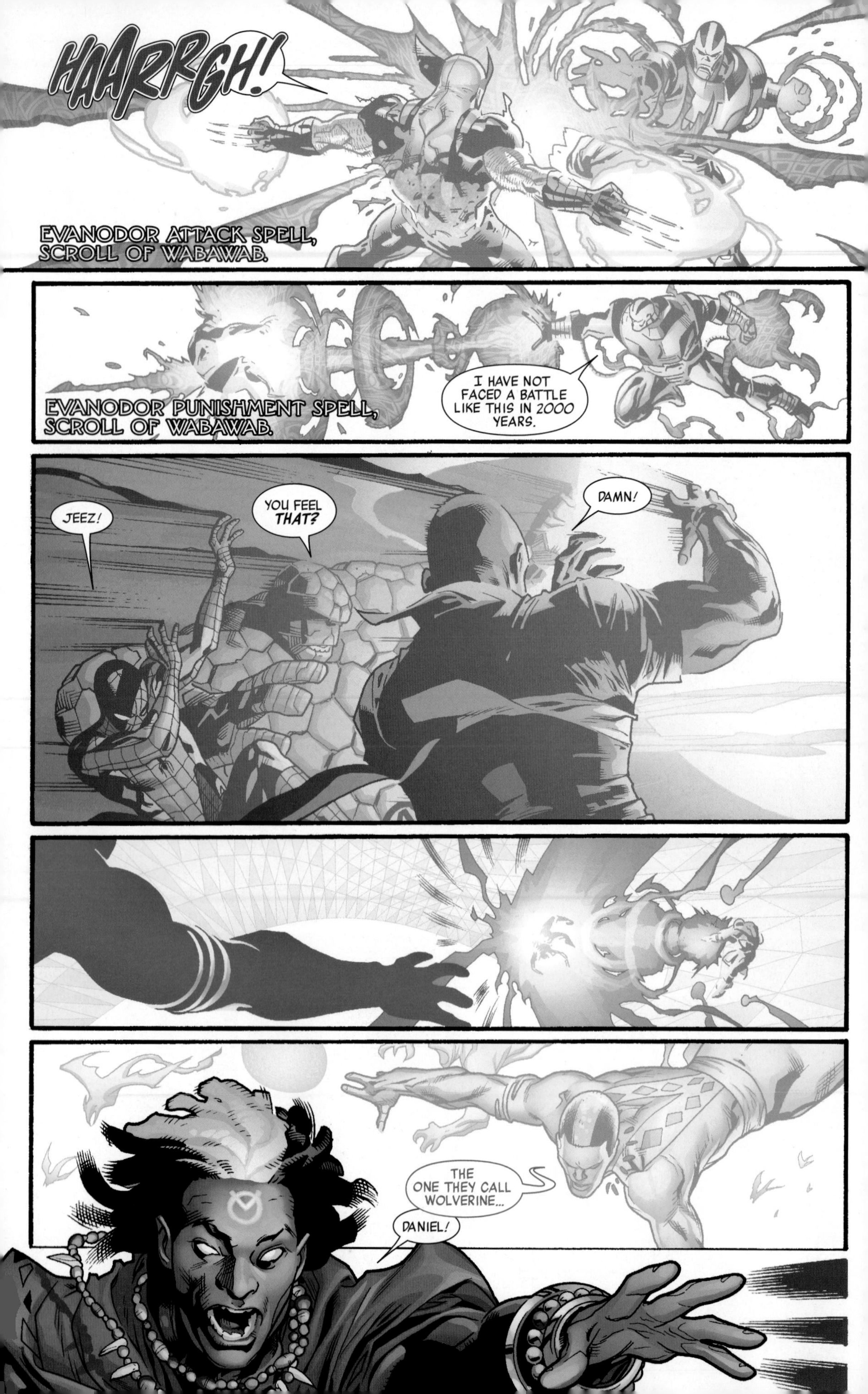
HAARRGH!
EVANODOR ATTACK SPELL, SCROLL OF WABAWAB.
EVANODOR PUNISHMENT SPELL, SCROLL OF WABAWAB.
I HAVE NOT FACED A BATTLE LIKE THIS IN 2000 YEARS.
JEEZ!
YOU FEEL THAT?
DAMN!
THE ONE THEY CALL WOLVERINE...
DANIEL!

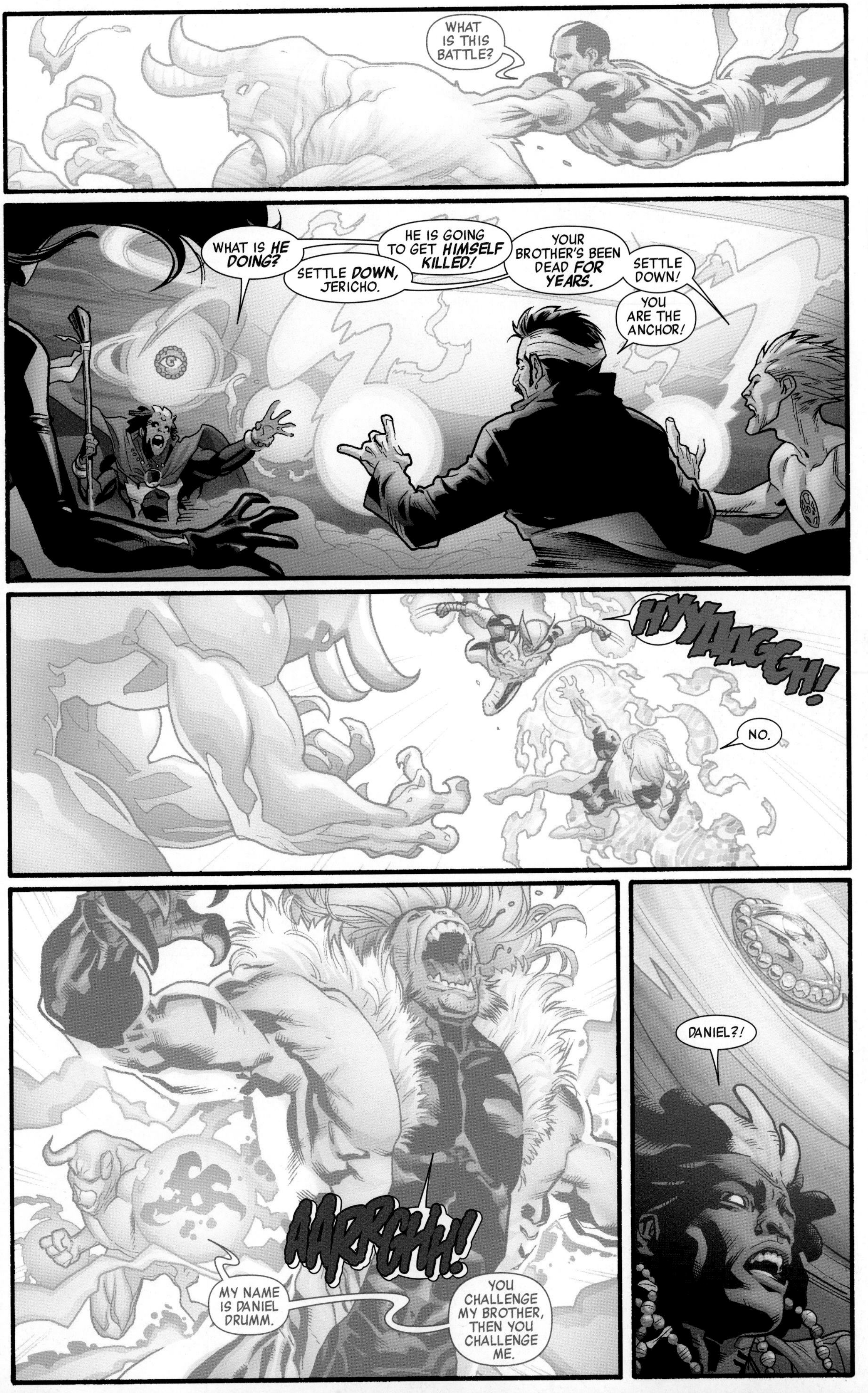
WHAT IS THIS BATTLE?
WHAT IS HE DOING?
HE IS GOING TO GET HIMSELF KILLED!
SETTLE DOWN, JERICHO.
YOUR BROTHER'S BEEN DEAD FOR YEARS.
SETTLE DOWN!
YOU ARE THE ANCHOR!
HYYAAAGGH!
NO.
AARRGHH!
MY NAME IS DANIEL DRUMM.
YOU CHALLENGE MY BROTHER, THEN YOU CHALLENGE ME.
DANIEL?!

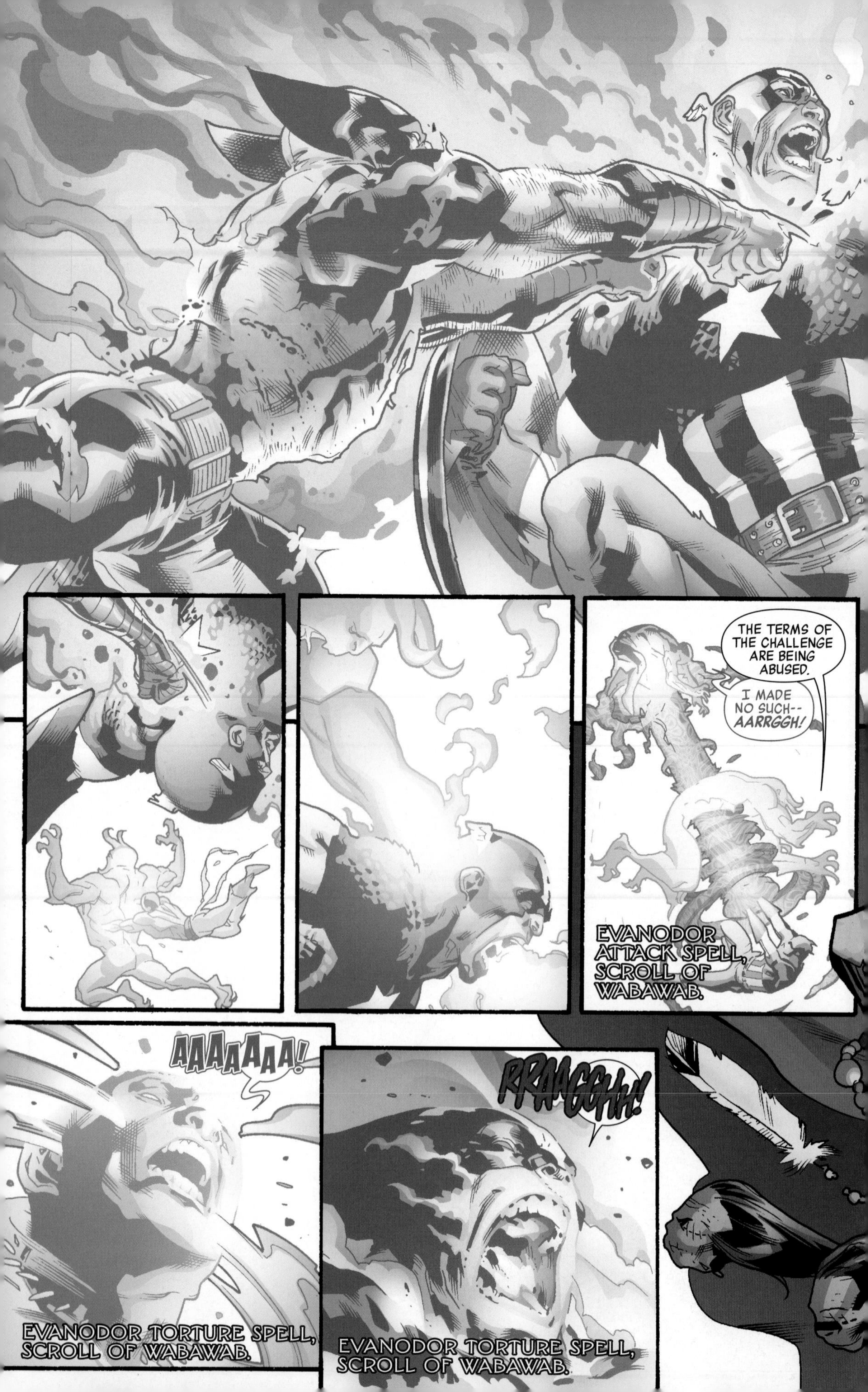
THE TERMS OF THE CHALLENGE ARE BEING ABUSED.
I MADE NO SUCH-- AARRGGH!
EVANODOR ATTACK SPELL, SCROLL OF WABAWAB.
AAAAAAA!
EVANODOR TORTURE SPELL, SCROLL OF WABAWAB.
RRAAGGHH!
EVANODOR TORTURE SPELL, SCROLL OF WABAWAB.

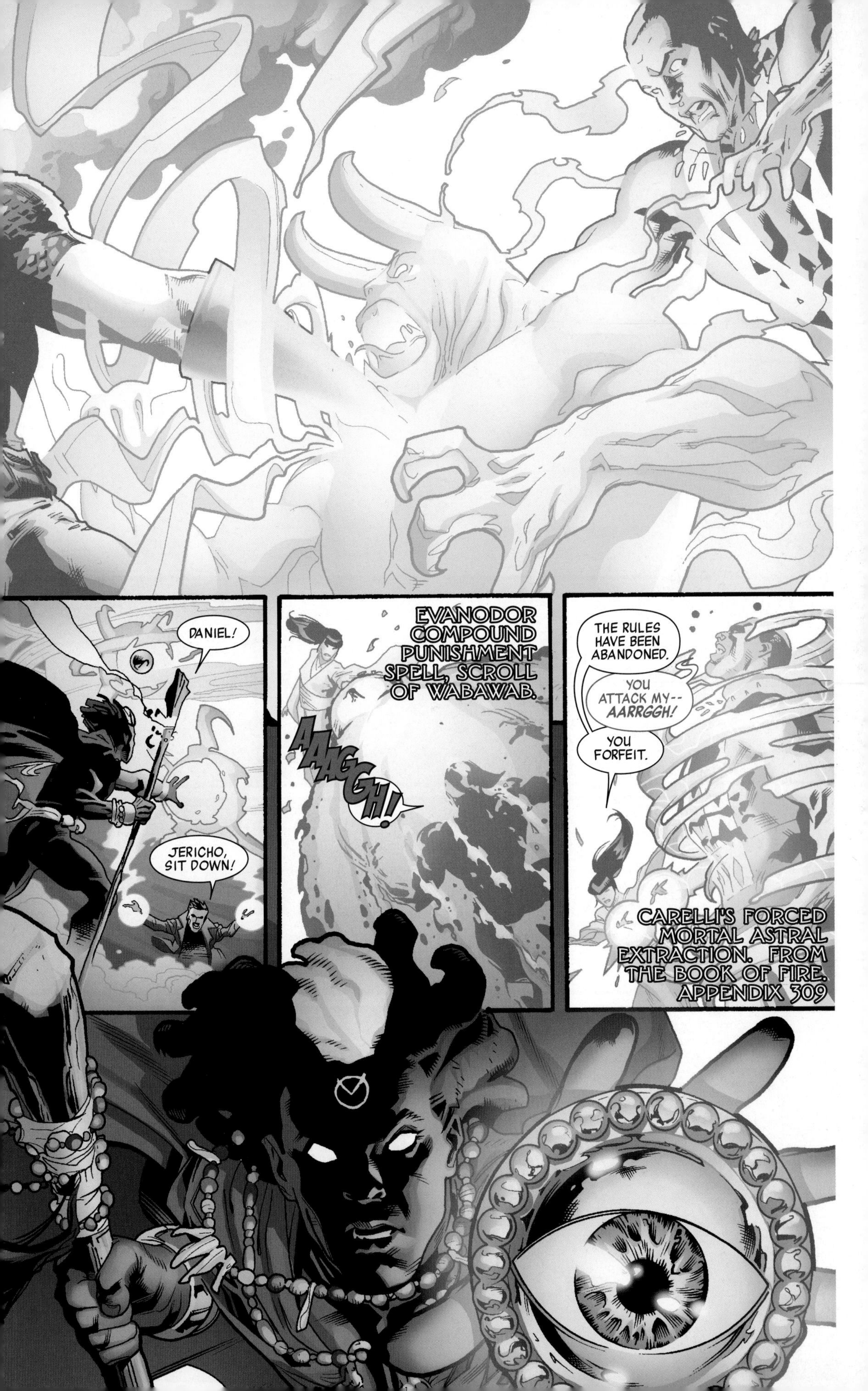
DANIEL!
JERICHO, SIT DOWN!
EVANODOR COMPOUND PUNISHMENT SPELL, SCROLL OF WABAWAB.
AAAAGGH!
THE RULES HAVE BEEN ABANDONED.
YOU ATTACK MY-- AARRGGH!
YOU FORFEIT.
CARELLI'S FORCED MORTAL ASTRAL EXTRACTION. FROM THE BOOK OF FIRE. APPENDIX 309

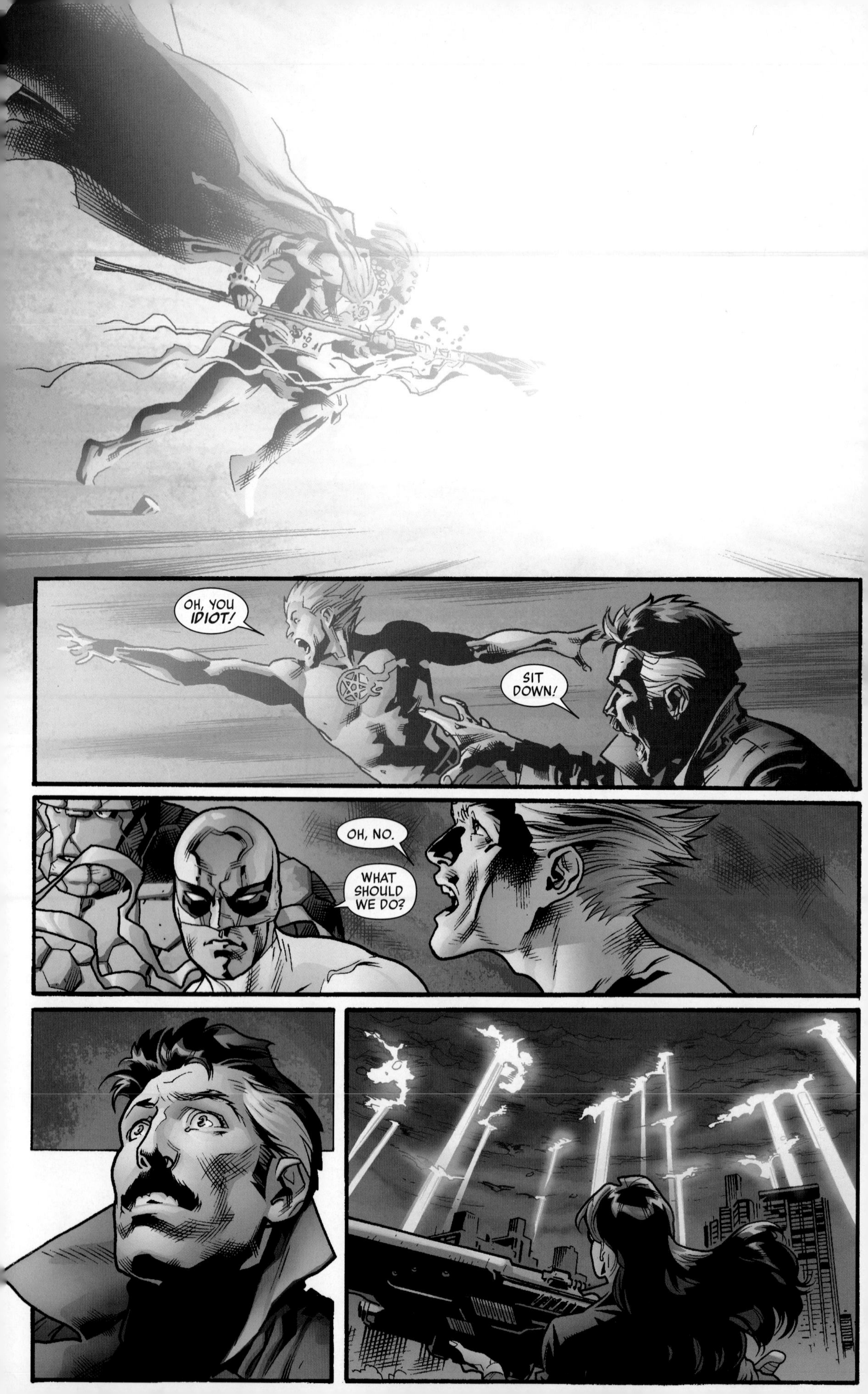
OH, YOU IDIOT!
SIT DOWN!
OH, NO.
WHAT SHOULD WE DO?

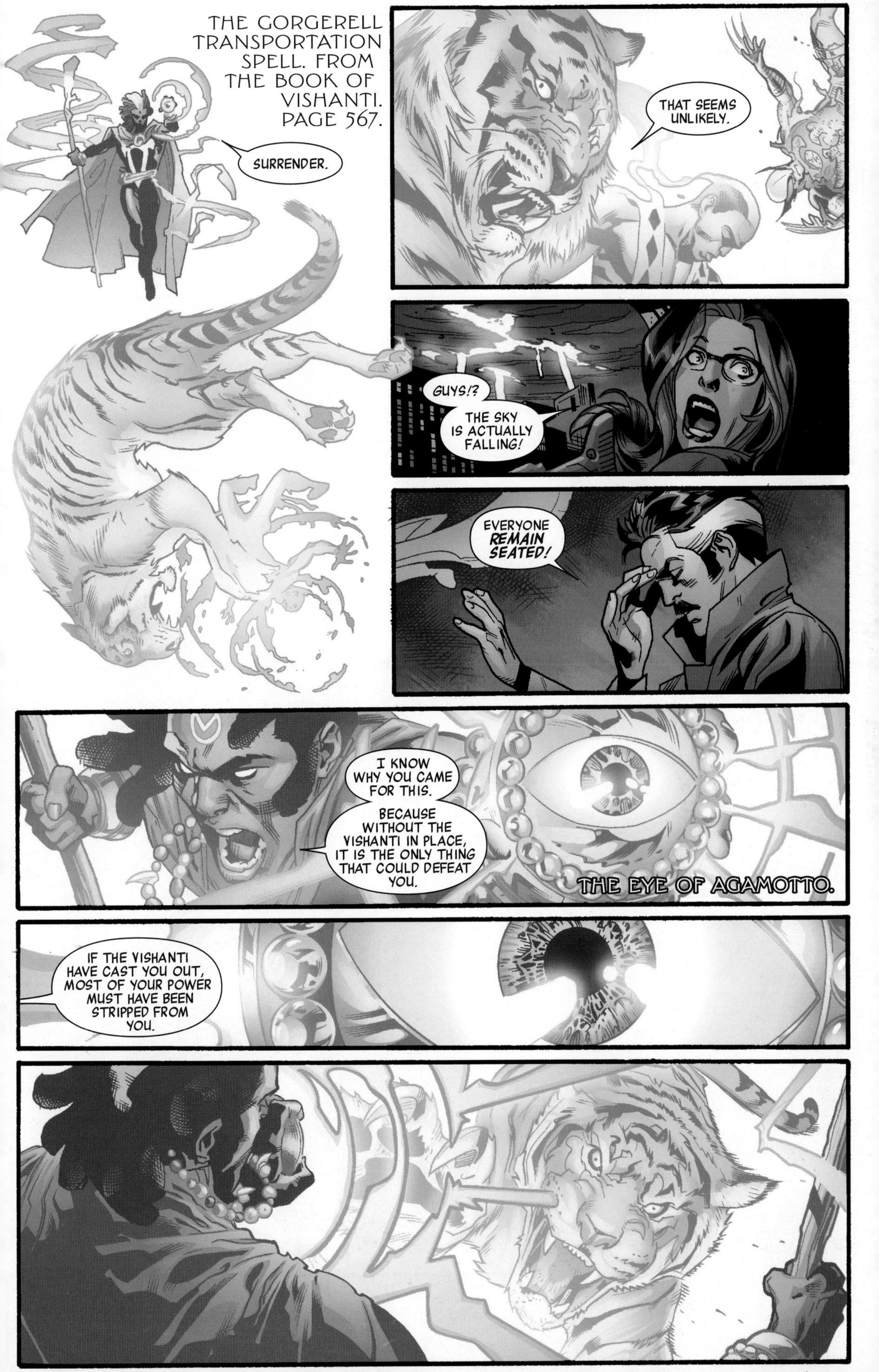
THE GORGERELL TRANSPORTATION SPELL. FROM THE BOOK OF VISHANTI. PAGE 567.
SURRENDER.
THAT SEEMS UNLIKELY.
GUYS!?
THE SKY IS ACTUALLY FALLING!
EVERYONE REMAIN SEATED!
I KNOW WHY YOU CAME FOR THIS.
BECAUSE WITHOUT THE VISHANTI IN PLACE, IT IS THE ONLY THING THAT COULD DEFEAT YOU.
THE EYE OF AGAMOTTO.
IF THE VISHANTI HAVE CAST YOU OUT, MOST OF YOUR POWER MUST HAVE BEEN STRIPPED FROM YOU.

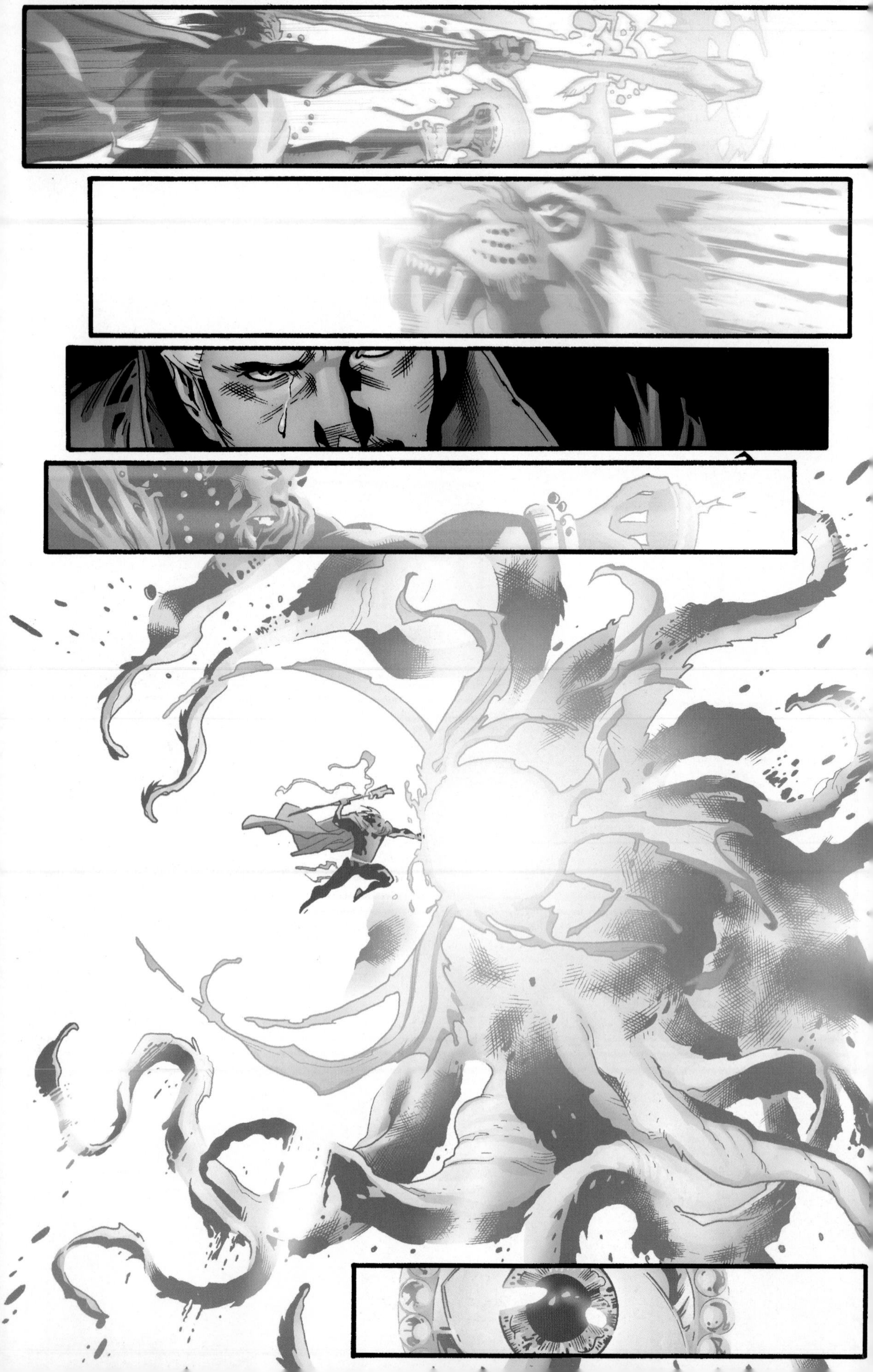

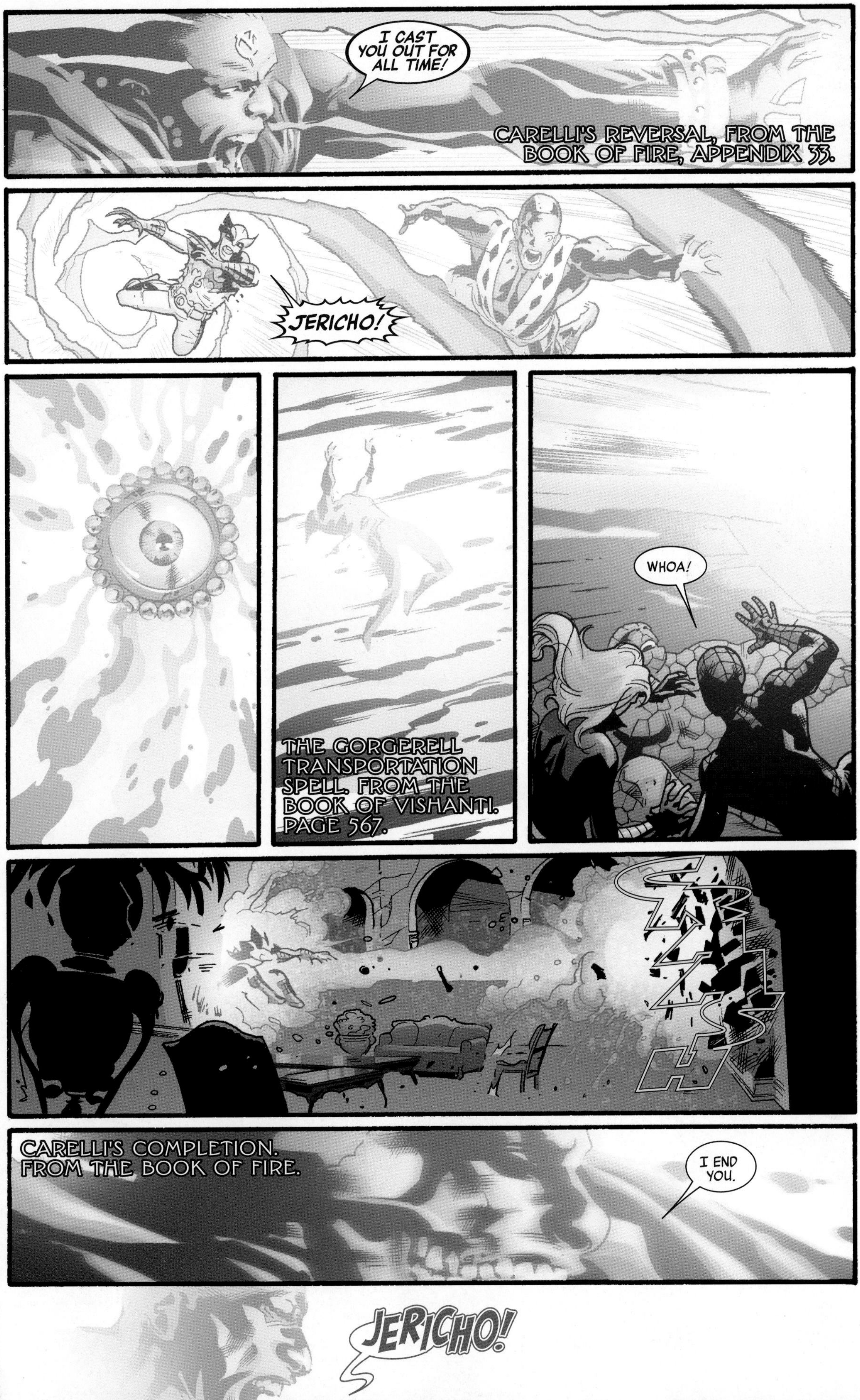
I CAST YOU OUT FOR ALL TIME!
CARELLI'S REVERSAL, FROM THE BOOK OF FIRE, APPENDIX 33.
JERICHO!
THE GORGERELL TRANSPORTATION SPELL. FROM THE BOOK OF VISHANTI. PAGE 567.
WHOA!
CRASH
CARELLI'S COMPLETION. FROM THE BOOK OF FIRE.
I END YOU.
JERICHO!

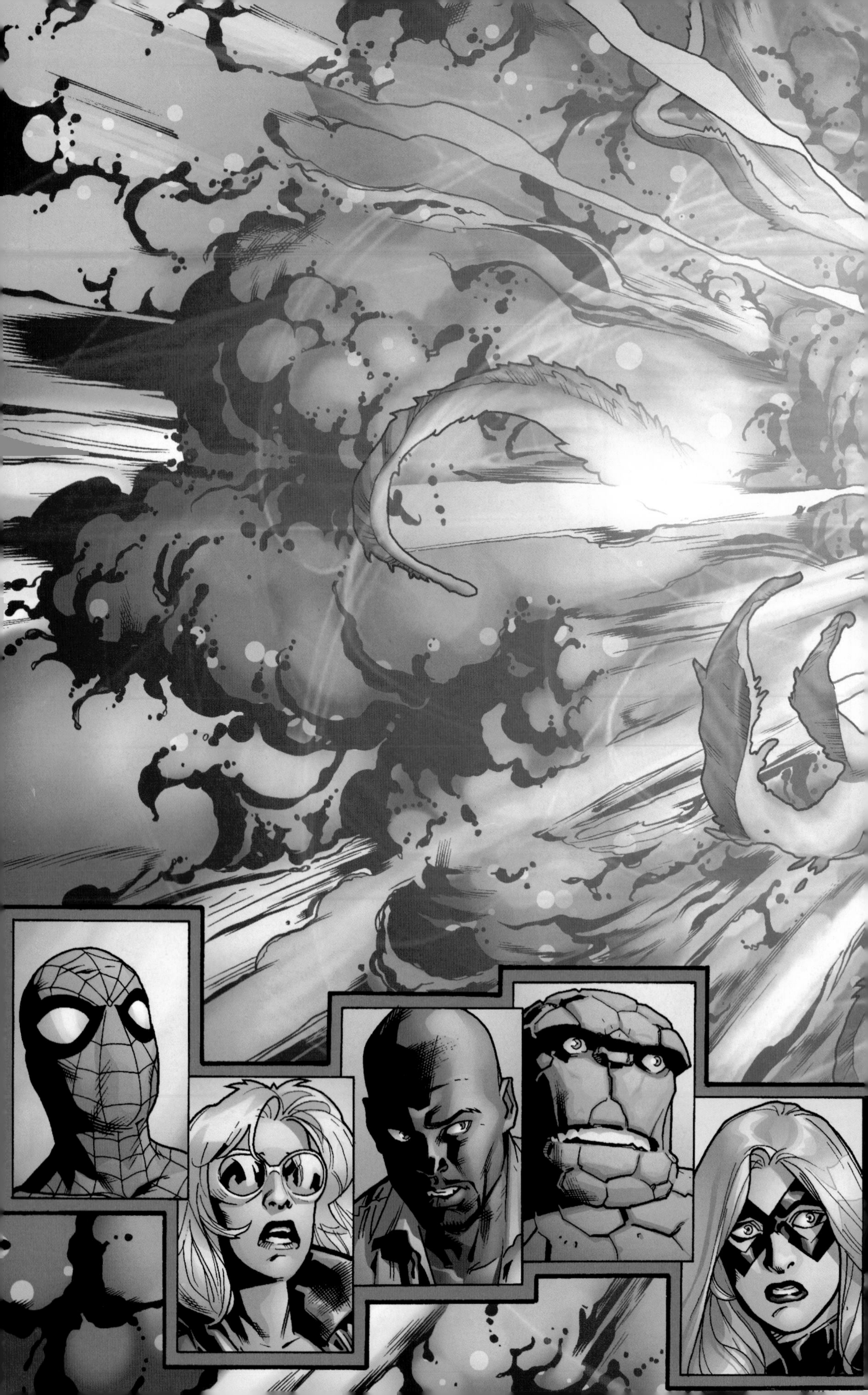

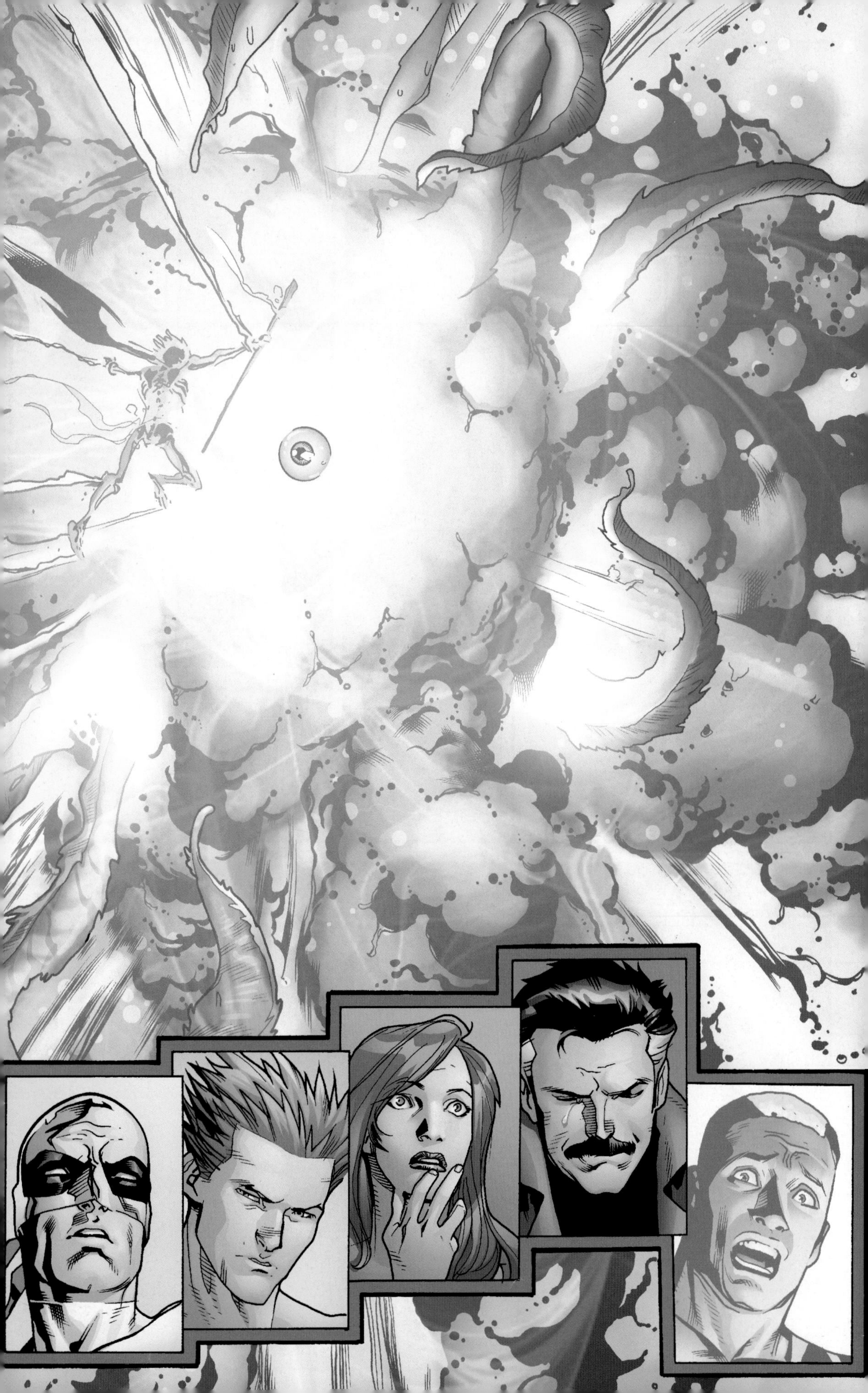

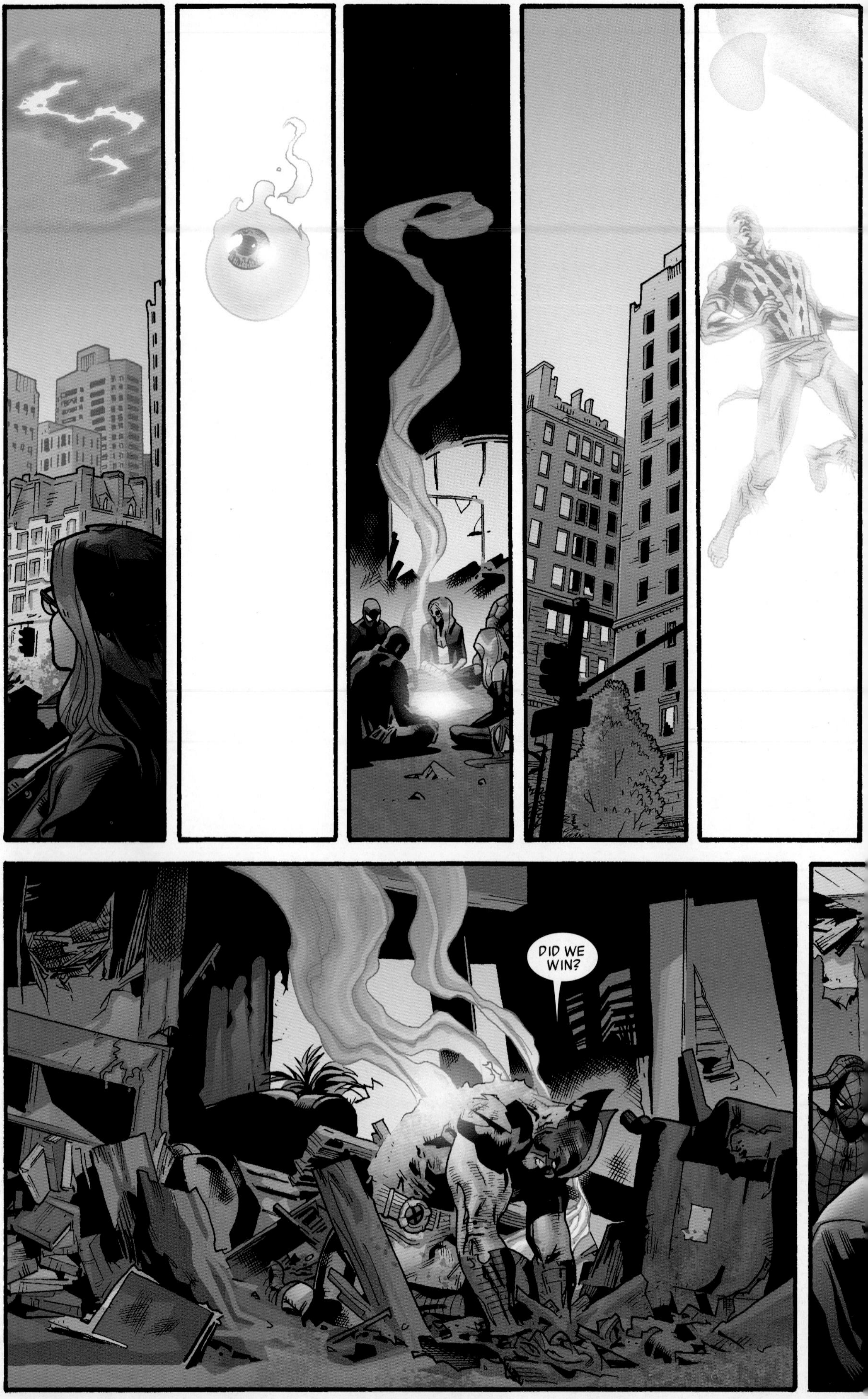
DID WE WIN?

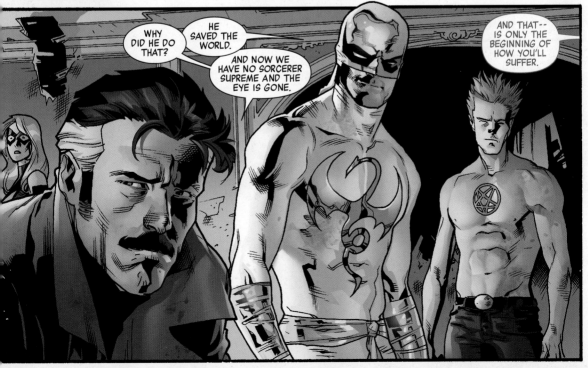

WHY DID HE DO THAT?

HE SAVED THE WORLD.

AND NOW WE HAVE NO SORCERER SUPREME AND THE EYE IS GONE.

AND THAT-- IS ONLY THE BEGINNING OF HOW YOU'LL SUFFER.

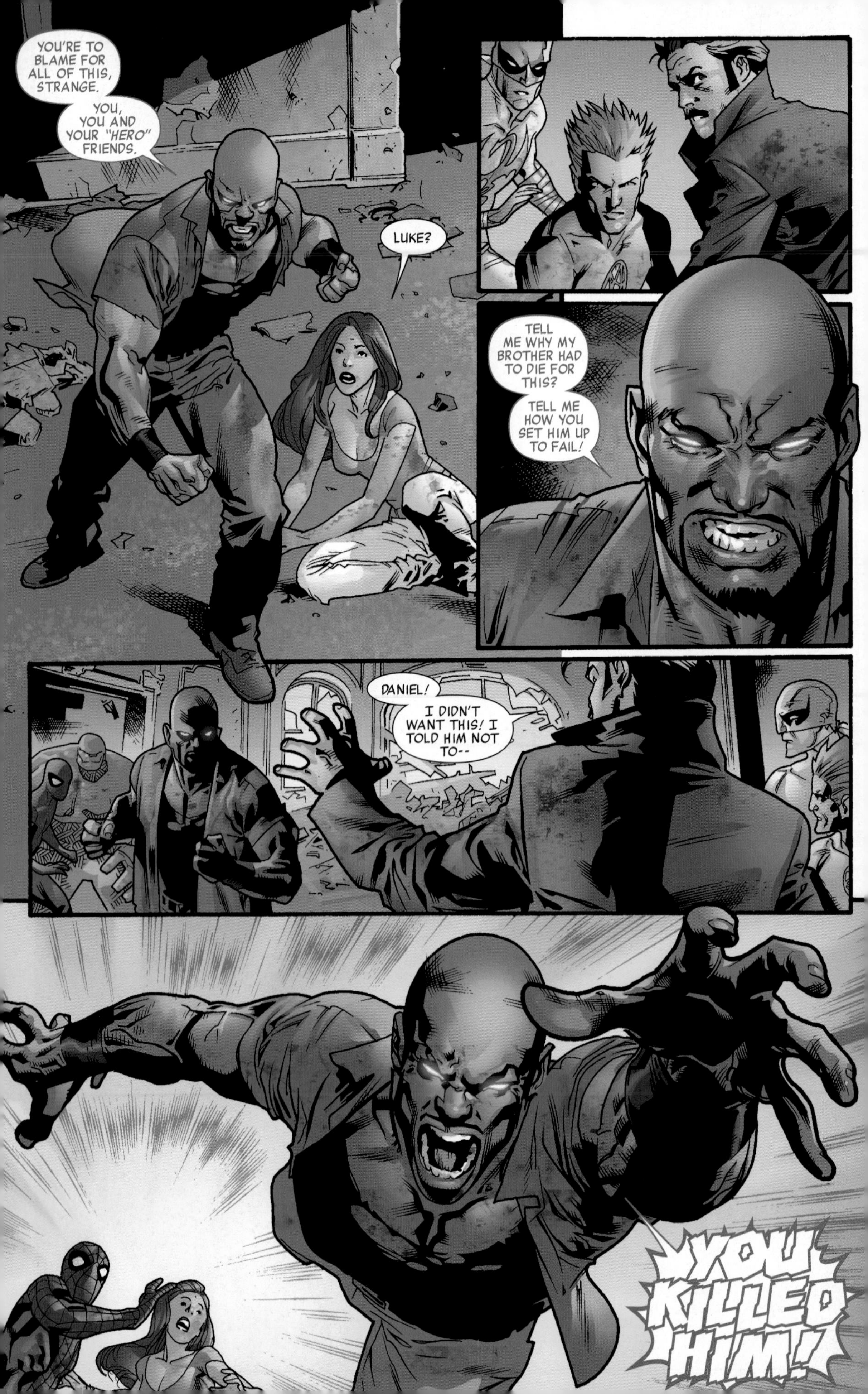
YOU'RE TO BLAME FOR ALL OF THIS, STRANGE.
YOU, YOU AND YOUR "HERO" FRIENDS.
LUKE?
TELL ME WHY MY BROTHER HAD TO DIE FOR THIS?
TELL ME HOW YOU SET HIM UP TO FAIL!
DANIEL!
I DIDN'T WANT THIS! I TOLD HIM NOT TO--
YOU KILLED HIM!

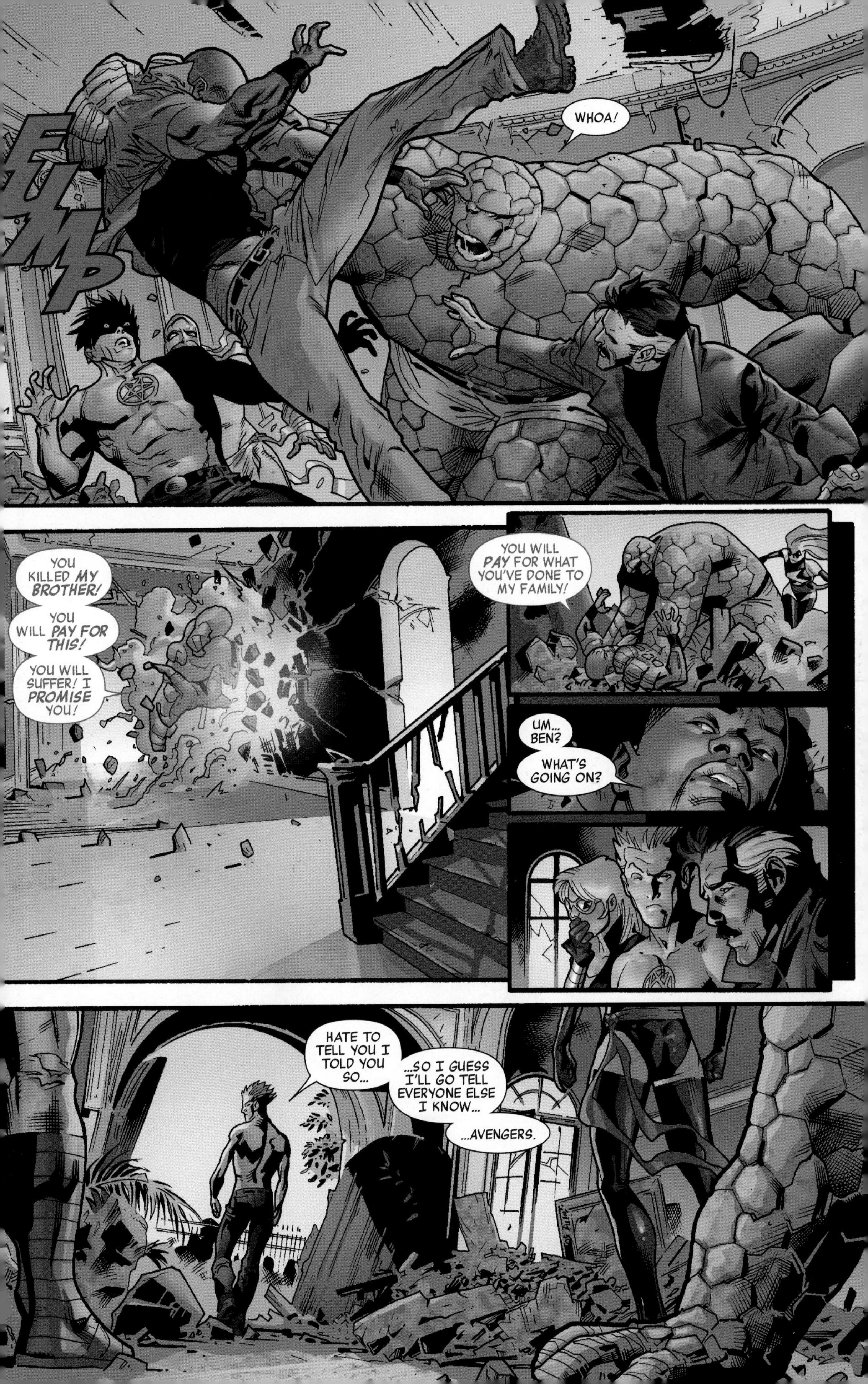

FUMP
WHOA!
YOU KILLED MY BROTHER!
YOU WILL PAY FOR THIS!
YOU WILL SUFFER! I PROMISE YOU!
YOU WILL PAY FOR WHAT YOU'VE DONE TO MY FAMILY!
UM... BEN?
WHAT'S GOING ON?
HATE TO TELL YOU I TOLD YOU SO...
...SO I GUESS I'LL GO TELL EVERYONE ELSE I KNOW...
...AVENGERS.

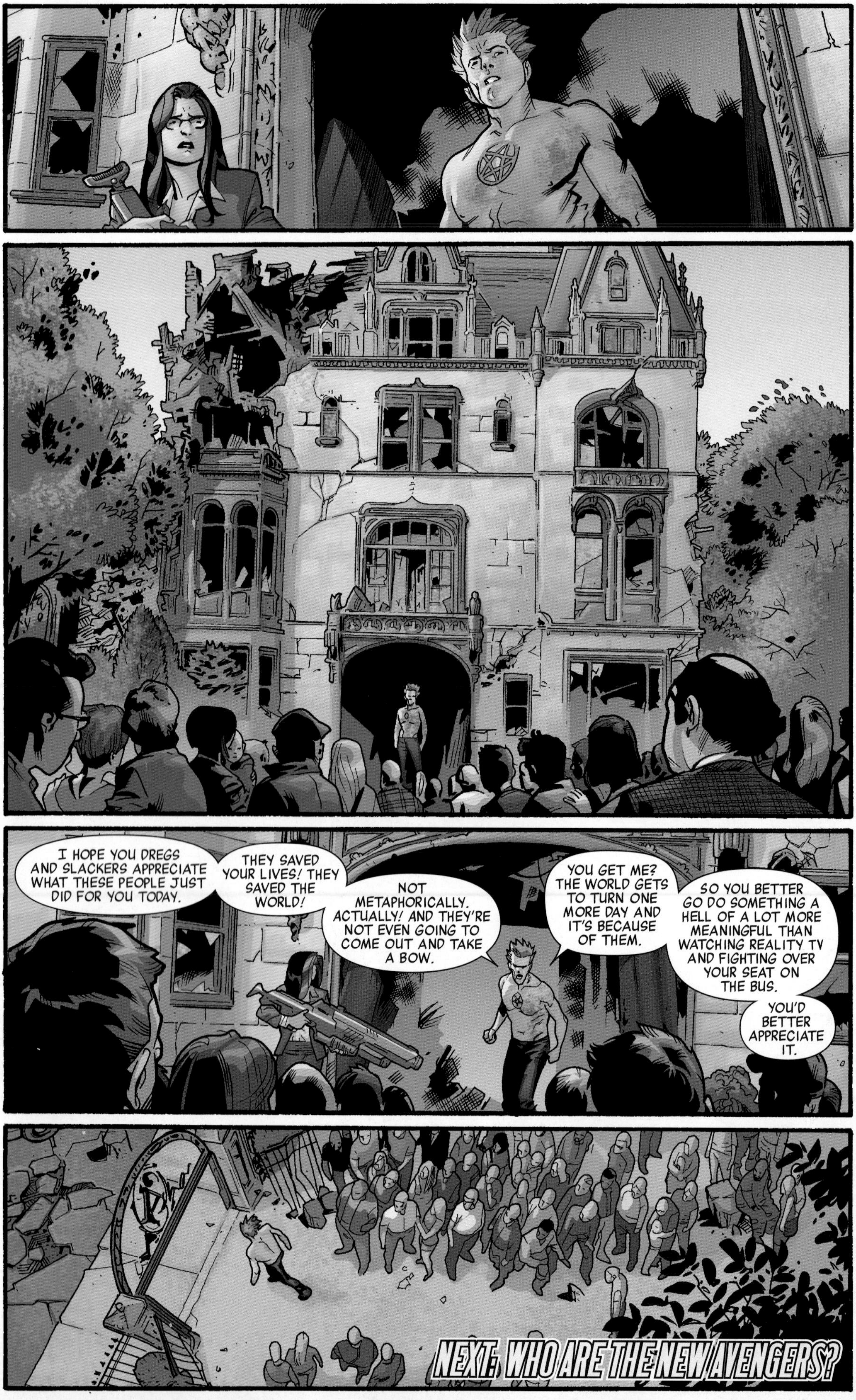
I HOPE YOU DREGS AND SLACKERS APPRECIATE WHAT THESE PEOPLE JUST DID FOR YOU TODAY.
THEY SAVED YOUR LIVES! THEY SAVED THE WORLD!
NOT METAPHORICALLY. ACTUALLY! AND THEY'RE NOT EVEN GOING TO COME OUT AND TAKE A BOW.
YOU GET ME? THE WORLD GETS TO TURN ONE MORE DAY AND IT'S BECAUSE OF THEM.
SO YOU BETTER GO DO SOMETHING A HELL OF A LOT MORE MEANINGFUL THAN WATCHING REALITY TV AND FIGHTING OVER YOUR SEAT ON THE BUS.
YOU'D BETTER APPRECIATE IT.
NEXT: WHO ARE THE NEW AVENGERS?

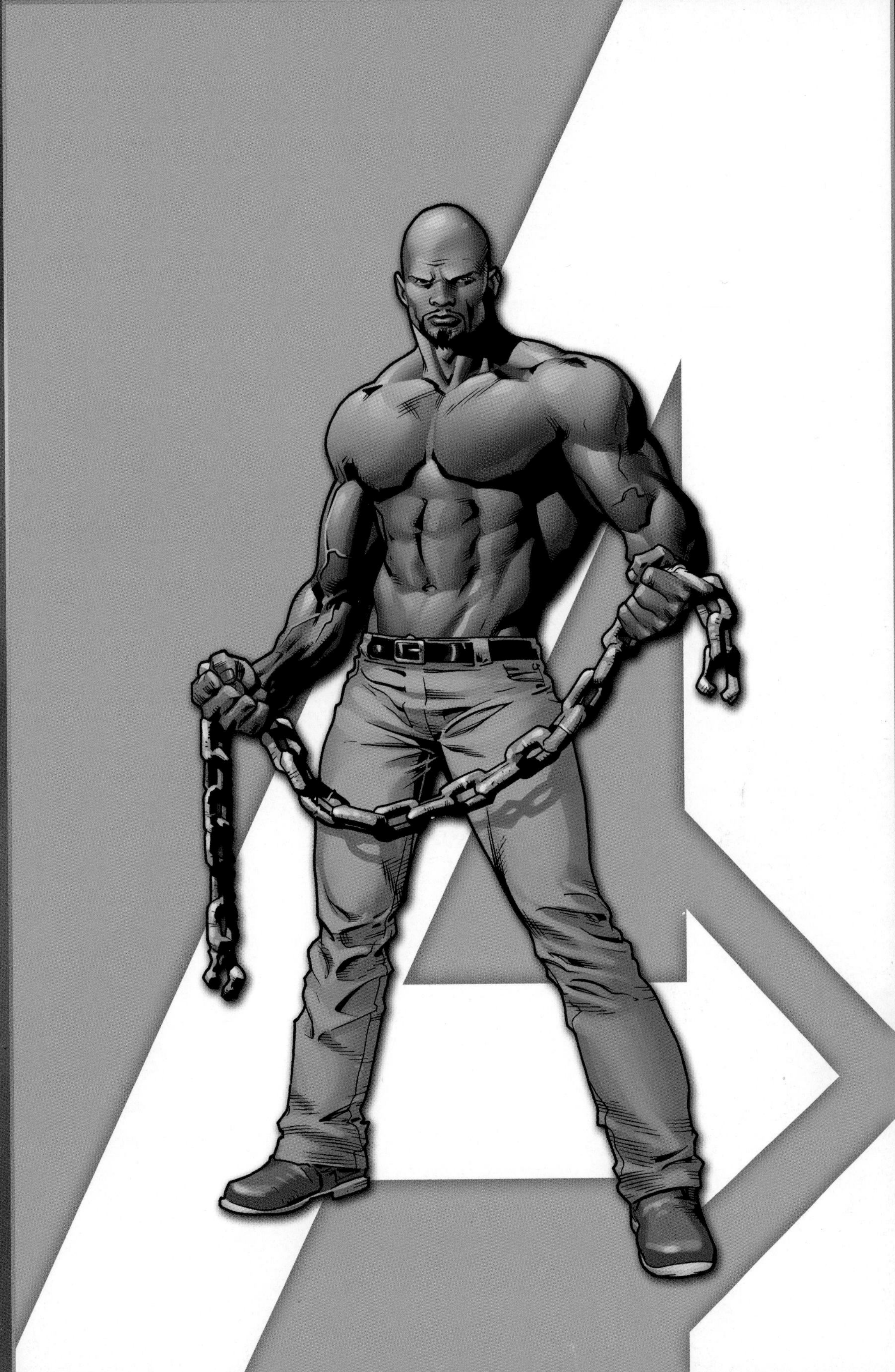

#1 VARIANT BY STUART IMMONEN,
WADE VON GRAWBADGER & LAURA MARTIN

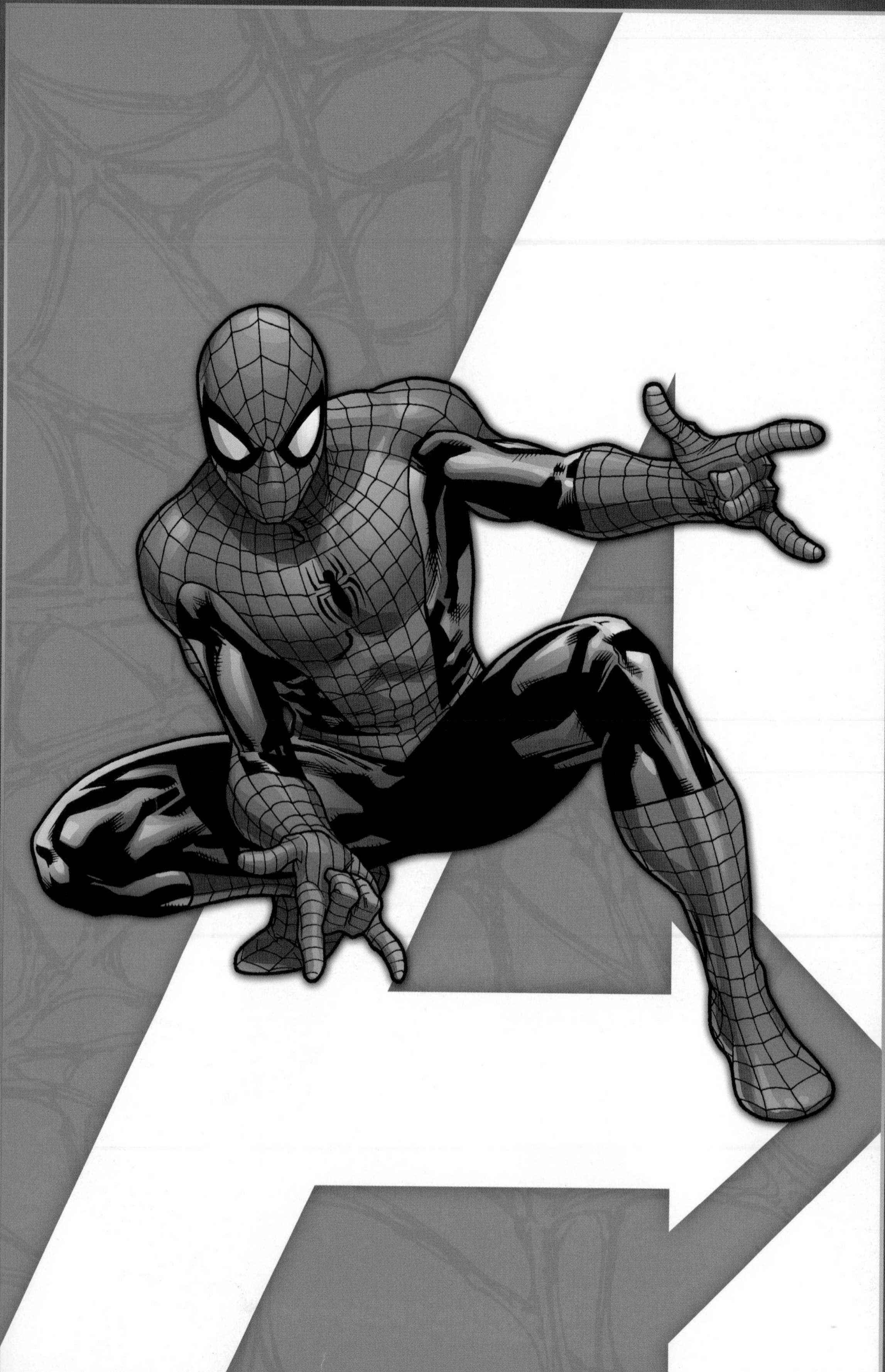

#2 VARIANT BY STUART IMMONEN,
WADE VON GRAWBADGER & LAURA MARTIN

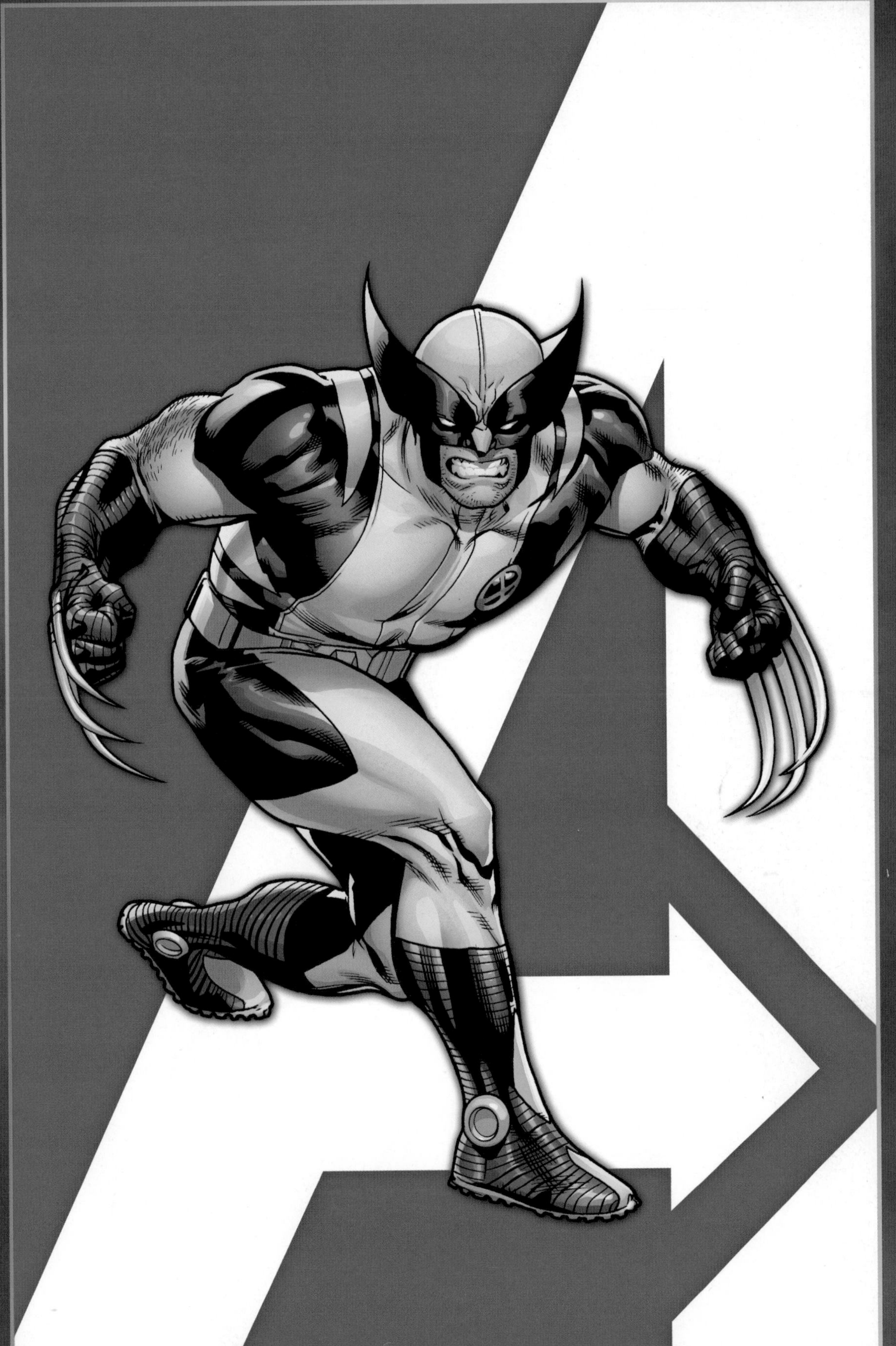

#3 VARIANT BY STUART IMMONEN,
WADE VON GRAWBADGER & LAURA MARTIN

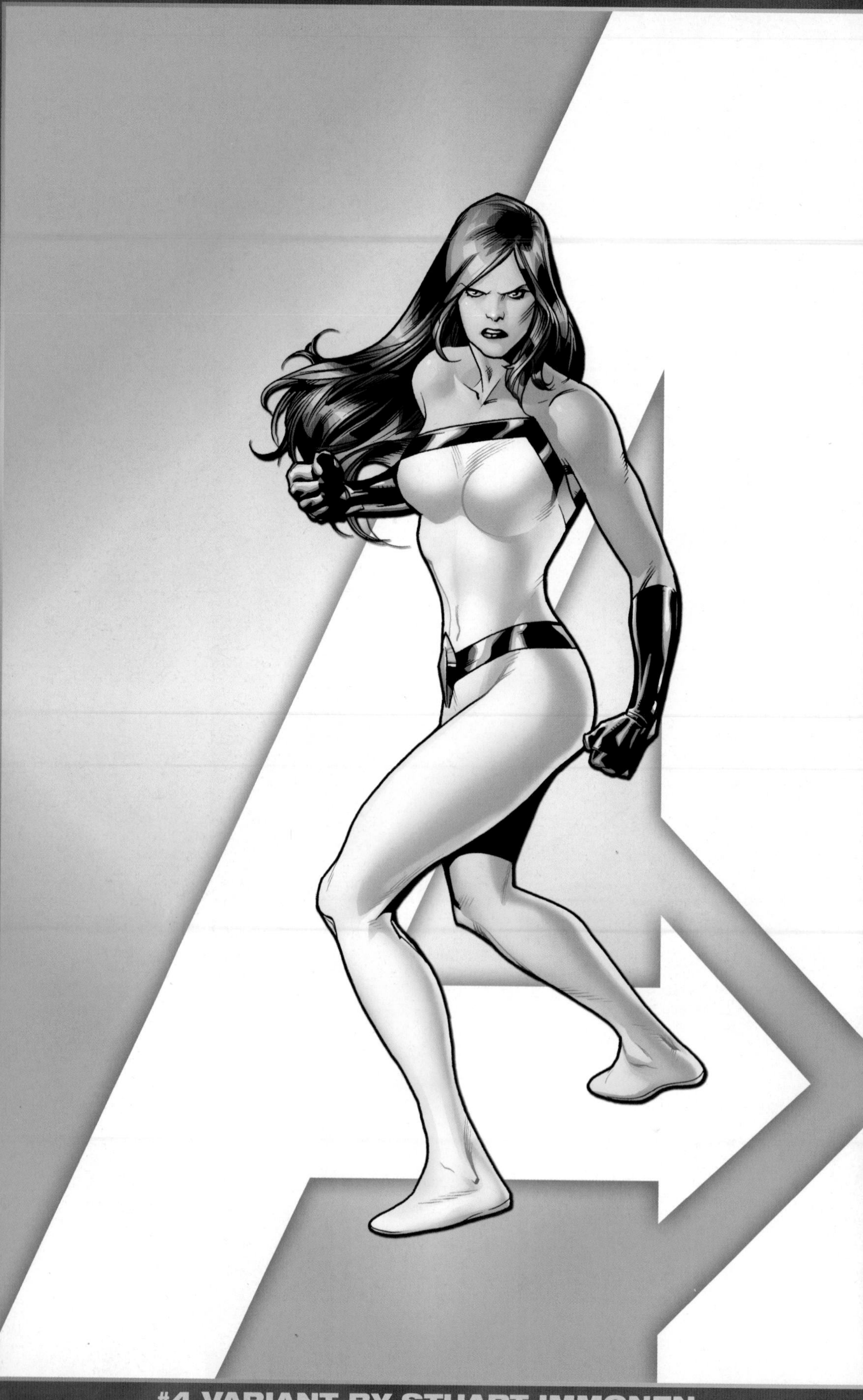

#4 VARIANT BY STUART IMMONEN,
WADE VON GRAWBADGER & LAURA MARTIN

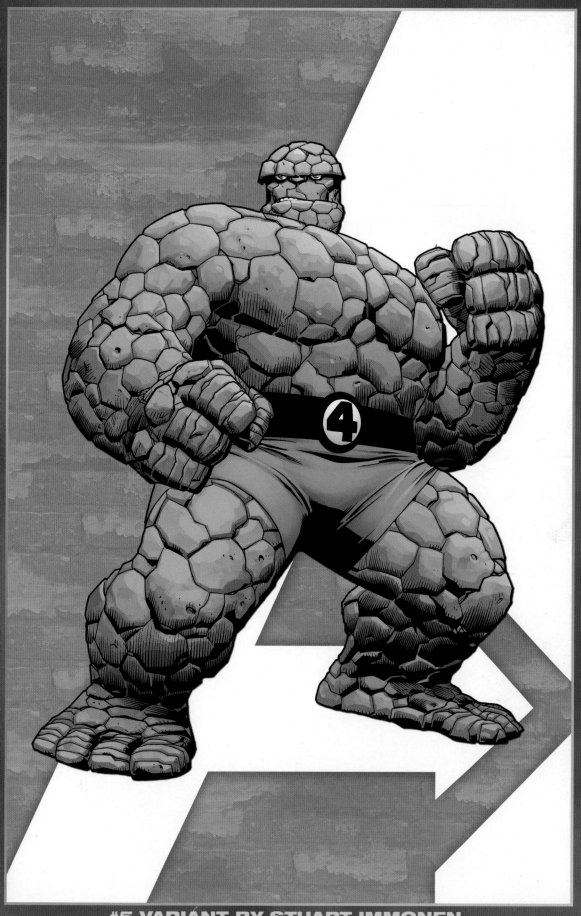

**#5 VARIANT BY STUART IMMONEN,
WADE VON GRAWBADGER & LAURA MARTIN**

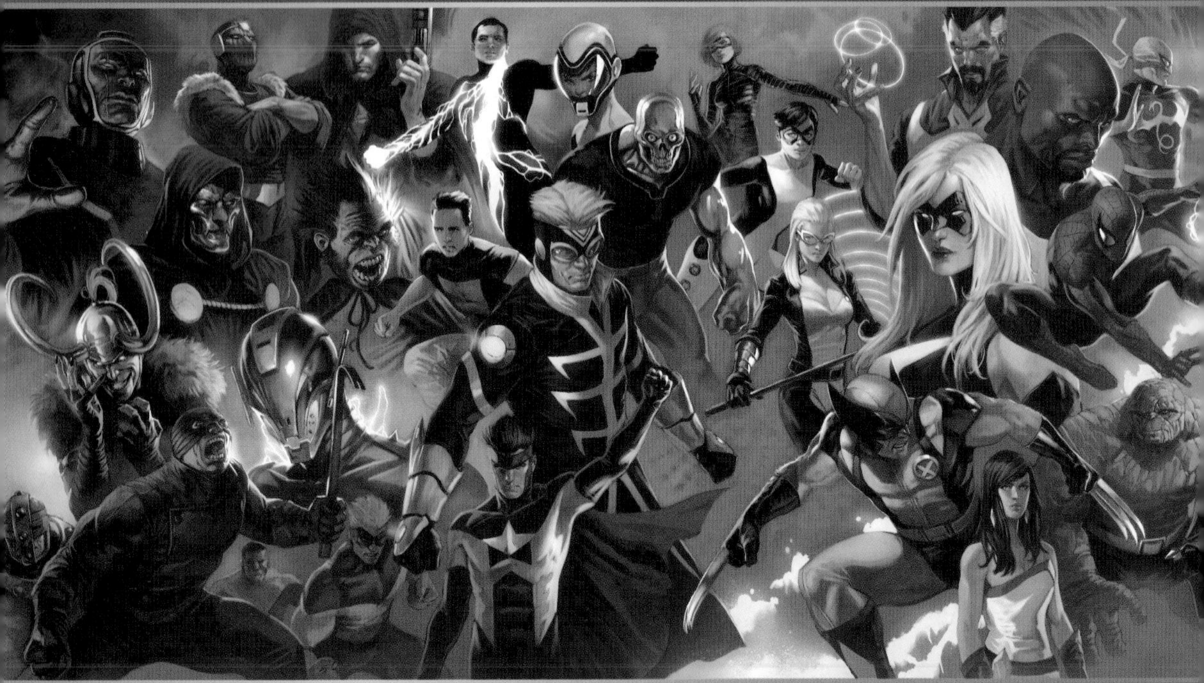

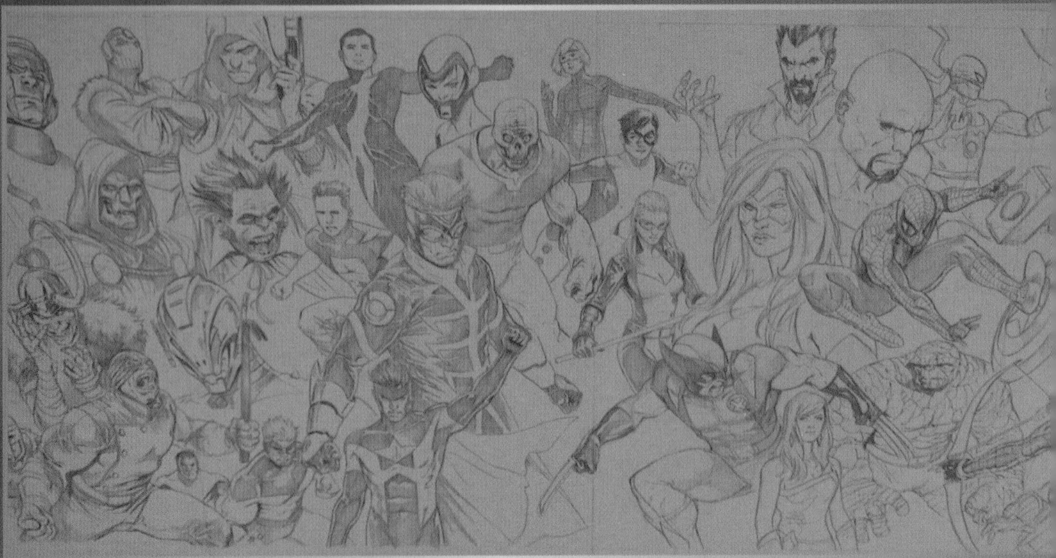

HAWKEYE & MOCKINGBIRD #1, AVENGERS ACADEMY #1, AVENGERS #1, NEW AVENGERS #1, SECRET AVENGERS #1 & AVENGERS PRIME #1

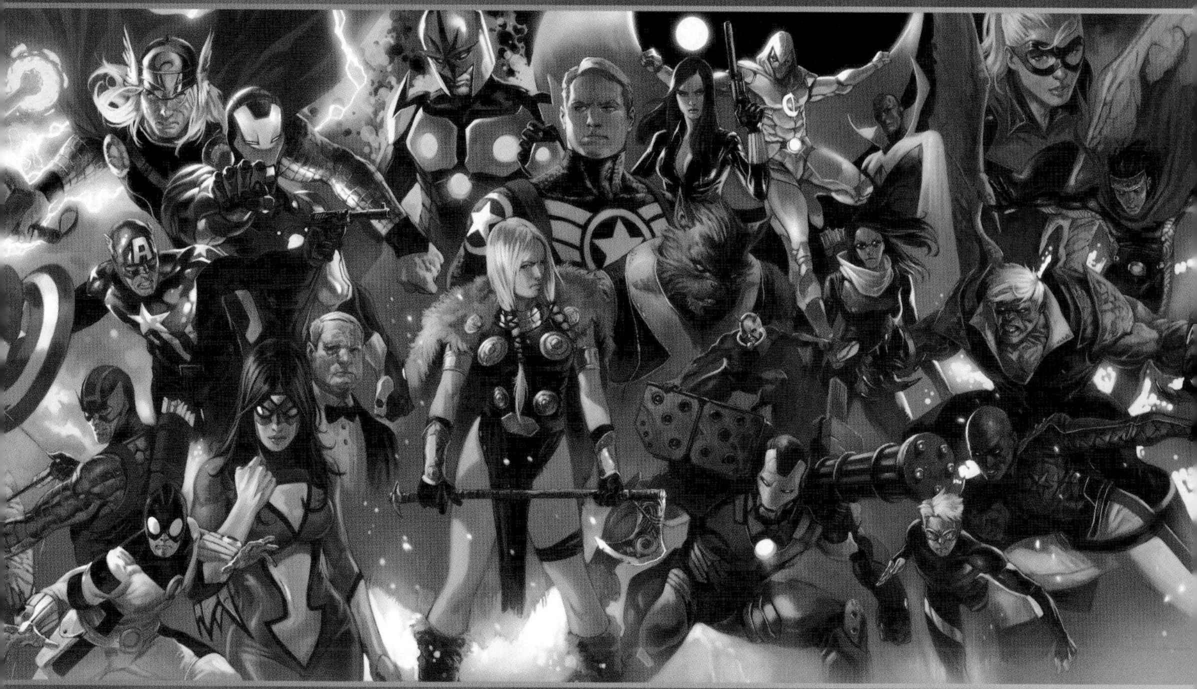

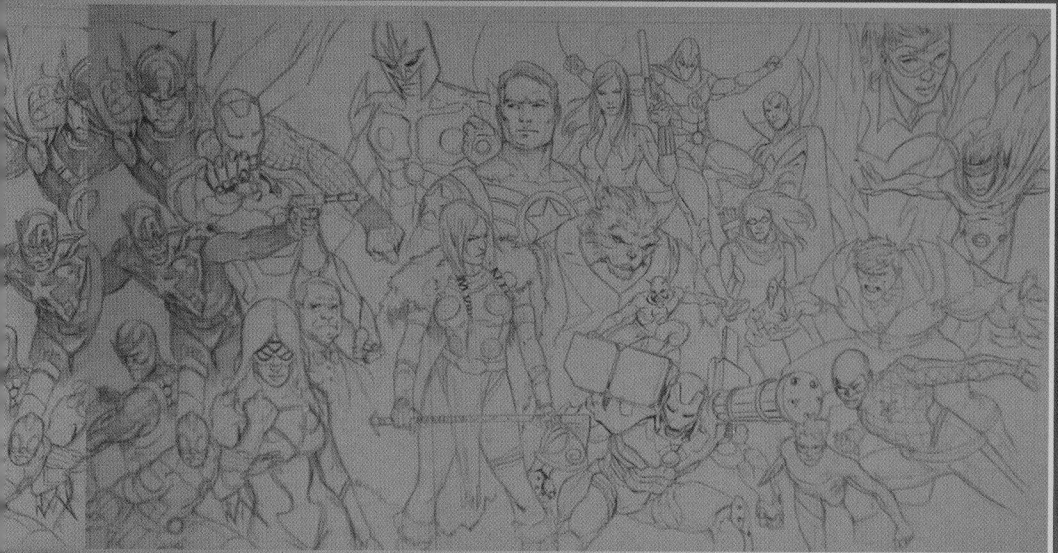

COMBINED VARIANTS
BY MARKO DJURDJEVIC

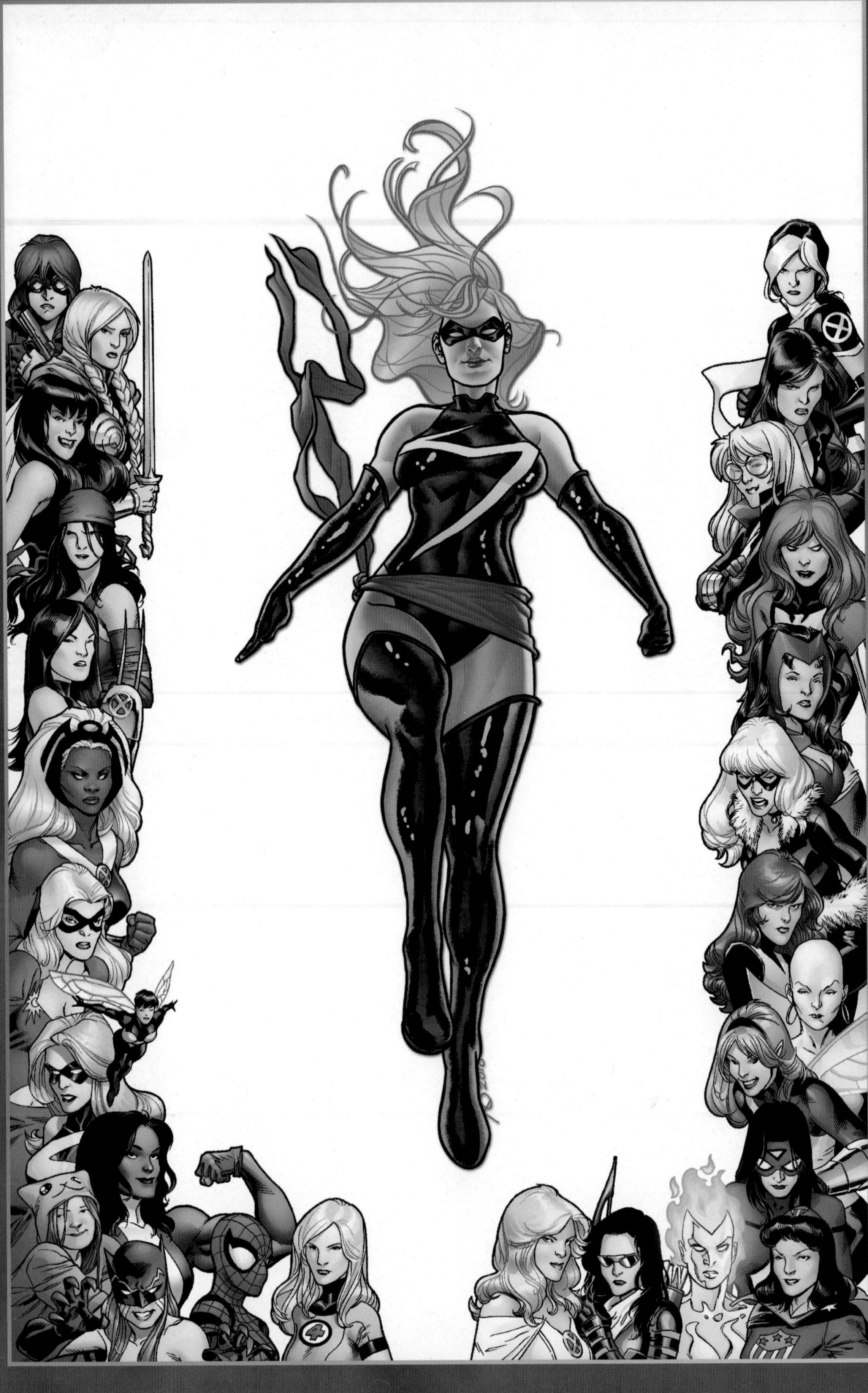

#3 WOMEN OF MARVEL FRAME VARIANT BY JOE QUINONES

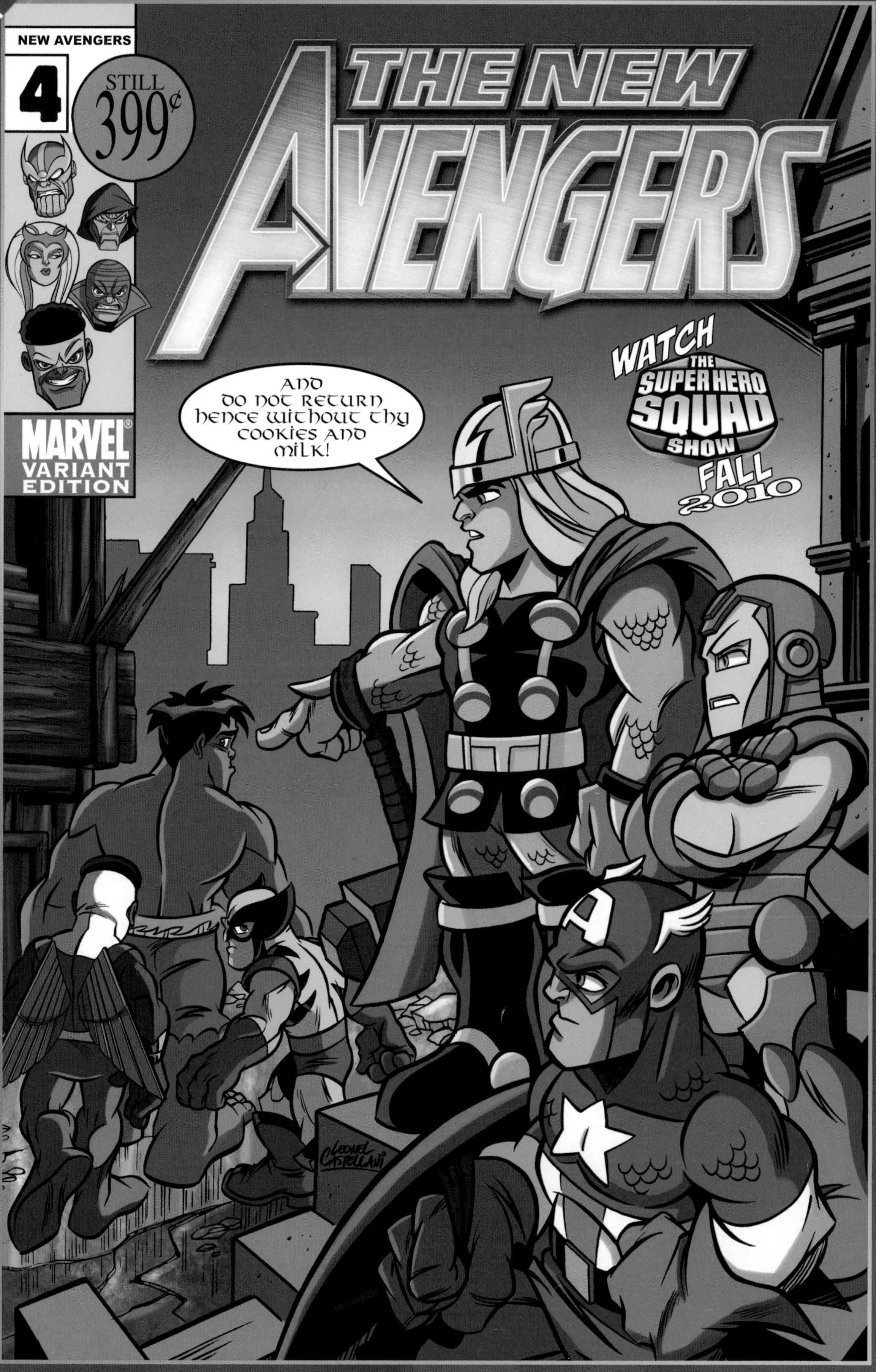
NEW AVENGERS
4
STILL 399¢
THE NEW AVENGERS
MARVEL VARIANT EDITION
AND DO NOT RETURN HENCE WITHOUT THY COOKIES AND MILK!
WATCH THE SUPER HERO SQUAD SHOW FALL 2010
LEONEL CASTELLANI

#4 SUPER HERO SQUAD VARIANT BY
LEONEL CASTELLANI & CHRIS SOTOMAYOR

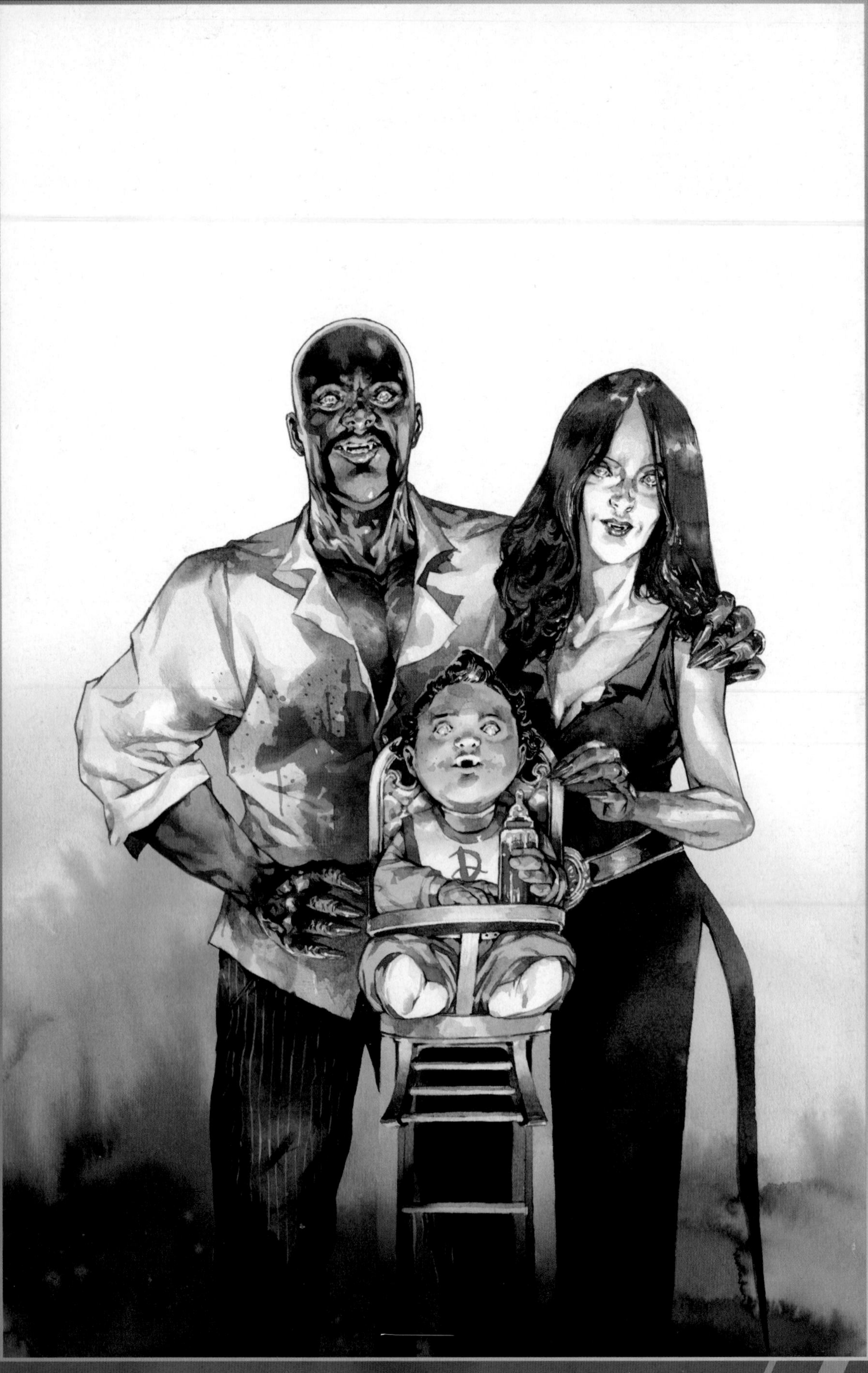

#5 VAMPIRE VARIANT BY STEPHANE PERGER